A STUDY MANUAL OF
PROFESSIONAL
COMPETENCE IN
ROAD HAULAGE

A STUDY MANUAL OF PROFESSIONAL COMPETENCE IN ROAD HAULAGE

11th edition

DAVID LOWE

KOGAN
PAGE

First published as *A Study Manual of Professional Competence in Road Transport Management* in 1978
Second edition 1980
Third edition 1983
Fourth edition 1984
Fifth edition 1986
Sixth edition 1988
Seventh edition 1989
Eighth edition 1991
Ninth edition 1995
Tenth edition 2001
Eleventh edition 2004
Reprinted 2005

Kogan Page Limited
120 Pentonville Road
London N1 9JN
United Kingdom
www.kogan-page.co.uk

British Library Cataloguing in Publication Data

A CIP record for this book is available from the British Library.

ISBN 0 7494 4304 9

Typeset by Saxon Graphics Ltd, Derby
Printed and bound by Creative Print and Design (Wales), Ebbw Vale

Contents

Preface

A further new syllabus for the professional competence examinations in road haulage was published by OCR (Oxford Cambridge and RSA Examinations) effective from 1 September 2002 and replacing the 1999 edition. This latest syllabus continues to reflect the requirements of EU Council Directive 98/76/EC which amended the previous Directive 96/26/EC.

The new style examination, first adopted in 1999, has been continued with candidates being required to provide written answers to some questions in addition to the multiple-choice questions. The examination is no longer purely a test of memory; it is much more complex, requiring both a good memory for facts and a greater understanding of individual topics, particularly in regard to their practical application to road haulage. The written questions require examinees to be able to relate what they have read to what might be a real-life scenario and to express their answers concisely, lucidly and in readable script, enabling the examiner to assess their knowledge of the topic.

This latest edition of the manual has been revised and restructured in line with the September 2002 syllabus and updated to reflect changes in legislation since publication of the previous (tenth) edition. Its contents follow the OCR syllabus with the text separated into individual subject headings and sub-headings referenced to both the EU Directive and the OCR syllabus. This layout system has been adopted rather than categorizing subjects under core, national and international headings to save the repetition that occurs within the syllabus. For example, the EU Directive reference E2 which covers different forms of credit actually appears in the syllabus three times (within the core, national and international units, namely modules 1, 2, 4 and 6). In this manual it appears just once in Section 5, E2.

To help the reader further, the Appendices contain 100 typical multiple-choice questions with correct answers and two OCR sample case study scenarios with questions and specimen marking.

The manual is written primarily for those studying for the national and international examinations in road haulage but since the module 1 syllabus is common to both road haulage and road passenger examinations, this part of the manual can be studied with equal benefit by passenger examination candidates. They may also find much of the other material useful and of interest, if not directly relevant to their studies.

Every effort has been made to ensure that the text of this manual is correct and sufficiently comprehensive and up-to-date at the time of writing. However, since changes are inevitable from time to time, the reader is advised to check that the information being studied is still current. Readers are invited to contact the author or the publisher if they have any doubts in this connection. Copies of the official syllabus may be obtained from OCR, Westwood Way, Coventry CV4 8JQ; Tel: 024 76 851509, e-mail: cib@ocr.org.uk; Web site: www.ocr.org.uk.

The reader should note that this manual is published for study purposes only and while the legislative content is intended to be accurate, it is not recommended as a legal work of reference for normal operational purposes. Other works by the same author, such as the annual publication *The Transport Manager's and Operator's Handbook* (Kogan Page), give much greater detail on specific points for operational guidance, but in the event of conflict with the law, proper legal advice should always be sought from a solicitor.

TERMINOLOGY

Many regulations are framed in negative terms rather than positive ones, for example: 'It is an offence to...' or, 'No person may...'. For the sake of brevity, frequent use is made in the text of the word 'must' in connection with legal requirements. Readers should, therefore, take the use of this word to mean one or both of the following: 1) that the law specifies certain actions to be taken; or 2) that the law specifies that an offence is committed if certain action is not taken.

To avoid over-complicating the study material, only limited reference, where absolutely essential, is made to the actual statutes themselves. Concentration has been on presenting the *facts* that are likely to comprise the answers needed to achieve an examination 'pass' result.

Masculine pronouns are used throughout this manual to avoid ugly and cumbersome language. No discrimination, prejudice or bias is intended.

Acknowledgements

Much of the success of this manual depends on the information available to me. In preparing the text a great deal of research has been carried out, and considerable help was provided by contacts and friends in many spheres of business in general, and transport in particular. It is not possible to list all those who made valuable contributions to both the original and to this latest edition, but I extend my sincere thanks to them all.

Reference was made to many books and documents in preparing the manual to check and cross-check facts, and while these cannot all be individually acknowledged, they included: *Your Lorry Abroad*, The International Road Freight Office, a host of statutory instruments, command papers and official publications and *The Highway Code*. Acknowledgement is also made to OCR whose syllabus and specimen case studies were the source of useful information.

Special thanks are due to my publisher whose persuasion and tolerance once again ensured the completion of a revised manuscript.

Since publication of the first edition of this manual in 1978 many readers have notified me of their successes in the examinations as a result of using it. It is particularly gratifying to receive such complimentary comments because they confirm the validity of the manual for the purpose for which it is intended. I also know that it has been widely used for reference by those studying at college and by home study means because many write with comments and to report their successes in the examination. I would like to thank these readers for taking the trouble to write to me and to others who also wrote in with helpful comments about the contents of earlier editions. These points have been included, where appropriate, in the revised editions.

Introduction

UK legislation (implementing EC Directive 561/74) specifying new standards of professional competence for those responsible for the operation of goods vehicles was originally introduced on 1 January 1978 as one of the conditions under which a Standard Operator's licence may be granted for carrying goods for hire or reward.

Provisions in the regulations originally enabled certain people in the road transport industry to claim their 'professional competence' on the grounds of qualifying experience gained by working in transport prior to 1975. This scheme finally ended on 31 December 1979. People who did not qualify under this 'Grandfather Rights' scheme may satisfy the requirements through membership, at specified grades, of certain of the professional transport institutes. For those who do not qualify by these methods, and for young people and other newcomers to the industry, an examination system provides a qualification to meet the legal requirements for professional competence.

This study manual is aimed principally at those people taking up positions in transport who need or want to become professionally competent by examination. Its purpose is to provide a comprehensive and self-contained course of study based on the official OCR syllabus, which leads the reader to a point where both the national and international examinations in road haulage may be taken successfully.

The manual enables examination candidates to study privately, at home and elsewhere, either when it is convenient to devote long periods to study or when just a few spare moments are available for revision. It is self-contained, providing sufficient knowledge of all the syllabus subjects to meet the examination requirements. To avoid unnecessary length and volume the information has been presented as briefly as possible, dispensing with irrelevant narrative and concentrating on the basic informative facts which the reader needs to learn to pass the examination.

The syllabus covers a broad subject range, from matters directly concerning legal and administrative aspects of road haulage operation to technical matters of goods vehicle construction, use and maintenance, and road safety measures, and then on to the much wider issues of management such as business administration, financial controls, marketing, legal knowledge, and the complexities of social legislation.

Overall, the extent of the syllabus is such that the successful examination candidate can justifiably claim to have acquired a sound grounding in the broader aspects of management and the running of a business, in addition to the more specialized knowledge of road haulage operation. It is this aspect of wider education which will undoubtedly induce many other managers in transport, who have qualified for professional 'competence' on the grounds of past experience, to attempt the examination to prove that they too can meet the demanding standards it imposes. Alternatively, they may just wish to brush up their knowledge even if they decide against the rigours of sitting the examination. For these people, the manual will make valuable reading and reference material.

While the scope of the study syllabus is broad and the nature of the examination such that the candidate's knowledge is tested in full, it should be recognized that there is much more to managing a road haulage fleet than just passing the professional competence examination. Prospective professional managers will need to broaden their knowledge further with more detailed reading on legal points, financial control and management techniques, marketing and the intricacies of industrial relations. But reading alone will not produce the truly professional manager. Transport is an industry where practical operating experience is a vital ingredient of success and examination candidates who read this manual should also seek ways of widening their practical knowledge.

Requirements for professional competence

A succession of European Union Council Directives since 1974 (ie 74/561/EEC, 89/438/EEC, 96/26/EC and most recently 98/76/EC) have set out requirements for admission to the occupation of road haulage operations. These provisions are currently implemented in the UK by means of the Goods Vehicles (Licensing of Operators) Act 1995 which in section 13 (3)[c] and Schedule 3 (7–15) requires that transport operators who wish to engage in the carriage of goods for hire or reward and, consequently, hold a standard operator's licence, must satisfy the requirement of professional competence with either the firm's proprietor holding the qualification or by the employment of a person who meets the qualification.

People who were responsible for road transport operations under an Operator's Licence before 1 January 1975 could qualify for professional competence by virtue of their experience (known as 'Grandfather Rights') but the issue of certificates (ie CPCs) under this scheme ended on 31 December 1979.

People who did not qualify under the Grandfather Rights provisions may gain 'exemption' through membership in an appropriate grade of one of the professional transport institutes (see page 193), thereby qualifying for professional competence.

Anyone else who did not qualify under the Grandfather Rights provisions or who is not exempt on the basis mentioned above must sit the official OCR examination in order to qualify for professional competence.

Transfer of professional competence qualification

Holders of the professional competence qualification gained in Great Britain can transfer the qualification to Northern Ireland or to any other member state of the European Union (ie Austria, Belgium, Denmark, Eire, Finland, France, Germany, Greece, Italy, Luxembourg, Netherlands, Portugal, Spain, Sweden and, from 1 May 2004, the new member states Cyprus, Czech Republic, Estonia, Hungary, Latvia, Lithuania, Malta, Poland, the Slovak Republic and Slovenia – ie the so-called 'acceding countries') should they wish to operate in road haulage or obtain a position as a transport manager in any of those states. A Certificate of Qualification for this purpose can be obtained on application (and on payment of the relevant fee) to a Traffic Commissioner. Similarly, any person holding nationality of an EU member state (as well as those from Northern Ireland) may obtain confirmation of their qualification in their own country and apply to use it in the UK.

CPC syllabus

This syllabus is effective from 1 September 2002. Please note that the numbering system in this syllabus relates to that used in the EU Directive. Also note that there is considerable overlap of topics in the official syllabus, but for this text core, national and international topics have been integrated.

A. CIVIL LAW

Relevant modules: 1, 2, 4 and 6

Assessment objectives

Candidates must:

A1. be familiar with the main types of contract used in road transport and with the rights and obligations arising therefrom (topics covered: Contracts: legal obligations; subcontracting; legal duties of agents, employers and employees);

A2. be capable of negotiating a legally valid transport contract, notably with regard to conditions of carriage (topics covered: Legal obligations: capacity to contract; specific performance; liability; lien; laws of agency);

A3. be able to consider a claim by his principal regarding compensation for loss of or damage to goods during transportation or for their late delivery, and to understand how such claims affect his contractual liability (topics covered: Performance: general and specific liabilities of principal, subcontractors and agents for the performance of a contract. Compensation: for losses relating to damage. Settlements: interim and full payments);

A4. be familiar with the rules and obligations arising from the CMR Convention on the contract for the international carriage of goods by road (topics covered: CMR liability and unwitting CMR: The requirements for consignment notes. Successive carriers. Limits of liability. Relevance of insurance).

B. COMMERCIAL LAW

Relevant modules: 1 and 4

Assessment objectives

Candidates must:

B1. be familiar with the conditions and formalities laid down for plying the trade, the general obligations incumbent upon transport operators (registration, keeping records) and the consequences of bankruptcy (topics covered: Trading law relating to: sole traders and partnerships; partnership agreements; rights and duties of partners; powers of partners; partners as agents; dissolution of partnerships. Company law: registered companies (private and public limited companies); AGMs; liquidation. Documentation: key legal documents including prospectus, memorandum of association; articles of association; certificate of incorporation);

B2. have appropriate knowledge of the various forms of commercial company and the rules governing their constitution and operation (topics covered: Types of business organization: sole traders; partnerships; private and public limited companies; co-operatives; Rules governing: partners, share capital, taxes, limited liability, duties of directors/company secretaries, role of the liquidators).

C. SOCIAL LAW

Relevant modules: 1, 4 and 6

Assessment objectives

Candidates must:

C1. be familiar with the role and function of the various social institutions which are concerned with road transport – trade unions, works councils, shop stewards, labour inspectors (topics covered: Role of: employment tribunals; trade unions; ACAS; arbitrators; associated Government departments. Employees' rights: trade union membership and activities);

C2. be familiar with the employers' social security obligations (topics covered: Relevant parts of current legislation relating to: health and safety; discrimination; employment protection; employment rights; pensions);

C3. be familiar with the rules governing work contracts for the various categories of worker employed by road transport undertakings – form of the contracts, obligations of the parties, working conditions and working hours, paid leave, remuneration, breach of contract (topics covered: Contracts of employment: content of written statement; time limits for the issue of contracts. Employment: rights of employers and employees including: full and part-time employees; casual employees; self-employed; agency staff; transfer of undertakings; remuneration and itemized pay statements; holiday entitlement; dismissal and unfair dismissal; notice to terminate employment; working time regulations, maternity and paternity information for employees);

C4. be familiar with the provisions on driving periods and rest periods laid down in Regulation (EEC) 3820/85, the provisions of Regulation (EEC) 3821/85 on recording equipment in road transport and the practical arrangements for implementing these regulations (topics covered: EU: the working week; driving time; breaks; daily and weekly rest periods; emergencies. Non-EU regulations: knowledge of AETR. Domestic hours' law: the working week; driving time; rest periods; emergencies. Tachograph legislation and operation: points of law; the records; driver and employer responsibilities; enforcement and inspection; calibration and sealing; malfunctions).

D. FISCAL LAW

Relevant modules: 1, 2, 4 and 6

Assessment objectives

Candidates must:

D1. be familiar with the rules governing VAT on transport services (topics covered: VAT – national operations: income threshold and registration; zero-rated goods and services; VAT returns; reclaiming

VAT. Turnover tax – international operations: registration for VAT; applying VAT; submitting returns; reclaiming VAT);

D2. be familiar with the rules governing motor vehicle tax (topics covered: Calculation of VED: basis for calculating motor vehicle taxation on general vehicles and vehicles used in special operations and conditions applied to them);

D3. be familiar with the rules governing the taxes on certain road haulage vehicles and tolls and infrastructure user charges (topics covered: National operation: charges and tolls on roads and bridges and the basis on which calculation is made. International operation: rules governing tolls and taxation of vehicles on international journeys);

D4. be familiar with the rules governing income tax (topics covered: Double taxation. Status: rules governing the status of employees and the self-employed and the imposition of income tax regulations. Employers' responsibilities: deduction and collection of income tax and National Insurance from employees; payment of income tax and National Insurance to Inland Revenue. Benefits: round sum allowances; expenses; benefits-in-kind; declaration).

E. BUSINESS AND FINANCIAL MANAGEMENT OF THE UNDERTAKING

Relevant modules: 1, 2, 4 and 6

Assessment objectives

Candidates must:

E1. be familiar with the laws and practices regarding the use of cheques, promissory notes, credit cards and other means or methods of payment (topics covered: payment methods: cash; cheques; credit cards; charge cards; promissory notes; debit systems and credit transfer. International operation – banking and payment systems including the electronic transfer of funds eg Swift, Eurocheques);

E2. be familiar with the various forms of credit (bank credit, documentary credit, guarantee deposits, mortgages, leasing, renting, factoring) and with the charges and obligations arising from them (topics covered: Different forms of credit: overdrafts; loans; documentary credit; guarantee deposits; mortgages; leases; rents; factoring);

E3. know what a balance sheet is, how it is set out and how to interpret it (topics covered: Determine: fixed assets; net current assets; current assets; long-term liabilities; current liabilities. Interpretation and calculation);

E4. be able to read and interpret a profit and loss account (topics covered: Determine: direct and indirect costs; gross [or operating or trading] profit; net profit; interpretation and calculation and their effect on a business);

E5. be able to assess the company's profitability and financial position, in particular on the basis of financial ratios (topics covered: Determine: capital employed and return on capital employed; liquidity ratios including working capital; cash flow. Use of ratios: (current ratio working capital ratio); quick assets ratio [acid test ratio]);

E6. be able to prepare a budget (topics covered: Construct budgets from data supplied. Use of budgets: to monitor and control performance, budgetary control; variance analysis);

E7. be familiar with his undertaking's cost elements (fixed costs, variable costs, working capital, depreciation) and be able to calculate costs per vehicle, per kilometre, per journey or per tonne (topics covered: From data supplied: identify and/or calculate fixed costs; variable running costs; overhead costs; depreciation. Determine: time and distance costs);

E8. be able to draw up an organization chart relating to the undertaking's personnel as a whole and to organize work plans (topics covered: Prepare an organization chart for an: organization; department; function; unit; or depot. Organizing, planning and measuring work);

E9. be familiar with the principles of marketing, publicity and public relations, including transport services, sales promotion and the preparation of customer files (topics covered: Market research – primary and secondary; segmentation; product promotion and sales and publicity; marketing; public relations; media relations. Customer: relations; research; files; profiles);

E10. be familiar with the different types of insurance relating to road transport (liability, accidental injury/life insurance) and with the guarantees and obligations arising therefrom (topics covered: Insurance: risk assessment; cover; claims, risk management and improvement of risk. Types of insurance: fidelity; goods in transit; CMR level; employers' liability; public liability; professional negligence; motor; plant; travel; health; property; consequential loss; cash in transit. Risks: guarantees; obligations; liability and role of trustees). Legislation;

E11. be familiar with the applications of electronic data transmission in road transport (topics covered: Legislation: Data Protection Act. Information Technology including electronic vehicle status monitoring; electronic data transmission; real-time information systems; customer information systems; depot readers; GPS; route and load planning systems; vehicle and staff scheduling; data analysis; data information systems);

E12. be able to apply the rules governing the invoicing of road haulage services and know the meaning of Incoterms (topics covered: Transactions: the purpose of documents including quotations, orders, consignment notes. Invoices – identify information required including Tax point, VAT details, payment methods and terms; Incoterms: principal provisions of incoterms applying to any mode of road transport, including multimodal.) NB: Incoterms are agreed trading terms with legal definitions, eg FOB;

E13. be familiar with the different categories of transport auxiliaries, their roles, their functions and, where appropriate, their status (topics covered: Agents: various agents who assist in ensuring freight is properly and correctly transferred, eg freight forwarders, shippers, clearing houses, groupage operators).

F. ACCESS TO THE MARKET

Relevant modules: 2, 4 and 6

Assessment objectives

Candidates must:

F1. be familiar with the occupational regulations governing road transport for hire or reward, vehicle rental and subcontracting, and in particular the rules governing the official organization of the occupation, admission to the occupation, authorizations for intra- and extra-Community road transport operations, inspections and sanctions (topics covered: National operation: role of Traffic Commissioners and enforcement agencies; statutory procedures concerning operator licensing; requirements for vehicle maintenance; regulations governing domestic operation. International operation: statutory procedures concerning operator licensing; regulations governing international operations);

F2. be familiar with the rules for setting up a road transport undertaking (topics covered: Rules for setting up a road transport undertaking: statutory procedures and rules concerning operator licensing);

F3. be familiar with the various documents required for operating road transport services and be able to introduce checking procedures for ensuring that the approved documents relating to each transport operation, and in particular those relating to the vehicle, the driver and the goods, are kept both in the vehicle and on the premises of the undertaking (topics covered: Documents and their administration: operator licences and vehicle discs; vehicle authorizations; tachograph records; waybills/consignment notes; driving entitlement; maintenance documents; insurance documents; systems for document checking and control procedures);

F4. be familiar with the rules on the organization of the market in road haulage services, on freight handling and logistics (topics covered: Market organization: regulatory powers of the Secretary of State, the Office of Fair Trading; the Monopolies and Mergers Commission. Main provisions of third country traffic and cabotage);

F5. be familiar with frontier formalities, the role and scope of 'T' documents and TIR carnets, and the obligations and responsibilities arising from their use (topics covered: 'T' documents, their status and rules of use. Carnets, rules governing their use. Exemptions: most practical use of various exemptions obtained by the use of various documents and the implications for operators and their customers).

G. TECHNICAL STANDARDS AND ASPECTS OF OPERATION

Relevant modules: 2, 4 and 6

Assessment objectives

Candidates must:

G1. be familiar with the rules concerning the weights and dimensions of vehicles in the member states of the European Union and the procedures to be followed in the case of abnormal loads which constitute an exception to these rules (topics covered: Terms used to identify the differing weight conditions. Statutory limits: weights and dimensions. Formulas used for various calculations concerned in weights and dimensions of vehicles. Role of local government and government agencies regarding the movement of abnormal loads. Main rules and most common weights and dimensions used internationally. Approvals for movement of abnormal indivisible loads through EU states);

G2. be able to choose vehicles and their components (chassis, engine, transmission system, braking system, etc) in accordance with the needs of the undertaking (topics covered: Vehicle specifications that will improve road safety, economy and reduce impact on the environment. Vehicle specifications to take into account for UK commercial and international operations).

G3. be familiar with the formalities relating to the type approval, registration and technical inspection of these vehicles (topics covered: Main provisions within current legislation relating to C&U, vehicle lighting and safety. Powers of enforcement agencies);

G4. understand what measures must be taken to reduce noise and to combat air pollution by motor vehicle exhaust emissions (topics covered: Main provisions of the C&U regulations; EU Directives and environmental legislation);

G5. be able to draw up periodic maintenance plans for the vehicles and their equipment (topics covered: Maintenance programmes: planned preventative; methods of maintenance; operator's obligations and liabilities to maintain vehicles and equipment in a safe, roadworthy condition; responsibility for vehicles whose maintenance is contracted out. Guide to maintaining roadworthiness; be familiar with the content and application of this document);

G6. be familiar with the different types of cargo-handling and loading devices (tailboards, containers, pallets) and be able to introduce procedures and issue instructions for loading and unloading goods (load distribution, stacking, stowing, blocking and chocking) (topics covered: Risk analysis and safe operations: requirements for various loads and procedures to ensure safe operations; Instructions: including intended audience, detail of actions, reporting guidance, appropriate language. Procedures: including logical sequence, appropriate language, use of appropriate diagrams);

G7. be familiar with the various techniques of 'piggy-back' and roll-on/roll-off combined transport (topics covered: Safety requirements; vehicle specifications charging methods);

G8. be able to implement procedures for complying with the rules on the carriage of dangerous goods and waste, notably those arising from:
   - Directive 94/55/EC on the approximation of the laws of the Member States with regard to the transport of dangerous goods by road;
   - Directive 96/35/EC on the appointment and vocational qualification of safety advisers for the transport of dangerous goods by road, rail and inland waterway;
   - Regulation (EEC) 259/93 on the supervision and control of shipments of waste within, into and out of the European Community;
   (topics covered: National: main provisions of regulations and their incorporation into a procedure to meet with current requirements. International: main provisions of regulations are identified and incorporated into a procedure to meet current requirements);

G9. be able to implement procedures for complying with the rules on the carriage of perishable foodstuffs, and in the case of international operation, notably those arising from the Agreement on the International Carriage of Perishable Foodstuffs and on the special equipment to be used for such carriage (ATP) (topics covered: Procedures to ensure correct compliance with legislation and best practice);

G10. be able to implement procedures for complying with the rules on the transport of live animals (topics covered: National and International: procedures to ensure correct compliance with legislation and best practice).

H. ROAD SAFETY

Relevant modules: 2, 4 and 6

Assessment objectives

Candidates must:

H1. know what qualifications are required for drivers – driving licences, medical certificates, certificates of fitness (topics covered: Vocational entitlements: different categories, types and qualifications for driving licences and entitlements. Procedures: relating to the issue, renewal, revocation and production of licences and removal of entitlements. Disciplinary matters: procedures and appeals. Driving tests: scope and conduct and sequence of theory and driving tests. International driving permits: issue and validation);

H2. be able to take the necessary steps to ensure that drivers comply with the traffic rules, prohibitions and restrictions in force in the United Kingdom and in the different member states of the European Union – speed limits, priorities, waiting and parking restrictions, use of lights, road signs (topics covered: Traffic regulations: signs and signals; variation in weights, dimensions and speed of road haulage vehicles in EU member states and non-member countries. Restrictions: imposed on the movement and speeds of road haulage vehicles);

H3. be able to draw up drivers' instructions for checking their compliance with the safety requirements concerning the condition of the vehicles, their equipment and cargo, and concerning preventive measures to be taken (topics covered: Write instructions for inspection, defect reporting and the safe use of vehicles and equipment, including cargo. Instructions: including intended audience, detail of actions, reporting guidance, appropriate language. Risk assessment for health and safety, basic principles, identify risk, controls in place, monitor control, review);

H4. be able to lay down procedures to be followed in the event of an accident and to implement appropriate procedures for preventing the recurrence of accidents or traffic offences (topics covered: Accident procedures: introduce measures to inform appropriate authorities and personnel of accidents; take appropriate action to minimize further dangers and to relieve suffering. The use of European Accident Statements. Legislation: Road Traffic Acts. Accident prevention: risk analysis and the introduction of preventative measures).

Correlation: EU Directive reference codes and OCR syllabus units and modules

Table 0.1

Directive References	National Unit 1 Module 1	Unit 2 Modules 2 and 4	International Unit 3 Module 6
Civil Law			
A1	*		
A2	*		
A3		*	*
A4		*	*
Commercial Law			
B1	*	*	
B2	*	*	
Social Law			
C1	*		
C2	*		
C3	*		
C4		*	*

Table 0.1 *continued*

Directive References	National Unit 1 Module 1	Unit 2 Modules 2 and 4	International Unit 3 Module 6
Fiscal Law			
D1		*	*
D2		*	*
D3		*	*
D4	*		
Business and Financial Management			
E1	*		*
E2	*	*	*
E3	*	*	
E4	*	*	
E5	*	*	
E6		*	*
E7		*	*
E8		*	
E9		*	
E10		*	*
E11		*	
E12		*	*
E13		*	*
Access to the Market			
F1		*	*
F2		*	*
F3		*	*
F4		*	*
F5			*
Technical Standards and Operations			
G1		*	*
G2		*	*
G3		*	*
G4		*	*
G5		*	
G6		*	*
G7		*	*
G8		*	*
G9		*	*
G10		*	*
Road Safety			
H1		*	*
H2		*	*
H3		*	
H4		*	*

The official examination

Examinations for professional competence in road haulage operations are conducted at registered centres throughout the country on behalf of the official examining body, namely OCR.

Normally, examinations will be held four times a year, usually in March, June, October and December, on dates which are published by OCR.

The examinations comprise:

Module 1 (Unit 1) (core) taken by both road haulage and road passenger candidates, which lasts for 30 minutes and comprises 20 multiple-choice questions with a 70 per cent pass mark.

Module 2 (Unit 2) (national road haulage) which lasts for one hour and comprises 40 multiple-choice questions with a pass mark of 70 per cent.

Module 4 (Unit 2) (national road haulage) is a case study examination which lasts 90 minutes, during which the candidate must study a given scenario and answer a variety of questions. These may require a short answer, a longer analytical response, the need to draw up schedules, and interpretation of data, and numerical calculations. Notional pass mark 50 per cent.

Module 6 (Unit 3) (international road haulage) lasts for 60 minutes and comprises two sections:

- Section A containing up to 14 questions each requiring a written direct answer with a 70 per cent pass mark; and
- Section B containing an average of three questions each requiring a short written response and with a 50 per cent pass mark.

NB: Candidates must pass both of these two sections at the same examination sitting to obtain a pass in Module 6.

Examination questions are of the multiple-choice type whereby the candidate has to choose a correct answer to each question from a number of given alternatives. Additionally, the candidate has to complete a case study having been given a scenario which he must read and then answer questions relating to. Examples of typical questions of the type used in the examinations are included in this manual with the correct answers shown at the end of the book.

OCR states in its syllabus that candidates who are successful in achieving Units One and Two (assessment modules 1, 2 and 4) will be awarded a Certificate of Professional Competence in National Road Haulage Operations. Candidates who are successful in achieving Units One, Two and Three (assessment modules 1, 2, 4 and 6) will be awarded a Certificate of Professional Competence in International Road Haulage Operations.

Certificates will be designed to meet the requirements of the EU Directive in terms of the wording used and the information presented on them. Certificates will carry both the OCR logo and a logo that represents the UK (Department for Transport (DfT)).

Candidates are not required to pass all of the assessment modules at the same sitting. OCR profile certificates are awarded to candidates who achieve fewer than the total number of assessment modules required for a full certificate. Candidates may re-sit assessment modules in which they were unsuccessful. When a candidate has achieved all of the required combination of modules, profile certificates may be returned to OCR and replaced by a full Certificate of Professional Competence in National Road Haulage Operations or Certificate of Professional Competence in International Road Haulage Operations.

Results, reports and certificates will normally be issued to centres within eight weeks of the date of the examination. It is the centre's responsibility to inform individual candidates of their results and to forward certificates where appropriate.

Full details of the examination and copies of the current syllabus which includes details of the examination regulations may be obtained from: OCR, Westwood Way, Coventry CV4 8JQ; Tel: 024 76 851509, Fax: 024 76 421944; e-mail: cib@ocr.org.uk; Web site: www.ocr.org.uk.

Fees for the examinations from 1 September 2003 are as follows:

Module 1 (core) – £10.45
Module 2 (national) – £19.05
Module 4 (national) – £30.50
Module 6 (international) – £37.50.

Additional local administrative fees will be charged by examination centres.

Unsuccessful candidates may apply for details of their performance using an application form obtainable from OCR.

SPECIAL NOTE TO READERS

This manual has been prepared in accordance with the official OCR syllabus for the professional competence examinations in national and international road haulage. However, despite the author's efforts to ensure conformity with the syllabus, experience has shown that occasionally questions are included in the examination that may not appear to be taken from within the published syllabus material. The examination has been criticized in the past for the inclusion of questions that are believed to be outside the stated scope of the syllabus. The author and publisher, therefore, will be pleased to hear from readers who can provide information or advice on any such questions so that they can be included in new editions for the benefit of future readers and examination candidates.

PART 1

Civil law

This part covers Directive items A1 and A2 in Unit 1 and A3, and A4 in Units 2 and 3.

INTRODUCTION TO LAW

Although not specifically part of the civil law syllabus material, it is useful in this introduction to explain the basic principles of law and the legal institutions as a background to the study of contracts, legal liabilities and the liabilities of employers, employees, subcontractors and agents, and the CMR contract.

Law is a word that describes a general rule of conduct. In the context of our study it may be defined as 'the body of principles recognized and applied by the State in the administration of justice' (Sir John Salmond, *Jurisprudence*). 'The law as a body has as its aim the attainment of justice in society' (R S Sim and D M M Scott, 'A' *Level English Law*).

Relationship of common law, statute law and legal precedent

The laws observed in operating transport are derived from common law or statute law and also legal precedent. Additionally, European Union law and the requirements of international agreements and conventions, to which the UK is a signatory, must be observed.

Common law

Common law is established by practice or custom over a long period of time rather than being enacted by the State, but many aspects of common law or 'practice' have become absorbed into our legal system as a result of being adopted by courts in the past as the basis for judgements. Once customs and practices are adopted by the courts they become precedents which other courts either *must* follow (binding precedents) or *may* follow (persuasive precedents).

Before 1873, law existed in the form of common law and equity, which was a system designed to overcome defects in the common law system. The Judicature Acts 1873/75 were responsible for drawing together the processes of common law justice and equity, which had previously been separately administered – common law in the common law courts and equity in the Chancery Court.

Statute law

Statute law is created by Act of Parliament to which, after the due processes of debate and approval in both the House of Commons and the House of Lords, the Sovereign gives approval with the Royal Assent. Legislation is law enacted by Parliament, in which all legislative power in the UK is vested. Parliament has the power to enact any law and remove or repeal any law (but cannot overrule or fail to implement EU law). In legislating, Parliament may delegate legislative powers to other bodies and even to individuals. For example, an Act of Parliament may authorize the Privy Council to legislate, it may authorize a Minister of the State to make 'provisional orders' that later require legislative confirmation by Parliament, or it may authorize a minister to make regulations. These are published as Statutory Instruments and have the statutory force of law.

Precedent

A precedent or judicial precedent is a statement or judgement of interpretation of the law by a court. It is recorded in law records and is followed by other courts when dealing with future cases in similar circumstances. Precedents may be authoritative pronouncements on the law setting standards for future judgements.

Precedents are usually binding for cases where similar matters are at issue in courts below that which set the precedent. Therefore, for example, a House of Lords decision on a particular matter will set the pattern to be followed for judgements in identical circumstances in the Court of Appeal, the High Court and the County Courts.

However, not all the pronouncements made in a court become 'binding'. A judge may make a particular decision in a case but may also make additional comments and observations which are recorded. While these ancillary comments may be studied and considered in future cases, they are not part of the actual judgement and are not 'binding' on other courts. They are only 'persuasive' (ie they give an indication of the line of thinking that may be followed).

Judicial precedents form what is known as 'case law'. A substantial amount of case law exists in Britain; in effect every case which comes before the courts is likely to be prejudiced by particular judgements in previous instances. However, judges exercise discretion in taking into account all the information available, and make reasoned decisions based on the facts of the particular case *and* observing the principles of any precedents that apply.

Parliament and the courts

It is Parliament's role to establish the law (except where EU law directly applies) and the courts' role to interpret it. In transport terms, this means that if you ring a government department (the Executive of Parliament) and ask an official to tell you what a particular regulation means, you will be told it means what it says (an official is not permitted to interpret the law). If a case is brought before a court, it is for that court to interpret the law and say how it should be applied. In particular, the courts may determine the definition of words used in law. As a transport example, a court will determine the meaning in particular cases of words like 'danger' and 'nuisance' which occur in the C&U regulations.

Formation of statute law

New law is created by the publication of a bill, which is placed before Parliament for consideration. Such bills may be put forward by the Government through its respective departments and Secretaries of State or they may be put forward by Members of Parliament as private members' bills.

Bills are debated by the House of Commons sometimes in committee first. The committees are formed from representatives of the major political parties, and they work their way through each section in detail and agree on the principles and the final wording before re-submitting the matter to the House.

After three readings in the Commons, where the bill is accepted either in its original or in an amended form, it passes to the House of Lords for consideration and, here again, debate can result in changes and the bill goes back to the Commons.

When the bill is approved, it gains the Royal Assent and is published as an Act of Parliament. An Act may detail new law which is effective on a specific date, or it may give powers to Secretaries of State or statutory bodies to make regulations by publishing Statutory

Instruments. In the latter case, the Act would be generally termed 'enabling legislation'.

When regulations are made under powers conferred by an Act, they are placed before Parliament (ie 'placed on the table of the House') for 21 days, after which time they become law on the date specified. Statutory Instruments specify the date made, the date laid before Parliament and the date of their enforcement.

Some items contained in Acts may remain dormant for many years before they are brought into use by regulations or may never be effected (eg Section 65 and Schedule 9 of the Transport Act 1968 providing for transport managers' licensing).

Redundant legislation is repealed by the inclusion, in subsequent Acts or regulations, of provisions which specifically repeal sections of earlier legislation or complete Acts or regulations (eg the goods vehicle plating and testing requirements, originally specified in the 1967 Road Safety Act, section 9, were repealed by the 1972 Road Traffic Act, Schedule 9, and replaced by section 45 of that Act and subsequently by section 49 of the Road Traffic Act 1988).

Subordinate legislation

As previously explained, legislation is created by Acts of Parliament which may either state the law or confer powers on the Executive (Secretaries of State or statutory bodies) to make regulations. Regulations and orders made by the Executive are referred to as 'subordinate legislation'. This form of legislation is applied extensively to road transport where we see fewer Acts (the Transport Act 1968 and the Road Traffic Acts 1972, 1974 and 1988 being just a few of the significant ones) but there are a great many regulations which set out the detailed requirements on a broad range of subjects, as follows:

- operators' licensing;
- driver licensing;
- drivers' hours and records;
- construction and use of vehicles;
- vehicle plating and testing;
- vehicle lighting;
- road traffic controls;
- excise duty.

Regulations are frequently published as Statutory Instruments to amend existing legislation (eg to increase statutory fees for licences or testing) or to introduce sections of Acts not previously implemented where the Secretary of State has been given powers to do so.

EU law

Since the UK is a member of the European Union we are bound to comply with the requirements of EU law. This takes two forms: *directives* which member states must apply in principle by means of their own domestic legislation, and *regulations* which have direct impact and must be applied to the letter, needing no domestic legislation to bring them into force (eg the EU drivers' hours and tachograph regulations – Regulations 3820/85/EEC and 3821/85/EEC).

International agreements/conventions

The UK is party to many international agreements or conventions that must be followed and are usually incorporated into British law. Examples in transport are the ADR agreement covering the carriage of dangerous goods by road, the ATP agreement covering the carriage of perishable foodstuffs by road, and the CMR agreement which applies to the carriage of goods for hire or reward on international journeys – these are all dealt with in detail in other parts of this manual.

Interpretation of statutory law

As previously explained, it is the role of the courts to interpret the law. Prosecutions for criminal acts (offences specified in statute law in general terms) are brought by the police (mainly via the Crown Prosecution Service – CPS), the Director of Public Prosecutions or by other specific authorities, like the Consumer Protection Officer representing the local authority. In presenting their case they cite the specific regulation or regulations that have been breached. It is then for the defendant to plead 'guilty' or 'not guilty'; if he pleads 'not guilty' then the court has to determine whether the defendant or the prosecution is right. This may be a straightforward matter, but complications may arise if, for example, the case depends on differing interpretations by the police and the defendant of a particular regulation. The court must then decide how the regulation should be interpreted, taking account of appropriate precedents and all the relevant facts of the matter.

If the defendant loses the case, he is either convicted and receives the appropriate penalty (fine, imprisonment, driving licence endorsement or disqualification) or is committed to a higher court (the Crown Court) for trial by jury.

The Courts

Initially, most transport related offences are dealt with in the lowest level of court – magistrates' courts or courts of summary jurisdiction. More serious offences are dealt with by the Crown Courts and appeals against their decisions are heard by the Court of Appeal. In complicated cases where satisfaction is not obtained from the Court of Appeal, the matter may be taken to the highest court in our legal system, the House of Lords or, where appropriate, to the European Court of Justice which supersedes even the House of Lords.

Criminal versus civil action

There are two basic forms of legal action: 'criminal' action, which generally deals with offences committed in breach of statutory legislation, and 'civil' action, when one party feels aggrieved by the actions of another party and wishes to obtain some form of restitution by way of damages or restraint (for example, a haulier may seek an injunction to stop a union or a group of workers 'blacking' his vehicles). An injunction is usually only granted for a short period until the matter concerned can be properly dealt with by negotiation or in court.

Civil action includes the recovery of debts and deals with other claims concerning failure to comply with contracts. Where small sums of money are involved these matters may be settled in the county court and in most instances no legal representation is necessary; the plaintiff can make his own case and produce his evidence personally to the district judge. Where larger claims are to be settled the matter is dealt with in the High Court where legal representation of the claimant (plaintiff) and defendant is usual but not essential.

Traffic Commissioners and the Transport Tribunal

There is a further system of legal control that the transport operator must understand. The controlling authorities for operators' licensing and related professional competence requirements are the Traffic Commissioners (one for each traffic area) appointed by the Secretary of State for Transport. The TCs have powers to administer these regulations, call operators to appear before them and impose penalties (such as suspension, revocation or curtailment of a licence).

Any transport operator dissatisfied with a decision of a TC regarding the grant of a licence or the refusal to grant a licence, or with any penalty imposed, can appeal to the Transport Tribunal (see module B part 3/1).

Other tribunals

Tribunals deal with certain areas of transport operation and other business, rather than the courts. For example, claims for redundancy payments, unfair dismissal and other employment matters (such as claims relating to sexual discrimination and equality, race relations and so on) are dealt with by employment tribunals.

A1. CONTRACTS

Contracts and conditions of carriage

The business of road haulage is conducted by means of contracts between hauliers and their customers who require them to carry, and sometimes store, goods on their behalf. These contracts are not always formally constituted in writing, more often being the consequence of a telephone call in which the customer asks the haulier to pick up and deliver a load of goods. Nevertheless, no matter how casual the arrangement, a contract does exist as described below.

Legally enforceable contracts
An enforceable contract must contain the following essential points:

- An offer and an acceptance.
- Details of a consideration (ie a benefit or payment).
- An intention for the parties to be legally bound by the contract (this is always assumed by the courts unless there is a written provision to the contrary).

A contract exists when an offer has been made and accepted – there is no requirement for it to be in writing.

Capacity to contract
It is important that contracts are made only between those persons and parties who have a legal capacity to contract. In the case of persons this generally means that contracts are made between adults – a minor (ie aged up to 18 years) does not have capacity to contract. Mental patients and those persons afflicted by drunkenness do not have capacity to contract. Limited companies (ie corporate bodies) have capacity to contract so long as this authority is given in the rules of the company as stated in its Memorandum of Association.

Performance of contracts
Contracts may be discharged by 'performance'. However, in general terms there are four classes of performance:

1. Entire performance is when both parties have fully performed the obligations placed on them by the contract (eg the haulier to carry and deliver the load, the customer to have paid the haulier's account for the job).
2. Substantial performance is a term used when a dispute over non-completion of a contract is referred to court and the court determines that

one party is not required to perform every term of the contract for the other party to be made liable. For example, the defendant may be required to pay for work done but may counterclaim against the contractor for 'defect in performance' (ie for work not done).
3. Partial performance is where one party is prepared to accept and pay for something less than full (ie entire) performance of the contract.
4. Frustration is where a contract proves impossible to fulfil from the outset and is therefore void (ie impossible of performance).

Discharge of contracts

Discharge of a contract is when the parties to it are freed from their mutual obligations under the contract. This may be either: lawfully – by agreement, by performance (see above), by frustration; or unlawfully – by breach of the contract.

Compensation for loss through damage

Where there is a breach of contract for the reasons given above, damages may be claimed by the plaintiff (ie the party who suffered the loss and who sues the defendant for compensation). These damages, if awarded by the court will normally fall into one of the following categories:

- Ordinary damages. These arise naturally from the breach of contract and in tort (see page 29) for losses which cannot be positively proved or ascertained. The amount of damages awarded will depend on the court's view of the nature of the plaintiff's injury (ie loss).
- Special damages. These are losses that do not arise naturally from the breach of contract and are awarded in tort for losses that can be positively proved or ascertained (ie where specific amounts of loss can be stated).
- Exemplary and aggravated damages. These are additional damages above those awarded for actual loss and are intended to punish the defendant and to deter him, and others, from similar conduct in the future. Hence they are invariably referred to as 'punitive damages'.

Carriers' liability for goods – private/common carriers

In road haulage operations the operator enters into a contract each time goods are accepted from a customer to be carried to a specified destination. In most cases he accepts these goods in the role of *private* carrier, whereby his liability is limited to the terms specified in his conditions of carriage, which are either printed on the back of his business paper or quotation sheets, or are posted in the office. If he has no conditions of carriage and holds himself out to carry for all and sundry without reserving the right to refuse to carry goods tendered, he undertakes the role of *common* carrier (basically under the terms of the Carriers Act 1830) and his liability for loss of or damage to the goods, irrespective of the degree of negligence, is unlimited.

Conditions of carriage

When goods are carried under a specific contract between the owner of the goods and the haulier (in the role of private carrier as opposed to common carrier), the haulier limits his liability by applying conditions of carriage, which are the terms on which a contract is made with the owner of the goods. By contracting to carry goods in accordance with specified conditions of carriage, the haulier limits his liability under the terms of those conditions.

Road hauliers' power to restrict legal liability

The road haulier may include in his conditions of carriage appropriate and easily understood terms and clauses that define the limits of his liability. If this is done, the haulier then remains liable only for his own negligence and that of his servants.

The haulier is also liable for loss or damage which the consignor suffers as a result of unreasonable delay of the goods in transit (*in transitu*) where such loss was reasonably foreseeable (eg if fruit were consigned to a market it would be known beforehand that delay might result in the market being missed and the fruit becoming worthless). The haulier is not liable if delay is caused by the consignor stopping delivery of the goods while in transit because he does not wish the buyer to receive them due to the buyer's possible inability to pay (for example, because of his insolvency).

Similarly, the haulier is liable for wrongful delivery of goods if this is due to wilful misconduct by his servants, but not if it is merely a negligent misdelivery. The haulier is not liable in respect of dangerous goods where he did not know that the goods were dangerous; had he known, he could have either refused to carry them or imposed special conditions or charges.

In making an offer to consign goods via the haulier, the owner implies acceptance of the conditions where they have been drawn to his attention, directly or otherwise (they may be printed on the back of the quotation or they may be referred to on the haulier's letter heading, literature or consignment notes) prior to the movement taking place.

The conditions of carriage limit the haulier's responsibility for loss or damage to the goods as a result of his own or his servants' negligence, up to a maximum limit of value (usually £800/£1,300 or more per tonne). He is not liable for loss or damage to the goods in excess of this value unless he has been informed of their value and undertakes to carry them and become the insurer of the excess amount over the standard conditions. If the haulier is advised that goods to be carried exceed this value, extra cover should be arranged with the Goods in Transit insurers.

Breach of contract

While the haulier can limit his liability as described previously, he cannot include in the contract a clause that exempts him from liability for a *fundamental breach of contract*. In other words he cannot fail to do what he has contracted to do and then avoid liability for this failure (eg by failure to deliver goods which he has contracted to deliver, although he could avoid liability for failure to deliver at, say, a specific time).

Rights to lien and bailment

The road haulier has a right to lien (ie possession) over goods entrusted to him for carriage until the carriage charges are paid.

Lien falls into two categories: particular lien means that a specific consignment of goods may be held until the carriage charges in respect of that particular consignment are paid, and general lien means that any goods may be held until charges for previous consignments have been paid.

Particular lien is a standing right in law, but the right to general lien is only applicable if specified in the haulier's conditions of carriage. The right to lien only confer a right to detain goods, not to charge for their storage to enforce the lien and not to dispose of them in order to recover lost carriage charges unless such actions are specifically forewarned in the conditions of carriage.

A haulier may detain goods which are consigned for carriage but which cannot be delivered for some reason known as 'bailment'. He then becomes a 'bailer' of the goods and, as such, has a duty to avoid them becoming lost or damaged through negligence. The goods may be held until the carriage charges are paid, either on his vehicle or in his yard, and if his conditions of carriage include the necessary provision, demurrage (ie delay) charges may be raised.

A2. LEGAL OBLIGATIONS

Torts and liabilities

Torts – negligence

A road transport operator, when under contract with a third party, is, in the execution of that contract, liable for his own negligence and, in many instances, the negligence of his employees. Negligence means that proper care was not exercised in dealing with other people's goods or property, or in maintaining vehicles on which goods are carried or premises in which goods may be held or stored.

The operator's liability for torts (a legal term for 'breach of duty', in other words negligence, redressable by a claim for damages by the person who suffers as a result of that breach) in many particular aspects is important.

The operator must exercise proper care in carrying and storing the goods belonging to his customers to ensure that they are not lost or damaged because of his negligence. Negligence could be attributed to such acts as failing to secure the load adequately on the vehicle, failing to sheet the load to protect it from the weather, or failing to maintain the vehicle so that as a result of mechanical failure the goods are damaged. Other instances concern delay so that if loss or damage occurs through unreasonable delay the operator is liable. Similarly he is liable for negligence if the load is transhipped in his yard and damage is caused through failure to use suitable lifting equipment, or if the goods are left outside and are damaged by the weather.

Legal proceedings for negligence

The customer (the plaintiff) can institute legal proceedings against the carrier (the defendant) for negligence if he has suffered damage or loss through the defendant's negligent actions or omissions. Without evidence of damage or loss there can be no case. Where there is a case and the court accepts this, it will award 'damages' (ie monetary recompense).

Nuisance

Public nuisance

It is a crime to cause a public nuisance: a person affected by a public nuisance to the point where he has suffered a loss beyond the discomfort or inconvenience suffered by the public at large may take action in tort against the person causing the public nuisance. A public nuisance may result, for example, from causing obstruction on a highway or public right of way, causing excessive noise at unsociable hours or creating exceptional noise or smell.

For an action to be called a public nuisance it must affect the reasonable comfort and convenience of the life of a 'class' of people. Therefore an action is not normally a public nuisance if it affects only one or two people, although the number which constitutes a class is not defined.

In the case of transport, for example, if all the people in a row of houses were subject to excessive noise at night from a vehicle workshop, this could be classed as a public nuisance and the people have recourse to law as well as having the opportunity to make an environmental representation against the operator's 'O' licence.

Private nuisance

If one person only is affected by an unlawful act concerning land, this can be termed 'private nuisance'. This might arise, for example, when the offender interferes with a person's enjoyment of land occupied by him by obstructing access to the land, by blocking light from the land or by allowing that person's land to be affected by noise, smells, water, germs or physical objects (eg rubbish).

Obstruction of the police
It is an offence to obstruct the police in the execution of their duties. Obstruction in this instance could include failure or refusal to provide information in response to police enquiries about alleged offences and crimes, in connection with the use of vehicles for example, or with any other police investigation. Almost any refusal to follow the direction of a police officer could result in prosecution for obstruction. For example, failure to move a vehicle to or from a particular place, refusal to produce a driving licence or other documents, or even making face-tious replies to questions or sarcastic comments when apprehended by an officer could be considered obstruction of the police and could lead to prosecution.

Employers' liability for the actions of their employees

An employer is liable for the wrongful or negligent acts of his employees when such acts are committed within the scope of their terms or position of employment. For example, if an employee is a salesman and commits any wrongful or negligent act in his selling capacity, this would be the responsibility of the employer.

However, if the employee committed a wrongful act in some other respect that could be termed 'deviation or departure' from duty, the employer would not be held liable. Consider the case of a television or a washing machine salesman who, on visiting a customer, strips down or attempts to repair the customer's old machine, having assured the customer that he 'knows about these things'. In the event of a claim, the employer could say that the employee was working outside the terms of his employment as a salesman; the employer could therefore not be held liable for any claim resulting from such action. Such action is generally referred to as the employee engaging in a 'frolic of his own'.

The employer is not completely free of liability if he merely pro-hibits an employee from doing certain things, or from doing certain things for specified third parties if this is part of his general terms of employment. For example, if a mechanic who services cars was expressly forbidden by his employer to service the car of Mr X but the employee disregards this instruction and a claim results, the employer cannot escape liability by virtue of the instruction to the employee not to commit that act.

Where an employee fails to meet specific legal requirements (for exam-ple, relating to his job as an LGV driver), the employer is also held to be responsible for the employee's failure should any claim result and he can also be prosecuted for offences relating to his employee's failure to comply with statutory requirements.

Occupiers' liability

Occupiers of premises encounter two types of person on their land: visitors and employees, who are there with explicit or implied permission, and trespassers, who have no authority to be there.

The occupier owes a common duty of care towards visitors and employees (under the Occupiers' Liability Acts of 1957 and 1984), to ensure that they are reasonably safe in using the premises for the purpose for which they are invited or permitted to be there. This can be achieved by giving adequate warning of any dangers attached to being on the premises.

It is particularly important to assess the role of children in relationship to this point. The occupier must be prepared for children to be less careful than adults and he becomes liable if child visitors are not protected from being attracted to dangerous objects or areas on the premises, although in the case of very young children the occupier may only need to give sufficient warning to the adult or a competent person accompanying the child.

It is also illegal (under the Guard Dogs Act 1975) to allow guard dogs to roam loose on premises or indeed to have such a dog on premises at all unless a notice clearly warns of the danger.

Trespass

Trespass may be defined as interference with the possession of another person's land without lawful justification. To constitute trespass, the interference must be forcible and direct and therefore to walk on another person's land constitutes trespass, as does remaining on the land after permission to stay has ended.

NB: This definition is peculiar to English law. In Scotland different circumstances can apply although the same general principle may be effective in similar circumstances.

The transport operator's legal responsibility to trespassers on land which he occupies prevents him from setting traps or other discouraging devices (see also below). The operator has a duty under common humanity to give warning to trespassers of the dangers on his land or to warn them to take reasonable steps to avoid the dangers.

If activities on a transport operator's land are likely to cause danger, even to unauthorized trespassers, the land should be fenced. The operator can be held liable for negligence if a trespasser suffers injuries while on his land.

A3. PRINCIPALS AND SUBCONTRACTORS

Principals and agents

A special legal relationship exists between principals and agents. An agent is not an employee of the principal but is authorized to act on his behalf. However, an employee may be an agent of the principal.

There are broadly two types of agent: 1) special agents who have authority from the principal to act for a special (ie defined) purpose only; and 2) general agents who have general authority to act for their principals (perhaps across the whole range of the principal's business interests).

An agency arrangement may be created by a deed, in writing, or orally, or it may be implied by the relative actions of the principal and the agent.

An agent's role is to act on behalf of and represent the business interests of his principal. For example, a firm (the principal) may wish to have another firm (the agent) or person act as a selling agent in a location where it does not have its own employed sales representatives.

In legal terms an agent is a firm or person who has agreed, on behalf of the principal, to conclude a contract between the principal and a third party. Once the authority to act is given to the agent by the principal, the principal becomes responsible for the agent's actions or omissions.

The extent of an agent's authority to act on behalf of his principal depends on the authority expressly conferred on him by his principal, or implied by the principal from his words or actions towards the agent. Agents cannot, generally, delegate their powers or duties to another person without authority from the principal, who is entitled to expect his agent to carry his business personally.

Any contract established by an agent is a contract between the principal and the third party (ie the customer). The agent is only a link between one and the other and is not a party to the contract. However, the principal is bound by the acts of his agent so long as such acts are within the agent's authority to act (ie either by general or express authority). Similarly, the principal can enforce contracts made by his agent so long as these were made within the agent's authority.

A principal's responsibility or liability for the actions of his agent cannot be terminated merely by telling the agent not to act. Therefore, if the agent continues to act for the principal in an unauthorized capacity (ie by still selling goods to third parties after having his employment as the agent terminated – this *does not* relate to employment as a pure employee), those people contracting with the agent have the right to assume that the agent is still authorized to act until they are informed otherwise.

If the employer or principal wishes to terminate the responsibility of an agent, he should take steps to inform all potential customers that the agent is no longer authorized to act on his behalf. This can be a long-term, extensive and very costly operation involving newspaper and trade paper advertisements, direct mail letters to existing and potential customers and so on.

Duties of agents
Agents have certain duties as follows:

- to use ordinary care and skill in carrying out their agency duties;
- to use their judgement and discretion honestly;
- to maintain confidence about information that comes to their notice;
- to ensure their own interests do not conflict with the duties to their principals;
- to keep accurate accounts of moneys received and paid out;
- to refuse bribes, secret commissions or benefits not known to their principals (see also below).

In return, agents may expect to be:

- remunerated in accordance with their contract with the principal;
- reimbursed for their legitimate outlays and expenses;
- indemnified against liabilities incurred in carrying out their authorized duties.

Agents have a right of lien over their principal's property in respect of all legal claims against their principal. But conversely, an agent is personally liable if he does not disclose the name of his principal when carrying out acts on behalf of the principal but, generally, he may not be liable if he discloses the existence of an (unnamed) principal.

Secret profits
It is illegal under the terms of a principal/agent relationship for the agent to make secret profits in his dealings with the principal's customers. In the event that such profits are made they must be returned to the principal or alternatively the principal can sue the agent for their return – they do not have to be returned to the customer.

Contractors and subcontractors

In haulage terms, a subcontractor is a vehicle operator who accepts instructions to deliver goods that a principal contractor has agreed to deliver. He is neither a servant nor an employee of the contractor (ie the principal). Usually the principal contractor subcontracts work when his own fleet is fully utilized, when the delivery is outside his normal working territory or when the price is poor but he still feels obliged to accept instructions for delivery. The responsibilities on both sides are as follows.

Main/principal contractor

The customer expects him to ensure that the goods are properly carried on a suitable vehicle with a reliable driver, are properly protected against loss or damage and adequately insured.

The customer will expect the goods to be delivered to the right place on time and will require proof of delivery.

The contractor should vet the haulier who is carrying the goods (ie the subcontractor) to ensure he is reliable, has proper vehicles, is licensed to do the work, has a properly licensed driver and, most important, is adequately insured.

The main contractor is fully liable to the consignor (ie the customer) for loss or damage to the goods even if this occurred when they were in the possession of a subcontractor whose fault the loss or damage may have been. In turn, he must seek redress from the subcontractor.

Subcontractor

The subcontractor has responsibility to ensure that instructions given regarding collection and delivery and other matters are followed.

The subcontractor must ensure that the load is carried without risk of loss or damage and is adequately covered by insurance.

The subcontractor should provide proof of delivery by producing a signed receipt note for the principal contractor when sending the invoice.

If the shipper (ie the customer or the consignor of the goods) has to make a claim for loss or damage, this claim will be made to the principal contractor who in turn will seek redress from the subcontractor. In acting as an intermediary only, the principal contractor does not (in fact legally cannot) escape responsibility for the safe-keeping and proper delivery of the goods.

A4. CMR LIABILITY

Operators carrying goods for hire and reward on international journeys must comply with the Convention on the Contract for the International Carriage of Goods by Road 1956 (CMR – *Convention Merchandises Routiers*) which relates to carriers' liability and documents to be carried on vehicles. The Convention was adopted in the UK under the Carriage of Goods by Road Act 1965.

The following countries in addition to the UK are party to the CMR Convention:

Austria	Greece	Romania
Belarus	Hungary	Russian Federation
Belgium	Italy	Serbia and Montenegro
Bosnia-Herzegovina	Kazakhstan	Slovak Republic
Bulgaria	Latvia	Slovenia
Croatia	Lithuania	Spain
Czech Republic	Macedonia	Sweden
Denmark	Moldova	Switzerland
Estonia	Morocco	Tajikistan
Finland	Netherlands	Tunisia
France	Norway	Turkey
Germany	Poland	Turkmenistan
Gibraltar	Portugal	Uzbekistan

The Convention applies to all contracts for the carriage of goods by road for hire or reward between one country and another, as long as one is a party to the Convention.

Exemptions apply in the case of:

- own-account operations;
- carriage under an International Postal Convention;
- furniture removals;
- funeral consignments.

CMR is not applicable in respect of international haulage operations between the UK (including Northern Ireland) and the Republic of Ireland. Also, a recent High Court ruling stated that CMR conditions do not apply to contracts for the carriage of goods between the UK mainland and the Channel Islands (ie Guernsey, Jersey, Alderney, Sark and Herm. *NB:* Vehicles are not normally allowed on the latter two islands in any case). Such operations are not legally classed as being international journeys.

The principal conditions of the Convention are as follows:

1. The Convention terms apply to the complete carriage, whether this is wholly by road or partly by road and partly by rail, sea or inland waterway, as long as the goods remain in the original vehicle.
2. The carrier is responsible under the Convention for the actions and omissions of his agents and any other persons whose services are used in carrying out the movement.

3. The contract of carriage is confirmed by making out a CMR consignment note (see page 39) in three original copies, which should be signed by the carrier and the sender. Both keep one copy and the third copy travels with the goods.

4. If the goods are carried in different vehicles or are divided owing to their different nature, the carrier or the sender can specify that a separate consignment note should be made out for each vehicle or load of goods.

5. The consignment note must contain certain details (see page 40) but may also contain additional information of use to the parties to the contract.

6. The sender is responsible for all expenses, loss and damage sustained by the carrier as a result of inaccuracies in completion of the consignment note in relation to information supplied by the sender.

7. On receipt of the goods, the carrier must check the accuracy of details in the consignment note and the condition of the goods and their packaging.

8. The sender is liable to the carrier for damage and expenses due to defective packing of the goods unless the defects were known to the carrier when taking over the goods.

9. The sender must attach to the consignment note or make available to the carrier the necessary documents to complete Customs formalities.

10. The sender has the right of disposal of the goods and may stop transit of the goods or change the delivery address up to the time of delivery to the consignee unless he has stated on the consignment note that the consignee has this right. Once the goods are delivered to the address on the consignment note, the consignee has the right of disposal.

11. A carrier who fails to follow the instructions on the consignment note or who has followed them without requesting the first copy of the consignment note to be produced is liable for loss or damage caused by such failure.

12. The carrier must provide the consignee with a second copy of the consignment note at the time of delivering the goods.

13. If the carrier cannot follow the instructions on the consignment note for any reason, he must ask the sender or the consignee (depending on who has the right of disposal – see condition 10 above) for further instructions.

14. The carrier is liable for the total or partial loss of the goods and for any damage to them occurring between the time when he takes over the goods and the time of their delivery unless the loss, damage or delay was caused by a wrongful act or neglect of the claimant. The burden of proof in this case rests with the carrier.

15. Failure to deliver goods within 30 days of a specified time limit, or within 60 days from the time when the first carrier took them over if

there is no time limit for delivery, results in the goods being considered to be lost.

16. When goods of a dangerous nature are consigned, the carrier must be informed of the nature of the danger and the precautions to be taken.

17. Calculation of compensation in the event of loss or damage is related to the value of the goods at the place and time they were accepted for carriage but will not exceed a set value (ie related to SDR – see page 39 for explanation).

18. Carriage charges, Customs duties and other charges in respect of the carriage are refunded in the case of total loss of the goods and proportionately in the case of partial loss.

19. Higher levels of compensation may be claimed where the value or a special interest in delivery has been declared or where a surcharge has been paid in respect of a declared value exceeding the limit mentioned in condition 17.

20. In the case of damage the carrier is liable for the amount by which the value of the goods has diminished.

21. The claimant may demand interest in respect of the amount of any claim at 5 per cent per annum from the date on which the claim was sent to the carrier.

22. A carrier cannot avail himself of exclusions or limiting clauses if damage to goods was caused by his wilful misconduct or default that constitutes wilful misconduct.

23. The consignee is considered to have accepted the goods in a satisfactory condition if he does not indicate his reservations at the time of delivery or within seven days (excluding Sundays and public holidays).

24. In legal proceedings, the plaintiff may bring an action in any court or tribunal of a contracting (ie CMR contracting) country or of a country in which the defendant is normally resident or has his principal place of business, or of a country where the goods were taken over by the carrier or where they were designated for delivery, and in no other courts or tribunals.

25. The period of limitation for an action under the Convention is one year, or three years in the case of wilful misconduct.

26. Where successive road carriers are involved in a contract under the Convention, each is responsible for the whole operation as a party to the contract. Each successive carrier must give the previous carrier a dated receipt and must enter his name and address on the second copy of the consignment note.

27. A carrier who has paid compensation arising from a claim may recover the compensation plus interest, costs and expenses from other carriers who were parties to the contract subject to:
    (a) the carrier responsible for the loss or damage paying the compensation;

(b) each carrier responsible for loss or damage jointly caused shall be liable to pay proportionate compensation or compensation proportionate to their share of the carriage charges if responsibility cannot be apportioned.

28. If a carrier who is due to pay compensation is insolvent, his share must be paid by other carriers who are parties to the contract.

CMR liability insurance

Transport operators in Britain normally carry goods either under their own conditions of carriage or under those of the Road Haulage Association, and consequently carry Goods in Transit (GIT) insurance cover in respect of their liability under those conditions. The cover usually varies between about £800 per tonne as a minimum and £1,300 per tonne (the current RHA standard).

In international road haulage operations (but *not* own-account operations), the carriage automatically comes within the terms of the International Convention on the Carriage of Goods 1956, known as CMR. Under this Convention the carrier's liability is determined by comparison with a measure known as 'special drawing rights' (SDR), whereby compensation must not exceed 8.33 units of account per kilogram of gross weight short (gws). Special drawing rights are defined by the International Monetary Fund and are converted to the national currency of the country in which any claim is dealt with in court and is assessed as to value on the date of the judgement or on a date agreed to by the parties. To gain a rough idea of what this value represents, on 30 March 2004 a conversion of SDR to sterling represented approximately £6,723 per tonne (ie £1.00 ÷ 1.239000 x 8.33 units x 1,000 kg = £6,723.164). The daily rate for SDR can be found in the *Financial Times* (Companies and Markets section – currency rates).

NB: The value or exchange rate of SDRs on the date of judgement or agreement referred to above must not be confused with the date of calculation of the value of the goods which are subject to the claim as referred to in item 17 on page 38).

With changing values it is essential that the current value should be established at any particular time, and adequate insurance cover to at least this level of liability should be carried.

Since all international road haulage movements are subject to CMR and a CMR consignment note accompanies the transit, operators should be aware that with any such movement their liability is for the CMR levels and that they need appropriate cover.

However, there are circumstances when a domestic haulier could unwittingly be involved in an international movement. These may arise when a haulier is asked, for example, to carry a loaded trailer or container from one place in the UK to another place in the UK. If the trailer or container has entered the country from abroad and has not been unloaded, any internal movement in the UK is still part of the international journey and is therefore still subject to CMR. The UK haulier who moves such a trailer or container may not be aware of this, particularly if the facts are not drawn to his attention or the relevant documentation is not pointed out, and he may only have standard GIT or RHA levels of insurance cover. Similarly, a haulier may be involved in an international haulage journey within the UK by taking a loaded trailer to a port for onward shipment or even to an inland clearance depot. If the trailer goes forward loaded the haulier should realize that he needs to be covered for CMR levels of liability despite the fact that his tractive unit and driver do not leave this country.

CMR consignment notes

The following details must be entered on CMR consignment notes:

1. The date of the consignment note and the place at which it is made out.
2. The name and address of the sender.
3. The name and address of the carrier and subsequent carriers.
4. The place and date of taking over the goods and the place designated for delivery.
5. The name and address of the consignee.
6. A description in common use of the nature of the goods and the method of packing (in the case of dangerous goods, their generally recognized description).
7. The number of packages and their special marks and numbers.
8. The gross weight of the goods or their quantity otherwise expressed.
9. Charges relating to the carriage (carriage charges), supplementary charges, Customs duties and other charges incurred from the making of the contract to the time of delivery.
10. Appropriate instructions for Customs and other formalities.
11. A statement that the carriage is subject, notwithstanding any clause to the contrary, to the provisions of the CMR Convention.

Where applicable, the consignment note should also contain the following information:

1. A statement that transhipment is not allowed.
2. The charges that the sender undertakes to pay.
3. The amount of COD charges.
4. A declaration of the value of the goods and of the amount representing special interest in delivery.
5. The sender's instructions to the carrier regarding insurance of the goods.

6. The agreed time limit within which the carriage is to occur.

7. A list of those documents handed to the carrier.

Any other particulars which the parties to the contract feel will be useful may be added to the consignment note.

The CMR consignment note must be carried by the driver on all hire and reward journeys abroad.

Blank sets of CMR consignment notes can be obtained from the Road Haulage Association and the Freight Transport Association.

PART 2

Commercial law

This part covers Directive items B1 and B2 in Units 1 and 2.

B1. TRADING LAW

Types of business organization

Business is conducted in many forms, the simplest organizational structure being the person working on his own account as a sole trader or sole proprietor. Larger organizations are usually formed into partnerships or into limited liability companies and many of the largest national and international firms are formed into public limited companies. Each of these various forms of commercial organization differs in the nature of the legal obligations to be met and each has relative advantages and disadvantages depending on size, the nature of the trade or commercial activity in which they are engaged, their financial needs and the wishes of the owners. The main legal differences and requirements and the relative advantages and disadvantages of each are briefly described here.

Sole traders
The simplest form of business is the sole trader. Any person can start a business in this way very cheaply and with the minimum of fuss. Set-up costs are negligible, legal requirements are minimal and the owner is mainly only responsible to himself and his customers.

The advantage of operating as a sole trader is the freedom from the need to comply with Companies Act legislation, which requires legal registration and other complex formalities to be followed, including the need for accounts to be kept in a proper form and audited annually and completed returns of directors and shareholders to be sent to Companies House.

The disadvantage is that the proprietor has no protection against his personal liabilities for meeting creditors' demands for payment if the business should fail. In this event the proprietor's belongings and even his house may be sold to help pay off what is due to creditors.

If the business succeeds it will need capital for expansion and consequently assistance from the bank, for which security has to be provided. Usually the bank will want to take a second charge on the proprietor's home (if he owns it or is buying it on mortgage). Thus if repayments cannot be made, the bank holds the house and could sell it to recover any outstanding balance on the loan.

All profits made by the business become the proprietor's income (ie rewards for the business risks taken and the effort put into the business), from which he both derives his livelihood and builds up capital resources for future asset replacement or expansion. He must, of course, declare these profits for taxation purposes and pay any tax due.

Partnerships

This form of business is an expansion of the sole trader structure. Instead of one person owning the business two or more people own it, sharing the ownership, the work and the profits either equally or in unequal proportions. The partners are, however, personally liable for any debts incurred by the partnership business.

Individual partners are agents for the partnership (usually referred to as a firm – as opposed to a company as described below) and as such can bind the other partners in contracts whether specifically authorized to do so or not. The partnership firm can be sued in its business names or by separate writ to each of the partners individually. Should a partner be sued individually, he may be entitled to a contribution towards any damages awarded against him from the other partners whether they have been individually sued in the same action or not.

A partnership business cannot buy and have land conveyed to it as such, only to one or more of the partners as individuals who can *declare a trust for sale* for all the partners in equity (ie who own equity in the business).

While most partnerships are constituted as general partnerships with all partners being equally liable for the business debts as mentioned above, the Partnership Act 1907 allows a form of limited partnership under which individual partners' liabilities for the debts may be limited to the amount of capital they invested in the business. However, in such cases there must still be at least one general partner with unlimited liability.

Usually the partners in a business have a legal agreement setting out their responsibilities and liabilities (ie for the partnership debts) in proportion to their share of the ownership of the business, and any profits made which are not retained for future use in the business are shared proportionately in accordance with the terms of the agreement.

In the absence of a partnership agreement the law in the form of the Partnership Act 1890 will imply terms under which it (and the Inland Revenue) will look upon the partners as all having equal shares but with each person 'jointly and severally' liable for any debts of the partnership – in other words, if the other partners have no personal assets one partner with assets could be left to meet the tax liabilities and all the other debts of the partnership should the business fail.

Many professional firms such as accountants, solicitors, surveyors, estate agents and consulting engineers operate as legally constituted partnerships (solicitors and accountants, for example, cannot by law limit their liabilities so they have no choice but to operate as partnerships). In contrast, the road haulage industry comprises many partnerships based on little more than friendship, mutual trust or family relationships (eg father and son, husband and wife, etc).

The advantages of a partnership are that there are more people to contribute initial finance and more people to share the work, the decision making and the worries. The burden of providing security is also shared.

The disadvantages of partnerships are that people do not always agree, and argument and distrust can lead eventually to the failure of a business. Another major aspect of contention is that profits have to be shared in proportion to ownership rather than in proportion to the work and effort put into making the business a success.

On dissolution of a partnership, which may be due to business failure or perhaps as a result of irreconcilable differences of opinion among the partners, the assets of the business must be sold and the funds used to pay off outstanding commercial debts and loans and to meet other liabilities such as the tax and National Insurance contributions of the partners and employees (a priority) and other employment liabilities. Should there be a shortfall of funds from the realization of assets, the partners will have to personally meet any outstanding amounts from their own resources (ie sale of their own personal assets including, if necessary, their car or even their home) as described above. Conversely, if there is a surplus after the disposal of assets, this may be shared among the partners either equally or in proportion to their individual share of the partnership business.

On the death of a partner, which may in itself be a reason for dissolution, the remaining partner/s must account to that late partner's personal representative (ie the executors to his estate) for the amount of his interest in the firm (ie the value of his share of the business). In these circumstances, all tax due under the old partnership (ie up to the time of the death) will normally become due immediately, except where special arrangements are made with the Inland Revenue about continuation of the partnership with the remaining partners.

Recognizing that such an event may occur, it is usual for partnerships to be advised to take out appropriate insurance cover to provide sufficient funds to meet payments due to the IR and to the deceased partner's estate should the eventuality arise.

Limited liability companies

If a person (or persons) forming a business wishes to remove the risk of loss of personal property and possessions in the event of the business failure, he can form a private limited liability company under the provisions of the Companies Act 1985.

This is a legally constituted corporate body (ie a 'company') formally registered with the Registrar of Companies in which the parties to the business hold shares in equal or unequal proportions. The owners of the business are therefore the shareholders (or members) of the company. The company has a registered name, which must be approved by the Registrar of Companies, and not be a name which may be confused with that of any other registered company or which is either sensitive (eg implying royal connections or suggesting that the company is a national body or authority), or offensive. The word 'limited' must be added as the last word of the name.

The legal requirement is for a minimum of two shareholders. One person must be appointed a director of the company (who may or may not be a shareholder) and one person must be the company secretary (who also need not be a shareholder and must not be the only director). Invariably, in small companies the secretary is both a shareholder and director. The company secretary is known as the legal officer of the company upon whom all legal notices are served. If the company is prosecuted for offences committed by the company itself, its directors as individuals or its employees, this is done through the company secretary; he may not be personally liable but he is the officer of the company who is ultimately answerable to the court on behalf of the company (the company may, of course, be legally represented in such cases). This person also has responsibility under the Companies Act for ensuring that all statutory requirements are met, for recording the minutes of board meetings, ensuring that annual accounts and a balance sheet are produced, and making the necessary annual returns to Companies House.

In forming the business or in raising capital for expansion, friends or relatives may be asked to invest funds in return for shares in the company *but it is not permitted to advertise for the public to invest in or buy the shares of a private limited company*. Some or all of the shareholders may be elected to be directors of the company (ie the people who control the business and make the important decisions). The directors can choose a chairman from among themselves for the purpose of conducting meetings of the board of directors. The chairman usually has a casting vote, which is intended to resolve any 'stalemate' situations in voting decisions.

When a company is formed, the subscribers (the founders) decide on the amount of shares that will form the legally constituted 'share capital' of the business. This may be, for example, 100 shares at £1 each to make it a £100 share-capital company. These shares are divided among the subscribers according to their contribution and according to the decision on who is to have the controlling interest. One shareholder may have 51 shares and the second one 49 shares, or they may have 50 each, which means neither has a controlling interest.

Once the share capital and the holdings of each of the subscribers are determined, this becomes the maximum limit of their personal liability if the business goes into liquidation. So if their shares are fully paid up, the shareholders do not have to make any other contribution towards the debts of the company.

Often the share capital of a company is not fully paid up. For example, two people could form a £100 company of which only two £1 shares are 'issued' or 'paid up' (one each). In the event of liquidation they become liable to pay the balance of their allocation of shares (another £49 each if they have equal shares).

Company directors carry considerable legal responsibilities and can be held liable for a whole range of company law-related offences (some 200 in all). They have a fiduciary duty to the company (ie duty of trust to safeguard its property and assets). They must act in good faith and must not allow their personal interests to conflict with those of the company. Besides this duty to the company (not necessarily to the shareholders) they also have a duty to the employees. The Directors are responsible, under the Companies Act 1985, for the preparation of financial statements for each accounting year which give a true and fair view of the state of affairs of the company as at the end of the year, and of the surplus or deficit for the year.

In preparing those financial statements the Directors are required to:

- select suitable accounting policies and then apply them consistently;
- make judgements that are reasonable and prudent;
- state whether applicable accounting standards have been followed, subject to any material departures disclosed and explained in the financial statements; and
- prepare the financial statements on a going concern basis unless it is inappropriate to presume that the company will continue in business.

The Directors have responsibility for ensuring that the company keeps accounting records which disclose with reasonable accuracy the financial position of the company at any time and which enable them to ensure that the financial statements comply with the Companies Act 1985. They also have general responsibility for taking such steps as are reasonably open to them to safeguard the assets of the company and to prevent and detect fraud and other irregularities. If they fail in their duties the directors can be held personally liable for any loss that is attributable to their negligence, or to any act outside their authority or in breach of duty or trust – in other words they could be forced to pay compensation out of their own pockets.

Public limited companies

When a company becomes very large and needs to raise more capital for expansion by investment rather than by borrowing, it seeks to become quoted on the stock market so that its shares can be sold on the market to all and sundry and it can become 'public'. In this instance companies are required to put the letters 'plc' (public limited company) after the company name.

The money that the new shareholders pay for their shares provides the required capital for the business and the new shareholders become part-owners of the business along with the original shareholders. The shares which are sold may be new issue shares if the share capital is increased or they may have belonged to the founders of the business (perhaps a family) who decided to sell all or a proportion of their shares (but in this case the money goes to them rather than into the company).

Shares may be divided into a number of classes (particularly into voting and non-voting shares). Normally shares carry the right to vote and usually the right is for one vote per share. The chairman of the board of directors, as mentioned above, frequently is granted an additional casting vote to avoid stalemate situations.

A limited company needs an authorized share capital of at least £50,000 before it goes 'public'. (A second category of plc is the unlisted securities market. A minimum share capital of £12,500 is needed for trading.) It must have at least two shareholders and must show a satisfactory history of performance and stability and good future prospects with sound management in order to satisfy the stock market.

Once a company has become 'public' its shares are quoted on the Stock Exchange and fluctuations in value are recorded daily and are usually published in the financial columns of the daily press.

Insider dealing in shares, which is the use of knowledge or confidential information of companies' plans, etc, to make financial gains on the stock market, is an illegal act for which severe penalties can be imposed.

Apart from its size and the more rigorous inspection of its activities, accounts, financial dealings and management, which result from a much larger body of shareholders (they could number thousands), a public limited company is very similar in structure to a private limited company.

Companies limited by guarantee

Non-profit-making organizations (such as professional organizations, sports clubs, etc) may form a type of limited liability company which is limited not by the shareholdings of its members (ie its shareholders), but by a guarantee of its members (who are not shareholders) who agree to pay a small amount in the event of collapse and/or liquidation of the organization (often a nominal sum of £1 each).

Cooperatives

Cooperatives are a type of business organization usually formed and run by a group of people each of whom has a financial interest in its success and a say in its management. Basically cooperatives are owned and jointly run by the members with all profits (after ploughing back an amount to develop the business) being shared among the members (ie they are not called shareholders). Management is usually by an elected committee of the members.

Such organizations were common in Communist countries, and are often found in agriculture where individual farmers cannot afford to buy expensive machinery or indulge in large-scale production. In other spheres they are found in management buyout situations where existing management and employees join together to take over an ailing firm in the interests of protecting their jobs (sometimes called worker cooperatives). In retailing, cooperatives are usually owned by the customers.

B2. COMPANY LAW

Formation and registration of a company

Limited companies may be formed specially to suit the requirements of a particular business, or 'ready-made' companies may be purchased 'off the shelf'. In both cases the formation procedure is the same, but the latter method provides quicker protection from liability and saves some money as such companies are formed by firms specializing in this business. Many of these have offices near Companies House and they can easily make the necessary searches to ensure that the name required has not already been used.

These off-the-shelf companies already have their share capital established, their name registered and their Articles of Association and Memorandum printed, plus all the other legal formalities completed for immediate operation, and are sold to anybody wishing to obtain limited liability for a business operation very quickly.

Against the advantages of speed and cheapness, ready-made companies are restrictive because the company name may not be suitable and the Articles may not cover exactly what is required. For this reason a new company may be formed. Usually an accountant or solicitor is employed to deal with a company formation and often his office is quoted as the registered office of the company. In forming a company, the following factors have to be established:

- A name (which must be acceptable to the Registrar of Companies – see above) followed by the word 'Limited'.
- The share capital (eg 100 £1 shares, 1,000 10p shares, etc).
- The names of the original subscribers (at least two persons).
- The names of the first directors and company secretary.
- The registered office for the company.
- The Articles of Association and Memorandum.

The Articles and Memorandum of Association jointly form the 'rule book' for the company because they define the company exactly, its name and the objects for which it was formed. Specifically this document (it is usually combined) contains the following information:

Memorandum of Association

- Name of company followed by the word 'Limited'.
- Where the registered office is situated (eg in England and Wales, or Scotland).
- The objects for which the company was formed (ie what it can and cannot do by way of trade).
- A statement that the liability of the members (ie shareholders) is limited.
- The amount of the share capital divided into a number of shares of a certain value each.
- The names of the original subscribers and their respective share holdings.

Articles of Association

- A statement that the provisions of the Companies Act 1985 apply (as amended 1989).
- Details of the capital structure of the company, the types of shares of which it is comprised and how they may be transferred.
- The voting rights of shareholders.
- Matters relating to the appointment and duties of directors.
- The borrowing powers of the company.
- The appointment of a company secretary.
- The requirements for notifying company meetings (how, when and to whom details must be circulated).
- The names of the first directors (not less than one and not more than seven for a private limited company).

- The names and addresses of the original subscribers (ie shareholders or members).

When the company is registered with the Registrar of Companies it is given a number, and it must have an official seal which is used on legal documents and share certificates. A Certificate of Incorporation is provided showing the company name, registration number and the date of first registration. This must be displayed at the company's registered office.

When the formation is complete, printed sets of the Articles and Memorandum are lodged with the Registrar of Companies along with other formation documents.

It is usual also for a company's bank to require copies of the Articles and Memorandum when it is providing finance by way of overdrafts and loans so it, too, can see what the company's borrowing powers are and any legal restrictions on its operations.

Legal operation of companies
A limited liability company must be operated within the requirements of the Companies Acts. Among these requirements are the following:

1. The Certificate of Incorporation must be displayed at the Registered Office.
2. The company name must be shown on the outside of all its business premises and on all its documentation including cheques.
3. All business paper must show the following information:
   (a) the registered office address if different from the trading address;
   (b) the registration number;
   (c) whether registered in England and Wales, or Scotland (or Northern Ireland);
   (d) the names of the directors *may* be shown provided the list includes *every* individual director of the company together with their first names or initials;
   (e) the VAT number if VAT registered (not a requirement under the Companies Act but a legal requirement of HM Customs and Excise).
4. The annual accounts for the company must be audited by a professional auditor (ie by a chartered accountant or by a member of the Association of Certified Accountants – but not if he is an employee of the company) who must also prepare a trading account and balance sheet.
5. An annual meeting (ie the AGM) must be held at which the directors and shareholders approve the annual accounts.
6. An annual return of directors, a copy of the minutes of the annual meeting and the accounts must be lodged with the Registrar of

Companies. Small companies (turnover not exceeding £350,000 annually) may produce simplified accounts in the form of a 'compilation report' for this purpose.

7. The Registrar of Companies must be notified of any changes of secretary, shareholders, directors or of the registered address.
8. Details of any charge or mortgage against the company or against property it owns or other assets must also be recorded at Companies House.

Records relating to limited companies, including their accounts and balance sheets and details of any charges and mortgages, etc, can be examined at Companies House by any interested body or person on payment of a small fee. Alternatively company search specialists based at Companies House will undertake this task and send copies of all documents, for a fee.

Duties and liabilities of company directors

Directors of a public limited company have similar responsibilities as described previously (see page 46) for directors of private limited companies. They owe an individual duty to every other director to act in accordance with legal requirements, in particular in regard to the interests of shareholders, employees and other people with whom the company comes into contact. They have a fiduciary duty to the company, acting as trustees of its assets and must not allow their personal interests to conflict with or supersede those of the company. They must act honestly and in good faith in all their dealings for the company.

They must not indulge in or allow the company to indulge in wrongful or fraudulent trading and may be held personally liable should the company become insolvent and go into liquidation as a result. Similarly, they must not seek or be party to any arrangement to make secret profits and may be made liable personally to compensate anybody who legitimately suffers loss as a consequence.

Besides these responsibilities, directors have statutory duties to:

- keep proper accounts and prepare annual accounts;
- file legal documents with Companies House as required;
- maintain the company's statutory books;
- disclose company contracts in which they have a personal interest;
- not accept or make loans to directors exceeding £5,000 (not totally banned, but they can raise problems);
- not accept or make substantial personal property investments in connection with the company (ie over £100,000 value or exceeding 10 per cent of the company's value);
- exercise care and skill in the operation and management of the company;
- be honest with shareholders and not mislead them as to the activities or profits of the company or its share value;

- not make negligent mis-statements or misrepresentations about the company in any promotional literature.

Liquidation of a business

If financial difficulties reach a point where a business cannot meet the demands of its creditors, it must cease trading – in other words, when it is insolvent. It is illegal to continue trading whether as a sole trader, a partnership or a limited liability company once this position is reached (under The Insolvency Act 1986).

When a business has to cease trading, various courses of action are open to the owners. The first stage may be an agreement with creditors whereby they accept reduction of the debt or a scheme for deferred payment. The next stage may be imposition of an administration order, which preserves the firm intact and prevents creditors making it bankrupt while the appointed administrator tries to rescue the business or sell it off as a going concern. If these alternatives are not relevant a receiver can be appointed voluntarily to take charge of the affairs of the business (ie voluntary liquidation) and pay off the creditors so far as realization of the assets permits, followed by winding up of the business (in the case of a limited liability company, when its name would be struck off the Companies Register). Alternatively, one or more of the creditors (or all of them collectively) may appoint a receiver. The former is a much more acceptable means of bringing a business to an end. In many instances creditors take action to make a firm bankrupt without prior notice.

Following the collapse of the business, charges may be brought against the proprietor, partners or directors (who may also be disqualified from taking part in the management of any company under the Company Directors Disqualification Act 1986) for misappropriation of funds for example, or for trading when insolvent, and they could be adjudged personally bankrupt.

Once the receiver is appointed he becomes legally responsible for collecting debts due to the business, for selling the company's assets and for paying off creditors (and the employees' wages) so far as possible. The amount paid to creditors depends on the resources available and on their status. Preferential creditors such as banks who have lent money against security, the Inland Revenue (for tax and National Insurance owing) and HM Customs and Excise (for VAT and any customs duties owing), and debenture holders are among those who have a first share of any money paid out. The receiver is permitted to charge his fees first.

When all the assets have been realized and distributed and the shareholders of a limited company have met any outstanding commitment on their shares, that is the end of the matter for them. In the case of non-limited firms the receiver becomes responsible for securing the personal assets of the proprietor or the partners including, where necessary to meet liabilities, forcing them to sell their home, their car and any luxury items such as TV sets, hi-fi systems, works of art and so on, until all claims are met. In the latter case, the individual may be left with nothing more than the barest amount of essential furniture (a bed, chair, table, etc). A similar misfortune may befall a director of a limited liability company who has given personal guarantees or secured his personal assets (ie home, insurances, other savings/investments, etc) against business loans.

PART 3

Social law

This part covers Directive items C1, C2 and C3 in Unit 1, and C4 in Units 2 and 3.

INTRODUCTION TO SOCIAL LAW

Present-day transport managers need to be concerned with many aspects of business operation and administration beyond those relating solely to owning and running haulage vehicles.

The employment of staff for driving, and to work in workshops, warehouses and offices, brings the manager into contact with a very broad and complex body of social legislation that has been built up over many years.

In this section we are concerned with the following key issues:

- employment law;
- the role of employment tribunals, ACAS and the trade unions;
- employment rights;
- current legislation on health and safety;
- EU and domestic drivers' hours law, record keeping and tachograph requirements;
- EU working-time regulation.

Current UK employment law is to be found in the following principal Acts of Parliament:

- Employment Protection (Consolidation) Act 1978 (as amended).
- Trade Union and Labour Relations (Consolidation) Act 1992.

- Trade Union Reform and Employment Rights Act 1993.
- Employment Relations Act 1999.
- Employment Act 2002.
- Employment Relations Bill (which will amend the provisions of the 1999 Act of this name and is expected to become law by Autumn 2004).

These Acts consolidate employees' rights in regard to:

- trade union membership;
- trade disputes and picketing;
- contracts and written statements of terms and conditions of employment;
- itemized pay statements;
- guarantee payments;
- suspension on medical grounds;
- time off for union duties and activities and for public duties;
- maternity rights;
- statutory sick pay (SSP);
- rights on termination of employment;
- dismissal and unfair dismissal;
- redundancy;
- time off for job seeking or to arrange training.

C1. TRIBUNALS AND TRADES UNIONS

Tribunals

A number of bodies are concerned with arbitration and providing conciliation in employment issues and disputes and there is also a facility for appeal to a higher authority. These are described here.

ACAS – The Advisory, Conciliation and Arbitration Service

ACAS is an official body that deals with employment disputes. It is staffed by civil servants and has a council comprising a full-time chairman and nine other members. Three of these members are appointed after consultation with employers' organizations, three after consultation with trade unions, and three are independent members, usually academics.

In cases where a worker makes a complaint to an employment tribunal, it is the statutory duty of ACAS to endeavour to secure a settlement if possible (by conciliation between the parties – employee and employer), to avoid the need for a tribunal hearing.

Generally, the role of ACAS is to:

- offer advice to employers, employers' associations, individual employees and trade unions on industrial relations matters and employment policies;

- provide a conciliation service to help settle employment disputes;
- provide, where necessary, conciliation officers who will endeavour to settle complaints both before and after matters are taken to employment tribunals; and where this is not possible –
- refer matters in dispute to arbitration or to the Central Arbitration Committee (CAC);
- inquire into employment relations generally or to examine particular industries or employment sectors;
- publish codes of practice and other advisory literature for employers, trade unions and others concerned with employment issues.

Employment tribunals

Employment tribunals are a type of court, in this case specifically convened to deal with employment disputes, where matters are considered, not by a judge and jury, but by a chairman (with legal training) and two other 'lay' members. They are intended to provide a less formal way of resolving employment disputes and to provide employees with a solution to situations where firms are in breach of their statutory duties towards employees.

Employment tribunals deal with the following employment and related issues:

- discrimination on grounds of sex, race and disability;
- equal pay;
- employment protection and employee rights;
- transfer of undertakings;
- payment of the national minimum wage;
- breaches of working-time regulations;
- wrongful or unfair dismissal;
- health and safety at work.

Central Arbitration Committee (CAC)

Principally, the CAC acts as an arbitrator in wage/pay disputes and in assisting recognized trade unions in exercising their statutory rights to obtain information for collective bargaining purposes from firms that employ their union members.

Certification Officer

The Certification Officer is an independent statutory authority responsible for ensuring:

- the independence of trade unions;
- that trade unions and employers' associations keep accounting records, have their accounts properly audited and submit annual returns;

- periodical actuarial examination and separate funding of members' superannuation schemes;
- observance of the statutory procedures for transfers of engagements, amalgamations and changes of name;
- supervision of the statutory requirements as to the setting up and operating of political funds, dealing with complaints by members about breach of the rules governing political funds (including the requirements on balloting) and trade union elections;
- the refund of certain costs incurred by independent trade unions in the holding of secret ballots for specified purposes;
- the availability of documents, including annual returns and rule books of trade unions and employers' association for public inspection.

Commissioner for the Rights of Trade Union Members
The Commissioner's role is to assist trade union members who intend to take, or are already taking, legal action against their unions (ie in connection with balloting, elections and political expenditure).

Trade union membership

Recognized trade unions
A 'recognized' trade union is one that is recognized by an employer or a group of employers for the purposes of collective bargaining on wages and other employment terms and conditions. It is also one that is recognized by the parties to a union agreement within the firm, or one which ACAS recommends as being one which should be recognized.

Right to belong or not to belong to a trade union
Employees have the right not to be victimized or discriminated against as individuals (short of dismissal) for the purpose of:

- preventing or deterring them from becoming members of a trade union;
- preventing or deterring them from taking part in trade union activities at any appropriate time (ie outside working hours or at a time when the employer gives permission for employees to take part in those activities);
- compelling them to be or become a member of a trade union. Employees who genuinely object on religious grounds have the right not to have action taken against them (short of dismissal) for the purposes of compelling them to belong to a trade union.

An employee can complain to an employment tribunal if any such action is taken against him. The complaint must be made within three months of the action complained of. The tribunal can award compensation that is just and equitable in relation to any loss suffered by the employee.

Trade disputes and picketing

A trade dispute is a dispute between an employer and his employees relating to, or in the main relating to:

- the terms and conditions of employment or the actual physical conditions in which employees are required to work;
- the engagement or non-engagement of one or more workers, the termination or suspension of their employment or the duties of their employment;
- the allocation of work or the duties of employment between employees or groups of employees;
- matters of discipline among employees;
- membership or non-membership of a trade union;
- the provision of facilities for trade union officials;
- the machinery for negotiation or consultation and other procedures relating to any of the above matters, including recognition by employers or employers' associations of the right of a trade union to represent workers in any such negotiation or consultation or in carrying out such procedures.

Trade disputes involving industrial action may take place between employers and employees or between groups of employees. Such disputes will be the subject of legal steps only if they have not been agreed in secret ballot requiring workers to make a straight 'Yes' or 'No' vote to the action. Without a properly conducted ballot the trade union and its officers have no legal immunity if they take or incite industrial action.

Secondary industrial action where a person is induced to take industrial action against an employer who is not party to a trade dispute in most cases can result in legal action for damages.

Picketing staged in furtherance of a trade dispute is legal if its purpose is to peacefully communicate information or peacefully persuade a person to refrain from working (or conversely to work) and provided it is carried out at or near the place of work. It is not illegal to picket elsewhere but this may result in a claim for damages by those who suffer loss as a result (eg by a firm which cannot get goods or employees into or out of its premises). In the cases described above, those who suffer loss may seek an injunction to put a stop to the action complained of and may also seek damages for the torts (wrongful actions) committed against them to compensate for their losses.

C2/C3. EMPLOYMENT AND HEALTH AND SAFETY

Terms and conditions of employment

Contracts and written particulars of employment

A contract of employment exists as soon as a job offer has been made and accepted by the prospective employee. Acceptance of the terms described verbally at the interview or contained in a letter of confirmation will be assumed if the employee reports at the due time to start the job. The contract does not have to be in writing.

Within two months of starting employment an employee must be given a written statement detailing:

- the parties to the contract;
- the date when employment began (and if for a fixed term, when it will end);
- the date when continuous employment began (eg after any probationary period);
- rates of pay;
- when payment is to be made (eg weekly or monthly);
- hours of work (normal and otherwise);
- holiday entitlements and pay;
- sick pay and provisions;
- pensions and pension schemes;
- notice of termination required;
- job title;
- if the job contract is only temporary, how long it may be expected to last;
- if the job is a fixed-term contract, the date of termination;
- where the job is outside the UK for more than one month, details of the length of the posting, the currency in which payment will be made, details of any additional benefits which accrue due to the posting, and terms and conditions relating to return to the UK;
- disciplinary rules (unless fewer than 20 persons were employed when continuous employment began);
- the name of the person to whom appeals on disciplinary matters can be referred;
- the name of the person to whom the employee can apply to seek redress of grievances;
- how such applications must be made.

If the terms of employment set out in the written statement are changed the employer must give the employee details of these in writing within one month.

Part-time workers

The Part-time Workers (Prevention of Less Favourable Treatment) Regulations 2000 introduced new rights for part-time workers which ensure that Britain's part-timer workers are not treated less favourably than comparable full-time employees in regard to the terms and conditions of their employment, unless it is objectively justified. This means, for example, that part-timers are entitled to:

- the same hourly rate of pay as their full-time colleagues;
- the same access to company pension schemes;
- the same entitlements to annual leave and maternity and parental leave on a pro rata basis;
- the same entitlement to contractual sick pay; and
- no less favourable treatment in access to training.

Itemized pay statements

When wages are paid the employee is entitled (on or before the pay day) to an itemized pay statement in writing showing:

- the gross amount of pay;
- amounts of any deductions and the reasons for deductions (except if fixed deductions are regularly made and a standing statement has been given plus a cumulative statement of the deductions);
- the net amount payable;
- where the net amount is paid by different means (eg part cheque/part cash), the method of payment of each different part of the total pay.

Guarantee payments

If the employer cannot find work on any day for an employee who has been employed continuously for at least one month, the employee is entitled to be paid a guaranteed payment for that workless day (ie 24 hours from midnight to midnight). This does not apply if the workless day occurs as a result of a trade dispute. Also, payment need not be made if the employee was offered alternative work which he unreasonably refused, or the employee does not comply with reasonable requirements to ensure that his services are available.

Limits are placed on the amount of guarantee pay due and the number of days for which it is due (eg five days in any three-month period for a five-day-week worker). Further, payment of guarantee pay does not affect the right of the employee to receive any other pay under his contract of employment.

An employee can complain to an employment tribunal if the employer fails to pay all or part of the guarantee pay due. If the tribunal upholds the complaint the employer will have to pay the amount due.

Suspension on medical grounds

If an employee is suspended from work by his employer on medical grounds as a result of legal requirements or recommendations based on Health and Safety at Work Codes of Practice, he must be paid for up to 26 weeks.

The employee is not entitled to such payment for any time when he is unable to work if:

- he had not been continuously employed for at least one month prior to commencement of the suspension;
- the employment is under a fixed-term contract not exceeding three months;
- he is suffering disease or bodily or mental disablement;
- the employer has offered suitable alternative work; or
- he does not comply with reasonable requirements to make his services available.

The amount of remuneration payable is one week's pay for every week's suspension starting on the day before the suspension begins, and proportionate payment for part-weeks.

An employee can complain to an employment tribunal if the employer fails to make any such payment. If the tribunal upholds the complaint it will order the employer to pay the amount due.

Time off

In certain circumstances as described below, employees must be given time off from work either with or without pay.

Trade union duties

An employee must be given (paid) time off work if he is an official of a recognized trade union for the purpose of:

- carrying out the duties of such an official concerned with industrial relations between the employer and the employees;
- undergoing training in industrial relations which is:
  - relevant to the duties mentioned;
  - approved by the union or the Trades Union Congress (TUC).

The amount of time which may be taken off for trade union duties is that which is 'reasonable in all the circumstances'. When an employer permits an employee to have time off for these purposes he must be paid for that time on the basis of normal pay for the time (where pay does not vary), or average pay for the time (where pay does vary).

Trade union activities

Employees (other than union officials) must be given (unpaid) time off to take part in the activities of a union which is recognized and of which the employee is a member, *excluding* activities which consist of industrial action in relation to contemplation or furtherance of a trade union dispute. The amount of time which may be taken off is that which is 'reasonable in all the circumstances'.

Any employee can complain to an employment tribunal if the employer fails to permit the employee to have such time off. If the tribunal upholds the complaint it will award just and equitable compensation to the employee.

Public duties

Employees who fulfil certain public duties as listed below must be given a reasonable amount of (unpaid) time off to attend to such duties:

- A Justice of the Peace (JP – ie a magistrate).
- A member of a local authority (but not elected councillors).
- A member of a statutory tribunal.
- A member of a regional or area health authority (in Scotland, a health board) or of a family practitioner committee.
- A member of the managing or governing body of an educational establishment maintained by a local education authority (in Scotland, a school or college council or central institution of education).
- A member of the National Rivers Authority.

For these purposes duties include attending meetings and discharging other functions. The amount of time off to be given is that which is 'reasonable in all the circumstances', having regard to how much time is required to fulfil the duties, the amount of time off already taken in this respect, and the effect on the employer's business of the employee's absence.

A complaint can be made to an employment tribunal (within three months) if the employer fails to allow such time off to be taken.

NB: Although not part of this legislation, employees listed for jury service must be allowed appropriate time off for such purposes – without pay.

Looking for work or arranging for training

An employee who has been given notice of dismissal by reason of redundancy (ie after two years' continuous employment) must be given, before the expiry of the notice, reasonable time off during working hours to look for new employment or to make arrangements for training for future employment. An employee who is allowed time off for these purposes must be paid at the appropriate rate. If the employer unreasonably refuses time off the employee is entitled to an amount equal to the pay he would have been entitled to, had he taken time off.

A complaint can be made to an employment tribunal (within three months) if the employer refuses time off for such purposes and compensation of up to two-fifths of a week's pay can be awarded.

Maternity rights

This section provides only basic information on the key aspects of maternity rights. Fully detailed explanatory booklets are available free of charge from local offices of the Department of Trade and Industry (DTI) or from the DTI Web site at: www.dti.gov.uk/er.

An employee who is absent from work due wholly or partly to pregnancy or confinement is entitled to:

- 26 weeks continuous leave before and/or after childbirth;
- paid time off for antenatal examinations;
- no risk of dismissal during the period of pregnancy and maternity leave other than in exceptional circumstances wholly unconnected with the pregnancy;
- preservation of her contractual rights during the maternity leave;
- pay at the sick-pay rate during the period of maternity.

Maternity leave

Pregnant employees are entitled to 26 weeks' ordinary maternity leave, irrespective of how long they have worked for their employer. This leave is normally paid. Pregnant employees who have completed 26 weeks' continuous service with their employer by the beginning of the 14th week before their expected week of childbirth (EWC) can also take additional maternity leave starting immediately after the ordinary maternity leave and continuing for a further 26 weeks, making a total of 52 weeks in all.

A pregnant employee must notify her employer that she intends to take maternity leave by the end of the 15th week before her EWC, unless it is not reasonably practicable to do so. She must tell her employer:

- that she is pregnant;
- the date of the week in which her baby is expected to be born; and
- the date when she wants her maternity leave to start.

She can change her mind about when she wants to start her leave providing she tells her employer at least 28 days in advance unless it is not reasonably practicable to do so.

A woman who intends to return to work at the end of her full maternity leave entitlement is not required to give any further notification to her employer but if she wants to return to work *before* the end of her maternity leave she must give her employer 28 days' notice of the date of her return to work.

Maternity pay
Women are entitled to statutory maternity pay (SMP) if they were:

- employed by their present employer in the 15th week before the birth of their baby; or
- employed by that employer for at least 26 weeks into the 15th week before the birth; and
- earning enough on average for it to be relevant for National Insurance purposes (ie £77 per week from April 2003).

Alternatively, if they do not qualify for SMP pregnant women who have been recently employed or self-employed can apply (to a Jobcentre Plus) for maternity allowance (MA) for 26 weeks.

Employee's right to return to work
An employee's right to return to work after pregnancy or confinement is subject to the specified conditions of her return. It must be:

- to the original employer or his successor;
- in the job in which she was previously employed;
- under the original contract of employment;
- on terms and conditions no less favourable than those applicable had she not been absent.

If, because of changed circumstances (eg redundancies) the employer or his successor cannot permit her to return to the original job, she must be offered any suitable alternative vacancy under a new contract of employment that provides suitable work and is not substantially less favourable than the original contract.

The employee wishing to exercise her right of return must notify the employer in writing at least 28 days before she proposes to do so. An employer can write to the employee up to 49 days after the notified date of confinement asking for written confirmation that she intends to return to work. If he does not receive a reply in 14 days the right to return to work is lost. The employer can postpone the return date for not more than four weeks provided he notifies the employee that the date is being postponed.

The employee, after giving notice of return, can postpone the return date for not more than four weeks – even if this goes beyond the 29 weeks. She must produce a medical certificate showing why she cannot return before the notified day of return or before the end of the 29 weeks.

Parental leave

Parental leave is available to employees who have, or expect to have, parental responsibility for a child. It is the right for parents to take time off work to look after the child or to make arrangements for the child's welfare, and particularly to spend more time with children and strike a better balance between their work and family commitments.

To qualify, employees must have one year's continuous service with their current employer after which they are entitled to 13 weeks leave in total for each child – if twins are born each parent will get 13 weeks leave for each child. Parents of disabled children get 18 weeks in total (for the purposes of parental leave a 'disabled child' is one for whom an award of disability living allowance has been made).

Employees may take parental leave in short or long blocks depending on agreement with their employer provided they give the correct notice to their employer.

Parental leave can be taken at any time up to the applicable cut off point, which generally means that, for example, parents of children born on or after 15 December 1999 can take leave up to their child's 5th birthday while adoptive parents of children placed for adoption between 15 December 1994 and 14 December 1999 can take leave up to 31 March 2005 (or the child's 18th birthday if that is sooner).

Termination of employment

Employment may be terminated either by the employee giving notice or by the employer giving the employee notice. In either case specified minimum periods of notice must be given.

Termination by the employer

If a person has been employed continuously for four weeks or more he must be given the following periods of notice of termination of employment:

Employment	*Notice*
Less than 2 years	1 week
More than 2 years but less than 12 years	1 week for each continuous year
More than 12 years	at least 12 weeks

Termination by the employee

An employee terminating his employment after four weeks or more of employment must give at least one week's notice irrespective of the length of employment service.

If a contract of employment stipulates shorter notice the above (legal minimum) still applies but either party may waive the right to notice or accept payment in lieu of notice.

Dismissal

Where the employer finds it necessary to dismiss an employee certain conditions must be observed depending on the circumstances of the case. Dismissal includes:

- termination of employment with or without notice;
- the term of a contract expiring without renewal;
- termination by the employee with or without notice due to the employer's conduct;
- failure by an employer to let an employee return to work after pregnancy or confinement.

Statement of reasons for dismissal

An employee is entitled to be provided on request, and within 14 days, with a written statement giving reasons for dismissal if:

- he is given notice of termination (unless the employment was for less than 26 weeks)
- he is dismissed without notice;
- a fixed-term contract expires without being renewed.

Where the employer fails to give such a written statement (or the reason given in writing is not adequate or is known to be incorrect) the employee can complain to an industrial tribunal (within three months of the date of dismissal) which will, if the case is well founded, declare the reason for dismissal and make an award that the employer pays an amount equal to two weeks' pay.

Fair and unfair dismissal

An employee has a right not to be unfairly dismissed. For an employee to be fairly dismissed the employer must show:

- the reason for dismissal;
- that the reason was within one of the following areas:
  - the capability or qualification of the employee for the work involved including his fitness to perform the work,
  - the conduct of the employee,
  - redundancy of the employee,
  - contravention of legal restrictions by the employee in connection with his work.

In showing that the reason for dismissal was within the items listed above, the employer must show that he acted reasonably in treating it as a sufficient reason for dismissing the employee.

Dismissal relating to trade union membership

It is unfair to dismiss an employee because that employee was, or proposed to become, a trade union member; had taken part, or proposed to take part, in trade union activities; or refused to become a trade union member.

Dismissal on redundancy

It is unfair to dismiss an employee on the grounds of redundancy if the employee was selected for dismissal for an inadmissible reason, or was selected in contravention of customary arrangements or agreed procedures.

Dismissal on pregnancy

It is unfair to dismiss an employee who is pregnant or for any reason connected with pregnancy except if the employee is incapable of doing her job because of the pregnancy, or cannot do her job due to her pregnancy without contravention of legal restrictions.

Dismissal on replacement

If an employee is engaged to replace a pregnant employee it is not unfair to dismiss that employee on the return to work of the former employee if the replacement employee was told that dismissal would then occur.

Dismissal on industrial action

It is unfair to dismiss an employee where at the date of dismissal the employer was conducting or instituting a lock-out, or the employee was taking part in a strike or other industrial action.

Qualifying period and age limit for dismissal

Claims for unfair dismissal can be made to an employment tribunal within three months of the date of dismissal. Unfair dismissal cannot be claimed:

- if the employment was in a firm with more than 20 employees and if –
- the employee was employed for less than two years – one year if the employment began before 1 June 1985 (if he worked for 16 or more hours per week); or
- the employee was employed for less than five years (if he worked for between 8 and 16 hours per week); or
- the employee was at the normal retiring age for an employee or if
  - a man, had attained the age of 65 years,
  - a woman, had attained the age of 60 years.

In the case of a firm with fewer than 20 employees, unfair dismissal cannot be claimed if the employment was for less than two years.

Remedy for unfair dismissal

An employee can make a complaint of unfair dismissal against an employer to an employment tribunal (within three months of the date on which the dismissal took effect) which, if the case is well founded, will order reinstatement or re-engagement (subject to the employee's wishes), or award compensation.

Redundancy

The need to make employees redundant arises either when a particular job ceases to exist, when the demand for a particular product or service falls or ceases, or when a business closes down altogether. In these circumstances the employee or employees are redundant. They are not redundant if they are replaced by new or other employees.

For an employee to claim a redundancy payment under employment legislation, he must have been continuously employed by that employer for at least two years since reaching the age of 18 years, and must not have unreasonably refused any alternative offer of suitable employment made by the employer.

The redundancy payment received by the employee depends on a number of factors: age, the length of service with the employer and the present weekly rate of pay. The scale of pay rates is as follows:

- Half a week's pay for each year continuously employed between ages 18 and 21 years.
- One week's pay for each year continuously employed between ages 22 and 40 years.
- One-and-a-half week's pay for each year continuously employed between ages 41 and 64 years.

Payment of the sum due under a redundancy arrangement is made by the employer unless he is insolvent, in which case it is paid by the Secretary of State for Education and Employment.

Redundancy payments made by employers are not recoverable from the Government.

Redundancy payments and payments in lieu of notice are not normally subject to income tax deductions.

The following are *not* entitled to redundancy payments:

- self-employed people;
- people who have been employed for less than two years continuously with their employers since reaching the age of 18 years;
- people aged over 65 years (ie both men and women);
- people normally employed for less than 16 hours per week;

- the husband or wife of an employer;
- people who are engaged on a fixed-term contract for two years or more and who have agreed to forfeit any right to redundancy;
- people outside Britain at the time of being made redundant, unless they normally work in Britain;
- share fishermen;
- merchant seamen (a master or seaman on a British seagoing ship with a gross registered tonnage of 80 tons or more);
- registered dock workers.

Consultation/disclosure

When an employer wishes to make an employee redundant he must *consult* that person's trade union representative about the proposed dismissal. It is important to note that the requirement is to consult, not to inform. Consultation should begin 30 days before dismissal when 10 or more employees are to be made redundant in a period of 30 days, and 90 days before dismissal when 100 or more employees are to be made redundant in a period of 90 days.

An employer is required to disclose to trade union representatives:

- the reason why the employees have become redundant;
- the number and description of employees whom it is proposed to dismiss as redundant;
- the total number of comparable employees at the establishment;
- the proposed method of selecting the employees to be dismissed;
- the proposed methods of dismissal, including the period over which they will take effect.

If trade union representatives ask for this information in writing employers should comply with the request, as there is a provision within employment legislation that can require the information to be posted to an address provided by the trade union. The employer is obliged to consider any representations made by the trade union representative during consultation, to reply to those representations and, if he rejects them, to state his reasons.

Failure to comply with these regulations enables the trade union to complain to an employment tribunal, which will make a protective award to the employee(s) if it finds the complaint well founded.

An employer is also required to notify the Secretary of State for Education and Employment of proposed redundancies at an establishment. This notification must be 30 days in advance when proposing to dismiss 10 or more employees and 90 days in advance when dismissing 100 or more employees.

Statutory sick pay

The Social Security Contributions and Benefits Act 1992 legislates for the statutory sick pay (SSP) scheme under which employers are required to make sickness payments to employees. The employee must satisfy rules on periods of incapacity, entitlement periods and qualifying days. Certain small employers may reclaim the full payments made to employees (including National Insurance contributions) by deductions from his payments of National Insurance contributions to the Inland Revenue – Small Employers' Relief (SER). State sickness benefit still applies for certain special cases – such as those who have to be regularly off work for long-term medical treatment and those who do not qualify for or who have exhausted their SSP entitlements.

Employees qualify for SSP after a specified period of incapacity for work (PIW) – four consecutive days – due to physical or mental illness or disablement. A number of periods can be linked if each is of a minimum of four days. The first *three* days of each PIW are waiting days – sickness payment is only made in respect of qualifying days, which count from the fourth day onwards. The maximum entitlement to SSP in any period of incapacity for work is 28 weeks, after which a new PIW will start.

Notification of sickness can be by use of the DSS self-certification form, by submitting a doctor's medical certificate or by the employer instituting his own scheme of self-certification of sickness.

The amount of SSP which must be paid is based on the employee's average gross weekly pay and is set at a specified limit by the Government.

The national minimum wage

The National Minimum Wage Act 1998 came into force in the UK from 1 April 1999 and has been subsequently amended to reflect increases in the minimum hourly rates payable to workers.

The current minimum rate of pay for workers (other than self-employed persons) aged 22 years and over is at least £4.50 per hour, and for workers aged from 18 to 21 years at least £3.80 per hour – rates effective from 1 October 2003 and due to increase again from 1 October 2004. The minimum wage applies to most workers in the UK including agency workers (eg agency drivers), part time and casual workers and those paid on commission basis.

Assessing minimum pay

For the purposes of assessing minimum pay, payments to employees comprising bonuses, incentives, and performance related awards count as part of the pay package, but other allowances not consolidated into an employee's pay are not counted. Similarly, overtime payments and shift payments do not count. Benefits in kind, such as the provision of overnight subsistence, meals, uniforms and workwear allowances, are also excluded.

Gross pay, with all deductions and reductions subtracted, should be divided by the number of hours worked to determine whether the resulting hourly pay rate at least matches, if not exceeds, the national minima stated above.

Types of work

The work hours for which an employer has to pay is calculated according to the type of work employees are engaged upon. Mainly these are as follows:

- Time work – where an employee is paid for working a set number of hours or a set period of time;
- Salaried work – where an employee has a contract to work a set number of basic hours annually in return for an annual salary paid in equal instalments;
- Unmeasured work – where employees are paid to do specific tasks (eg driving), but are not set specific hours for the work.
  NB: In this case the employer must agree with the employee (in writing) a daily average of hours to be spent carrying out the assigned tasks. The employer must be able to show that the number of hours agreed is realistic.

Enforcement and penalties

Enforcement of the minimum wage provisions is by the Inland Revenue and by the employees themselves who have a right to complain if they are not being paid the national minimum wage.

Employers should keep accurate records of the hours worked and hourly rates paid to employees in case such information is called into question later – for a minimum of three years. An employee (or any other qualifying worker) may make a written request for access to his/her own records, and this must be allowed within 14 days unless extended by agreement. Should a dispute arise, the burden of proof is on the employer to show that the national minimum wage has been paid, not on the employee to prove that it has not.

Refusal to pay the national minimum wage is a criminal offence carrying a maximum fine up to £5,000 on conviction. Dismissal of an employee who becomes eligible for the national minimum wage or for a higher rate of pay will constitute unfair dismissal with no qualifying period to be served by workers to secure protection against this form of unfair dismissal.

Discrimination

A range of legislation is applied to prevent discrimination against workers on account of sex, colour, race or creed in relation to their recruitment or training for employment, selection for promotion, their pay and terms of employment or other working conditions.

Equal Pay Act 1970

Any employer who employs women, in whatever capacity, is affected by the Equal Pay Act 1970 (as amended by the Equal Pay (Amendment) Regulations 1983) which was introduced to prevent discrimination between men and women with regard to terms and conditions of employment.

The Act requires employers to ensure that the terms and conditions of employment for men and women who are employed on 'like work' or 'work rated as equivalent' are 'not in any respect less favourable than those of the other'. A term of the contract under which a woman is employed at an establishment in Great Britain must be that she shall be given equal treatment to men in the same employment.

The employer's problem lies in establishing what is 'like work', or 'work rated as equivalent'. In the Act, 'like work' is defined as work of the same or broadly similar nature and the difference, if any, between the work a woman does and the work a man does is not of practical importance in relation to the terms and conditions of employment. Also, in comparing a woman's work with a man's, regard must be given to the frequency with which any differences occur in practice as well as to the nature and extent of the differences.

'Work rated as equivalent' is intended to mean that the woman's job has been given equal value to the man's job in terms of effort, skill and decision.

Employers are required to define clearly 'female' jobs and, where necessary, mixed staff arrangements in offices should have been changed if the jobs of the men and women in these offices were to remain unequal after the Act took effect. For example, in a large accounts/invoices/costs/wages office both male and female clerks may be employed on work that could easily be defined as 'broadly similar' by the staff or their union.

The employer must consider the requirements of the Act when negotiating any pay deals, because the Act states that discrimination between men and women must be eliminated from any collective agreement, pay structure or wage regulation order made before commencement of the Equal Pay Act. This means that separate rates of pay for men and women employed on similar jobs should have ceased by the end of 1975 and should have been replaced by one rate for the job, applicable to both men and women.

A person who is aggrieved under the terms of this Act and who wishes to make a claim must take his or her case to an employment tribunal within six months of termination of his or her employment or at any time while still employed by the employer. If his or her case is successful he or she can be awarded up to two years' arrears of pay.

Sex Discrimination Acts 1975 and 1986

Under these Acts (which apply only to firms with more than five employees) it is an offence for anyone to discriminate between people on the grounds of their sex or marital status in relation to employment, selection for training and promotion and other employment benefits, as well as for dismissal.

The sexes must be given equal opportunities in terms of work, training and promotion, and for many employers the most significant factor arises when advertising vacancies. The advertisement placed must not be worded in a way which suggests that applicants of only one sex should apply. There are instances when it is clearly necessary to show discrimination in advertising and these are generally exempt from the provisions of the Act. The most obvious is recruitment of females for the women's branches of the armed forces or attendants for toilets (male or female), but the transport operator must exercise care against wording advertisements such as 'tea lady required', 'attractive young lady required as receptionist' or 'female invoice clerk required', all of which will provoke complaints under the Act. Even when seeking driving, maintenance, warehouse or traffic office staff, careful wording is essential to avoid the direct suggestion, for example, that *only* males will be employed. It is permissible to state that the duties are arduous or include heavy lifting, which by implication means that mainly men should apply, but would not exclude a strong woman who wished to apply.

In general, the media will not accept advertisement copy that infringes the Act but the employer should consider, too, the dangers of ambiguous framing of employment requests or opportunities which might be posted internally on noticeboards or in staff newsletters, for example.

Disabled persons

The Disabled Persons (Employment) Acts of 1944 and 1958 and the Disability Discrimination Act 1995 (commonly abbreviated to the DDA) make provisions to enable persons handicapped by disablement to secure employment or to work on their own account, and be protected from discrimination because of their disability.

A disabled person for these purposes is either an individual who was registered as disabled under the Disabled Persons (Employment) Act 1944 on both 12 January 1995 and 2 December 1996; or a person who has or has had a disability as defined in the DDA as, 'a physical or mental impairment which has a substantial and long-term adverse effect on their ability to carry out normal day-to-day activities'.

NB: To be protected under the Act, a person must satisfy its four main conditions of disability as outlined above.

Physical and mental impairment
Physical impairment includes impairments that affect hearing or sight while mental impairment is defined as an impairment resulting from or consisting of a mental illness, but only if the illness is a *clinically well-recognized* illness (ie one that includes manic depression, schizophrenia and severe and extended depressive psychoses). A clinically well-recognized illness is one that is recognized by a body of respected medical practitioners such as the World Health Organization.

Impairments for these purposes do not include such conditions as alcoholism, nicotine and substance addictions, arson, thieving, exhibitionism and voyeurism, and physical or sexual abuse of other persons.

Discrimination against the disabled
Discrimination against a disabled person by an employer may occur in two ways: 1) if for a reason which relates to a disabled person's disability the employer treats that person less favourably than he treats or would treat others who do not have a disability and he cannot show that the treatment is justified; 2) if the employer fails to make a 'reasonable adjustment' in relation to the disabled person and cannot show that such failure is justified.

Complex definitions relating to the circumstances in which less favourable treatment of disabled person may be justified, and to the employer's duty to make 'reasonable adjustments' for such persons, are included in the 1995 Act, as are examples of reasonable adjustments, such as:

- making adjustments to premises;
- allocating some of the disabled person's duties to another person;
- transferring him or her to fill an existing vacancy;
- altering his or her working hours;
- assigning him or her to a different place of work;
- allowing him or her to be absent during working hours for rehabilitation, assessment or treatment;
- giving, or arranging for him or her to be given, training;
- acquiring or modifying equipment;
- modifying instructions or reference manuals;
- modifying procedures for testing assessment;
- providing a reader or interpreter;
- providing supervision.

Remedies for discrimination against disabled persons
A disabled person may make a complaint of discrimination due to their disability to an employment tribunal within three months of an act of such discrimination occurring (or longer if the circumstances are 'just and equitable'). In cases where other employees discriminate against a disabled per-

son, the employer is held liable, unless he can show that he has taken reasonably practicable steps to prevent this happening.

In the event of a successful claim for discrimination by a disabled person, the discriminator will be required to take reasonable action to end such discrimination and compensation may be awarded (with no ceiling on the amount).

Race Relations Act 1976

This Act (following on from earlier Acts of the same name), as most recently amended in 2003, effectively prohibits discrimination in employment on racial grounds between people of different racial groups.

Specifically, the aims of the Act are to make it illegal for a person to treat another person less favourably on racial grounds, or to apply requirements or conditions to a person or proportion of people of different racial groups, which are not shown to be justifiable irrespective of the colour, race, nationality or ethnic or national origins of the person or people to whom they are applied.

It is illegal to discriminate against a person on racial grounds in respect of offering employment, the terms on which employment is offered, or refusal of employment. Further, it is also illegal to discriminate against employees by offering or refusing to offer opportunities for promotion, training, benefits or services on racial grounds and to dismiss a person or subject him to other detriment on the same grounds.

Fair Employment (Northern Ireland) Act 1989

This Act (replacing a 1976 Act of the same name), which applies solely to the province of Northern Ireland and which came into effect on 1 January 1990, is intended to ensure that Catholic and Protestant workers in Northern Ireland have equal job opportunities. It established a new Fair Employment Commission and a Fair Employment Tribunal and requires compulsory registration of employers with the Commission. Employers are required to review their recruitment, training and promotion practices and monitor their workforces and job applicants to ensure the aims of the Act are upheld. Failure to comply with the Act can result in both criminal penalties and economic sanctions (eg loss of government grants and contracts) and victims of religious discrimination can be awarded compensation by the new Tribunal (currently up to £30,000). The Commission is to draw up a code of practice for use by employers in establishing and reviewing their employment policies.

Public disclosure

An employee can officially 'shop' an employer who, in various ways, contravenes the law. Under the so-called 'whistleblowers' Public Interest

Disclosure Act, effective from 1 January 1999, employees are legally protected from detrimental treatment when they disclose information in the reasonable belief that the employer is contravening the law, and particularly so where such disclosure may be seen to be in the public interest. For example, in road transport this might be the disclosure of information about such matters as:

- the use of ill-maintained or unsafe vehicles;
- the use of unlicensed, untaxed or uninsured vehicles;
- encouragement by an employer for drivers to speed or overload vehicles;
- the employer setting unreasonable work/delivery schedules that contravene the law;
- the use of illegal 'red' diesel fuel in road vehicles;
- drivers being encouraged or coerced into exceeding the drivers' hours limitations;
- the falsification or fraudulent use of tachographs;
- contravention of other aspects of transport or employment legislation.

Disclosure may be by any worker, including agency workers, and need not be of a case where positive proof is available. It is sufficient for the person disclosing the information to have a reasonable belief that:

- A criminal offence has been, is being or is likely to be committed.
- A person has failed, is failing or is likely to fail to comply with a legal obligation.
- A miscarriage of justice has occurred, is occurring or is likely to occur.
- The health and safety of any individual has been, is being or is likely to be endangered.
- The environment has been, is being, or is likely to be, damaged.
- Information showing the above has been, is being or is likely to be deliberately concealed.

A 'protected disclosure' is one that is made:

- in good faith to an employer;
- to another person where the malpractice relates to the other person's conduct;
- to another person with legal responsibility for the subject matter of disclosure;
- where the worker uses an employer's authorized procedure;
- where the worker seeks legal advice;

- where the worker, in good faith, makes a disclosure to regulatory authorities;
- to anybody
  - if the disclosure is made in good faith,
  - if the disclosure is made without the purpose of personal gain,
  - if the disclosure contains true information,
  - if disclosure to the employer might result in the complainant suffering detrimental treatment,
  - if the complainant believes that disclosure to his employer would result in evidence being concealed or destroyed, and
  - if the complainant has reported the matter to his employer previously without any response.

Employers are not permitted to prevent or persuade their employees or workers from making public interest disclosures, nor may they make contracts with employees/workers that prohibit disclosure. Any such arrangement would be legally invalid. Instead, they must establish procedures to deal with complaints of malpractice, including proper investigation and action to remedy any such complaints.

Dismissal of any employee or worker for making a public disclosure would be considered to be unfair and lead to a compensatory award by an industrial tribunal for an unlimited amount.

Working time

Council Directive 93/104/EC of November 1993 (commonly referred to as the 'Working Time Directive') introduced a number of new provisions to control working time for employees, including the concept of a maximum 48-hour working week and shift working restrictions under which night workers may not work more than an average of 8 hours in any 24-hour period. This Directive specifically excluded the transport sector (eg road, rail, sea, air, inland waterway, etc) – by implication meaning that while drivers may be excluded, other workers employed in associated transport operations such as warehousing, vehicle maintenance and administrative functions may not be excluded.

The Working Time Regulations 1998 (amended 1999) came into force on 1 October 1998 implementing the Directive provisions in Great Britain only (ie Northern Ireland is excluded) in respect of most workers except those employed in road, rail, sea and air transport, inland waterway and lake transport, sea fishing and other work at sea, and doctors in training. In this context, while goods vehicle drivers are clearly exempt from the working time requirements and are, in any event, covered by other controlling legislation as described in this chapter, the matter is currently not clear in regard to other workers employed in transport (eg loaders, etc).

These regulations impose a range of legal obligations on employers, enforceable by both the Health and Safety Executive (HSE) and by local authorities for premises for which they are responsible. Failure by an employer to comply with any of the statutory provisions in this legislation is an offence under the Health and Safety at Work Act, which may result on summary conviction in a fine of up to £5,000 and on indictment by the Crown Court for more serious cases, the risk of imprisonment.

Duty of employers

Employers are specifically required by the regulations to:

- limit average weekly working time to a maximum of 48 hours, including overtime, calculated over successive periods of 17 weeks (ie four months), or for the period of employment where this is less than 17 weeks. Workers may agree individually, or by means of a collective or workforce agreement, that the maximum should not apply to them, but detailed working records must be kept;
- limit night working to no more than eight hours' in 24 hours taken as an average over a 17-week reference period. For night workers (ie those who work for at least three hours at night) whose work involves special hazards or heavy physical or mental strain the limit is a straight eight hours in 24 with no averaging-out;
- provide free health assessments for night workers, and the opportunity to transfer to day work if their health is affected by night working;
- allow workers a daily rest period of at least 11 consecutive hours in each 24-hour period and an uninterrupted rest break of at least 20 minutes when their daily work exceeds 6 hours;
- allow workers a weekly rest period of not less than 24 hours in each seven days;
- allow workers who have been employed continuously for 13 weeks at least four weeks paid annual leave which may not be exchanged for payment in lieu, except where it occurs on termination of the employment;
- keep records of workers' hours of work which are adequate to show that the legal requirements are complied with and retain them for at least two years from the date on which they were made.

The regulations set more restrictive standards for young workers and exempt certain special classes of worker such as Crown servants, the police, trainees and agricultural workers.

The Working Time Directive (WTD) mentioned above was amended by the so-called Horizontal Amending Directive (HAD) (Directive 2000/34/EC) which set rules for those sectors that were expressly excluded from the original WTD, such as non-mobile transport workers and mobile workers not covered by the EU drivers' hours rules (for example, light vehicle drivers).

Finally, from 23 March 2005 we shall have the Road Transport Directive – the RTD – (Directive 2002/15/EC) – which deals specifically with working time for those persons performing mobile transport activities within scope of the EU drivers' hours rules. This will be the main area of concern for hauliers and own account transport operators.

It is important to note here that the RTD supplements both the current EU drivers' hours regulation 3820/85/EEC and the AETR Agreement, so drivers who fall within the scope of these regulations when driving a goods vehicle must also take note of and comply with the provisions of the RTD.

Unfair dismissal

The Employment Rights Act 1996 is amended by the addition of new provisions to make it unfair to dismiss an employee for refusing to comply with a requirement contrary to these regulations, or to forgo their rights.

The national minimum wage

The national minimum wage provisions introduced by the National Minimum Wage Act 1998 came into force in the UK from 1 April 1999. An amendment from 1 October 2003 requires that workers (other than self-employed persons) aged 22 years or over must be paid at least £4.50 per hour, and workers aged from 18 to 21 years at least £3.80 per hour. The minimum wage applies to most workers in the UK including agency workers (eg agency drivers), part-time and casual workers and those paid on commission basis.

New workers aged 22 years or over who receive accredited training must be paid at least £3.50 per hour for the first six months. In this case, the employer will have to come to an agreement with the worker, committing him to providing training on at least 26 days during that six-month period.

Assessing minimum pay

For the purposes of assessing minimum pay, payments to employees comprising bonuses, incentives and performance-related awards count as part of the pay package, but other allowances not consolidated into an employee's pay are not counted. Similarly, overtime payments and shift payments do not count. Benefits in kind, such as the provision of overnight subsistence, meals, uniforms and workwear allowances, are also excluded.

Gross pay, with all deductions and reductions subtracted, should be divided by the number of hours worked to determine whether the resulting hourly pay rate at least matches, if not exceeds, the national minima stated above.

Types of work

The work hours for which an employer has to pay is calculated according to the type of work employees are engaged upon. Mainly these are as follows:

● time work – where an employee is paid for working a set number of hours or a set period of time;
● salaried work – where an employee has a contract to work a set number of basic hours annually in return for an annual salary paid in equal instalments;
● unmeasured work – where employees are paid to do specific tasks (eg driving), but are not set specific hours for the work. NB: In this case the employer must agree with the employee (in writing) a daily average of hours to be spent carrying out the assigned tasks. The employer must be able to show that the number of hours agreed is realistic.

Enforcement and penalties

Enforcement of the minimum wage provisions is by the Inland Revenue and by the employees themselves who have a right to complain if they are not being paid the national minimum wage.

Employers obviously need to keep accurate records of the hours worked and hourly rates paid to employees in case such information is called into question later – for a minimum of three years. An employee (or any other qualifying worker) may make a written request for access to his own records, and this must be allowed within 14 days unless extended by agreement.

Should a dispute arise, the burden of proof is on the employer to show that the national minimum wage has been paid, not on the employee to prove that it has not.

Refusal to pay the national minimum wage is a criminal offence carrying a maximum fine up to £5,000 on conviction. Dismissal of an employee who becomes eligible for the national minimum wage or for a higher rate of pay will constitute unfair dismissal, with no qualifying period to be served by workers to secure protection against this form of unfair dismissal.

Health and safety

Stringent UK legislation on health and safety at work implements the EU's 'Framework Directive', namely EC Directive 391/1989. The overall objective of this Directive is to impose on employers a duty to encourage improvements in the health and safety of people at work.

The main legislation is contained in the Health and Safety at Work, etc Act 1974, plus the regulations listed below – the so-called 'six pack' – which were introduced to implement the 'Framework Directive':

1. Management of Health and Safety at Work Regulations 1999
2. The Workplace (Health, Safety and Welfare) Regulations 1992

3. Manual Handling Operations Regulations 1992
4. Health and Safety (Display Screen Equipment) Regulations 1992
5. Provision and Use of Work Equipment Regulations 1998
6. Personal Protective Equipment at Work Regulations 2002

Additionally, there are many other relevant provisions dealing with such matters as fire protection and safety signs. Collectively, this legislation has largely replaced both the Factories Act 1961 and the Offices, Shops and Railway Premises Act 1963 which formerly applied. There are also the Lifting Operations and Lifting Equipment Regulations 1998.

The Health and Safety at Work, etc Act 1974
The Health and Safety at Work, etc Act 1974 applies to all persons at work including employers and self-employed persons, but with the exception of domestic servants. It replaces certain parts of both the Factories Act 1961 and the Offices, Shops and Railway Premises Act 1963 (which still remain in force), but adds other provisions.
   The main aims of the Act are:

- to maintain and improve standards of health, safety and welfare for people at work;
- to protect people other than those at work against risks to their health or safety arising from the work activities of others;
- to control the storage and use of explosives, highly flammable or dangerous substances, and to prevent their unlawful acquisition, possession or use;
- to control the emission into the atmosphere of noxious or offensive fumes or substances from work premises;
- to set up the Health and Safety Commission and the Health and Safety Executive.

Approved codes of practice set up under the Act (particularly those that cover working with lead and other hazardous products, and working with excessive noise) have special status in providing a simple and flexible extension of the law. Consequently, while a person is not rendered liable to proceedings if a code is not observed, it could have a bearing on the matter in legal proceedings if advice given in a code has been ignored.

Duties of employers under the Act
The Act prescribes the general duties of all employers (with five or more employees) towards their employees by obliging them to ensure their health, safety and welfare while at work. This duty requires that all plant and methods of work provided must be reasonably safe and without risks

to health. A similar injunction relates to the use, handling, storage and transport of any articles or substances used in connection with the employer's work.

It is the duty of the employer to provide all necessary information and instruction, supported by proper training and supervision.

Workplaces generally, if under the employer's control, must be maintained so that they are safe and without risks to health, have adequate means of entrance and exit, and provide a working environment that has satisfactory facilities and arrangements for the welfare of the people employed there.

Additionally, employers and self-employed persons must ensure that their activities do not create any hazard to members of the general public. In certain circumstances, information must be made publicly available regarding the existence of possible hazards to health and safety.

Written policy statement

The employer must (unless he has fewer than five employees) draw up and bring to the notice of all the workforce a written statement of the company policy regarding health and safety at work, together with all current arrangements for its implementation. The statement must be updated as the need arises and all alterations must be communicated to employees.

Safety representatives and committees

Safety representatives in firms should be appointed by the union (*not* by the management) from among the workforce and joint safety committees must be established as required by the safety representatives (at the request of two or more) in situations where employees are organized in recognized trade unions. Safety representatives should be persons who have been employed by the firm for at least two years or who have had two years' experience in similar employment 'so far as is reasonably practicable'. In other cases the employer should voluntarily set up a safety committee comprising employees and management.

Duties of employees

The Act states in general terms the duty of an employee to take reasonable care for the safety of himself and others and to cooperate with others in order to ensure that there is a compliance with statutory duties relating to health and safety at work. In this connection no person shall interfere with or misuse anything provided in the interests of health, safety or welfare either intentionally or recklessly.

Summary of duties of employees at work

It shall be the duty of every employee while at work:

- to take reasonable care for the health and safety of himself and of other persons who may be affected by his acts or omissions at work, and
- as regards any duty or requirement imposed on his employer or any other person, to cooperate with him so far as is necessary to enable that duty or requirement to be performed or complied with.

No person shall intentionally or recklessly interfere with or misuse anything provided in the interests of health, safety or welfare.

General duties of employers and self-employed to persons other than their employees

It is the duty of every employer and of every self-employed person to conduct his undertaking in such a way as to ensure so far as is reasonably practicable that persons not in their employment are not thereby exposed to risks to their health and safety.

It is the duty of every employer and of every self-employed person to give to persons not in their employment who may be affected the prescribed information about such aspects of the way in which he conducts his undertaking as might affect their health and safety.

Improvement and prohibition notices

An improvement notice may be served on a person by a health and safety inspector in cases where he believes (ie is of the opinion) that the person is contravening, has contravened, or is likely to continue contravening any of the relevant statutory provisions. Such a notice must give details of the inspector's reason for his belief and requires the person concerned to remedy the contravention within a stated period.

A prohibition notice with immediate effect may be served by an inspector on a person under whose control activities to which the relevant statutory provisions apply are being carried on, or are about to be carried on, if he believes that such activities involve or could involve *a risk of serious personal injury*. A prohibition notice must specify those matters giving rise to such a risk, and the reason why the inspector believes the statutory provisions are, or are likely to be, contravened. The notice must direct that the activities in question shall not be carried on unless those matters giving rise to the risk of serious personal injury, and any contravention of the regulations, are rectified.

Remedial measures

Both improvement and prohibition notices may include directions as to necessary remedial measures and these may be framed by reference to an approved code of practice and may offer a choice of the actions to be taken. Reference must be made by the inspector to the Fire Authority before serving a notice requiring, or likely to lead to, measures affecting means of escape in case of fire.

Withdrawal of notices and appeals

A notice, other than a prohibition notice with immediate effect, may be withdrawn before the end of the period it specifies, or an appeal against it made. Alternatively, the period specified for remedial action may be extended at any time provided an appeal against the notice is not pending.

Penalties for health and safety offences

Conviction for an offence under the Health and Safety at Work. etc Act 1974 may lead to a fine of £20,000, but where the case is tried in the Crown Court the fine which may be imposed is unlimited. However, it should be stressed that while generally the fine imposed is intended to reflect the gravity of the particular offence and the employer's attitude towards health and safety matters, the court will also bear in mind the offender's resources and the effects of a heavy penalty on his business, and may reduce the penalty accordingly.

Corporate manslaughter

In a situation where a death is caused through the negligence of an employer, whether health and safety related or as a result of a road accident, the employer risks facing a charge of corporate manslaughter.

It has been ruled by the courts that for an indictment on such a charge to be sustained, three key issues must be established by the jury as follows:

1. The defendant owed a duty of care to the person killed.
2. The defendant had breached his duty of care and that breach of care led to the death.
3. The defendant's negligence was so gross that a jury would consider it justified to bring in a criminal conviction.

The management of health and safety

The new 'management' regulations are both wide ranging and general in nature, overlapping with many existing regulations. They have to be viewed as a 'catch-all' regulation, sitting astride other more specific health and safety provisions. The Health and Safety Executive, in its Approved Code of Practice, advises that where legal requirements in these management regulations overlap with other provisions, compliance with duties imposed by the specific regulations will be sufficient to comply with the corresponding duty in the management regulations. However, the HSE says, where duties in the Management of Health and Safety at Work Regulations 1999 go beyond those in the more specific regulations, additional measures will be needed to comply fully with the management regulations. Specifically, these regulations cover:

- Requirements for employers (and self-employed persons) to make assessments of the risks to the health and safety of employees while they are at work, and other persons not in their employ, arising out of or in connection with their conduct or the conduct of their undertaking.
- Employers with five or more employees must record the significant findings of their risk assessment (ie make an effective statement of the hazards and risks which lead management to take relevant actions to protect health and safety).
- Employers and self-employed persons must make and give effect to such arrangements, as are appropriate to the nature of their activities and the size of their undertaking, for the effective planning, organization, control, monitoring and review of preventive and protective measures.
- Health surveillance must be provided for employees as appropriate to the risks to their health and safety as identified by the assessment.
- Employers must appoint one or more (competent) persons to assist them in undertaking the measures necessary to comply with the requirements and prohibitions of this legislation.

The workplace regulations
These new regulations (see item 2 in the list of new legislation on p 80) add further to existing legislation on workplaces. They apply to new workplaces as of 1 January 1993 and to any modifications or conversions to existing workplaces started after this date. Existing workplaces (ie which are unaltered) must comply from 1 January 1996.

Specifically the regulations impose requirements on the:

- maintenance of workplaces;
- ventilation of enclosed workplaces and temperatures of indoor workplaces and the provision of thermometers;
- lighting (including emergency lighting);
- cleanliness of the workplace, and of furniture, furnishings and fittings (also the ability to clean floors, walls and ceilings) and the accumulation of waste materials;
- room dimensions and unoccupied space;
- suitability of workstations (including those outside) and the provision of suitable seating;
- condition of floors, and the arrangement of routes for pedestrians or vehicles;
- protection from falling objects, and from persons falling from a height, or falling into dangerous substances;
- material of and protection of windows and other transparent or translucent walls, doors or gates, and to them being apparent;
- way in which windows, skylights or ventilators are opened and their position when left open and the ability to clean these items;

- construction of doors and gates (including the fitting of necessary safety devices), and escalators and moving walkways;
- provision of suitable sanitary conveniences, washing facilities and drinking water (including cups and drinking vessels);
- provision of suitable accommodation for clothing and for changing clothes, for rest and for eating meals.

Factories Act 1961

The Factories Act 1961 (which although partially replaced by the HSW Act still remains in existence) is concerned with the health, safety and welfare of people employed to carry out manual labour in *any* premises (including open-air premises). It is also concerned with regulating and controlling the employment of women and young people in such premises.

A factory, for the purposes of the Act, is defined as any premises in which people are employed in any process in manual labour. It includes docks, wharves, quays, warehouses with mechanical power, and building and civil engineering premises.

The Act contains the following important provisions:

- *Cleaning/painting.* Premises should be cleaned daily, floors must be cleaned at least once a week and walls and ceilings should be washed with hot water and soap or by other approved methods every 14 months; or whitewashed or colour-washed if they are not painted or varnished; if these surfaces are painted or varnished, they should be repainted or re-varnished at intervals of not more than seven years.
- *Overcrowding.* Each workroom must provide a minimum of 11 cubic metres of space for every person employed, measured within a height of 4.2 metres from the floor (ie any space above 4.2 metres is discounted).
- *Temperature.* Where workers are required to sit down to do work which does not involve serious physical effort, the temperature must be maintained at least at 16°C (60°F) after the first hour. A thermometer must be placed in a suitable position in every workroom. The maximum temperature permitted (other than in domestic premises or where industrial processes require more heat) is 19°C (66.2°F).
- *Ventilation.* Workrooms must be provided with an adequate supply of air, sufficient to render harmless any injurious fumes or dust generated in the course of work carried on in that room.
- *Injurious fumes or dust.* Where processes are carried out which result in injurious dust or fumes being generated, measures must be taken to protect workers against inhalation of the dust or fumes by the use of exhaust appliances.

- *Lighting.* Sufficient natural or artificial light must be provided and windows and skylights should be kept clean on both sides and free from obstruction, although these may be whitewashed or shaded.
- *Drainage of floors.* Provision must be made for draining floors.
- *Toilets.* Suitable separate toilets for both sexes must be provided and kept clean. There should be at least one toilet for every 25 female employees and one for every 25 male employees, with four toilets for the first 100 male employees and, provided there is sufficient urinal accommodation, toilets need only be provided on the basis of one for every further 40 male employees in excess of 100. (For example, there should be five toilets for 140 male employees and a minimum of eight toilets for 260 male employees.)
- *Meals in dangerous trades.* Food or drink must not be taken into workrooms in which poisonous substances such as lead or arsenic are involved in processes or where the work carried out produces siliceous or asbestos dust.
- *Lifting excessive weights.* Workpeople must not be employed to lift, carry or move any load which is heavy enough to cause them injury.
- *Lead processes.* Young people and females must not be employed in workrooms where processes connected with lead manufacture are carried out or where any other process involving the use of lead compounds is carried out which results in dust or fumes being produced.
- *Notification of industrial diseases.* Where any worker is affected by poisoning or disease as a result of working in dangerous trades such cases must be reported to the Factories (ie Health and Safety) Inspector.
- *Notification of accidents.* Accidents causing loss of life or disabling a worker from earning full wages for more than three days must be reported immediately to the Factories Inspector and entered in a General Register (ie Accident Book) kept in the workroom. The General Register should contain details of people employed in the workroom and information regarding the cleaning and painting of the workroom in addition to space for describing every accident and case of industrial disease which occurs (see also page 87 regarding RIDDOR). A certificate from the fire authority relating to the means of escape in the case of fire should also be attached to the General Register.
- *Fencing.* The moving and working parts of all machinery and other dangerous mechanical parts in the workshop must be securely guarded and such guards must be kept in position while the machinery is in motion or in use.
- *Power cut-offs.* Means must be provided to enable the power for transmission machinery to be cut off promptly.
- *Training of young people.* Young people must be fully instructed about the danger and the precautions to be observed when working on dangerous machines, and they must have had adequate training by an expe-

rienced person before working on such machines or must be supervised while working. Young persons under 18 years must not clean, lubricate or adjust dangerous machinery if this exposes them to risk of injury from the machine being worked on or from nearby machinery.

- *Hoists and lifts.* All hoists and lifts must be in good mechanical condition and of adequate strength, and must be properly maintained. They must be thoroughly examined once every six months by a competent person and his report must be kept with the General Register. They must be suitably protected by enclosures and gates with efficient locking devices and the safe working load must be marked conspicuously on them.

- *Air receivers.* Air receivers (ie air compressors) and their fittings must be cleaned and examined every 26 months. The safe working pressure must be shown clearly and a safety valve and pressure gauge must be fitted.

- *Chains, ropes and lifting tackle.* Chains, ropes and lifting tackle must be of good construction, of adequate strength and free of patent defect. Such equipment must be examined by a competent person once every six months and must be tested and certified before being used for the first time. Chains must be annealed at least once every 14 months. Tables of safe working loads must be displayed except in the case of equipment which has the safe working load clearly displayed on it. A register of all chains, ropes and lifting tackle except fibre rope slings must be kept and so too must certificates of their tests.

- *Cranes.* Cranes and other lifting machines and all their parts and working gear, including anchoring appliances, must be of good construction, sound material, adequate strength and free from patent defect, and must be properly maintained. All such equipment must be thoroughly examined by a competent person once every 14 months. The safe working load must be shown on every lifting machine and in the case of cranes with a jib, an automatic indicator or a table of safe working loads must be attached to the crane.

- *Construction of floors.* All floors, steps, stairs, gangways and passageways must be soundly constructed and kept free from obstruction and any substance likely to cause people to slip. Ladders must be soundly constructed and properly maintained; openings in floors must be fenced and stairs must have handrails.

- *Safe access.* A safe means of access to every place in which a person works must be provided.

- *Fire.* All premises in which more than 20 persons are employed or which have been constructed or converted for factory use and in which more than 10 persons are employed on any floor other than the ground floor or in which explosive or inflammable materials are stored or used, must have an adequate means of escape in the case of fire. The means of escape must have been approved by the fire authority and a certificate to this effect issued. It must be properly maintained and kept free from obstruction. Effective fire alarms must be provided and should be tested or examined every three months and a report on this attached to the General Register.

- *Protection of eyes.* If any process is carried out which involves risk of injury to the eye from particles or fragments (eg from grindstones), suitable goggles or effective screens must be provided.
- *Drinking water.* An adequate supply of fresh drinking water and suitable drinking containers must be provided.
- *Washing facilities.* Clean hot and cold water, soap and towels and other means of cleaning and drying must be provided.
- *Accommodation for clothing.* Adequate facilities must be available for hanging clothing not worn during working hours, together with reasonably practicable arrangements for drying clothing.
- *Facilities for sitting.* Where workers have an opportunity to sit down during working time they must be provided with suitable facilities.

Manual handling

The Manual Handling Regulations 1992 are intended to reduce back and other injuries suffered through the manual handling of loads. Employers must reduce the risk of injury to employees by using more mechanical aids, by providing training in load handling and by providing precise information about load weights, centres of gravity and the heaviest side of eccentrically loaded packages.

Employers must avoid having employees undertake manual handling operations which involve risk of injury, or where it is not possible to avoid this, they have a duty to assess potential injury risks and to take steps to reduce them to the absolute minimum or, better still, to find an alternative way of achieving the same objective which does not involve manual handling – for example, by mechanization of certain handling tasks or by eliminating some activities altogether.

Where such activities must take place, the employer should ensure that employees are well trained in good handling techniques, understand how operations have been designed to ensure their safety, and make proper use of systems of work provided. In particular employees should understand:

- how potentially hazardous handling operations can be recognized;
- how to deal with unfamiliar operations;
- the proper use of handling aids;
- the proper use of personal protective equipment;
- features of the working environment that contribute to safety;
- the importance of good housekeeping;
- factors affecting individual capability;
- good handling techniques.

Training in good handling techniques should be tailored to the particular handling operations likely to be undertaken, beginning with relatively simple examples and progressing to more specialized handling operations. It is especially useful to train employees to:

- recognize loads whose weight, shape and other features, and the circumstances in which they are handled, might cause injury;
- treat unfamiliar loads with caution and not assume that apparently empty drums or other closed containers are, in fact, empty;
- test loads first by attempting to raise one end;
- apply force gradually when lifting or moving loads until undue strain is felt, in which case an alternative method should be considered, or it is clear that the task can be accomplished without injury.

Display screen equipment

For the purposes of these regulations a display screen is any form of alphanumeric or graphic display screen regardless of the process involved – generally termed Visual Display Units (VDUs). Under the regulations employers are required to protect VDU users (ie those who habitually use VDUs for a significant part of their normal work) from the risks associated with habitual VDU use – mainly visual fatigue, mental stress, backache and upper limb pain. This must be done by controlling the design of workstations and actual working conditions.

Employers must make an assessment of the risks to which VDU users are exposed and reduce these to the lowest, reasonably practicable level. Work at VDU screens must be periodically interrupted by breaks or a switch to other work and employers must provide eye and eyesight tests for relevant employees and, where necessary, also provide special corrective appliances (ie spectacles) where normal spectacles cannot be used. Both existing and new VDU users must be given health and safety information about, and training in the use of, the workstation.

Provision and use of work equipment

The Provision and Use of Work Equipment Regulations 1998 require employers and the self-employed to ensure that equipment provided for use at work complies with the regulations. The law applies to owned, hired, leased and second-hand equipment and all machinery, appliances (including cranes, lift trucks and vehicle hoists), apparatus, tools or component assemblies so arranged as to function as a whole unit.

Work equipment must be:

- suitable for its intended purpose;
- assessed as to any risks associated with the equipment;

- subject to a recorded inspection where such an inspection would assist in identifying health and safety risks;
- maintained in efficient working order, in an efficient state and in good repair, and a maintenance log kept.

Personal protective equipment

Employers are required to provide suitable personal protective equipment (PPE) to employees where there are risks to their health and safety which cannot be adequately controlled by other means – it is a last resort measure. Self-employed persons must provide their own protective equipment where necessary.

PPE is not suitable unless:

- it is appropriate for the identified risks;
- account has been taken of the environment that it will be used in;
- ergonomic factors such as the nature of the job, the need for communication and the health of the wearer, have been considered;
- it fits the wearer correctly and comfortably and is capable of being adjusted; and
- it is effective, so far as is practicable, against the risks it is intended to control.

PPE is described as being any equipment designed to be worn or held by persons to protect them from one or more risks, including against extreme temperatures, poor visibility and adverse weather, but work clothing and uniforms, sports equipment and road safety protective wear such as crash helmets are excluded.

A recent fatal accident to a lorry driver on a motorway hard shoulder has highlighted the need for drivers, and others, to wear high visibility clothing when working in vulnerable situations. In this particular case the driver was criticized for being careless with his own safety in not wearing his reflective jacket.

Lifting operations

The Lifting Operations and Lifting Equipment Regulations 1998 apply to all lifting equipment which is defined as 'work equipment for lifting and lowering loads and includes its attachments used for anchoring, fixing or supporting it'. These regulations obviously apply to fork-lift trucks and to automated goods storage and retrieval systems and front-end loaders on tractors.

It is important to note that these regulations also apply to tipping vehicles and in this context it is important that the operator ensures he receives from the manufacturer adequate information about safe operation and correct methods of use, and that such information is passed on to the driver who should also be properly trained as per all health and safety requirements.

The Regulations make provisions regarding the:

- strength and stability of lifting equipment;
- safety of lifting equipment for lifting persons;
- way lifting equipment is positioned and installed;
- marking of machinery and accessories for lifting, and lifting equipment which is designed for lifting persons or which might so be used in error;
- organization of lifting operations;
- thorough examination and inspection of lifting equipment in specified circumstances;
- evidence of examination to accompany it (ie the lifting equipment) outside the firm's premises;
- exceptions for winding apparatus at mines;
- making of reports of thorough examinations and records of inspections;
- keeping of information in the reports and records.

First aid

Employers must advise their employees about first-aid arrangements and provide training as necessary. A first-aid box or cupboard containing only first-aid requisites must be provided in every factory and workshop. In low hazard operations there must be one trained first-aider for every 150 employees. In high hazard operations there must be one trained first-aider for 50–150 employees and an additional first-aider for every further 150 employees. In small establishments a responsible person must be able to take charge in the event of accident or injury.

A first-aid room should be provided in high hazard operations where more than 400 persons are employed.

Offices, Shops and Railway Premises Act 1963

This Act is concerned with provisions for the health, safety and welfare of people employed in offices, shops and certain railway premises.

The main provisions of the Act are similar in detail to the conditions required under the Factories Act (see page 81).

Reporting of accidents (RIDDOR)

Employers are required to report accidents or dangerous occurrences to the Health and Safety Executive under legislation commonly referred to as RIDDOR (the Reporting of Injuries, Diseases and Dangerous Occurrences Regulations 1995) – see also page 82 (Notification of accidents). Reports must be made of the following occurrences:

- fatal accidents;
- major injury accidents/conditions;

- dangerous occurrences;
- accidents causing more than three days' incapacity for work;
- work-related diseases;
- matters concerning the safe supply of gas.

Full records of all such accidents and occurrences must be maintained by the employer and kept for at least three years.

COSHH Regulations

The Control of Substances Hazardous to Health Regulations are intended to control the exposure of employees to hazardous substances at their places of work. In particular, the regulations require employers to make assessments of the use of such substances in their work places and to implement suitable control and monitoring procedures for each substance which falls under this heading (largely all toxic, corrosive, irritant and other harmful substances). The employer has a duty to inform his employees (and specifically provide training where appropriate) about the dangers which exist in handling such substances and the precautions to be taken to ensure safe handling.

C4. DRIVERS' HOURS AND TACHOGRAPHS

Drivers' hours regulations

Goods vehicle drivers in Great Britain are restricted in the number of hours they may drive and work and must observe minimum requirements relating to breaks during the driving day and rest periods between working days and weeks. These requirements are specified in EU Regulation 3820/85 on drivers' hours and the Transport Act 1968 (as amended). The rules that apply in particular circumstances are as follows:

- International driving (ie journeys within the EU) – EU hours rules apply.
- National driving (ie journeys exclusively within UK) – EU hours rules apply.
- Domestic driving (ie exempt from EU provisions) – 1968 Transport Act rules apply.
- Mixed driving (ie a combination of any two or three driving categories mentioned above in the same week) – a set of mixed rules apply.
- International journeys outside the EU – AETR rules (see page 99) apply.

Exemptions to EU rules

Certain vehicles and specialized transport operations as listed below are specifically exempt from the EU rules. However, it should be noted that exemption from these rules does not mean total exemption; the British domestic rules may apply instead (see page 99). Also, there is no exemption for short period or short distance driving operations. If the EU rules apply, because there is no exemption, then they must be followed from the moment a vehicle is driven on the road.

NB: Examination candidates should note that while it is not necessary to learn this list of exemptions 'parrot fashion', it is important to have a sound understanding of the type of operation that is exempt and that which is not.

Exemptions in international transport operations:

- Vehicles not exceeding 3.5 tonnes maximum permissible weight including the weight of any trailer drawn.
- Passenger vehicles constructed to carry not more than nine persons including the driver.
- Vehicles on regular passenger services on routes not exceeding 50 kilometres.
- Vehicles with legal maximum speed not exceeding 30kph (approximately 18.6mph).
- Vehicles used by armed services, civil defence, fire services, forces responsible for maintaining public order (ie police).
- Vehicles used in connection with sewerage; flood protection; water, gas and electricity services; refuse collection and disposal; highway maintenance and control; telephone and telegraph services; carriage of postal articles; radio and television broadcasting; detection of radio or television transmitters or receivers.
- Vehicles used in emergencies or rescue operations.
- Specialized vehicles used for medical purposes.
- Vehicles transporting circus and funfair equipment.
- Specialized breakdown vehicles.
- Vehicles undergoing road tests for technical development, repair or maintenance purposes, and new or rebuilt vehicles which have not yet been put into service.
- Vehicles used for non-commercial carriage of goods for personal use (ie private use).
- Vehicles used for milk collection from farms and the return to farms of milk containers or milk products intended for animal feed.

Exemptions in national transport operations:

- Passenger vehicles constructed to carry not more than 17 persons including the driver.

- Vehicles used by public authorities on or after 1 January 1990 to provide public services which are not in competition with professional road hauliers. This exemption applies only if the vehicle is being used by:
  a) a health authority in England and Wales, a health board in Scotland or an NHS Trust
    i) to provide ambulance services in pursuance of its duty under the NHS Acts or
    ii) to carry staff, patients, medical supplies or equipment in pursuance of its general duties under the Acts;
  b) a local authority to fulfil social services functions, such as services for old persons or for physically and mentally handicapped persons;
  c) HM Coastguard or lighthouse authorities;
  d) harbour authorities within harbour limits;
  e) airports authorities within airport perimeters;
  f) British Rail, London Regional Transport, a Passenger Transport Executive or local authority for maintaining railways;
  g) British Waterways Board for maintaining navigable waterways.
- Vehicles used by agricultural, horticultural, forestry or fishery undertakings for carrying goods within 50 kilometres radius of the place where the vehicle is normally based including local administrative areas the centres of which are situated within that radius. (To gain the exemption the vehicle must be used to carry live fish or to carry a catch of fish that has not been subjected to any process or treatment (other than freezing) from the place of landing or to a place where it is to be processed or treated.)
- Vehicles used for carrying animal waste or carcasses not intended for human consumption.
- Vehicles used for carrying live animals from farms to local markets and vice versa or from markets to local slaughterhouses.
- Vehicles specially fitted for and used:
  - as shops at local markets and for door-to-door selling;
  - for mobile banking, exchange or savings transactions;
  - for worship;
  - for the lending of books, records or cassettes;
  - for cultural events or exhibitions.
- Vehicles not exceeding 7.5 tonnes maximum permissible weight carrying materials or equipment for the driver's use in the course of his work within 50 kilometres radius of base, providing the driving does not constitute the driver's main activity and does not prejudice the objectives of the regulations.
- Vehicles operating exclusively on islands not exceeding 2300 sq km not linked to the mainland by bridge, ford or tunnel for use by motor vehicles.

- Vehicles not exceeding 7.5 tonnes maximum permissible weight used for the carriage of goods propelled by gas produced on the vehicle or by electricity.
- Vehicles used for driving instruction (but not if carrying goods for hire or reward).
- Tractors used after 1 January 1990 exclusively for agricultural and forestry work.
- Vehicles used by the RNLI for hauling lifeboats.
- Vehicles manufactured before 1 January 1947.
- Steam propelled vehicles.

EU rules covering national and international transport operations

EU Regulation 3820/85 applies to drivers of relevant (ie non-exempt) vehicles on both national and international transport journeys within the EU. The provisions of the regulations are as follows:

- Maximum daily driving: 9 hours, which may be increased to 10 hours on two days in a week.
- Maximum driving before break: 4½ hours in aggregate.
- Breaks: 45 minutes after 4½ hours' driving or other breaks of at least 15 minutes each spread throughout the driving period to equal 45 minutes minimum.
- Minimum daily rest: 11 hours (normally).
- Reduced daily rest: daily rest may be reduced to 9 hours on three occasions in a week (reduced time to be made up by end of next following week).
- Split daily rest: daily rest taken in two or three periods:
  - one minimum 8 hours;
  - other periods minimum 1 hour each;
  - total rest 12 hours in 24 hours.
- Interrupted daily rest: daily rest may be interrupted provided (ie on ferries and trains):
  - part of rest taken in terminal and part on board ferry or train;
  - not more than 1 hour between parts;
  - driver to have access to bunk/couchette for both parts of rest;
  - total rest period in a day to be increased by 2 hours.
- Maximum weekly driving: 6 driving shifts in a week.
- Maximum driving in two weeks: 90 hours.
- Minimum weekly rest: 45 hours (normally).
- Reduced weekly rest: weekly rest may be reduced to:
  - 36 hours when vehicle/driver at base;
  - 24 hours when taken elsewhere reduced time to be made up *en bloc* by the end of the third following week.

Double-manned vehicles

When a vehicle is double-manned each driver must have had 8 hours of continuous rest in each period of 30 hours. One driver must not be taking his *rest* period while the vehicle is being driven by the other (see point below about rest) but he may take a *break*.

Day/week

For the purposes of these regulations a 'day' is any period of 24 hours (ie rolling period) and a 'week' is a fixed week starting at 00.00 hours Monday to 24.00 hours (midnight) on the following Sunday.

Breaks

Drivers are required by law to take a break or breaks if in a day the aggregate of their driving time amounts to 4½ hours or more. If the driver does not drive for periods amounting in aggregate to 4½ hours in the day there is no legal requirement for him to take a break during that day.

Break periods must not be regarded as parts of a daily rest period and during breaks the driver must not carry out any 'other work'. However, waiting time, time spent riding as passenger in a vehicle or time spent on a ferry or train, is not counted as 'other work' for these purposes.

The requirement for taking a break is that immediately the 4½ hour driving limit is reached a break of 45 minutes must be taken, unless the driver commences a rest period at that time (see below). This break may be replaced by a number of other breaks of *at least* 15 minutes each distributed over the driving period or taken during and immediately after this period, so as to equal at least 45 minutes and taken in such a way that the 4½ hour limit is not exceeded. To re-emphasize the point, once the 45 minutes break requirement has been met, the slate is effectively wiped clean and the next 4½-hour driving period can begin.

A break period which was otherwise due in accordance with this requirement does not have to be taken if immediately following the driving period the driver commences a daily or weekly rest period, so long as the 4½ hours' aggregated driving is not exceeded.

According to DETR examples, the driver could legally operate the following procedures:

- Drive 1 hour, 15 minutes' break, drive 3½ hours, 30 minutes' break, drive 1 hour, 15 minutes' break, drive 3½ hours, commence daily rest period.
- Drive 1 hour, 15 minutes' break, drive 1 hour, 15 minutes' break, drive 2½ hours, 15 minutes' break, drive 2 hours, 30 minutes' break, drive 2½ hours, commence daily rest period.

- Drive 3 hours, 15 minutes' break, drive 1½ hours, 30 minutes' break, drive 3 hours, 15 minutes' break, drive 1½ hours, commence daily rest period.

Rest periods

A daily rest period must be taken once in each 24 hours. Weekly rest must be taken after six daily driving periods or may be postponed until the end of the sixth day so long as the weekly driving limit is not exceeded. Weekly rest commenced in one fixed week and continuing into the next may be attached to either week.

During rest periods the driver must be 'free to dispose of his time as he wishes'. The driver may take his rest period in a vehicle so long as it is fitted with a bunk and is stationary for the whole of the time.

Made-up rest

Made-up (ie compensated) rest must be attached to other rest periods of at least 8 hours' duration. Made-up *daily* rest can be split when adding to other daily or weekly rest periods (eg if 4 hours to be made up from previous week this could be taken as 2+2 or 3+1) but when making up for reduced *weekly* rest periods the time must be added *en bloc* to other daily or weekly rest periods. Compensated rest must be taken at the place chosen by the driver (ie at home or away), not as dictated by the employer.

Emergencies

Under the EU regulations there is an exemption from the need to follow the stated requirements in emergency situations. In such circumstances, a driver may depart from the rules to the extent necessary to enable him to reach a suitable stopping place, if the safety of persons, the vehicle or its load must be ensured, providing road safety is not jeopardized. The nature of the emergency and the reasons for departing from the rules should be shown on the tachograph chart.

Prohibition on payments

It is prohibited under the EU rules to make any payment to wage-earning drivers in the form of bonus or wage supplement related to distances travelled and/or the amount of goods carried, unless the payments are such that road safety is not endangered.

Employers' responsibilities

Employers have a duty under the regulations to organize drivers' work in such a way that the hours' law is not broken. They must also make regu-

lar checks to ensure the regulations are complied with and take appropriate steps to prevent any repetition if the law is found to have been broken.

AETR agreement

When drivers are engaged on international journeys that extend beyond
the territories of EU member states and involve travel into or transit
across the territories of national states which are signatories to the AETR
agreement, the AETR drivers' hours rules must be observed *for the whole
of the journey*. In fact, the AETR rules are now fully aligned with those of
the EU as contained in EU Regulation 3820/85 referred to above.

The European Agreement Concerning the work of Crews of Vehicles
Engaged in International Road Transport 1971 (AETR) was established
by the Economic Commission for Europe to control the hours of work
and rest for drivers engaged in international road transport operations to
or from third countries that are contracting parties to the Agreement (see
below), or in transit through such countries for the whole of the journey
where such operations are carried out by vehicles registered in an EU
member state or in one of the contracting countries.

This Agreement arose from a need to increase the safety of road traffic and the requirement to make regulations governing certain conditions
of employment (notably in respect of driving time, breaks and rest periods, etc) in international road transport in accordance with the principles
of the International Labour Organization.

Parties to the agreement
The AETR Agreement has been signed (ie ratified by) the EU member
states plus the following non-EU countries:

Belarus	Moldova
Bosnia-Herzegovina	Norway
Bulgaria	Poland
CIS	Romania
Croatia	Serbia and Montenegro
Czech Republic	Slovakia
Estonia	Slovenia
Latvia	

British rules applicable to domestic driving

Drivers of vehicles not exceeding 3.5 tonnes maximum permissible
weight (including the weight of any trailer drawn) and of other vehicles

which are exempt from the EU regulations (see list above) must follow the British domestic drivers' hours rules set out in the Transport Act 1968 as amended, unless they are exempt as shown below.

Exemptions

Total exemption from the rules (ie the daily driving and duty limits) is given to the following:

- Drivers of vehicles used by the armed forces, the police and fire brigades.
- Drivers who always drive off the public highway.
- Private driving not in connection with any trade or business or with any employment.
- When the driving does not amount to more than four hours on each day of the week.

Driving and duty limits under British domestic rules

Maximum daily driving 10 hours. Maximum daily duty 11 hours.

For the purposes of these regulations, 'driving' means time spent behind the wheel actually driving and the limit applies to such time spent driving on public roads. Driving on off-road sites and premises such as quarries, civil engineering and building sites and on agricultural and forestry land is counted as duty time not driving time. The daily duty limit does not apply on any day when a driver does not drive.

Special note: readers should note that under the domestic rules there are no limits on continuous duty, weekly duty or on daily spreadover times. There are also no break period and no daily or weekly rest-period requirements.

Light vehicle driving

Drivers of light goods vehicles not exceeding 3.5 tonnes maximum permissible weight (including the weight of any trailer drawn) must conform to the British domestic limits stated above (although there are no record-keeping requirements – see below – so the enforcement authorities have no sure means of verifying whether the limits are observed), but where such vehicles are driven in connection with the following activities only the 10-hour maximum daily driving limit need be observed:

- by doctors, dentists, nurses, midwives or vets;
- for any service of inspection, cleaning, maintenance, repair, installation or fitting;
- by a commercial traveller and carrying only goods used for soliciting orders;
- by an employee of the AA, RAC or the RSAC;
- for the business of cinematography or of radio or television broadcasting.

Emergencies

Daily driving and duty limits may be suspended when an emergency situation arises. This is defined as an event requiring immediate action to avoid danger to life or health of one or more individuals or animals, serious interruption in the maintenance of essential public services, for the supply of gas, water, electricity, drainage, or of telecommunications and postal services, or in the use of roads, railways, ports or airports, or damage to property. Details of the emergency should be entered in the record sheet when the rules are exceeded.

Postal vehicles

Special requirements apply to postal vehicles which carry parcels traffic and which are over 3.5 tonnes maximum permissible weight. Drivers of such vehicles must comply with the British domestic driving hours rules on daily driving and duty limits even though their vehicles are required to be fitted with tachographs under the EU rules.

Mixed driving

In certain circumstances a driver may, in a day or a week, drive vehicles or be engaged in operations which come within the scope of both the EU rules and the British domestic hours' rules. When this arises he may choose to conform strictly to the EU rules or alternatively take advantage of the more liberal domestic rules. If he decides on the latter and combines the two sets of rules he must watch the following points:

- Time spent driving under the EU rules cannot count as an off-duty period for the domestic rules.
- Time spent driving or on duty under the domestic rules cannot count as a break or rest period under the EU rules.
- Driving under the EU rules counts towards the driving and duty limits for the domestic rules.
- If any EU rules' driving is done in a week the driver must observe the EU daily and weekly rest period requirements for that day and that week.

Penalties for drivers' hours offences

Drivers who are found to be in breach of any of the various hours rules provisions (ie EU or British) are liable to face prosecution and heavy fines on conviction in Britain. On the continent such breaches may incur heavy on-the-spot fines that must be paid immediately, otherwise the vehicle may be impounded and the driver held until the fine is paid. The employer is also likely to face prosecution for failing to cause the driver to observe the law and heavily fined on conviction. Also, convictions for such offences may result in penalty against the driver's LGV driving entitlement and the employer's goods vehicle 'O' licence.

Hours of work records

Vehicles covered

Official records of hours worked, driving time, rest and break periods must be kept by drivers of all goods vehicles except the following, who are exempt:

- Drivers of goods vehicles not exceeding 3.5 tonnes gross weight.
- Drivers who, on a working day, do not drive a vehicle to which the driving hours' regulations apply.
- Drivers engaged on domestic work who, on any day, do not drive for more than four hours *and* who do not travel outside a 50 kilometre radius of the vehicle operating centre.

Type of record

Drivers engaged in domestic transport operations must keep written records in a simplified record book issued by the employer. Drivers engaged in national and international transport operations within the scope of the EU rules (ie EU regulations 3820/85 and 3821/85) must keep records by means of a tachograph.

Record keeping under the British domestic rules

Where the driver has only one employer, that employer must issue him with a record book. Where the driver has two employers, it is the first employer who must issue the book. In this case, each employer must make available to the other details of the driver's working and rest times.

When a record book is issued the employer must:

- complete the details on the front of the book:
  - the company name,
  - address,
  - telephone number,
  - operator's licence number;
- give the driver instructions about the use of the book (instructions for use are printed in the book).

On receipt of a record book the driver must:

- write his name (surname and first name(s)) on the cover;
- fill in his address;
- record the date when the book was first used.

When the book is completed, the driver must write the date of the last sheet on the cover and then return the book to his employer after retaining it for 14 days for inspection by an authorized examiner if required.

There is space on the front cover of the record book for the name, address and telephone number of any other employer of the driver to be entered (where employers have an official stamp this can be used in the space provided).

Method of completion

A new record sheet must be used for each week covering the period from 00.00 hours Monday to 24.00 hours on the following Sunday. A duplicate record must be made by means of 'carbon paper or otherwise' and entries in the record must be made in ink or with a ballpoint pen. The driver must enter his name in box 1 and the dates when the week commences and ends in box 2 at the top of the weekly sheet. He must then complete the following information on the sheet (in boxes 3–9) for each day on which he drives, making the entries at the beginning and end of the day as appropriate:

- Registration number of vehicle(s).
- Place where vehicle(s) are based.
- Time of going on duty.
- Time of going off duty.
- Time spent driving.
- Time spent on duty.
- Signature of driver.

When the week's sheet has been completed, the driver must return the book to the employer who issued it within seven days to enable the employer to examine and sign the records. The employer signs in box 10 to the effect that he has examined the entries, adds his signature (to both top copy and the duplicate) and the position he holds (eg transport manager). He must detach the duplicate sheet and return the book to the driver 'before he is next on duty'.

Owner-drivers

Owner-drivers (provided they are operating under the British domestic rules – and there are not many of them) should complete the details on the front cover of the book, putting their business address in Section 4 where employers enter their information and this is the address where their duplicate record sheets should be returned after completion. They should complete the record sheets in the same way as employed drivers. On completion, record books should be retained by owner-drivers for 12 months counting from the date when the book was completed or ceased to be used.

Signatures

Weekly record sheets must be signed by the driver against each day's entry and later by the employer after they have been checked.

Examination of records

The employer must collect the duplicates of used weekly record sheets from drivers within seven days of completion, check them for accuracy, sign them, and retain them for inspection for 12 months counting from the date when the sheets were returned by the driver. Used record books must also be retained for the same period.

Police constables and other authorized Department of Transport officials may request a driver to produce a current weekly record sheet and record sheets for the previous two weeks for inspection.

Delays

In the event of exceptional delay during a journey caused by unforeseen circumstances, a driver should enter full details on the record sheet for future reference. Despite delays, the driver is still bound by the driving and working hours' regulations unless the reason comes within the category of 'emergency'.

Summary of employers' obligations

Employers must issue their drivers with record books, enter appropriate details on the front cover of the book, collect, check and sign completed duplicate weekly sheets and collect completed books 14 days after the date of the last entry.

All records must be retained, available for inspection, for 12 months counting from the date when they were returned by the driver.

Employers must give their drivers specific instructions as to the use of record books and the hours of work and rest periods.

A record book, issued to a driver who subsequently leaves the employer's service, or who no longer has any use for it, may be re-issued to another driver if it contains a supply of unused sheets.

If discrepancies or false entries are found by an employer on a driver's record sheet a written notice and a warning should be given to him in advance of any disciplinary proceedings.

Record-keeping offences

It is an offence for a driver to fail to keep records and for an employer to fail to cause a driver to keep records. The employer can avoid conviction if he can show to the court that he took all reasonable steps to ensure that the driver did keep proper records. On conviction for such offences heavy fines may be imposed and both the driver's LGV driving entitlement and the employer's 'O' licence are put in jeopardy.

Tachographs

Record keeping by tachograph

Drivers of vehicles operating within scope of the EU drivers' hours rules must keep records of their driving times, breaks and rest periods by means of a tachograph under the provisions of EU Regulation 3821/85.

Vehicles covered
Tachographs must be fitted to all vehicles used for the carriage of goods by road and registered in member states except those vehicles exempt from the EU driving hours' law specified in Regulation 3820/85 (see page 93).

Types of tachograph
The tachographs referred to in these regulations are those which meet the detailed specifications laid down in the EU regulations and no other type.

Installation and inspection
Tachographs must be fitted and repaired only by fitters or workshops approved by the official authority in each member state. In Britain this authority is the Department of Transport which requires tachograph centres to be quality approved to the ISO 9000 standard.

On inspection (calibration) by an approved fitter or workshop, a plaque must be fixed to the vehicle and the instrument must be sealed and specially marked. Details of these markings must be recorded and given, together with a list of approved fitters and workshops, to other member states.

When presented for calibration, vehicles must be in normal road-going trim complete with body and fixtures. They must be unladen and the tyres must be inflated to manufacturers' recommended pressures.

Calibration and sealing
Tachographs are calibrated and sealed, firstly to ensure the accuracy of the recordings on the charts in respect of the vehicle in which the instrument is fitted, and secondly so that any tampering with the instrument to give false readings can be readily detected.

Permitted tolerances
The EU regulations specify permitted limits of accuracy for tachograph equipment, as shown in Table 3.1.

These tolerances are based on real speed and real distance of at least one kilometre.

Table 3.1

	During Bench Tests	On Installation	In Use
1. Speed	+3 kph	+4 kph	+6 kph
2. Distance	+1 per cent	+2 per cent	+4 per cent
3. Time	+2 minutes per day or +10 minutes per seven days		

Breakage of seals

The regulations are specific about where seals must be located and which ones may be broken in an emergency. Seals must be fitted at:

- the installation plaque;
- the two ends of the link between the recording equipment and the vehicle;
- the adaptor itself and its point of insertion into the circuit;
- the switch mechanism on vehicles with two or more rear axle ratios;
- the links joining the adaptor and switch mechanism to the rest of the equipment;
- the instrument casing to protect its internal parts from tampering;
- any cover giving access to the means of adapting the constant of the recording equipment to the characteristic coefficient of the vehicle.

Only the seals at the second, third and fifth points above may be broken in an emergency and a written record of the reason for breakage should be made.

Tachograph checks and recalibration

Vehicles must be submitted to a DETR approved tachograph centre for a statutory tachograph 'check' or 'inspection' every two years and a full recalibration every six years unless these have been carried out following repair or re-sealing in the interim. The two-year and six-year periods count from the previous 'check' or 'calibration' date.

Use of equipment

Both the employer and the driver are responsible for ensuring that a tachograph functions properly and that the seals remain intact. The seals may be broken only in a case of absolute necessity, which must be proved (see above).

The employer is responsible for issuing drivers with tachograph charts – called record sheets in law. These must be of a type which are 'type approved' for the particular make/model of instrument in use. It is an offence to use charts which are not type approved for a particular instrument.

A sufficient number of sheets (charts) must be issued by the employer and when they are returned to him (no later than 21 days after use) they must be retained for one year and produced at the request of any authorized inspecting officer.

Drivers must not use dirty or damaged charts, but if one chart becomes damaged it must be attached to the sheet/chart which replaces it.

Time

The driver must ensure that the time recorded on the sheet agrees with the official time in the vehicle's country of registration (ie tachographs fitted in British-registered vehicles operating in Europe where the time difference applies should show British time, not the local European time).

Use of mode switch

Drivers must operate the mode switch on the tachograph to indicate the activity in which they are engaged while recordings are being made, as shown in Figure 3.1.

Continuous records

The tachograph must be kept running continuously from the time the driver takes over the vehicle until finishing the day's work with the vehicle. A continuous record for a 24-hour period must be made and, while drivers are away from the vehicle, their activity must still be recorded either automatically or manually.

Entries on charts

Drivers must enter the following information on the chart:

- Their surname and first name.
- The date and place when use of the chart begins and ends.
- The registration number of each vehicle driven.
- The distance recorder (odometer) reading:
  - at the start of the first journey on the chart;
  - at the end of the last journey recorded on the chart;
  - in respect of any other vehicles driven.
- The time of any change of vehicle.

Production of charts

Drivers must be able to produce to an authorized inspecting officer on request a chart or charts giving full details of all relevant periods (eg driving times, other work, breaks and rest periods) for not less than the current week and the last day of the previous week in which they drove (but not going back more than 21 days).

Drivers must return used charts to their employer no later than 21 days after use.

Activity	Symbol	
	⊚	Driving
	⊢	Break/rest period
	⋇	Active work (not used officially in UK)
	⊠	Passive work (attendance at work in the UK)

Figure 3.1

Breakdowns

If the tachograph breaks down it must be repaired by an approved fitter or at an approved workshop as soon as reasonably practicable. If the vehicle does not return to base within one week (seven consecutive days), the necessary repairs must be carried out en route at an authorized tachograph repair and calibration station (ie by the seventh day).

While the tachograph is broken, drivers must manually enter details of their driving times, other work, breaks and rest periods on the charts.

Retention of charts

Charts must be retained by employers for a minimum of one year after use and be made available for inspection by authorized examiners. Police and authorized examiners may enter premises at any reasonable time to examine tachograph charts.

The instrument

A tachograph is a speedometer with mechanical or electronic drive incorporating an integral electric clock and a chart recording mechanism. It is fitted on the vehicle dashboard. The instrument indicates and records time, speed and distance. In particular the recordings on charts show the following information:

- The speed at which the vehicle was driven.
- The total distance travelled, the distance between stops and other intermediate distances.
- The number of hours of driving time and the time taken to drive between intermediate points.
- The number of hours of standing time in total and during the working day.
- Whether driving was steady and economical or fast and erratic and consequently wasteful in fuel and in wear and tear on the vehicle.
- Whether a continuous record was made or if there are unexplained gaps in the recording.

Recordings

Recordings are made inside the instrument by three styli on special circular charts, each chart covering a period of 24 hours. One stylus records distance, another records speed and the third records driver activity in the time mode. The styli press through a wax recording layer on the chart, revealing the carbonated layer between the surface and the backing paper.

Charts are pre-marked with time, distance (in kilometres) and speed (in kph) reference radials, and when the styli have marked the chart these factors can be easily identified and interpreted.

Movement of the vehicle creates an easily identifiable broad running line on the chart, recording accurately (normally readable to within about one minute) when the vehicle started running and when it stopped. After the vehicle has stopped, the clock stylus continues to mark the chart but with an easily distinguishable thinner black line. The speed trace gives an accurate recording of the speeds attained at all times throughout the journey. The distance recording is made between five radials on the chart, each upward and each downward stroke representing five kilometres travelled. After every five kilometres, the stylus reverses direction to form a 'V' for every 10 kilometres travelled. To calculate the total distance covered, the 'V's are counted and multiplied by 10 and odd tail-ends of the trace are added in.

NB: Examination candidates should take the opportunity to examine a number of tachograph charts to ensure they are fully familiar with the recording areas printed on them and the actual recordings made by the instrument.

Second-man recording

When a second chart is located in the rear position of a two-man tachograph, only a time recording of the second man's activities (ie other work, break or rest) is shown. Traces showing driving, vehicle speed or distance cannot be recorded on this chart.

Interference with recordings

Precautions against interference with the readings are incorporated in the instrument. It is opened with a key and a security mark is made on the chart every time the instrument is opened. When checking the chart it can be easily established at what time the instrument was opened and thus whether this was by an authorized person or not. Interference with the recording mechanism to give false readings, particularly of speed, can be determined quite simply by an experienced chart analyst.

Faults

Tachographs are generally robust instruments, but listed below are some of the faults that may occur:

- Failure of the cable drive at the vehicle gearbox.
- Failure of the cable drive at the tachograph head.
- Failure of the adaptor/corrector/triplex gearbox.
- Cable breaking or seizure.
- Electrical fault affecting lights in the instrument or the clock.
- Incorrect time showing on the 24-hour clock (eg day-shift work becomes shown against night hours on the charts).
- Failure of the internal workings of the tachograph head.
- Damage to the recording styli.

- Failure of the distance recorder.
- Damage to charts because of incorrect insertion.

Fiddles

A key feature of tachograph recordings is that careful observation will show results of the majority of faults in recordings as well as fiddles and attempts at falsification of recordings by drivers.

The main faults likely to be encountered will show as follows:

- Clock stops – recordings continue in a single vertical line until the styli penetrate the chart.
- Styli jam/seize up – recordings continue around the chart with no vertical movement.
- Cable or electronic drive failure – chart continues to rotate and speed and distance styli continue to record on base line and where last positioned respectively. Time group recordings can still be made but no driving trace will appear.

Attempts at falsification will appear as follows:

- Opening the instrument face will result in a gap in recordings.
- Winding the clock backwards or forwards will leave either a gap in the recording or an overlap. In either case the distance recording will not match up if the vehicle is moved.
- Stopping the clock will stop the rotation of the chart so all speed and distance recordings will be on one vertical line.
- Restricting the speed stylus to give indications of lower than actual speed will result in flat-topped speed recordings, while bending the stylus down to achieve the same effect will result in recordings below the speed base line when the vehicle is stationary.
- Written or marked-in recordings with pens or sharp pointed objects are readily identifiable by even a relatively unskilled chart analyst.

Chart reading and checking

Employers have a responsibility under EU regulations (EU 3820/85) for 'periodically' checking tachograph charts to ensure that drivers have observed the regulations, have complied with statutory limits on driving time and such like, and have been notified when the law has been breached. The regulations require employers to 'take appropriate action to prevent any repetition of such breaches' in these circumstances.

The principal items to be checked are:

- that the chart has been properly produced;
- the driving time, indicated by a broad band;

- break and rest periods between driving periods;
- periods of other work;
- distances travelled, measured by reference to a series of radials set to indicate five kilometres for each full stroke.

To enable drivers to keep track of their times employers must give them, on request, a copy of their daily tachograph charts.

Chart analysis

Detailed analysis of the information on the tachograph charts provides valuable data for increasing the efficiency of the vehicle operation and for establishing productivity payment schemes for drivers. Tachograph manufacturers can supply accessories to enable detailed chart analysis to be carried out. For example, a simple chart analyser magnifies the used chart to the extent that detailed analysis, beyond the scope of a normal visual examination, can be made of the vehicle's minute-by-minute and kilometre-by-kilometre progress.

Analysis of charts by means of electron microscope allows for highly detailed evaluation of vehicle progress in accident situations. This is a specialized facility that cannot normally be undertaken by operators themselves or even on their premises.

Digital tachographs

A new generation of digital tachographs, in which the driver has to insert his personal 'smart' card to record his driving and working activities, breaks and rest periods, were due to be officially introduced under amended EC regulations from 5 August 2004. However, due to hitches in the technical procedures this start date was expected to be deferred until 2005.

The long-awaited digital (ie so-called 'smart card') tachograph regulations (Regulation 1360/2002/EC – amending Regulation 3821/85/EEC) and the technical specification in its Annex 1B were published in the Official Journal of the European Communities (the OJ) on 5 August 2002. This date signalled the start of an official 24-month countdown to the date when such instruments were to be legally required in new goods vehicles and certain older vehicles when their existing tachograph instruments fail and need to be replaced.

From the due date (as yet to be determined – see above) all new goods vehicles exceeding 3.5 tonnes gross weight (except those specifically exempt under the regulations) will need to be fitted with the new-type digital instruments in which the driver inserts his or her own, personalized, micro-chip 'smart' card on which their driving, working and rest activities will be held, along with vehicle speeds and distances driven, for up to 28 days.

There is no requirement for retrospective fitment of digital tachographs to existing vehicles except where, after 5 August 2004, a pre-existing vehicle exceeding 12 tonnes gross weight suffers tachograph failure requiring replacement, that replacement will have to be a new-type digital instrument.

The new regulations have been introduced for a number of reasons including:

- to prevent infringement and fraud in application of the driving hours rules;
- to monitor automatically driver performance and behaviour;
- to overcome problems of monitoring compliance due to the numbers of individual record sheets (charts) which have to be held in the vehicle cab;
- the need to introduce advance recording equipment with electronic storage devices and personal driver cards to provide an indisputable record of work done by the driver over the last few days and the vehicle over a period of several months; and
- to devise a system which ensures total security of the recorded data.

Definitions for digital tachographs and ancillaries

The new-type equipment will feature a number of key components defined in the regulations as follows:

- *Recording equipment* is amended to mean the total equipment intended for installation in road vehicles to show, record and store automatically or semi-automatically details of the movement of such vehicles and of certain work periods of their drivers. This equipment includes cables, sensors, an electronic driver information device, one or two card readers for the insertion of one or two driver memory cards, an integrated or separate printer, display instruments, facilities for downloading the data memory, facilities to display or print information on demand and facilities for the input of the places where the daily work period begins and ends.
- *Data memory* means an electronic storage system built into the recording equipment, capable of storing at least 365 calendar days from the recording equipment. The memory should be protected in such a way as to prevent unauthorised access to and manipulation of the data and detect any such attempt.
- A *'driver card with memory'* means a removable information transfer and storage device allocated by the authorities of the Member States to each individual driver for the purposes of identification of the driver and storage of essential data. The format and technical specifications

of the driver card must meet the requirements laid down in the technical annex to the regulations (not yet adopted).

- A *'control card'* means a removable data transfer and storage device for use in the card reader of the recording equipment, issued by the authorities of the Member States to competent authorities to get access to the data stored in the data memory or in the driver cards for reading, printing and/or downloading.
- A *'company data card'* means a removable data transfer and storage device issued by the Member State's authorities to the owner of vehicles fitted with recording equipment. The company data card allows for displaying, downloading and printing of the data stored in the recording equipment fitted in the company's vehicle(s).
- *'Downloading'* means the copying of a part or of a complete set of data stored in the data memory of the vehicle or in the memory of the driver card, but which does not alter or delete any stored data, allows for the origin of downloaded data to be authenticable and to be kept in a format that can be used by any authorized person and which ensures that any attempts to manipulate data are detectable.

Functions of digital instruments
The regulations require digital instruments to be able to record, store, display and print-out specified statutory information as follows.

Recording and storing in the data memory
The instrument will be required to record and store:

- distance travelled by the vehicle with an accuracy of 1 km;
- speed of the vehicle:
  - momentary speed of the vehicle at a frequency of 1 second for the last 24 hours of use of the vehicle;
  - exceeding the authorized speed of the vehicle, defined as any period of more than one minute during which the vehicle speed exceeds 90 km/h for N3 vehicles or 105 km/h for M3 vehicles (with time, date, maximum speed of the over-speeding, average speed during the period concerned);
- periods of driving time (times and dates), with an accuracy of one minute;
- other periods of work or of availability (times and dates) with an accuracy of one minute;
- breaks from work and daily rest periods (times and dates) with an accuracy of one minute;
- for electronic recording equipment which is equipment operated by signals transmitted electrically from the distance and speed sensor, any interruption exceeding 100 milli-seconds in the power supply of the

recording equipment (except lighting), in the power supply of the distance and speed sensor and any interruption in the signal lead to the distance and speed sensor, with date, time, duration and driver card issue number;

- the driver card issue number with times and dates of insertion and removal;
- for each driver card that is inserted for the first time after it was used in another item of recording equipment:
  - current driving time since the last break or rest period;
  - driving time for the day after the last rest period of at least eight hours;
  - driving times for the day between two rest periods of at least eight hours for the preceding 27 calendar days with date, time and duration;
  - total of the driving times for the current week and the preceding week and the total of the driving times of the two completed preceding weeks;
  - rest periods of at least eight hours' duration for the day and the preceding 27 calendar days in each case with date, time and duration;
  - the VRN (vehicle registration number) of the vehicles driven;
- date, time and duration of driving without an inserted or a functioning driver card;
- data recorded on the places at which the daily work period began and ended;
- automatically identifiable system faults of the recording equipment with date, time and driver card issue number;
- faults in the driver card with date and time and driver card issue number;
- workshop card number of the authorized fitter or workshop with date of at least the last installation inspection and/or periodic inspection of the recording equipment;
- control card number with date of control card insertion and type of control (display, printing, downloading). In case of downloading, period downloaded should be recorded;
- time adjustment with date, time and card issue number;
- driving status (single/crew driving – driver/co-driver).

Storing on the driver card
The driver card must be capable of storing:

- the essential data for a period of at least the last 28 calendar days combined with the VRN identification of the vehicle driven and the data as required above;

- the events and faults mentioned above with the VRN identification of the vehicle driven;
- the date and time of insertion and removal of the driver card and distance travelled during the corresponding period;
- the date and time of insertion and removal of the co-driver card with issue number.

Data must be recorded and stored on the driver card in such a way as to rule out any possibility of falsification.

Recording and storing for two drivers
Where vehicles are used by two drivers the driving time must be recorded and stored on the driver card of the driver who is driving the vehicle. The equipment must record and store in the data memory and on the two driver cards simultaneously, but distinctly, details of the information listed above.

Displaying or printing for an authorized examiner
The equipment must be capable of displaying or printing, on request, the following information:

- driver card issue number, expiry date of the card;
- the surname and first name of the driver who is the cardholder;
- current driving time since the last break or rest period;
- driving time for the day after the last rest period of at least eight hours;
- driving times for the day between two rest periods of at least eight hours for the preceding 27 calendar days on which the driver has driven, with date, time and duration;
- total of the driving times for the current week and the preceding week and the total times for the two completed preceding weeks;
- the other periods of work and availability;
- rest periods of at last eight hours' duration for the day and the preceding 27 days in each case with date, time and duration;
- VRN identification of vehicles driven for at least the last 28 calendar days with the distance travelled per vehicle and day, time of first insertion and last removal of the driver card and the time of change of vehicle;
- time adjustment with date, time and card issue number;
- interruption of power supply to the recording equipment with date, time, duration and driver card issue number;
- sensor interruption with date, time, duration and driver card issue number;
- the VIN and/or VRN identification of the vehicle driven;
- driving without driver card as defined above for the last 28 calendar days;

- details of the information stored concerning the driver;
- recorded data on the places where the daily work period began and ended;
- the automatically identifiable system faults of the recording equipment with date, time and driver card issue number;
- the faults in the driver card with date and time and driver card issue number;
- control card number with date of control card insertion and type of control (display, printing, downloading). In the case of downloading, period downloaded should be recorded;
- exceeding the authorized speed as defined above, with date, time and driver card issue number for the current week and in any case including the last day of the previous week;
- summary reports to permit compliance with the relevant regulations to be checked.

Smart cards

Crucial to the whole system is the driver ('smart') card (a credit-card sized plastic card with an imbedded microchip) that is personal to the individual and carries identification information and other essential data about him/her. It has a capacity to store relevant data on driving and working times, breaks and rest periods covering at least 28 days and will comprise the legal record in place of the current tachograph chart. The card itself must be tamper proof and strict regulatory systems are to be established by national governments to prevent fraudulent issue, use and transfer of cards within their territories.

PART 4

Fiscal law

This part covers Directive items D1, D2 and D3 in Units 2 and 3, and D4 in Unit 1.

D1. VALUE ADDED TAX

VAT is a tax on consumer spending. It is collected on business transactions and imports by VAT 'registered persons' and, in the UK, paid to HM Customs and Excise (C&E).

Most business transactions involve supplies of goods or services. VAT is payable if they are:

- supplies made in the UK or the Isle of Man;
- by a taxable person;
- in the course or furtherance of business; and
- are not specifically exempted or zero-rated.

Taxable persons
A taxable person is an individual, firm, or company that is, or is required to be, registered for VAT. A person who makes taxable supplies above a certain value (currently £56,000 in the previous 12 months) must be registered.

Out-of-scope supplies
Supplies are outside the scope of VAT if they are:

- made by someone who is not a taxable person;

- made outside the UK and the Isle of Man (unless they are of certain international services); or
- not made in the course or furtherance of business.

Current VAT rates
There are currently three rates of VAT in the UK:

- a standard rate, currently 17.5 per cent;
- a reduced rate of 5 per cent on domestic fuel and power; and
- a zero rate on which no VAT is payable although items to which they apply are treated as taxable supplies in all other respects.

VAT exempt supplies
Some supplies are exempt from VAT:

- building and civil engineering services;
- exports;
- land and buildings;
- education and training;
- financial services;
- certain insurance services.

No tax is payable on these supplies, and the person making the supply cannot normally recover any of the VAT paid on their own purchases.

Zero-rated supplies
Certain supplies are zero rated for VAT purposes. Examples include:

- food and drink for human consumption;
- some healthcare services (drugs, medicines, etc);
- some insurance services;
- certain transport and cargo-handling services;
- sewerage and water supply;
- construction of buildings;
- imports and exports;
- children's clothing and footwear;
- gold and bank notes;
- charitable and cultural services.

VAT categories
VAT is divided into two categories: output tax and input tax.

Output tax
Output tax is the tax due on taxable supplies made by a registered person. The tax value of a supply is the amount on which VAT is due, the amount

of tax payable being the tax value of the sales/supply invoice multiplied by the tax rate (currently in the UK 17.5 per cent, except as stated above).

Input tax

Input tax is the VAT charged on business purchases and expenses (with certain exceptions such as on car purchase, business entertainment and certain building articles), including:

- goods and services supplied in the UK;
- goods imported from outside the EC;
- goods acquired from another taxable person within the EU;
- goods removed from a warehouse; and
- certain services received from abroad (eg banking, financial, consultancy, legal, data and information, engineering, advertising).

Input tax paid is reclaimable by a VAT-registered person by deduction from the amount of output tax payable and is accounted for on the VAT (assuming the output tax is greater than the input tax).

VAT registration

People who are in business making taxable supplies above the threshold of annual taxable turnover (currently £52,000) must register for VAT within 30 days of becoming liable to register (broadly, once you are aware that your taxable turnover will exceed the threshold). Once registered you will be known as a registered person. However, it should be noted that where a person is registered for VAT for business purposes, he cannot recover VAT paid on non-business purchases. Also, it is illegal for a non-VAT-registered person to charge VAT on supplies of goods or services.

VAT invoices/receipts

Taxable supplies must be accompanied by a VAT invoice showing details of the supplier and his VAT number, the date and amount (ie tax value) of the supply and the relevant amount of VAT. These invoices are evidence of output tax. To reclaim input tax on purchases, it is necessary to obtain a receipt/invoice showing the supplier's VAT number, date and amount of the supply and the amount of VAT charged.

VAT records

VAT-registered people must keep records of all taxable supplies made or received (ie both standard and zero-rated supplies and exempt supplies) and a summary of the totals of output and input tax for each period (ie VAT accounts). Records can be kept manually (ie in writing) or on computer – so long as C&E inspectors can easily check the figures (they can order that changes are made to the system if they cannot do so).

VAT returns

Returns of VAT and payment of tax due must be made for each tax period (usually quarterly). A tax return is sent out by C&E and this must be completed and returned with any tax payable by the due date (stated on the form). It is an offence to fail to submit a VAT return by the due date (or at all!) or to pay the tax due by the relevant date. Heavy penalties, including default surcharges, are imposed on late payers and other offenders.

D2. VEHICLE EXCISE DUTY

The Vehicle Excise and Registration Act 1994 requires that all mechanically propelled vehicles, whether used for business or private purposes, which are driven or parked on public roads in Great Britain (also in Northern Ireland under the Vehicles (Excise) Act (Northern Ireland) 1972) must have and display current and valid excise licences unless they are being driven, by previous appointment, to a place for their annual test.

It is an offence to use or keep (ie park) an unlicensed vehicle (or trade licensed only vehicle) on a road even for a short period of time.

Exceptions

Exceptions apply to certain official vehicles such as those belonging to fire brigades and ambulance services, those operated by the Crown, snow clearance and certain other public utility vehicles.

One other exemption applies when vehicles used solely for forestry, agriculture or horticultural purposes travel on public roads for not more than 1.5 km per journey between land occupied by the same firm or person who is the registered owner of the vehicle. An 'exempt' disc is provided for display on the vehicle windscreen.

Concessionary tax classes

Special and concessionary rates of VED apply to special vehicles over 3.5 tonnes. This class includes mobile cranes, digging machines, works trucks, road rollers and showmen's goods and haulage vehicles. The 'special concessionary' class includes agricultural machines (including tractors and ploughing engines), mowing machines, gritters and snowploughs, electric vehicles and steam-driven vehicles.

Documents for licensing

When licensing a vehicle, the following documents must be provided:

1. The registration document (form V5) for the vehicle (in Northern Ireland the logbook).

2. A current certificate of insurance (or a temporary cover note, but not the policy).
3. A current MOT or goods vehicle test certificate (where applicable).
4. A completed application form:
   - form VE55 for first registration;
   - form V10 for renewal.
5. The type approval certificate (for first registration only).
6. A reduced pollution certificate (where relevant).
7. The appropriate amount of duty.

On first registration of the vehicle, a registration number will be allocated. This must be made into plates to be displayed on the front and rear of the vehicle.

A circular windscreen disc is also provided to indicate that duty has been paid (the colouring of these discs is varied to provide ready indication whether or not they are out of date). This disc must be displayed on the vehicle windscreen on the nearside, where it can be easily seen. Failure to display the disc (even if the duty has been paid) is an offence.

Rates of excise duty

VED is payable either annually or at six-monthly intervals in accordance with scales of duty. Under the present scheme of VED, duty for goods vehicles is payable in accordance with a published scale. The amount of duty payable depends on the vehicle type, its gross (ie 'revenue') weight and the number of its axles. For goods vehicles over 3,500kg gross weight the duty is based solely on gross weight, and for vehicles over 12 tonnes gvw, also on the number of axles. Certain goods vehicles with approved low-emission engines or equipment qualify for lower rates of duty if they have been issued with a 'Reduced Pollution Certificate'. Vehicles are classed as follows for duty purposes:

- Private/light goods (PLG), which includes private cars and other privately registered vehicles, and all light goods vehicles up to and including 3,500kg gross weight.
- Goods vehicles not exceeding 7.5 tonnes gross weight.
- Goods vehicles (ie rigid and articulated vehicles) over 7.5 tonnes but not exceeding 12 tonnes gross weight.
- Rigid goods vehicles exceeding 12 tonnes gross weight divided into:
  - two-axle rigids;
  - three-axle rigids;
  - four or more axle rigids.
- Trailers exceeding 4 tonnes gross weight (ie drawbar trailers).
- Special types vehicles.

- Articulated vehicles exceeding 12 tonnes gross weight divided into:
  - two-axle tractive units used with *any* semi-trailer;
  - two-axle tractive units used with two or more axle semi-trailers only;
  - two-axle tractive units used with three or more axle semi-trailers only;
  - three-axle tractive units used with *any* semi-trailer;
  - three-axle tractive units used with two-axle semi-trailers only;
  - three-axle tractive units used with three or more axle semi-trailers only.
- Special concessionary vehicles.
- General haulage vehicles.
- Recovery vehicles.
- Trade licences.

Dual-purpose vehicles

If a dual-purpose (estate-type) vehicle is used for carrying goods in connection with a trade or business and it is over 3,500kg gross weight, the appropriate rate of goods vehicle duty must be paid.

The definition of a dual-purpose vehicle is a vehicle built or converted to carry both passengers and goods of any description, which has an unladen weight of not more than 2,040kg and:

- has four-wheel drive, or has:
- a permanently fitted roof;
- a permanently fitted single row of transverse seats behind the driver which are cushioned or sprung and have upholstered backrests;
- a window on either side to the rear of the driver and one at the rear.

The majority of vehicles generally described as estate cars, shooting-brakes, station wagons, Land Rovers (hard-top version only) and 'hatchback' saloons with fold-down seats are dual-purpose vehicles under this definition, and if these are used in connection with a trade or business (carrying deliveries or trade samples, etc) and are over 3,500kg gross weight, the appropriate goods vehicle rate of duty must be paid.

Reduced pollution vehicles

Reduced rates of vehicle excise duty (currently by up to £1,000 per year for the heaviest vehicles) apply to certain buses, haulage vehicles and heavy goods vehicles that have been built or adapted to ensure reduced pollution exhaust emissions under the provisions of the Vehicle Excise Duty (Reduced Pollution) Regulations 1998.

The reduced pollution requirement may be satisfied by:

- a new vehicle meeting the required standard;
- the fitting of a new engine to a vehicle; or
- the fitting of a type-approved device (catalyser) for which there is a Certificate of Conformity issued by the vehicle manufacturer.

The reduced pollution requirements are satisfied if the rate and content of a vehicle's particulate emissions do not exceed the number of grams per kilowatt-hour specified in Table 4.1.

Refunds of duty

Paid duty may be reclaimed for each complete month remaining on the licence when it is surrendered. Applications for refunds must be made by the last day of the preceding month and the licence disc must be surrendered.

Alteration of vehicles

If a vehicle is modified, the details must be notified to the Driver and Vehicle Licensing Agency (DVLA) at Swansea.

Fuel duty

Diesel fuel for road-going vehicles is subject to excise duty, whereas the same type of oil used, for example, on farms and sites is not. Duty-free diesel is dyed red (legally it is called 'rebated heavy oil' but is generally referred to as 'red diesel' or 'gas oil' – a green version is also available) and can easily be detected if used illegally in road-going vehicles. HM C&E conduct roadside checks of vehicles to ensure that the correct duty-paid fuel is being used.

Table 4.1

Instrument setting standard to which vehicle was first used	Rate and content of particulate emissions after adaptation (grams per kilowatt-hour)
1. Directive 88/77/EEC	0.16
2. Directive 91/542/EEC (limits A)	0.16
3. Directive 91/542/EEC (limits B)	0.08
4. European Commission Proposal (Com [97] 627) for a European and Council Directive amending Council Directive 88/77/EEC	0.04

Trade licences

Trade licences (commonly referred to as trade plates) may be obtained and used by motor traders (manufacturers, repairers or dealers in motor vehicles including motor vehicle delivery firms) and vehicle testers. The plates may be used on vehicles that are temporarily in their possession as motor traders, and on vehicles submitted for testing. Trade plates must not be used on recovery vehicles.

Applications for trade licences

Application must be made to local Vehicle Registration Offices (VROs) on form VTL 301. The licence is valid for one year (or for a lesser period, ie 6 to 11 months). If a trade licence is refused by the VRO an appeal can be made to the Secretary of State for Transport.

Trade plates

Two plates are issued with red letters on a white background; one has the triangular licence affixed to it. This plate must be attached to the front of the vehicle, and the other to the rear.

Use of trade plates

Trade plates may only be used in the following circumstances by bona fide motor traders and testers:

- for test or trial in the course of construction or repair of the vehicle or its accessories or equipment and after completing construction or repair;
- when travelling to or from a weighbridge to check the unladen weight or when travelling to a place for registration or inspection by the council;
- for demonstration to a prospective customer and when travelling to or from a place of demonstration;
- for test or trial of the vehicle for the benefit of a person interested in promoting publicity for the vehicle;
- for delivering the vehicle to a purchaser;
- for demonstrating the accessories or equipment to a prospective purchaser;
- for delivering a vehicle to, or collecting it from, other premises belonging to the trade licence holder or another trader's premises;
- for going to or coming from a workshop in which a body or equipment or accessories is to be, or has been, fitted;
- for delivering the vehicle from the premises of a manufacturer or repairer to a place where it is to be transported by train, ship or aircraft or for returning it from a place to which it has been transported by these means;

- when travelling to or returning from any garage, auction room or other place where vehicles are stored or offered for sale;
- when travelling to a place to be dismantled or broken up.

Goods may only be carried on a vehicle operating under a trade licence:

- when a load is necessary to demonstrate or test the vehicle, its accessories or its equipment – the load must be returned to the place of loading after the demonstration or test;
- when a load consists of parts or equipment to be fitted to the vehicle being taken to the place where they are to be fitted;
- when a load is built in or permanently attached to the vehicle;
- when a trailer is being carried for delivery or being taken to a place for work to be carried out on it.

The only passengers permitted to travel on a trade-licensed vehicle are:

- the driver of the vehicle, who may be the trade licence holder or an employee. Other persons may drive the vehicle with the permission of the licence holder but they must be accompanied by the licence holder or his employee – this latter proviso does not apply if the vehicle is constructed to carry only one person;
- persons required to be on the vehicle by law, such as a statutory attendant;
- any person carried for the purpose of inspecting the vehicle or trailer;
- any person in a disabled vehicle being towed;
- a prospective purchaser or his servant or agent;
- a person interested in promoting publicity for the vehicle.

Trade-licensed vehicles must not be left parked on public roads.

Recovery vehicles

Recovery vehicles may not be used for recovery operations on trade plates. A separate class of VED applies to these vehicles. Any vehicle used for recovery work that does not conform to the definition given below must be licensed at the normal goods vehicle rate according to its class and gross weight. Goods must not be carried on a recovery vehicle when in use, except essential tools or spares.

Definition of a recovery vehicle
For the purpose of this taxation class, a recovery vehicle is one that is 'either constructed or permanently adapted primarily for the purpose of lifting, towing and transporting a disabled vehicle or for any one or more

of those purposes'. A vehicle will no longer be a recovery vehicle under the regulations (ie Vehicle Excise and Registration Act 1994 Schedule 1 Part V) if at any time it is used for a purpose other than:

- the recovery of a disabled vehicle;
- the removal of a disabled vehicle from the place where it became disabled to premises at which it is to be repaired or scrapped;
- the removal of a disabled vehicle from premises to which it was taken for repair to other premises at which it is to be repaired or scrapped;
- carrying any load other than fuel and any liquids required for its propulsion and tools and other articles required for the operation of, or in connection with, apparatus designed to lift, tow or transport a disabled vehicle.

Plating and testing of recovery vehicles

Recovery vehicles licensed under the recovery vehicle taxation class are not exempt from goods vehicle plating and testing unless they satisfy the definition in the regulations of a 'breakdown vehicle' namely, 'a vehicle on which is mounted permanently fitted apparatus for raising a disabled vehicle from the ground and for drawing that vehicle when so raised, and which is not equipped to carry any load other than articles required for that operation, the apparatus for repairing disabled vehicles.

Operation of recovery vehicles

Licensed recovery vehicles are exempt from 'O' licensing, the EU drivers' hours rules and the tachograph requirements, but those persons who drive them must hold driving entitlements of the correct category (category C) and must comply with the British domestic driving hours rules.

D3. ROAD AND BRIDGE TOLLS

Certain roads, bridges and tunnels, both in the UK and in Europe, are available for use only to those who pay a toll which, in most cases, varies according to the type of user. These variations range from rates for pedestrians, cyclists and motorcyclists, motor cars and light goods vehicles, heavy goods vehicles and passenger vehicles.

Generally, the raising of a toll is to defray the high costs of construction and maintenance of the road, bridge or tunnel in question. However, there is a trend these days towards private financing (or combined government and private finance initiatives) of construction, maintenance and management of infrastructure facilities, so the toll also provides investment returns.

Road charging

More recently there has been considerable debate about the merits or otherwise of road charging, with the Government circulating consultation documents on the subject. The against lobby naturally sees any form of road toll as yet another tax on motorists, while the commercial user quickly points out that the costs can only be recovered through higher transport and delivery costs, which will filter through to increase the shelf price of goods.

However, the Government's case is that with ever-increasing congestion and the high costs of road provision and maintenance, some form of route selection and increased funding is required. Hence the possibility of road tolls on key routes in the future. Opponents quickly point out that raising tolls on motorways will drive many users to secondary routes through urban areas, causing additional congestion and greater accident risk to pedestrians and other road users.

UK toll bridges and tunnels

Currently, there are no such tolls on motorways in the UK, unlike France and Spain, for example, where motorway users pay heavily for the privilege, but we do have quite a number of tolled bridges and tunnels as follows:

- Dartford crossing (ie Dartford Tunnel northbound and the Queen Elizabeth II bridge southbound over the River Thames on the M25 motorway).
- Erskine Bridge over the River Clyde west of Glasgow on the A82.
- Forth Road Bridge over the Firth of Forth on the A90 between Fife and Lothian in Scotland to the west of Edinburgh (connecting with the M8, M9 and M90 motorways).
- Humber Bridge over the River Humber on the A15.
- Mersey Tunnel between Liverpool and Birkenhead.
- Severn Bridge – two crossings of the River Severn on the M4 and M48 motorways between England (Avon) and Wales (Gwent).
- Skye Bridge over the Kyle of Lochalsh on the A87 between the Scottish mainland and the Isle of Skye.
- Tamar Bridge over the River Tamar on the A38 between Plymouth and Saltash (toll payable eastbound only – ie into Cornwall).
- Tyne Tunnel under the River Tyne on the A1 to the east of Newcastle upon Tyne.

International vehicle taxes and tolls

Goods vehicle taxation
Goods vehicles are normally subject to the vehicle taxation system of any country through which they pass. However, as a result of Britain's

acceptance of the terms of the International Convention on the Taxation of Road Vehicles mentioned above and as a result of bilateral agreements, goods vehicles are exempt from paying further taxation *provided* that they are correctly taxed in the country of registration (see below for the list of countries where additional taxes are payable). To ensure that vehicles are correctly taxed to meet this requirement, valid excise licence discs must be displayed on the vehicle windscreen on all journeys abroad.

Countries where further lorry tax (ie excise duty) *has* to be paid are:

- Austria (tax payable on transit of goods vehicles over 12 tonnes).
- Hungary (where single-axle weight exceeds 10 tonnes or 16 tonnes on two axles).
- Switzerland (road tax payable based on gross weights and time in country).
- Turkey (transit tax payable).
- Former Yugoslavia (road tax payable for vehicles in transit).

Fuel duties

Generally, road fuel used to power vehicles carries tax/duty payable in the country of origin at the time of purchase and no further tax/duty is payable when it is carried into other countries in vehicle fuel tanks (the general allowance within the EU is 200 litres). However, since many vehicles used on international operations have high-capacity, long-range fuel tanks, some countries charge additional tax or duty above certain limits.

Motorway taxes (vignettes)

Goods vehicles exceeding 12 tonnes gross weight are subject to a motorway tax when travelling to or through Germany, the Benelux countries (Belgium, Luxembourg and Holland), and Denmark. A vehicle certificate (vignette) is issued upon payment of the sliding-scale tax depending on the number of axles (ie up to three and four or more) and the period of time for which the certificate is required (ie from one week to one year).

A road user charge is imposed in Poland. Motorway vignettes must be purchased in Slovakia for the use of motorways. Similarly, Slovenia charges for the use of certain routes.

NB: A scheme for lorry road charging in Germany – the LKW-Maut – destined to come into effect in August 2003 has been postponed until late 2004 or 2005 due to technical difficulties with the vehicle on-board equipment.

Britain's first toll motorway – the M6 Toll Road – formerly known as the Birmingham Northern Relief Road (BNRR), opened to traffic in December 2003. The new road is a 27-mile long, three-lane motorway designed to ease traffic and congestion through the West Midlands, one of the most congested sections of motorway in Europe. It should provide reduced journey times, greater fuel efficiency and a renewed commitment to delivery times, with time savings that are estimated to save businesses billions of pounds a year in wasted man hours.

D4. CORPORATE AND INCOME TAX

There is a saying that only two things are certain in life: death and taxes. It is certainly true that whether you are an income-earning employee or boss of a business you will need to pay taxes.

While there are many forms of taxation within our complex taxation system, in this section we are only concerned with two types of tax: income tax paid by individuals who may be employees or self-employed persons, and corporate taxation which is levied on the profits of limited liability companies.

Income tax

Employed individuals (who may be workers, managers or even directors of companies) and self-employed sole traders and partners in a partnership business are liable to pay income tax based on their earnings, but subject to certain minimum earnings concessions and various personal allowances.

Tax schedules

Income is assessed according to its source and depending upon which 'schedule' this is allocated to by the tax authority, namely the Inland Revenue. Broadly, there are four schedules:

- Schedule A, which applies to income from land and property (applicable to individuals and companies).
- Schedule D, which applies to income/profits from trade or a profession, interest on savings/investments, etc, rents and commissions (applies to both individuals and companies).
- Schedule E, which applies to wages and salaries from employment.
- Schedule F, which applies to dividends, etc, paid to shareholders by a UK company.

Payment of income tax

The method for paying income tax varies between the system by which tax is deducted from the pay of employees, namely Pay As You Earn (PAYE), and payment of tax by self-employed persons on a twice-yearly basis calculated on their annual income.

PAYE

Employers of wage- and salary-earning employees are required to operate a PAYE system under which they deduct from employees' gross earnings the relevant amount of income tax (determined by reference to a tax code issued by the IR, which takes account of the individual's statutory and declared allowances) and National Insurance contribution. These deductions are paid over by the employer to the IR on a monthly basis.

The personal allowances that are offset against tax due include a personal allowance for all individuals which may vary (ie increase) according to circumstances (eg single-child-one-parent families, blind person allowance, widow's bereavement allowance, medical insurance relief, life assurance relief).

Tax for the self-employed

Self-employed people are taxed on an earnings basis (ie on income and expenses due in the tax period rather than on income and expenses received and paid in that period) and account for their own tax under the 'self-assessment' system. They must keep records of their income and expenditure and make a return to the IR annually (with a tax return) showing this information. Either the individual or the IR assesses the amount of tax payable and this is due in two half-yearly amounts in January and July each year.

After the first year in business it is necessary to make two payments on account towards the annual tax bill, on 31 January and 31 July each year, a final payment of the balance of any tax due being payable on the following 31 January. This means that after the first year the self-employed person will have to pay a half-yearly tax bill plus another estimated half-year amount in advance, so, in effect, in that year he will pay one and half years' worth of tax.

Trading accounts for the self-employed

Self-employed persons are required to compile a record (ie account) of income received in a tax year. This record must be complete and accurate whether they prepare it themselves or use the services of an accountant, in which case the individual is still responsible for its accuracy.

The accounts may be in two parts: a profit and loss or trading account showing income and expenditure, and a balance sheet showing the assets and liabilities of the business.

For very small businesses (ie below £15,000 annual income before deduction of expenses) a simple three-line return will suffice (ie turnover, less expenses, equals net profit).

Expenses and allowances for the self-employed

Business expenses, which are offset against income to determine gross profit (ie before tax), are only allowable if they relate to business activities. Non-allowable expenses include:

- personal and domestic expenses;
- entertaining and hospitality;
- gifts and donations, fines and penalties;
- debts other than bad debts;
- life insurance and pension premiums on the proprietor of the business.

Employee benefits

Most benefits in kind provided to an employee in consequence of his employment are taxable. The general rule (subject to many exceptions) is that for employees who are company directors or whose annual income and benefits exceed £8,500, the benefit is assessable on the employee for an amount equal to the cost to the employer. For other employees, the employee fringe benefits are not usually assessed. The taxable benefits include:

- the provision of accommodation;
- gifts of assets and gift vouchers;
- loans;
- the provision of staff (eg chauffeur, nanny);
- childcare facilities;
- company car/van and fuel;
- luncheon vouchers;
- club memberships;
- use of mobile phones;
- share options;
- travel.

Certain benefits, including the following, can be provided free of tax:

- Canteen facilities, provided the same facilities are available to all employees.
- Car parking at or near the place of work.
- Chauffeur, provided he is only used on company business.
- Childcare facilities provided by the employer and which comply with local authority regulations.
- Clothes such as uniforms, safety clothing or bearing the company logo.
- Company car, covering use of a pool car only for company business.
- Education, full-time, but only where it meets certain criteria.
- Entertainment, but only where incidental to the employment.
- Gift, but only if unrelated to employment or not from the employer and not worth more than £150 a year.
- Housing – necessary to perform duty properly, customary for that employment, necessary for security, or free board for agricultural workers.

- Hotel bills, but only necessary food and accommodation (£5 a day personal expenses in the UK and £10 a day overseas).
- Laundry where the clothing qualifies for tax relief.
- Liability cover or payment, but not for a criminal offence.
- Long service awards for service of at least 20 years and not over £50 per year of service.
- Luncheon vouchers, but not if worth more than 15p per working day.
- Medical treatment incurred overseas or for a routine check-up.
- Mobile telephone, but not for personal calls.
- Outplacement counselling for an employee made redundant.
- Parties and functions provided cost does not exceed £75 per person.
- Pension contributions to an approved scheme.
- Relocation up to £8,000.
- Scholarships first awarded before 1983.
- Security measures necessary to protect an employee or his family (but not a vehicle or accommodation).
- Sports facilities provided by an employer.
- Training costs – related to an employee's work.
- Training expenses – for courses in the UK related to work and lasting four weeks or more.
- Travel and subsistence made in the course of work.

Tax records
Tax records (including all receipts, etc) must be kept for five years counting from the 31 January in the year following that to which the return relates – which effectively means keeping records for six years.

Corporation tax

Corporation or corporate tax is payable by UK-based companies based on their annual trading profits and on their capital gains.

The relevant figures are determined from the company's annual accounts which show sales or turnover and purchases and, by deduction of one from the other, the gross profit. Income may include overseas trading, investment income and dividends received. Purchases/expenditure may include normal business expenses, capital allowances, charitable covenants and patent royalties.

Corporation tax is currently (ie 1999/2000 tax year) 30 per cent, but for smaller companies with annual profits not exceeding £300,000 it is only 19 per cent, and where the profit is only £10,000 or less it is zero.

Small company corporation tax

Marginal relief eases the transition from the starting rate to the small companies' rate for companies with profits between £10,000 and £50,000. The fraction used in the calculation of this marginal relief will be 19/400. Marginal relief also applies to companies with profits between £300,000 and £1,500,000. The fraction used in the calculation of this marginal relief will be 11/400.

Double taxation

Double taxation is when the same income and gains are subject to tax in more than one country. Double taxation relief is given for this taxation by:

- means of a double tax treaty with the country concerned, whereby income is exempt from tax in one country and a credit granted for foreign taxes paid on other income;
- allowing the foreign tax paid as a credit against the total UK tax liability;
- the foreign tax being considered as a deductible expense in calculating the business profits chargeable to tax (ie the foreign tax being treated like an ordinary business expense).

Where relief is due under a double tax treaty, the treaty takes precedence over UK domestic legislation. In most cases, the full amount of income, including income from the overseas territory, is brought into account for calculating the income tax liability on the income for the tax year. The overseas tax paid on the relevant income is then offset as a credit against the total liability to income tax. The credit is limited to the income tax liability on the income that has been subject to overseas tax. There is no relief available for any excess foreign tax paid. Any unrelieved foreign tax cannot be carried forward or back and is therefore wasted. Generally, only direct foreign taxes are taken into account for the purposes of double tax relief.

National Insurance

Most people who work are liable to pay National Insurance contributions unless they come into one of the groups excepted from liability. There are five classes of contributions in all, and the class an individual needs pay depends on whether he is an employee, a self-employed person, a non-employed person or an employer. Depending on his status, a person may have to pay more than one class of contribution at the same time. Some contributions count towards benefits such as incapacity benefit and retirement pension.

Self-employed people are liable to pay two classes of contributions: Class 2 contributions, and Class 4 contributions, which are paid on profits and gains at, or above, a set level.

Class 2 contributions

Class 2 contributions are a flat rate payment collected by the Contributions Agency from persons who are normally self-employed, age 16 or over and under pension age (60 for a woman, 65 for a man).

Payment is made in arrears either by quarterly bill every 13 weeks or by direct debit every month.

These contributions do not count for Jobseeker's Allowance but they do count for incapacity benefit, retirement pension, widow's benefit and maternity allowance.

Class 4 contributions

Class 4 contributions are payable when an individual's profits exceed a certain amount. These contributions may have to be paid in addition to Class 2 contributions. They are based on a percentage of annual profits between a lower and upper profit level. The levels are set each year by the Chancellor in the Budget. For example, currently (ie 2003/2004 tax year):

- Percentage rate – 8.0%
- Lower profit level – £4,615
- Upper profit level – £30,940

Class 4 contributions are normally assessed and collected by the Inland Revenue together with Schedule D tax, based on the individual's profit assessment. As with tax, if payment becomes overdue, interest may have to be paid. These contributions do not entitle the payee to any benefit, but they do help to share the cost of funding the benefits paid to all self-employed people.

PART 5

Business and financial management

This part covers Directive items E1 in Units 1 and 3; E2 in Units 1, 2 and 3; E3, E4 and E5 in Units 1 and 2; E6, E7, E10, E12 and E13 in Units 2 and 3; and E8, E9 and E11 in Unit 2.

INTRODUCTION TO FINANCIAL MANAGEMENT

Maintaining strict control over the financial affairs of a business is vital for its success. For this reason there should be an organized system for dealing with payments received and made and for arranging credit where necessary. The methods by which this is done are described in E1 and E2 below. There must also be a similarly organized system of calculating and regularly monitoring direct costs, overheads, revenue and profit. In any event, it is usual at least once each year for a business to balance its books of account in order to prepare proper financial statements of these items as a reflection of its activities during the past year (as described in E3 to E7 below).

This enables the owners and shareholders of the business and other interested parties to see its performance during that time, what expenditure has been incurred, what revenue received, the value of assets owned, the liabilities of the business in terms of money owed and other commitments, and money owing to it by its debtors. Most important, the accounts also show the profit or loss made from the year's trading and the current value of the business (the so-called 'bottom line' figure).

These documents together provide a complete picture of the financial affairs of a business at a particular moment in time (ie at the end of the financial year). It is from these documents that shareholders are able to obtain a knowledge of how 'their' company has been managed, the company's bank manager can learn of the true financial state of the bank's client, and potential investors can obtain information that may encourage them to invest in the company (in the case of public limited companies). The accounts are also of interest to other institutions and firms to whom the company may have applied for loans or other financial facilities, or with whom it hopes to do business.

For limited liability companies it is a legal requirement that annual accounts are prepared and independently audited and, of course, a return of income or profit must be made to the Inland Revenue (but advising expenditure is not compulsory!) for tax assessment purposes by all businesses, ranging in size – and income – from the sole trader to public limited companies.

Annual accounts comprise many separate documents in the case of a large organization, but for simplicity of explanation we are concentrating on just two documents – the profit and loss (or sometimes called the trading) account and the balance sheet – which are found in all accounts whether for a very large company or the smallest (see E3 and E4).

E1. PAYMENT METHODS

The methods used in payments of accounts and expenses comprise a variety of alternative arrangements, it not always being convenient or even sensible (for security reasons) to deal in cash, although this method does have its merits in certain circumstances.

Cash

Perhaps the oldest and simplest means of paying for what you want, and a useful constraint against buying what you cannot afford, is to use cash (hard currency). The disadvantages of doing so are first, the need to use cash received in respect of work done or goods sold, which could lead to shortcomings in the accounting system, or having to call repeatedly at a bank to draw more funds; and second, the inherent risk of loss or theft when handling and holding large sums of money in banknotes and coins.

The dubious advantages are that additional discount on the purchase price may be negotiated for immediate cash payments, and one often comes across the illegal practice where a lower price is offered for cash purchases, reflecting the fact that the recipient is not meeting his income tax responsibilities and is also avoiding VAT registration.

Cheques

Cheques are a simple means of paying for purchases without the risk or inconvenience of carrying large amounts of cash. They are, of course, only available to those who have a current account with a bank, and sufficient funds in their account to meet the cheques drawn, or an agreed overdraft facility that allows them to exceed their own funds up to a set limit. For small purchases a cheque guarantee card, issued by the bank and guaranteeing cheques up to £50 or £100 in value, will ensure that the recipient (ie the payee) is certain to receive payment, irrespective of the state of the payer's account. Cheques usually take at least three working days to clear, giving purchasers a small margin of credit between obtaining the purchase and actually seeing the amount deducted from their bank account.

Credit/debit cards

Confusion sometimes surrounds the differing uses of these two types of card. Credit cards provide holders with a pre-set credit facility which they may use to make purchases but which, if they do not repay the amount owing within the set time (usually up to a maximum of about six weeks – the period of credit), will incur interest charges on the outstanding balance. The interest charge is invariably set at a high rate compared to some other forms of credit, but shopping around will provide competitive alternatives. Exceeding the maximum credit level and/or failure to make regular payments could lead to loss of the facility.

Credit cards also have an advantage with certain purchases in that the card-issuing company provides a degree of insurance or guarantee should the purchased item not perform as expected.

Debit cards provide no credit. They are issued by banks to account holders as an alternative to cheques, enabling purchases to be made with the amount due being taken directly from the purchaser's bank account by the retailer or supplier. This method saves the task of writing out cheques, but it does mean that any advantage provided by the three-day cheque clearance delay is lost.

Charge cards

Charge cards are a form of credit card usually issued to a person holding an account with a supplier, but payable in full when the invoice or statement is presented. They are not usually valid for use with more than one supplier and do not normally offer extended credit terms. However, defaulting on payment can result in abnormally high interest rates and penalties being applied. Typical of charge cards are the so-called 'store cards' issued by High Street retailers and designed to enhance loyalty to that particular store.

Promissory notes

These are quite simply notes that contain a promise to pay a specified person/firm a specified amount of money either on demand or on a specified date. In essence they are like a cheque but usually carry more information. They may, for example, refer to the details of the transaction.

Bills of exchange

Bills of exchange are used in international trade to pay for goods or services. They are an unconditional order in writing from one person to another to pay a specified amount within a given time scale (usually either on sight, or within 60 or 90 days from the date of its issue). Due to its security of payment when due, the holder may be able in the meantime to raise credit on the bill.

Debit systems

The system of bank debit cards has been described above.

Direct debit is a service whereby the bank is authorized to pay amounts direct from a client's accounts, usually on a regular basis (eg monthly, quarterly or annually), on application by the client's debtors (eg for mortgage payments, hire purchase or leasing repayments). This service helps the bank client by saving him the job of writing out cheques every time a payment is due and avoids the problem of remembering to make the payment and ensures it is paid on time.

Credit transfer

This is an arrangement whereby money can be transferred within the banking system without the need for cheques. Many firms these days pay their employees by means of credit transfer – in other words pay the money direct to the employees' bank account. This saves the firm the problems of handling cash and writing cheques and ensures more rapid payment for the recipient.

NB: Readers should note the difference between credit transfer and direct debit – the former puts money automatically into an account, the latter automatically takes it out.

E2. CREDIT AND BORROWING

Bank loans

Bank loans are generally provided, against security, for the establishment of a new business or for financing expansion of existing businesses. Banks invariably require security in the form of deposits, personal guarantees given by individuals employed in or with an interest in the business, charges over freehold property or the lodgement of insurance policies with a guaranteed surrender value, or debentures. Repayment of bank loans is invariably by regular amounts over a fixed period of time. Such loans are usually for mid- to long-term periods and are not subject to recall at short notice like overdrafts, provided repayments are made in accordance with the terms of the agreement.

Overdrafts

Overdrafts are provided by banks for short-term use in day-to-day business operations to overcome the problems of fluctuating cash flows. They are not intended for long-term capital requirements because they are subject to recall at short notice if, among other things, the Government or the Bank of England places restrictions on credit. Besides the intention, the use of overdraft facilities for capital purchases is not recommended because it reduces credit (ie the availability of ready cash) for more immediate needs such as weekly wages, meeting fuel bills on delivery of new supplies, etc. Security in some form is normally required to cover overdraft facilities or at least the surety of a substantial inflow of funds in a short time.

Documentary credit

A documentary (letter of) credit is a means of the importer paying the exporter for goods to be despatched to him. It is an agreement under which the importer's bank agrees to pay the exporter (ie the supplier of the goods) usually via his own or a nominated bank in his home country. Payment is invariably tied to pre-established conditions as set out in the letter of credit being met by the exporter. Letters of credit are useful where the seller does not know the buyer and has little means of establishing his ability to pay for the goods ordered.

Guarantee deposits

Guarantee deposits are simply a form of payment whereby the buyer (ie the importer abroad) pays in advance for the goods by means of a guaranteed bank deposit, which is released to the seller (ie the exporter) when the goods are received.

Mortgages

Mortgages are a means by which loans are made, usually to a purchaser of property (but mortgages are also made on boats) under which the property itself acts as security for the loan – ie the lender takes a legal charge on the property so that if the buyer defaults on payment the lender can recover the property and sell it to realize the outstanding debt. In the context of small haulage businesses, operators who raise a mortgage on their own home (or obtain bank loans secured on their home) to provide business finance, risk losing their home should the business fail.

Leases

A lease is a means by which the use of property can be obtained without actually purchasing it. Leases are usually long-term arrangements and can be transferred to another leasee, in which case a premium is usually charged (ie sale of a lease). They are legally prepared and contain all the terms and conditions relating to use of the property, often its maintenance, and any exclusions as to the occupancy or use of the premises (called covenants). A lessee wishing to prematurely opt out of a leasing agreement may find difficulty due to its inherent penalty and forfeiture clauses unless, as stated above, the remaining term of the lease can be sold (with the leasor's agreement) to another lessee.

Rents

Premises occupied on a short-term tenancy basis are usually subject to a rental arrangement rather than the legal complexity and expense involved in negotiating a lease. Payment is in the form of rent which may be by cash, monthly cheque or by a banker's order/direct debit arrangement through the bank. Termination is usually by giving the landlord the requisite (ie pre-determined) period of notice.

Factoring

When poor cash flow causes a business financial problems, one source of short-term finance to alleviate this difficulty is the factoring of sales invoices. Factoring companies will pay cash against invoices they consider acceptable, with the deduction of a percentage of the face value for their charges. By this means, prompt payment of invoices is obtained, which improves cash flow and saves the extended periods of delay in waiting for payment, but the amount received is reduced, often substantially. This scheme is not usually acceptable where the firm is working on small profit margins, as in haulage operations, because the commission payable to the factors virtually (or completely) eliminates the profit margin on each invoice. It does not help, either, with doubtful payers; the factoring house will not accept such invoices.

Hire purchase and leasing

These two long-term financing facilities provide capital for the acquisition of specific assets: motor vehicles, workshop equipment, office machines, etc. In the case of hire purchase, the finance house lends the money required, the borrower makes the purchase and then repays the loan plus interest over an agreed period of time. At the end of the payment period the asset belongs to the borrower but even while payments are being made he still has title to the goods. In the case of leasing, the lessor provides the money and retains ownership title to the goods while the lessee has their full use during a given period but never actually becomes the owner. The advantage of leasing is that the use of essential items of equipment is obtained with a minimum of capital outlay; a regular predetermined amount is repaid over a period and the item used does not appear on the balance sheet as an asset or as an outstanding debt (hence the term 'off-balance sheet financing') – however, under new accounting rules this situation is being changed so that such items do appear on balance sheets and trading accounts to give a more accurate reflection of a firm's activities in regard to leased assets and leasing commitments.

Other funds

Finance for establishing and running business activities is available from a number of sources as described below, each of which has particular advantages depending on the purpose for which the finance is used.

Proprietor's and shareholder funds

When businesses are originally founded it is usual for the founder proprietor to introduce some, at least, of his own capital, although this may be topped up by business loans and funds from other sources. In the case of limited liability companies the initial capital will come from the shareholders, although again this may be increased by funds from other sources. It is quite common for banks and other institutions to invest in new concerns where the ideas are good and the prospects are sound. These original funds are looked upon as being long-term investments.

Retained profits

The usual, principal source of funds for the operation and expansion of an established business is the use of retained profits (ie those made in previous years through successful trading, which have been retained in the business, not having been distributed to shareholders). This is the ideal method of funding development of a business but in times of recession and during the business's formative years profits may not be sufficient to meet all of its financial needs, so recourse to other sources becomes necessary.

Debentures

These are long-term loans (sometimes called loan stock) secured against the assets of the business (eg by individuals or investment firms) and are repayable with agreed rates of fixed interest added, usually after a specified period of time. Frequently, the issue of a debenture or loan stock is tied in with a charge on the firm's fixed assets or part of them (its freehold premises for example). In the event of collapse of the company debenture holders have priority over normal creditors and shareholders (but not over statutory claimants such as the Inland Revenue, the DSS, or HM Customs & Excise for VAT) when that particular asset is disposed of and in any share out of remaining funds, but invariably they lose their investment.

Investment funds

When a business is short of capital to meet development or expansion plans, to obtain more extensive premises, to purchase additional equipment or to meet equipment replacement programmes, assistance may be obtained from a number of sources including merchant banks, investment groups, the ICFC (Industrial and Commercial Finance Corporation) and the 3is company as well as individual investors (possibly under the former Business Expansion Scheme – now the Enterprise Investment Scheme (EIS) – whereby if all the qualifying conditions are met they receive taxation benefits). In return for the provision of long-term capital (often termed 'venture capital') the investor will usually want to take a share in the equity of the business, which means that the original owners have to surrender part of their holding and thus some of the control of the business.

Use of funds

In assessing the various merits of financial sources as described in outline above, it is necessary to consider the uses to which the money is to be put. There is no point in raising fresh capital from shareholders and surrendering part of the equity of the business just to meet short-term demands. These can normally be covered by short-term borrowing and overdrafts with no loss of equity or without tying up valuable securities such as legal charges on freehold property. On the other hand, facilities for short-term borrowing should not be used for expenditure on major capital projects or long-term development as this reduces the availability of ready funds to meet urgent or unexpected short-term needs. Careful financial planning in these matters is essential and this is where the management skill lies in running a successful business, whether large or small.

E3. BALANCE SHEETS AND ASSETS

Balance sheet

A balance sheet is a statement of the cumulative 'worth' of a business over its whole life, shown at a certain time (ie at the end of the financial year – and only then). The values of the fixed and current assets of the business are shown, including buildings, land, equipment, money in the bank and money owed to it by debtors, the value of stock on hand (in a haulage firm: diesel in a bulk tank, spares and tyres in the workshop stores as well as stationery in the cupboard) and liabilities of the business including tax owed to the Inland Revenue, amounts due to creditors, outstanding loans and other debts.

The balance sheet entries are in two columns, those on one side being all the assets plus any trading profits (carried forward from the trading and profit and loss account – see above) and those on the other being its liabilities and any trading losses (see also above). Both sides of the balance sheet are totalled at the bottom and one figure is deducted from the other to show a plus or minus balance that represents the value of the business, the so-called 'bottom-line figure'. From the balance sheet it is possible to determine the current assets and current liabilities of the business.

A simple balance sheet may appear as follows:

Fixed assets	*Current liabilities*
Freehold premises	Mortgage
Motor vehicles	Accounts payable (ie creditors)
Plant and equipment	Hire purchase repayments
Fixtures and fittings	Bank loan repayable
	Bank overdraft
	Tax liability

Current assets
Accounts receivable (ie debtors)
Stocks
Cash at bank
Petty cash on hand

Trading profit brought forward	Trading loss brought forward
Total assets	Total liabilities

It should be noted that not all of these items would necessarily appear on a particular balance sheet. For example, there would not be both a trading profit and a loss figure brought forward, similarly there may not be hire purchase repayments, a bank loan and an overdraft, and a firm may not have cash in the bank and an overdraft – usually (but not always) the credit cash balance would eliminate the overdraft. Premises may be rented rather than owned so while the value would not be shown on the assets side no mortgage liability would be shown on the other side (rents for rented property would appear as expenditure on the profit and loss account only).

Assets

It is important to understand the role of assets in a business and the difference between fixed assets and current assets.

Fixed assets are property and equipment owned by a business, which represent a value shown on the balance sheet but one which is not readily realizable for cash in the event of a shortage of funds or an urgent need for cash to meet liabilities. Fixed assets include property owned by the business, motor vehicles, mobile and fixed plant and equipment, tools, office equipment and furniture, and fixtures and fittings in buildings.

Current assets are represented by cash held by the business in its bank account and in petty cash in the office, by 'accounts receivable', in other words money owed for work done (or goods or services supplied) and invoiced, and by stocks of goods which could, if necessary, be quickly sold to raise cash to meet liabilities.

Net current assets are the value of current assets as described above less current liabilities (see below) or debts owing. Once a firm has paid all its debts (met all its liabilities) what it has left by way of credit bank balances, cash in hand and stocks that could be sold are its net current assets. It is when current liabilities exceed current assets that a business is in trouble and is, in effect, insolvent and should cease trading.

Liabilities

Liabilities are, in effect, debts owed by a business to its suppliers, its banks or any other provider of funds. There is nothing wrong in a business having liabilities provided that it has assets to cover those liabilities, otherwise it is effectively insolvent (ie it cannot meet its liabilities). To calculate the solvency of a business it is necessary to add together all the current liabilities and deduct these from the total of the current assets to show (hopefully) a positive (plus) balance.

The fact that a business may have a strong asset base and a good order book does not mean that it could still not find itself in trouble if its cash flows are such that current liabilities cannot be met.

Debtors and creditors

Here it is important to point out the difference between debtors and creditors. The examination candidate should ensure he clearly understands which is which – it can have a significant bearing on answers to questions in this section.

Debtors are people, firms or organizations owing money to a company. They show on the balance sheet as current assets. Creditors are people, firms or organizations including banks and financial institutions to which a company owes money. They show on the balance sheet as current liabilities. Ideally, a company's balance sheet should show the value of debtors to be greater than that of creditors so that if all moneys owing were received and all debts paid there would be a surplus of funds rather than a deficit.

Legal responsibilities

As mentioned earlier in this section, limited liability companies are required to have their annual accounts audited by professional (ie chartered) accountants and to show copies of the profit and loss account and balance sheet to shareholders each year. They must also submit copies to the Registrar of Companies (at Companies House) where they are retained on file and are available for inspection by *any* person wishing to see them, on payment of a small statutory fee.

There is no legal requirement for non-limited, sole proprietorships and partnership businesses to have their business accounts audited annually but they must prepare satisfactory annual financial records and submit a statement of their income to the Inland Revenue for tax assessment purposes (see previous note about there being no legal requirement to notify expenditure – p130).

E4. PROFIT AND LOSS ACCOUNTS

The profit and loss (or trading) account identifies the trading activity of the business for the year, showing on one side of the account payments received for work done or goods supplied (termed 'sales' or 'sales turnover', just 'turnover' or 'revenue' – and invariably shown as a single figure) and on the other side a record of all expenditure incurred by the business in its trading activities including purchase of materials, administrative and operating costs, salaries, etc (usually broken down into many individual headings).

When both sides of this account are balanced it will show whether revenue exceeded costs or vice versa. If it is the former then the figure indicates a *trading profit*, otherwise there is a *trading loss*. These are not true profits/losses of the business because other factors such as depreciation and other allowances may need to be taken into account later, which can alter the situation but, nevertheless, the (gross) trading profit or loss figure gives a good indication of performance.

Interpreting profit and loss accounts is a key function for a business manager, ie having the ability to quickly assess how a business operation stands financially and the likelihood of its future success. Clearly, profitability is a measure of business success whereas a firm showing losses, whilst not totally doomed, is nevertheless unlikely to inspire confidence in its future prosperity.

Two particular points should be borne in mind about the profit and loss account. First, any increase or decrease in business expenditure items (such as local authority rates or rents on premises, fuel prices, or wages) will appear and have a direct affect on this account – not elsewhere. Second, debtors and creditors *cannot* be established from the profit and loss or trading account, nor can business asset values, bank overdrafts, the value of shareholder funds or other liabilities. These items will be deduced from the balance sheet.

E5. PROFITABILITY AND FINANCIAL RATIOS

Most businesses, certainly those in the road haulage sector, exist to provide profit for their owners (the proprietor, the partners or the shareholders, depending on the structure of the business). It is this type of business that we are concerned with here.

But it is important to mention that other types of business exist that do not have profit as their primary motive. They are established to provide public services or are charitable organizations intended to help worthy causes. In these cases the objective is to break even or achieve a 'surplus'. Break even means ensuring that income at least matches the amount of expenses incurred in running the operation; a surplus is an income at a level above the costs of operation.

Assessing profitability is a key role both for a business' owner and for others with an interest in its viability, such as the firm's bank and other lenders.

Ratios for assessing financial performance

In financial management, a number of basic and very simple calculations are used (as by an accountant or bank manager) to quickly assess business performance. The important ones are as follows.

Working capital ratio
This is otherwise known as liquidity ratio or acid test, and indicates how readily a business could settle its liabilities. It is calculated thus:

$$\frac{\text{liquid working capital (ie current assets)}}{\text{current liabilities}} = \frac{\text{liquidity/working}}{\text{capital ratio}}$$

Current ratio
This is basically the same as the working capital ratio as shown above and is a measure of a company's current assets in relationship to its current liabilities, and is calculated in the same way, namely:

$$\frac{\text{current assets}}{\text{current liabilities}} = \text{current ratio}$$

The result of this calculation should ideally be at least 2:1 so that the assets are double the liabilities, but in practice the results may vary from 1:1 (acceptable but not good) or less (which spells problems because basically the firm cannot meet its liabilities), to a much higher figure, particularly in seasonal trading conditions, which indicates a surfeit of funds and which should be placed on deposit to earn interest or used for other investment purposes.

Return on capital
This is a means of measuring whether sufficient profit is being made in relationship to the capital invested in the business, and is calculated thus:

$$\frac{\text{net profit}}{\text{capital employed}} \times 100 = x\%$$

Example:
$$\frac{£30,000}{£300,000} \times 100 = 10\%$$

Working capital

A business needs money to operate on a day-to-day basis, paying its suppliers, staff wages, office rent, heating, lighting, telephone bills and so on. The money used for this purpose is called working capital (ie the money that enables a business to function). This includes money in the bank, cash in hand and the value of debtors' invoices, which are a quickly realizable asset, less any moneys owing to creditors. In other words it is the excess of current assets over current liabilities.

Total capital employed

This is the total of all the money (ie assets) employed in a business. It includes the proprietors'/partners'/shareholders' initial investment, which may have been spent on fixed assets such as land and buildings, on plant, equipment and vehicles, on other assets such as office furniture and company cars. It also includes current assets such as cash in the bank and other (perhaps invested) reserves. It is against this yardstick of total fixed and current assets employed in the business that the owners or managers can assess trading or financial performance in the form of return on capital invested.

Cash flow

Today, control of cash flow is one of the most vital elements of business management. Many firms, especially large ones, have progressively to reduce the speed at which they pay their outstanding debts causing other (usually small) firms to suffer the severe problems arising from a lack of available funds to meet their immediate needs, such as payment for essential supplies and wages. These problems can quickly result in closure (ie liquidation) of a business (see page 52) despite the fact that it is giving its customers good service and may even be showing annual profits.

Planning finances, or budgeting, to ensure a regular cash flow is therefore important. It is done by assessing the levels of revenue to be invoiced and the frequency at which payment is likely to be received, then assessing expenditure which has to be made over the same period. If the latter is greater than the former, plans have to be made to cover the shortfall. These could include measures to ensure faster payment by debtors, to obtain longer periods of credit with suppliers or to obtain bank overdraft facilities to bridge the gap. Net cash flow, which the bank may ask about, is the difference between cash received in and cash paid out by the business on a day-to-day or week-to-week basis or over longer periods.

Cash-flow forecasting is necessary to ensure the availability of cash to meet future needs. Particularly, a bank manager being asked to provide overdraft facilities to meet short-term cash deficiencies may want to see a cash-flow forecast to indicate the levels of overdraft needed, when it is needed and over what period of time. The forecast would also show him what funds were expected in, and when, to balance the planned overdrawing on the account. Some banks provide blank forms specially designed for completion of cash-flow projections. The time and effort required to produce such a document is well worth while because it provides the business proprietor with a guide as to when and what revenues he has to come and when he can and should – and should not – incur expenditure. It would also indicate to him the months of the year when his cash flow looked deficient, giving him the opportunity to consider possible ways of rearranging work to overcome any financial shortcomings.

E6. BUDGETS

A budget is quite simply a plan for the future. Home owners budget for their expenditure, deciding what has to be spent on essential services (gas, water, electricity, rent and rates, etc) and supplies (eg food and clothing). So, too, must a business budget for its expenditure.

Mainly, budgets are of a financial nature but an operational plan needs to be made in order to establish what work is to be done to earn a certain level of revenue at a calculated cost (eg a haulier may have work for a vehicle that requires it to work for x days in the year covering x miles, consuming x litres of fuel and involving the driver in x hours of work at given rates of pay).

From this operating plan the haulier can budget for his likely earnings (a revenue budget) and the likely costs of running the vehicle plus his other related costs (an expenditure budget). If a project requires a new vehicle or other new plant this would involve making a capital or capital expenditure budget (ie how much capital expenditure – investment – the potential earnings from the project will stand). With the revenue and expenditure budgets calculated a cash-flow budget can also be established.

A cash-flow budget will show, on a month-by-month basis, *projected income* arising from invoices issued and haulage work scheduled to be done (or supplies made), and *projected expenditure* arising from regular outgoings (fuel, wages, rents, vehicle taxes, insurances, telephone charges, electricity and water bills, etc), and from irregular or ad hoc (ie one-off) purchases (vehicle parts, repairs, etc).

The difference each month between cash due in and payments due to be made will indicate whether these can be accomplished within existing cash resources or whether an overdraft will be needed, and if so for how much and for how many months.

Purchasing and stock control

Control over expenditure is important in any business organization, particularly in transport where it is possible for staff to purchase indiscriminately spare parts for vehicles and accumulate excessive stocks of incorrect and redundant components, and thus have excessive amounts of capital tied up which could be put to more immediate use meeting day-to-day commitments. Over-stocking reduces available cash resources and can create liquidity problems if the stocks cannot be sold off quickly enough (or at an acceptable market price) to meet urgent demands (eg to reduce an overdraft quickly). For this reason the establishment of proper systems of purchasing and stock control are necessary involving, particularly so far as transport operations are concerned, the following:

- Placing limits on the value or volume of parts that individuals may purchase.
- Establishing budgets for expenditure, which must not be exceeded without authority.
- Determining the best time to buy in relation to the firm's cash-flow position and market forces (ie when prices are likely to be lower or discounts higher).
- Establishing recording systems for purchases and issues.
- Keeping regular checks on stock levels to ensure that stock holdings agree with the records (ie reconciliation).
- Making stock analyses and examining requisition notes to ensure that correct stock levels of individual items are held according to demand (ie slow-moving and fast-moving items).
- Checking on suppliers' prices and discount structures to ensure that purchasing is channelled to the most economic supply sources and that maximum discounts are being obtained.
- Ensuring that obsolete and redundant stocks plus surplus items are returned for credit as soon as possible.
- Checking supply invoices to ensure that correct prices are being paid and that credits, as appropriate, are being obtained.

It is important to be able to assess current stock levels from records (such as in the case of bulk diesel fuel storage facility) and this is done as follows:

Opening stock or balance	+	Deliveries or purchases	−	Issues or sales	= Current stock

E7. COSTS AND DEPRECIATION

Having the ability to calculate vehicle operating costs and road haulage rates, plus understanding the intricacies of accounting paperwork and dealing with payments, are important attributes for running a haulage business.

Vehicle costing

It is necessary to determine in advance the cost of owning and running commercial vehicles in order to establish the prices to be charged for haulage work and to ascertain whether a particular job can be carried out so that the revenue it will earn provides a margin for profit.

In own-account transport operations where profit is not the motive, costing is still necessary to determine whether vehicles are being operated efficiently and within the scope of any pre-budgeted financial limits for transport.

Methods of costing

Vehicle costing comprises a number of separate elements as listed below. These various costs can be further identified as *direct* costs (ie those costs directly attributable to the running of the vehicle such as fuel, maintenance, licences, insurance and so on) and *indirect* costs (ie those costs which relate to the operation of the haulage business rather than specifically to vehicles such as office rent, heating and lighting costs, telephone charges, bank charges, etc). It is important to be able to differentiate between these two types of cost item.

Standing or fixed costs

These are incurred from the time of ownership of a vehicle irrespective of the amount of use to which it is put. They are usually calculated on an annual basis, including the following items:

Licences	Vehicle excise licence (VED) and 'O' licence.
Insurance	Compulsory third party plus additional cover.
Wages	Drivers' wages plus costs of employment (National Insurance, pension, etc).
Rents and rates	A proportion of the costs incurred in the provision of land for vehicle parking (alternatively this could be dealt with as an overhead cost item).
Interest on capital	Provision for a return on the capital invested in the vehicle on the basis that had the money been invested elsewhere it would have earned a return

	by way of interest – alternatively this would cover the interest payable if a vehicle was being bought on hire purchase.
Depreciation	Provision for a reserve of capital to be built up from the vehicle earnings to pay for its eventual replacement. Usually calculated on a straight-line or on a reducing balance basis as follows:

Depreciation

Depreciation by straight-line calculation method over a fixed period of time (calculation made only once when vehicle is first purchased):

$$\frac{\text{Vehicle original cost} - \text{tyres} - \text{residual value}}{\text{Anticipated life (years)}} = \text{£x depreciation per annum}$$

To calculate depreciation by the reducing balance method, the amount to be depreciated is reduced by the chosen percentage each year. Say a five-year life is expected, then the figure can be reduced by 20 per cent in the first year and then each year the carried forward balance is reduced by 20 per cent thereby resulting in a progressively lower depreciation figure for each year. In theory the high early years' depreciation should coincide with low maintenance costs in the vehicle's early life (when there is also warranty protection) and the lower figure with the higher maintenance and downtime costs later in the vehicle life.

Example of calculation:
Total amount to be depreciated, say, £40,000, over five years:

Year 1	£40,000 x 20% = £8,000 = £32,000
Year 2	£32,000 x 20% = £6,400 = £25,600
Year 3	£25,600 x 20% = £5,120 = £20,480
Year 4	£20,480 x 20% = £4,096 = £16,384
Year 5	£16,384 x 20% = £3,276 = £13,108

Thus after the end of the fifth year the 'written down' value is £13,108.

To depreciate by a current cost accounting method, the calculation would need to be made at least once each year during vehicle life, often more frequently. On each occasion the current (ie as at today) new price for the vehicle would be used instead of the original invoice amount in the straight-line method calculation made above.

Running or variable costs

These are all the direct costs incurred through operation of the vehicle. They are usually calculated on a pence per mile/km basis, including the following items:

Fuel	Fuel consumed at x pence per mile/km.
Tyres	The cost of tyre usage, calculated by dividing the tyre costs by their life in miles/km to give a cost in pence per mile/km.
Maintenance	The cost of maintaining the vehicle including regular servicing, safety inspections, oil changes, unscheduled repairs and breakdowns, and the annual test.

NB: It may be preferable or even necessary to calculate running costs on a pence/km basis because most heavy goods vehicles now operate tachographs that indicate distance in kilometres only. Similarly, fuel calculations would need to be made on a pence/litre basis since most pumps are now calibrated to record litres only. So overall, fuel consumption figures may be increasingly referred to on a km/litre basis.

Overheads or establishment costs

These are the indirect costs of operating the business (ie they do not apply directly to the vehicle itself but to the business as a whole) including management and administrative costs, workshop costs, heat and light expenses, telephone and postage charges, salaries, company cars and so on, usually calculated on an annual basis. Every single item of expenditure by the business must be included (with a receipt and recorded in the books of account) to produce an accurate reflection of the costs of running the *business* (not the lorries). If any items are missed this can result in distorted cost calculations and lead to incorrect quoting of haulage rates as well as producing inaccurate trading accounts.

Total operating costs

These are a combination of standing costs, running costs and overheads brought together by calculating each item into a common denominator of time or mileage (km) to give a price per week, per day, per hour or per mile/km. These costs will vary in accordance with the distances run by the vehicle. Less miles/kms means higher cost per mile/km because the fixed costs are spread over fewer miles/kms, while more miles/kms means a reduced overall cost per mile.

Marginal costs

These are the costs of running the vehicle after the fixed and overhead costs have been recovered. For example, once a vehicle route has been costed, if an extra delivery has to be included, its cost would only be the marginal cost of the extra costs incurred after the fixed costs have been recovered (ie fuel and tyre wear, etc, plus the driver's extra time).

Profit

With a profit margin added to the total operating cost, this is the amount that a haulier needs to obtain for the operation of vehicles on a profitable basis. A figure of 25 per cent is a useful gross margin to add.

Calculation of haulage rates

Many hauliers accept (or have no choice but to accept) rates quoted to them by their customers. While this may be difficult to avoid, it is important that the operator should work out the cost of the operation by determining how much time it will take, how many miles, etc, and add a profit margin to check whether this falls within the scope of the rates being offered.

Rates are calculated by assessing the cost of operating the type of vehicle needed to carry out the work and adding a margin for profit. The resulting figure can be converted into an appropriate unit price to suit a customer's requirements (ie a rate per day, per hour, per load, per ton, per pallet, per cubic foot, per litre, etc). Rate schedules can be calculated on a mileage/kilometres or tonnage basis with progressively increasing amounts in radial distances and on a tonnage basis, starting with 'up to one tonne', increasing to full load prices.

Financial considerations

Exchange rates

In international transport and the export of goods, the financial aspects of operation take on particular significance because of the increased direct costs and the vagaries of exchange rates between the currencies of one country and another.

The values of the currencies of various countries in relation to each other change frequently and often without prior warning. In some instances the effect is of considerable consequence, especially where foreign currencies rise in value in relation to the pound sterling, and can seriously affect the British haulier's pricing of contracts. He should beware quoting prices too far in advance because sudden currency fluctuations could have a significant effect on his prices.

A 'strong' pound sterling reduces the operator's costs (because he gets *more* value in foreign currencies in exchange for his one pound sterling) whereas a 'weak' pound will result in higher direct costs of operation outside Britain, especially for such items as fuel and driver expenses (because he gets *less* value in foreign currencies in exchange for his one pound sterling). In order to understand the effects of exchange rates, it is useful to make a series of comparisons of the rates as published in the financial press.

European Currency Units (euros)

With the implementation of financial measures in connection with the Single European Market, a new universal currency, the euro (European Currency Unit), has been introduced. This will be useful in inter-EU trade because of the way it will help smooth out wide variations in individual national currencies. Haulage rates can be quoted in euros and the current daily value of these units is quoted in the financial press.

Costs involved in international haulage

The international haulier is confronted with many additional costs compared to his domestic counterpart. These include the following:

- The need for vehicles that meet the TIR specification or Community Transit requirements.
- The costs of employing staff experienced in international operations.
- The cost of preparing documents such as carnets and consignment notes.
- Additional insurance costs for vehicles.
- The cost of obtaining permits.
- Other fiscal charges.
- Cross-Channel ferry fares.
- Taxes, tolls and dues in foreign countries.
- The extra costs of communication.
- Driver expenses for food, accommodation, general expenses and cash for on-the-spot fines and 'gratuities'.
- The higher costs incurred in the event of vehicle breakdown.
- Insurance costs for CMR liability, green card, drivers' medical/accident cover and bail bonds.
- Drivers' extra costs for passport, international driving licence (where necessary) and visas.

Payment and collection of revenue

In transport operations it is usual for drivers to carry consignment and receipt notes, which give instructions regarding collection and delivery of the goods and other relevant information. The receipt copy enables the consignee to acknowledge with his signature the safe receipt of the goods. From these documents the job can be priced according to the nature of the goods carried, the vehicle used, the weight or volume of goods, the distance covered, the waiting time, etc.

When the price has been calculated, an invoice can be sent to the customer identifying the job, enclosing a copy of the receipt note if appropriate to prove delivery – POD – (or this can be retained for the carrier's future reference) and stating the price plus VAT as appropriate. Following the invoice a statement of the account can be sent, on which the customer will base his payment of the account. Some firms pay on receipt of the invoice, others do not pay until a statement is received.

It is becoming more common these days for firms, especially large firms, government departments and other authorities, to pay their suppliers by means of credit transfer whereby amounts owing are paid straight to the payee's bank account (direct from the payer's bank account) without the need for preparing, signing and posting individual cheques. This has the added advantage of speeding clearance of the amount into the payee's bank account by avoiding x number of days in the post and sitting on somebody's desk awaiting a trip to the bank.

E8. ORGANIZATION

What is an organization?

An organization comprises a number of people employed to fulfil various roles within a hierarchy of rules and procedures that determines the division of labour, all with the common purpose of achieving a set goal – in commercial organizations, a profit or a return on the capital invested.

Organization charts

An organization chart specifies the individual roles within an organization and their relative status to each other (a hierarchy of authority), and the lines of communication between them.

Organizations tend to have what is termed a 'stratified' or layered system with the 'boss' sitting on top of the pile. In fact, many forms of organization chart may be employed within firms, mainly depending upon the actual structure of the organization itself (ie the relative status of managers and their lines of reporting). However, taking a fairly typical medium-sized road haulage operation as an example, the two alternative structures shown in Figure 5.1 may emerge.

Planning and measuring work

Work plans set out the various individual tasks that have to be completed. Invariably such plans will specify the logical sequence for each task in relation to the others (a flow chart) and the timescale within which each task must be completed in order to achieve the final timescale (or meet the deadline) for the work as a whole. Such plans may be quite simple, particularly where only a few individual tasks need to be undertaken to complete the project. But they may be complex, where many individual tasks,

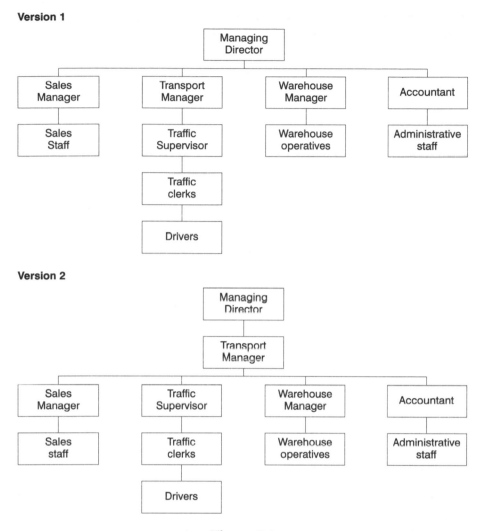

Figure 5.1

possibly overlapping each other, need to be undertaken, and complicated even further by the need to plan for the supply of relevant materials or components to each task within a timescale, ensuring that the work is not held up (ie just-in-time – JIT), and ensuring the removal of waste or empty containers that would otherwise impede progress on the work.

Measuring work is a system devised to determine the time it takes a worker to fulfil a particular, specified, work task. This may be a simple task measured as a whole, or a complex task that is broken down into a number of sub-tasks each of which is individually measured.

In transport operations, measurement generally relates to journeys comprising loading, delivery and running/travel time. Typically, a delivery journey may be broken down into the following sub-sections:

- driver/vehicle preparation time;
- loading (x units/pallets/stillages/roll-cages);
- securing load;
- travel time to destination;
- driver break;
- finding signatory/contact at delivery point;
- preparing for unloading (undoing securing devices, lowering tailboard, etc);
- unloading x units;
- obtaining signature for receipt of goods;
- re-securing and closing vehicle;
- travel time returning to base;
- driver signing-off time.

E9. MARKETING

What is marketing?

Road hauliers are dependent on marketing skills to win business from their road freight competitors and from other transport modes. Marketing is a function that has been defined in as many ways as it is possible to string words together. However, for the purposes of this text and certainly from the haulier's point of view it is the task of promoting his company and its services to customers (existing and potential) in such a way that the customer wants to use the services offered because the rates are set at the levels he is prepared to pay (the right price), because the service level offered is what he wants for the delivery of his goods (the right service), because he is convinced of the reliability and integrity of the haulier (the right place, right time and right quality of service), because the vehicles are right for his work, because the haulier's drivers are professional in their approach, and for many other reasons. It can be summed up as the function of identifying, anticipating and satisfying customer requirements – with profit for his business.

The point about marketing for the haulier is that he has to set out to convince customers that this is the level of service he provides – and more efficiently, more effectively and more economically than his competitors – and yet can still make a profit. This is essential because without the profit motive all the marketing skills would be to no avail. It is an unfortunate quirk, of course, that some customers appear only to be interested in obtaining the lowest price and that there is always a haulier who is prepared to work at the lowest (clearly uneconomical) rates.

The separate functions of marketing

Marketing is a complex and all-encompassing function (having an effect on all aspects of a business) but it can be separated into a number of individual functions, each one interrelated to the others, as follows:

- market research;
- marketing planning;
- sales (including sales promotion);
- advertising;
- public relations (to include customer relations).

It is useful to consider each of these briefly in turn.

Market research

Market research basically means finding potential customers and finding out what they want. The simplest form of market research is for the haulier to look in a local telephone directory and identify those firms that he thinks may be interested in the services he offers. He could then telephone them and ask what services, if any, they require. At the other end of the scale he could employ (if he could afford such a luxury) a market research consultancy that would, with its teams of researchers, conduct surveys of lists of pre-identified potential customers to find out precisely their transport services needs. In between these two extremes the haulier could obtain lists of firms to whom he could make approaches about the use of his services. The essence of market research is the task of finding out who may be interested in his services, what particular aspects of transport services they require, what special equipment they may need and what levels of price they may be prepared to pay.

Sources of market data

Market data can be obtained from many sources but the most obvious are telephone and trade directories, commercial gazetteers, chamber of commerce directories, trade journals, local newspapers and such like. Having identified potential contacts from these sources the next step is to start the data collection process. This involves person-to-person in-depth interviews, telephone interviewing or the use of postal questionnaires to find out what services are required, what aspects of service are important (or orders of priority), what factors influence decisions, and who makes the final decision. Importantly, too, information is needed on the aspects of service that are not required, not relevant or not important or which would mitigate against a decision.

Marketing planning

Marketing planning is planning to satisfy the requirements (or demands) of potential and existing customers. Having identified from market research what potential customers may want in the way of services, the haulier could plan, firstly, to see whether and how he could offer such services and, secondly, plan his positive methods of approach to those firms by way of advertising, direct selling and sales promotion, and indirectly via public relations. He would do this in the same way that a manufacturer of, say, consumer goods would determine what products to make and sell and how to package and present them and what price levels to set for them, bearing in mind his costs and what the market will bear (and in relation to what prices his competitors sell at) and the profit he wants or needs (to satisfy shareholders) to make.

Selling

Selling is the job of actually winning orders. Having identified potential customers and determined that the type, quality and price of service they require can be offered, the haulier has got to go out and 'sell' to them. Particularly, without criticizing them, he must show that he can improve upon the type, quality and price of service currently being offered to the firm by one of his competitors. In other words, the haulier must convince them that what he offers is what they want at the best price with the utmost reliability and so on, and get them to agree to use his services. To use salesmanship jargon, this is 'to close the sale'.

Selling techniques are specialized and involve many methods. A common approach is by direct mail, whereby personally addressed letters are sent direct to the relevant person. These letters would set out what the haulier has to offer, an explanation as to why he is better than the competition, and invite the potential client to try the service or at least to agree to a meeting to discuss their precise needs in more detail. Alternatively, the method adopted may be 'cold calling' (or cold canvassing) whereby a salesman calls at a potential customer's premises without prior appointment or introduction and chances getting in to see the relevant person to discuss his business. With a good salesman it can work, but otherwise it is a difficult task with a high risk of failure because of the turnaway rate – by executives who see nobody without an appointment.

Sales promotion

Sales promotion is an extension of the selling effort. It is the business of adding something to the selling message to sway the customer towards deciding to buy your services or your products. It includes the provision of brochures and supporting literature, the staging of exhibitions and other promotional campaigns, the distribution of logo-emblazoned stickers, balloons, hats and T-shirts, among other things. We are all familiar with sales promotion methods. In the supermarket they give you free plastic bags (with their name shouting to everybody where you did your shopping). Some firms merely give their customers calendars for the New Year, others give desk diaries, key rings, pens, ties and such like. In the big league, sales promotion may involve bigger and more prestigious gifts or free travel (eg weekend golf matches, trips to sports events – a day at a Grand Prix – or visits to factories abroad). All of this would come under the heading of sales promotion – the business of trying to win yet more orders by direct influence.

Advertising

Advertising is the business of trying to attract customers through the media (ie trade papers, journals, newspapers, even radio or television). Generally an advertisement does two things. First, it tells interested firms who you are, what services you offer and where you can be contacted – the basic ingredients of most normal adverts (seeing some magazine and TV adverts you may wonder what is on offer and by whom!). Second, the advert may be in the form of an invitation to potential customers to try your services. The added ingredient here is an attraction (a bonus offer such as 'two for the price of one') or an invitation for the reader to telephone or complete a tear-off strip or send in a reply-paid card requesting further details, or to have a salesperson call on him.

The latter is known as direct response advertising – that is, the success of the advert can be measured and its cost-effectiveness assessed by the number of replies in relationship to the circulation. Very often this may only be in the region of 1 or 2 per cent of a newspaper or magazine readership, perhaps 4/5 per cent for a really successful campaign. The secret of advertising lies in the ability to design a printed (or verbal or filmed in the case of radio and TV) message that catches the eye of the potential customer and holds his attention for sufficiently long for your name and the services you offer to register with him and, if appropriate, to note the telephone number, or fill in and send off the reply slip.

Public relations

To many people this is a complete mystery. It is simply ensuring that everybody who comes into contact with your firm (customers, the public, the authorities such as police, enforcement staffs, local authority, neighbours, employees, trade and professional people with whom it has dealings, etc) gains a good impression of it. The concept is for you to make them think that the firm is good, professional and reliable among other qualities and not just in its services to customers but in every other way. For example, with hauliers, being seen as being concerned for the environment and not creating pollution by noise or fumes or obstruction by scruffy lorries parked where they should not be, is good PR.

Media relations

Media relations is an adjunct to public relations in that while being part and parcel of the overall function of PR, it tends, these days, to form a specialization in its own right. University degree courses are devoted to it and many consultancy firms brand themselves as being purely media specialists. There is no doubt that 'dealing with the media' requires particular knowledge and skills to best exploit the massive publicity opportunities that exist in newspapers and magazines and on radio and television, and to avoid the adverse publicity that can arise from mis-handled news stories, product launches and such like.

Market segments in road haulage

In considering the road haulage industry at large, we are, of course, considering a very broad spectrum of road freighting activities, which differ widely in their specializations and operating methods and consequently in the equipment they use and the particular skills of the people they employ. They necessarily differ considerably, too, in their marketing approach and methods. In examining a list of such market sectors it has to be recognized that there is extensive overlap of specializations in many firms.

At one end of the scale is the firm (usually running small vans) that promotes the idea that it carries anything for anybody to anywhere at any time. This cannot be strictly true, of course, because limitations of weight capacity or vehicle suitability would ensure that it cannot carry 'anything', but the marketing message sounds good and it wins customers. At the other end of the scale, for example, is the specialist bulk road tanker operator who carries only dangerous substances. There is no point in him marketing his services to all and sundry, or of advertising in the mass media or on radio or television, because his existing and potential customers, taken all together, may only form quite a small group of chemical manufacturers and suppliers. His marketing efforts would be more effectively directed to public relations, convincing the public that when they see his vehicles they can rest assured they are completely safe, being driven responsibly and operating within the law.

There is a long list of other specialist sectors as follows:

- express parcels carriage (same-day, next-day services);
- bulk carriage in road tankers (chemicals/foodstuffs, etc);
- carriage of abnormal loads;
- furniture removals (domestic and industrial and new furniture);
- machinery carriage (including computers);
- livestock carriage;
- timber haulage;
- steel haulage (including rolled steel, billets and ingots);

- boat haulage;
- contract hire;
- distribution and storage;
- refrigerated transport (temperature-controlled);
- international haulage (specialized or general);
- groupage operations (plus export packing, labelling and shipment, etc);
- bulk tipping (minerals, fuels, aggregates, cement, grain, animal feeds);
- ready-mixed cement (ie truck-mixers);
- container haulage;
- vehicle/trailer hire/spot rental;
- distribution of motor vehicles (car transporters);
- motor parts.

Within these specializations there are to be found many sub-specializations. There are hauliers who provide only local or only long-distance services, those who cover only certain geographical regions within Great Britain, those who follow only particular routes (eg Glasgow–London–Glasgow), and those who serve only particular countries (eg UK–Republic of Ireland, UK–Spain).

It has to be recognized also that quite a number of haulage firms serve only a single customer either under a specific long-term contract or merely by long-established tradition. With these it becomes questionable as to how much marketing effort is necessary – perhaps very little market research and actual selling (although some sales promotion effort could be worthwhile); but a good public relations image remains essential and should be worked on.

E10. INSURANCE

Businesses are dependent on many specialized and professional services: insurance, for example, which is overlooked in many firms but is particularly important to protect the risks that occur in business activities. Insurance can cover buildings and property, vehicles and equipment, personal sickness and accident, and life. There is also ancillary cover such as insurance against loss of money, goods in transit and other special risks such as public liability, employers' liability and so on. The cover provided in return for premiums paid (so the insurance company shoulders the risk) reduces the risk of ruination of a business in the event of a serious fire, for example, or the death of a partner or major shareholder, or a substantial claim for damages resulting from the negligence of an employee (eg a driver causing death in an accident for which he was to blame).

It is important for the insured (the person or firm who has taken out the insurance) to be aware of any policy exclusions in any of the following policies that may prevent him from obtaining compensation when it may have been expected. In particular, on vehicle insurance the insured should note any actions that can invalidate the cover, such as operating the vehicle outside the requirements of the law (ie in a defective state or with unlicensed drivers). The main types of insurance, both compulsory and voluntary, are described in the following text.

Excess clauses

In many areas of insurance, and especially vehicle insurance, the insurers require the insured to bear the first portion of any claim. This may be the first £25, £100, £250 or more, depending on the particular circumstances. This amount is referred to as the 'excess' (ie the excess on the policy). Thus if a vehicle is damaged in an accident and requires £500 worth of repairs and the insured has a £100 excess on his policy, the insurance company will reimburse him only £400, leaving him to find the other £100 himself or reclaim this from whoever was responsible for the damage.

Fire (non-compulsory)

Insurance against fire provides cover in the event of loss of buildings, equipment, vehicles and other possessions. The fire brigade would generally need to be called to effect a claim for fire damage. If neighbouring premises catch fire and damage the insured's property, he must claim on his own insurance. His insurance company will in turn seek reimbursement from the neighbour's insurers.

Storm and flood (non-compulsory)

This is cover to provide compensation in the event of damage or loss sustained as a result of severe weather and flooding.

Theft (non-compulsory)

This type of insurance policy provides cover against loss of possessions by theft, but often to substantiate such a claim there needs to be evidence of forcible entry. Policy conditions vary but insurers may not accept claims unless there is sound evidence of a criminal act and the matter has been reported to the police.

Fidelity guarantee (non-compulsory)

When employees are put in responsible positions, particularly if they may be required to handle money or valuables, a firm can take out a fidelity guarantee insurance policy. The insurers investigate the employee's background and if acceptable they will then provide cover (by bond or guarantee) against the risk of the employee disappearing with money or valuables belonging to the employer.

Consequential loss (non-compulsory)

It is important to have insurance cover for any consequential loss resulting from an accident or fire. For example, if a warehouse was burnt down the buildings and stock may be covered, but not the resultant loss of trade and business profits. Consequential loss insurance would cover this. The same applies where a haulage vehicle was off the road for an extended period for repair following an accident: the repairs may be covered under the vehicle policy but not the resulting loss of business.

Employers' liability (compulsory)

Employers have a statutory duty to take out insurance cover (minimum cover £5 million) against the risk of injury to their employees while on the firm's premises or elsewhere (eg on the road in a company-owned vehicle – hence the reason why compulsory passenger cover on motor vehicle policies does not extend to employee passengers – see p 156). Usually such policies provide unlimited cover for any eventuality. A current certificate of insurance against employers' liability risks must be displayed on the employer's premises.

Public liability (non-compulsory)

In addition to cover against the risk of injury to employees, a firm should protect itself against claims for loss or injury from the general public. Public liability policies provide such cover. If a member of the public is injured or suffers loss while on a firm's premises or as a result of the action or negligence of its employees (eg a van driver letting a rear door swing open and hit and injure a passing pedestrian, or a heating-oil delivery driver leaving a pipe across a pavement so that an elderly person trips over it and is injured), that person has a right of claim for compensation. Such claims can be substantial these days so it is important to have adequate cover against such risks.

Life/sickness and accident/pension (non-compulsory)

The proprietor of a business is wise to take out personal insurance to cover the event of his premature death or against extended periods of incapacity due to sickness or accident. This protects (to an extent) his dependants and his business in the event of such a calamity by providing a cash sum (in the case of his death) or an income over a period (in the case of his incapacity), which may be sufficient to keep the business going until it can be sold or until he is fit to work again. Similarly he would be wise to provide for his eventual retirement by paying into a personal pension fund which can be provided via an insurance policy.

Motor vehicles (compulsory)

Basic motor vehicle insurance covers the insured against claims by injured parties for personal injury (ie death or bodily injury) and medical expenses. This, together with mandatory cover for passengers – except those in the employ of the vehicle owner/operator – and for damage to roadside property, is the minimum legal requirement (referred to as Road Traffic Act cover). Beyond this a policy may cover other third-party risks including damage to other property, loss of the vehicle by fire or theft, or it may be extended to become fully comprehensive cover to provide full protection against third-party claims and to provide compensation for damage to the vehicle.

Motor vehicles using the public highway must be covered against third-party claims – except those belonging to local authorities; belonging to, used or directed by the police or the armed forces, and certain vehicles of the NHS. The cover may be provided by means of a security of £500,000 deposited with the Accountant General of the Supreme Court (subject to the approval of the Secretary of State for Transport) or by means of an insurance policy taken out with an authorized insurer (a member of the Motor Insurers' Bureau – MIB) – Road Traffic Act (of 1988) cover. The insurance policy must:

> insure such person(s) or classes of person as may be specified in the policy in respect of any liability which may be incurred by him or them, in respect of the death or bodily injury to any person caused by, or arising out of, the use of the vehicle on a road; and must also insure him or them in respect of any liability which may be incurred by him or them relating to payment for emergency treatment.

The insured person or organization must have in their possession a current and valid certificate of insurance (the policy is not acceptable proof of cover) showing the cover provided and it must give particulars of any conditions subject to which the policy is issued; it should indicate:

- The vehicles covered by registration number or by specification.
- The persons authorized to drive the vehicle.
- The dates between which the cover is effective.
- The permitted use of the vehicle.

Claims to MIB

Third parties injured in motor vehicle accidents who find subsequently that the vehicle driver/owner was not insured, can seek compensation from the Motor Insurers' Bureau, for which purpose it was established.

Passenger liability (compulsory)

Passenger liability insurance cover for motor vehicles is compulsory. This requirement includes all vehicles which are required by the Road Traffic Act to have third-party insurance and the cover will extend to authorized passengers, other non-fare paying passengers and also to what may be termed 'unauthorized passengers' such as hitch-hikers and other people who are given lifts. It does not cover employees of the vehicle owner/operator (these are covered under the employers' liability policy).

The display in a vehicle of a sign which says 'No passengers' or 'No liability' does not fully indemnify the owner or driver against claims by unauthorized passengers for injury or damage as a result of negligence even if they agree to travel at their own risk, but the law ensures that such liabilities are covered within the vehicle policy.

Additional voluntary insurance

Any insurance cover over the minimum mentioned above is at the vehicle owner's discretion, but in many instances it is advisable for the protection it gives in the event of loss of the vehicle or severe damage to it.

Production of insurance certificate

The owner of a vehicle must produce a certificate of insurance if requested to do so by a police officer or following a road traffic accident. The certificate or a temporary cover note may be produced at any police station nominated by the vehicle owner or driver within seven days (five days in Northern Ireland) from the date of the police officer's request.

Application for an excise licence for a vehicle must be accompanied by a current certificate of insurance or an applicable temporary cover note.

The owner of a vehicle must give the police any information needed to determine whether a vehicle was being driven without third-party insurance in force.

Invalidation of cover

Insurance cover on a vehicle can be invalidated for a number of reasons including the non-payment of premiums, employment of unlicensed or incorrectly licensed drivers, using a vehicle without an excise licence or 'O' licence, the use of a vehicle in an unroadworthy condition, failing to report an accident to the insurers or admitting liability at the scene of an accident, or otherwise being in breach of policy conditions (eg operating the vehicle outside the terms of the stated cover).

Cancellation of insurance

When an insurance policy is cancelled the certificate(s) of insurance relating to that policy must be surrendered to the insurer within seven days of the cancellation date.

Goods in Transit (GIT) insurance cover

Vehicle insurance covers risks of loss or damage to the vehicle itself, but not the load it is carrying. This is covered by a GIT policy which provides protection against loss or damage to the load based on a standard valuation of at least £1300 per ton (ie in accordance with the RHA standard conditions of carriage). If the loads carried are of greater value per ton, the cover should be extended as necessary. Usually insurers need to be advised if exceptionally valuable or vulnerable loads are carried (spirits, cigarettes, etc). Failure to do so can result in invalidation of the cover or refusal by the insurers to pay out on claims. In any event the firm could lose heavily if it is not adequately covered.

GIT policies usually specify restrictive clauses that require vehicle owners to observe particular conditions as follows: vehicles must be fitted with anti-theft devices that must be put into operation when they are left – 'immobilizer clause'; and loaded vehicles must be left in a closed building or yard which is locked or guarded – 'night risk clause'.

CMR cover for international haulage journeys

The GIT cover described above is not sufficient or even legally acceptable where vehicles are engaged on international haulage work. In most cases, the provisions of the Convention on the Contract for the International

Carriage of Goods by Road commonly known and referred to as the CMR convention govern such operations. This Convention automatically applies where an international haulage journey takes place between different countries at least one of which is party to the Convention (with the exception of UK-Eire and UK mainland – Channel Islands journeys which are ruled not to be international journeys for this purpose).

Road hauliers who carry goods on any part of an international journey, whether they know it or whether they choose to or not, fall within the legal confines of the CMR Convention under which compensation levels for loss or damage to goods are much higher than the standard Conditions of Carriage GIT cover applicable in national transport operations. CMR levels of cover vary according to a set standard, which is published daily in the financial press. For this reason it is important to obtain adequate cover when involved in international transport.

Additionally, where hauliers undertake cabotage operations they should discuss the levels of cover required with their insurers – indeed they should see if extended cover is available to cover certain liabilities such as losses from unattended vehicles. Difficulties may arise where local conditions of carriage are imposed, and claims and legal wrangling arise under law other than English law – under French law, for example, minimum liability is set at a value equivalent to approximately £12,000 per tonne and as this is a domestic requirement it may not be covered by a UK haulier's CMR policy.

Insurance and carriers' liability

Adequate insurance is necessary against civil liability claims in respect of the use of motor vehicles on international journeys. Details of the requirements are specified in EU Directive 166/72 'Council Directive on the approximation of the laws of the member states relating to insurance against civil liability in respect of the use of motor vehicles, and to the enforcement of the obligation to ensure against such liability' as follows.

Definitions
- *Vehicle:* Any mechanically propelled motor vehicle intended for travel on land and any trailer, whether coupled or not.
- *Injured party:* Any person entitled to compensation in respect of any loss or injury caused by vehicles.
- *National Insurers' Bureau:* A professional organization which groups together insurance undertakings authorized by member states to conduct the business of motor vehicle insurance against civil liability. Such bodies are constituted in accordance with a recommendation of the

Road Transport Sub-Committee of the Inland Transport Committee of the United Nations Economic Commission for Europe.

- *Territory in which the vehicle is based:* The state in which the vehicle is registered.
- *Green card:* An international certificate of insurance issued on behalf of a national insurers' bureau (see above).

Other provisions of the Directive

It provides that member states need not see evidence of insurance in respect of vehicles based in other member states. Similarly, it provides for a relaxation of checks on the evidence of insurance for vehicles based in third countries when entering member states from another member state.

It specifies that member states must take all appropriate steps to ensure that civil liability (in the UK commonly known as third-party liability or Road Traffic Act cover) in respect of vehicles based in their territory is covered by insurance.

Member states must make sure that the insurance also provides cover for loss or injury caused in other member states according to the law in force in those states, and loss or injury suffered by nationals of member states during a direct journey between two territories in which the treaty establishing the EU is in force, if there is no national insurers' bureau responsible for the territory that is being crossed. In this case the loss or injury must be covered in accordance with the internal laws on compulsory insurance in force in the member state where the vehicle is normally based.

It allows for derogation (exemption) from the previous Article in certain respects. A list of exempted people must be drawn up by the member state and communicated to other member states and to the EU Commission.

Member states must ensure that compensation is paid in respect of loss or injury caused in the territory of other member states by vehicles belonging to the exempt persons.

Further, derogation also applies to certain vehicles having a special plate, but member states may still request sight of valid green cards for vehicles entering their territory or they can request that suitable insurance cover is obtained at the point of entry to the territory.

It also deals with action in the event of accidents. Member states are required to ensure that where an accident is caused in its territory by a vehicle normally based in another member state, the national insurers' bureau must be given details of the vehicle registration mark and the territory in which the vehicle is normally based, and details of the insurance of the vehicle from the green card or as they would appear on the green card. This information must be given to the national insurers' bureau of the state in whose territory the vehicle is normally based.

The Directive requires EU member states to ensure that vehicles normally based in third countries (ie non-EU members) or in the non-European territory of any member state are not used in their territory unless any loss or injury caused by those vehicles is covered in accordance with the various laws on compulsory insurance against civil liability in respect of the use of vehicles.

It further requires that vehicles from third countries must have a green card or a certificate of frontier insurance before entering EU member states unless the national bureaux of all member states guarantee, in accordance with their own national laws, settlement of claims in respect of accidents caused by such vehicles.

Green cards

An international motor insurance card (green card) issued by an insurance bureau (in the UK the MIB via insurance companies) provides evidence of insurance against compulsory insurable liabilities in those countries in which the card is valid.

While green cards are no longer essential for travel within the EU and in certain other countries, drivers should continue to carry a green card (or at least their British insurance certificate) because, although they will not be subjected to routine checks, they may need to produce it in the event of an accident or other incident.

European Accident Statement

It is usual for insurers to provide a copy of the European Accident Statement to operators who send their vehicles abroad. This document is a universally recognized form of words and layout for making a report (ie statement) of a motor vehicle accident. The document contains advice to drivers (eg 'don't get angry; be polite; keep calm') and instructions on completion of the form. It also instructs drivers to forward the form *without delay* to their own insurer (ie the vehicle insurer). It should *not* be sent to any other official body.

E11. ELECTRONIC DATA AND DATA PROTECTION

EDI – Electronic Data Interchange

Widespread computerization in the road freight, shipping and export/import industries and by HM Customs and Excise has led to the introduction of modern systems for passing shipping and export/import data via direct or indirect computer links, without the need for paper documents to pass or confirm information. This whole concept is known as Information Technology (IT) or EDI – Electronic Data Interchange, sometimes also called 'paperless systems of trading' and its use results in automatic handling and actioning of data. To ensure uniformity in this method of trading the United Nations has set a standard for EDI known as EDIFACT (Electronic Data Interchange for Administration, Commerce and Transport) under which there are standard procedures and messages for passing such matter as shipping instructions.

More recently, the development of e-commerce (transactions via computer) has become a major talking point following on from the e-mail revolution, particularly in respect of the home shopping (also termed on-line or Internet shopping) explosion. This latest trend for e-business has come about as a result of the combination of the latest technology in both telematics and computing power and is likely to lead to a whole new logistics concept where shoppers order via the Internet and expect their goods to be delivered direct to their home at a time to suit them – in effect replacing the usual shopping trip and the weekly visit to the supermarket.

Satellite-based communications systems

Technological developments in satellite-based communication systems provide facilities for long-range telephone, fax and paging links between base and vehicle, as well as positive vehicle tracking systems. Such systems are now widely used in North America and are of increasing interest to UK and European transport fleet operators. (In fact, the European Transport Council announced in 2002 the launch of the development phase of the European 'Galileo' global navigation satellite system – GNSS.) Using the same basic technology that puts instantaneous live pictures from sporting events and news reports on our television screens, the precise location of vehicles can be pinpointed and messages passed, but on a one-way basis only from base to vehicle, not vice versa, so drivers cannot abuse the system by calling friends and relatives worldwide.

The Global Positioning System

The Global Positioning System (GPS), originally devised by the US military to assist navigation of both ground and air crew, incorporates over 24 satellites orbiting the Earth in outer space. As the system developed, it has been utilized for civilian purposes, in particular the marine, leisure and commercial markets.

The nature of the satellite signal enables the GPS receiver, ranging in size from a standard mobile phone to a small television set, to track it accurately and efficiently. At least three satellites are in view of the receiver at any one time, and this decodes the information to display global position in longitude and latitude, and a number of different co-ordinate formats. Because it does not rely on radio signals GPS can be used anywhere in the world.

A relatively new use for GPS is for 'in-vehicle systems' which now are capable of incorporating CD, radio, and GPS in a single unit. For navigation purposes, it is just a case of entering a destination (eg the name of a road) and within seconds the distance, route and travel time is calculated and displayed. A voice gives commands for turning at the correct junctions and a map on the screen is a useful navigation aid.

The Blaupunkt system, for example, gives accurate information for navigation in the UK, but the system also incorporates CD ROMs that can be downloaded in seconds to allow navigation on almost any road in Europe.

Computerization in transport

The current trend is towards the development of on-board systems to allow vehicle drivers to remain in constant communication via computer with their base for transmitting data and instructions. Precise vehicle location (ie to within a few metres irrespective of where the vehicle is) can be determined via the GPS (global positioning satellite – see above) and other tracking systems – particularly useful for tracking high-value cargo vehicles and stolen vehicles.

Additionally a full range of data recording, information and analysis operations, including accounting, staff records, vehicle maintenance records and such like, can be carried out accessible by all relevant staff and management both in the office and away from base on laptop or hand-held computers, via an Internet connection, which they carry around with them.

The use of e-mail and Internet connection to the World Wide Web (WWW) has led to enormous improvements in business efficiency and information, providing rapid person-to-person communication and access to unlimited data on just about every subject under the sun.

Intelligent transport systems

Intelligent transport systems (ITS) using telematics (the combination of information technology and telecommunications) provide online (electronic) information and control systems for all modes of transport, including vehicle-based systems. Typical of such systems used in road transport are those which operate:

- variable message signs (VMS), for example on motorways;
- on-board route and traffic information, such as Trafficmaster;

- traffic control and enforcement signs, like the new-type digital speed cameras;
- electronic road charging;
- traffic monitoring;
- vehicle-to-base communications;
- electronic ticketing.

The Data Protection Act 1998

This Act is designed to protect living and identifiable persons from the misuse or unauthorized disclosure of any information, including expression of any personal opinion, about them. Thus firms or individuals such as self-employed road hauliers who hold personal data on file (especially in electronic – ie computerized – format) about employees, job applicants and customers, fall within scope of the Act. Exemptions apply when information is held:

- by persons for their own family or domestic purposes;
- for historical or statistical research;
- in certain instances relating to journalism, art and literature;
- for the purposes of national security.

In road haulage, if customer names and addresses held on file include an individual person (eg of the managing director or transport manager) then such data falls within the scope of the Act.

The Act defines data as information:

- being processed by means of automatic equipment;
- recorded to be processed by such equipment;
- recorded as part of a filing system, or with that intention; or
- relating to certain health and associated records.

Processing of personal data means obtaining, recording or holding information or data or carrying out any operation on it, including its:

- organization, adaptation or alteration;
- retrieval, consultation or use;
- disclosure by transmission, dissemination or otherwise making it available;
- alignment, combination, blocking, erasure or destruction.

Special rules apply to the processing of 'sensitive' data such as an individual's racial origin.

Any firm or individual holding personal data must register with the Data Protection Commissioner and conform to the data protection principles set out in the Act.

It is a criminal offence (punishable by a fine of up to £5,000) for an unregistered person to hold or disclose personal data about any person, and no processing of data should take place until after registration under the Act and an entry has been made in the Data Protection Register.

It is the responsibility of data controllers (those who process and who determine the use of personal data) to operate within the terms of their Register entries and they can be held liable to pay compensation for any damage or associated distress suffered as a result of holding or disclosing inaccurate personal data.

On registration a data controller must notify the Data Protection Commissioner of:

- the name and address of their principal place of business – in the case of limited companies the address of the registered office;
- the name and address of any nominated representative for the purposes of the Act where this differs from that of the company's registered office;
- a description of the personal data being or to be processed and the category or categories of data subject to which they relate;
- a description of the purpose or purposes for which the data is being or is to be processed;
- a description of recipients to whom data will be disclosed;
- the names of countries outside the European Economic Area (EEA) to which the data controller will directly or indirectly transfer the data.

It is illegal for a registered data user to:

- hold personal data of any description other than that specified in their entry in the Data Protection Register;
- hold any such data, or use any such data which they hold, for any purpose other than those described in their entry;
- obtain data, or information to be contained in such data, from any source which is not described in the Register entry;
- disclose the data which they hold to any person who is not described in the Register entry; or
- directly or indirectly transfer data they hold to any country or territory outside the EEA which does not have similar data protection laws.

The Act sets out eight 'data protection principles' under which registered data users must ensure that data is:

1. processed fairly and lawfully;
2. used only for specified and lawful purposes;
3. adequate, relevant and not excessive;
4. accurate and up-to-date;

Order

An order is a notification from a customer instructing the supplier to supply goods or services as specified. Full details of the customer's requirements should be specified on an order including the date or period of supply, the quantity of goods, the quality, method of supply, labelling and packing instructions and other special instructions ('loads must be sheeted', 'delivery only accepted between 8 am and 4 pm', 'notification required before delivery', etc).

Invoice

This is a notification from the supplier to his customer of the job done and/or the amount owing for the work. It should identify the job clearly and have supporting evidence of supply or delivery. It should show the date of supply, the quantity of goods, the price per unit (eg per tonne) and the total price less any discount offered and plus any VAT due. It is in effect a demand for payment of moneys due for goods or services supplied, or to be supplied where the agreement or practice is for payment in advance. Usually terms for payment are shown, for example, 'terms 30 days net'. A note of discounts offered for prompt payment can be added, such as '2.5 per cent discount for payment in 14 days'. Often invoices carry the letters 'E & OE'. This means errors and omissions excepted; in other words it gives the issuer the opportunity to go back to his customer for increased payment if he finds later that an inadvertent undercharge was made when preparing the invoice.

Unless clearly stated in the original contract for the job or on the original invoice (or in the case of a haulier, in his conditions of carriage), it is illegal to subsequently add interest charges to unpaid or late-paid accounts.

VAT tax point

Invoices must show VAT details including particularly the tax point or 'time of supply'. It is this point that determines in which period the VAT payable becomes due (ie by being included in the return for that period). Although there are variables that come into effect depending on circumstances, broadly the tax point is the date when goods are sent to a customer or the customer takes them away – in the case of road haulage operations which is the provision of a service, it is the date on which the service is performed. The tax point is not the date of the invoice for the goods or service as this may be made out and submitted to the customer either sooner or later than the actual tax point.

Invoices must show the price of the goods or service excluding VAT, the applicable VAT rate and amount of VAT and the total amount including VAT. They must also show the supplier's VAT number without which, effectively, the customer cannot reclaim the VAT paid (if he is VAT registered).

NB: It is an illegal act for a non-VAT registered person to add VAT to invoices for goods or services supplied.

Credit note

If goods are returned or accepted in a damaged state or are 'short' delivered or an overcharge is made, rather than refund money a supplier can make amends by giving the customer a credit note indicating a refund of part or all of any charge paid or due. This effectively says, 'I owe you some money', without actually paying it at that time. The recipient of a credit note may deduct the value of the credit from any amount he may owe the supplier or use it against payment for future supplies or, if there is an account between the two firms, the credit will be shown as a reduction of the total amount owing from one to the other.

Debit note

A debit note is effectively the opposite of a credit note or the same as an invoice. It advises the recipient that he owes some money to the issuer. If the issuer owes the recipient money the debit note says, 'I will reduce what I owe you by £x (the amount of the debit)'.

Statement

In full, 'statement of account'. A statement is sent out after invoices have been issued and acts as a reminder to the recipient of how the account stands with the supplier. In business transactions, a statement will progressively show outstanding amounts owing, less any payments received since the last statement was issued, plus whatever invoices have been issued since the last statement (ie the balance of the account). A total of debit or credit is shown and usually a statement will indicate amounts owing as follows: 'this month', 'owing over 30 days', 'owing over 60 days', 'outside our normal credit terms', 'immediate payment required', etc.

Consignment notes

Consignment notes are used in multiple sets which give details of consignor and consignee, the address for collection and delivery, details of the goods (description, weight, size, number of packages, markings), information regarding delivery, details of the vehicle and driver (registration number and driver's name), and a space for the recipient to sign acknowledging safe receipt (referred to as a 'clear signature') or receipt in a damaged condition or short delivery. Frequently, consignment notes are printed on the back with the firm's conditions of carriage. In international haulage operations, consignment notes are particularly significant and must conform to the CMR convention requirements (see page 35).

It is useful to emphasize here the distinct difference between *consignor* – the sender of the goods, and *consignee* – the recipient of the goods; also, *carriage paid* – where carriage charges are paid by the consignor or in advance by the consignee, and *carriage forward* where charges are to be paid by the consignee, either on an account basis on invoice or COD ('Cash on Delivery' – in other words, payment must be made before the goods are handed over).

E13. FREIGHT AGENTS

Working in road haulage operations will bring the reader into contact with other modes of transport and many other organizations such as freight forwarders, haulage subcontractors, transport clearing houses and groupage operators. It is important to understand the various different roles fulfilled by these organizations, as described below.

Freight forwarders

Many firms with goods to despatch, particularly to overseas destinations, use the services of freight forwarders. Their role is to provide a complete transport service in connection with the export or import of goods (as well as for inland movements) covering some or all of the following aspects:

- advice on the best method of movement (ie road, sea, air);
- advice on legal/commercial requirements;
- advice on the best services;
- making necessary bookings with appropriate transport services;
- completing all documentation;
- advising on and arranging packing and labelling;
- arranging insurance cover as necessary;
- arranging for collection and following through until delivery is effected;
- arranging Customs clearance for export/import consignments;
- ensuring that all charges are reasonable and presenting a comprehensive final account.

Clearing houses

A clearing house is an organization which arranges with shippers (ie consignors) of goods to move those goods by subcontracting the work to road haulage operators; ie it does not normally undertake the carriage itself. The clearing house agrees one price with the customer and another (lower) with the haulier and keeps the difference. Alternatively, it advises the haulier of the price to be paid by the customer then deducts a commission for handling and administrative charges from what is due to the subcontract haulier. Usually the commission is in the region of 10 per cent of the original rate but can be less if the rate is poor or substantially more if it is good. Hauliers seeking return loads for vehicles frequently accept loads from clearing houses to save searching around. There are problems on both sides. Unscrupulous clearing houses deduct excessive commission and take a long time to pay the haulier, thereby existing on finance owed to hauliers rather than on their own working capital. Hauliers sometimes pick up loads and deliver to the wrong place, or do not obtain proof of delivery, or take a long time to effect delivery (they may tranship loads in their own yard for delivery later). Sometimes, too, subcontract hauliers are not adequately covered by Goods in Transit insurance and if loads are lost or damaged and substantial claims arise, financial problems can result.

Subcontract hauliers

These are hauliers (often owner-drivers) who have no direct contact with customers but who pick up work from other hauliers and clearing houses. In other words, they undertake work that others have contracted to carry. This method of operating saves them the costs and efforts of marketing but it means they exist always on haulage rates reduced by the main contractor's commission, and they usually have to wait a considerable time for payment since they have no leverage on the customer. There is a significant legal aspect to subcontract haulage work, which is dealt with in detail in module A.3.

Groupage

This is the practice of bringing small consignments together (in industry terminology less than container loads – LCLs) and consolidating them into bulk loads for onward shipment (ie the trunk haul) in a large vehicle or container. Break-bulk is a term used to describe the unloading of consolidated loads ready for delivery of individual consignments to their respective destinations. In the case of import/export groupage, much of this work is carried out at inland clearance depots where HM Customs and Excise have a presence for clearing the necessary documentation for such loads.

PART 6

Access to the market

F1. OPERATOR LICENSING

The operators' ('O') licensing system is concerned with safety and this is achieved by regulating the 'quality' of goods vehicle operators entering the industry and is thus a quality licensing system. It is administered by the Traffic Commissioner (TC) for each of the traffic areas covering England, Wales and Scotland. Northern Ireland is dealt with separately: its Road Freight Operators' licensing system is administered by the Department of the Environment in the province.

Quality and quantity licensing

Quality licensing is a system whereby control is exercised on the basis of the quality of licence holders, that is, their ability to operate safely, legally and professionally. Quantity licensing, on the other hand, is based on restricting the number of licence holders or the total volume of freight that licence holders can move. The present UK system of 'O' licensing (and Northern Ireland road freight operators' licensing) is quality based.

Under the current licensing scheme, trade or business users of most goods vehicles over 3.5 tonnes maximum permissible weight must hold an 'O' licence for such vehicles, whether they are used for carrying goods in connection with the operator's main trade or business as an own-account operator (ie a trade or business other than that of carrying goods for hire or reward) or are used for hire or reward road haulage operations. Certain goods vehicles, including those used exclusively for private purposes, are exempt from the licensing requirements. Details of the exempt vehicles to which 'O' licensing does not apply are given on page 173.

The regulatory system

The original system of operators' licensing was established by the Transport Act 1968, the relevant provisions of which are now consolidated into the Goods Vehicle (Licensing of Operators) Act 1995. This Act states that no person may use a goods vehicle on a road for hire or reward or in connection with any trade or business carried on by him except under an operator's licence.

Regulations which took effect on 1 January 1978 made substantial changes to the 'O' licensing system, which had existed from 1970 to the end of 1977. These regulations, The Goods Vehicle (Operators' Licences) Regulations 1977, introduced a three-tier system of 'O' licensing in contrast to the previous single-tier system which applied similarly to both professional hauliers and own-account operators. From 1 June 1984 further significant changes to the system were introduced by The Goods Vehicles (Operators' Licences, Qualifications and Fees) Regulations 1984 (as amended 1986, 1987, 1988, 1990, 1993 and 1994) which, principally, gave Licensing Authorities (now called Traffic Commissioners) powers to consider representations to 'O' licence applications on the grounds that environmental nuisance or discomfort would be caused to local residents by the presence of goods vehicles at or operating from particular locations.

Further changes were made from 1 January 1996 when the system of continuous 'O' licensing was introduced whereby licences, once granted, remain valid indefinitely, provided the holder complies with all relevant conditions and pays the necessary fees on time – failure to do so bringing with it risk of loss of the licence – or unless a major variation of the licence is required (eg to increase the number of authorized vehicles or to change or add a new operating centre to the licence). The requirement for five-yearly licence renewals has been abolished for cases where details remain unchanged, although operating centres are subject to periodic reviews to ensure that they remain suitable.

Besides this principal change, the 1995 Act also provided new definitions for vehicle operating centres (they must be sufficiently large to accommodate all the vehicles used under the licence), where newspaper advertisements must be placed (ie in one or more local newspapers circulating in the locality), and the period of time in which objectors and environmental representors may make their case (five years for environmental representors). It also gives wider powers to TCs in road safety matters, particularly in regard to situations where vehicles may cause danger to the public.

From 1 October 1999 yet more changes were introduced as a result of new UK regulations implementing the provisions of EC Council Directive 98/76/EC of 1 October 1998, which amends Directive 96/26/EC. Principal among these provisions are stricter good repute requirements, increased financial commitments for new (and later for existing) operators, a more extensive professional competence examination syllabus and a tougher examination regime. All of this is to ensure higher levels of professionalism and law abidance in road haulage (similar steps are being applied in passenger transport) and a harmonized approach throughout all the member states of the EU.

Administration of licensing system

The 'O' licensing system, which is based on the concept of ensuring legal and safe operation and thus is a system of 'quality' as opposed to 'quantity' licensing, is administered on a regional (ie Traffic Area) basis throughout Great Britain. (Northern Ireland's Road Freight Operators' Licensing system is dealt with separately by the Department of the Environment in Belfast.) Six Traffic Area Offices (TAOs), each with its own TC, administer the eight Traffic Areas forming the networks, with two of the TCs carrying responsibility for two Traffic Areas (eg the TC in Leeds covers the North East and North West Traffic Areas, and the TC in Birmingham covers both the West Midlands and the Wales Traffic Areas).

These TCs are appointed by the Secretary of State for Transport and are 'independent quasi-judicial authorities' who have the statutory power to grant or refuse operators' licences, to place road safety and environmental conditions or restrictions on such licences where necessary, and subsequently to impose penalties against licences in the event of the holder being convicted for goods vehicle-related offences.

The Traffic Area Network (TAN) is now merged with the Vehicle Inspectorate (VI) to form VOSA, ie the Vehicle and Operator Services Agency.

The vehicle user

An 'O' licence is required by the 'user' of an appropriate vehicle (ie one that is not exempt). The 'user' is the person who operates and drives the vehicle in the case of an owner-driver, or who employs a person to drive the vehicle for him in connection with any trade or business that he carries on. Ownership of the vehicle is *not* a relevant factor in determining who is the user. In Northern Ireland own-account users of vehicles are exempt from road freight operators' licensing.

Definition of a goods vehicle

For the purposes of 'O' licensing, a goods vehicle is one which is used in connection with the trade or business of the licence holder and as such is a vehicle with a permissible maximum weight (pmw) of over 3.5 tonnes unless it is otherwise exempt.

Exemptions from 'O' licensing

The following small vehicles are exempt from 'O' licensing:

- Rigid vehicles plated at not more than 3.5 tonnes permissible maximum weight or unplated with an unladen weight of not more than 1,525kg.
- Drawbar combinations with plated weights totalling not more than 3.5 tonnes gross or unplated with a total combined unladen weight of not more than 1,525kg (trailers of not more than 1,020kg unladen weight need not be included in the calculation to determine whether an 'O' licence is needed).
- Articulated vehicles with a combined plated weight of not more than 3.5 tonnes gross or, if either is not plated, if the total of the unladen weights is not more than 1,525kg.

A number of further exemptions apply to specialized vehicles or vehicles used for specialized purposes, but these are not listed because OCR does not examine on the exemptions.

Restricted 'O' licences

Own-account operators who only carry their own goods or goods in connection with any trade or business carried on by them (other than that of professional haulier) may hold a restricted 'O' licence which allows them to operate both within the UK and internationally. The licence does *not* permit them to carry any goods for hire or reward, or in connection with a trade or business other than their own.

Standard 'O' licences – national operations

Professional haulage operators and own-account operators who wish to carry goods for hire or reward in addition to their own goods, solely within the UK, are required to hold a standard 'O' licence covering national transport operations.

The holder of a standard national 'O' licence may also carry his own goods (ie goods in connection with any other trade or business carried on by him) on international journeys as well as on national journeys.

Standard 'O' licences – international operations

Professional haulage (ie hire and reward) operators and own-account operators who wish to carry goods for others in addition to their own goods both nationally and internationally need to hold a standard 'O' licence covering both national and international operations.

Definition of international operations
For the purposes of the 'O' licence regulations the definition of international operations, which determines whether a standard international licence is required, is as follows:

> If the driver or the vehicle is engaged on a journey where the vehicle or part of the vehicle (ie a semi-trailer) leaves the UK in a loaded condition, or the vehicle or part of the vehicle has entered the UK in a loaded condition from another country, then that is an international operation. However, if the driver only takes a loaded trailer or semi-trailer to a British port for unaccompanied onward movement or collects an unaccompanied loaded trailer or semi-trailer from a port and does not leave the country himself, in these circumstances it has been ruled that a standard 'O' licence covering only national operations is required.

Conditions for the granting of restricted/standard 'O' licences

The conditions which an applicant must meet in order to obtain the grant of a restricted or standard 'O' licence are as follows:

- Restricted 'O' licences. The applicant must be a fit and proper person, and must be of appropriate financial standing.
- Standard national 'O' licences. The applicant must be of good repute, must be of appropriate financial standing, and must be professionally competent in national transport operations (see page 192).
- Standard international 'O' licences. The applicant must be of good repute, must be of appropriate financial standing, and must be professionally competent in both national and international transport operations.

In each case the licence applicant must additionally show he is willing and able to comply with the conditions of the declaration of intent on the 'O' licence application form GV 79. Further, the operating centre at which vehicles on the licence are based must be suitable for the purpose and environmentally acceptable (ie must not be likely to cause environmental discomfort to owners or occupiers of other land in the vicinity).

Number of 'O' licences

Only one 'O' licence may be held by a person/firm in any one traffic area. A separate 'O' licence is required in each traffic area in which goods vehicle operations are based.

Observance of legal requirements

It is a condition of 'O' licensing that operators must observe the law regarding drivers' hours and the keeping of drivers' records (including tachographs); the overloading of vehicles; the maintenance, roadworthiness and use of vehicles; vehicle plating and testing; speed limits and traffic rules (eg motorway driving); drivers' licensing; international road haulage permits; use of rebated fuel oil; parking restrictions and prohibitions on loading/unloading. They must also comply with the 'O' licensing conditions on the reporting of vehicle defects by drivers, the regular safety inspection of vehicles and the keeping of maintenance records (ie driver defect reports, safety inspection reports and defect repair records).

Declaration of intent

In making an application for an 'O' licence, or variation of an 'O' licence, the applicant is required to make a declaration of intent – a legally binding promise that the law regarding all the above-mentioned requirements will be strictly observed. This promise must be kept throughout the duration of the licence. Failure to fulfil promises made in the declaration of intent can leave the licence holder open to risk of penalty against his licence by the TC who has the power to curtail, suspend or revoke it if such action is considered appropriate.

The precise wording of the promises on Form GV 79 comprising the declaration of intent is shown on page 195.

Maintenance

Operators must make proper arrangements, acceptable to the TC, for the maintenance and repair of their vehicles. These arrangements may be the provision by the operator of his own workshop facilities or the use of the services of an outside repairer; the TC would want to see a proper written agreement between the operator and the repairer setting out details of the arrangement and the manner and frequency of the inspection and repairs. Although repairs may be carried out by other repairers, the vehicle user (ie the licence holder) remains fully and solely responsible for the mechanical condition of the vehicles on the road. Blame for faulty work cannot be transferred to the repairers so far as the 'O' licence is concerned.

Maintenance records

Maintenance records, whether prepared in an operator's own workshop or supplied by a repairer (depending on where the repair work is carried out), must be maintained and kept available for inspection for at least 15 months.

Fit persons/good repute

Applicants for an operator's licence are required to satisfy the TC that they are fit and proper persons to hold such a licence and in the case of standard 'O' licences are of 'good repute'. In order to determine this fact the TC requires details of any convictions which the applicant, any partners or any other directors of a limited company have had in connection with the operation of goods vehicles.

Under new rules introduced in 1999 good repute is automatically lost if a person is convicted of more than one serious offence or of road transport offences. A serious offence is one that incurs:

- more than three months' imprisonment; or
- a community service order of more than 60 hours; or
- a fine exceeding level 4 on the standard scale (currently £2,500).

Rehabilitation of offenders

The convictions that the TC is concerned with are those incurred during the five years prior to the date of the granting of the licence where a fine or community service order was imposed or, if such a conviction resulted in a prison sentence of not more than six months, up to seven years prior to that date and 10 years for a longer sentence. If the person concerned was under the age of 17 when any such conviction was made then the respective periods are two and half, three and a half, and five years. Convictions for offences prior to these periods are 'spent' under the terms of the Rehabilitation of Offenders Act 1974 and therefore do not count against the applicant. The rehabilitation period where an absolute discharge was granted is six months, where a detention centre order was imposed it is three years and where a borstal order was imposed it is seven years.

Financial status

Applicants for an operator's licence are required to satisfy the TC as to their financial status at the time of applying for the licence so that he can determine whether there is sufficient money available to enable the applicant to operate and maintain the licensed vehicles to the standards required by law. Detailed questionnaires (form GV 79F) are frequently sent out by TCs for completion, mainly by standard 'O' licence applicants, to obtain details of their financial resources and projected operating expenditure.

Operating centres and parking

When applying for an operator's licence the applicant is required to give the address of the place where the vehicles will normally be 'kept', which effectively means the place where vehicles are parked when they are not in use. This is termed the 'operating centre'. The TC will need to consider, in view of the facilities available and in conjunction with the local authority, the location and suitability of the premises for the parking of goods vehicles under provisions contained in the Transport Act 1982 (section 52 and schedule 4) amending the Transport Act 1968.

Under these provisions the definition of operating centre includes any place where vehicles are regularly parked, even if this is away from the normal depot. Therefore, when drivers regularly take vehicles home, the place where they park the vehicle may become an operating centre and the subject of an application for use of the place as such – complete with requisite newspaper advertisement (see below). This is then subject to TC approval and to representation by any local resident who is environmentally affected by such parking. This legislation enables representations to be made to TCs about the environmental effects of goods vehicle operating centres on land owned or occupied by the person making the representation in the vicinity of the nominated operating centre.

Powers of Traffic Commissioners

Applications for operators' licences have to be made to the TC for the area in which the vehicles to be operated are based.

The TC has the sole power (apart from appeal decisions of the Transport Tribunal – see page 191) of considering applications and of granting or refusing licences, and of placing environmental restrictions on the use of vehicles at operating centres.

The TC requires completion of the appropriate forms and needs to be satisfied of the following:

- That the applicant is of good repute and is a fit person to hold a licence.
- That he has suitable facilities or has made satisfactory arrangements for vehicle maintenance.
- That he has made satisfactory arrangements for ensuring that the law concerning drivers' hours and records and the overloading of vehicles will be complied with.

- That, where appropriate, he is professionally competent or employs somebody who is professionally competent.
- That he is of adequate financial standing.
- That the applicant has suitable parking facilities (with appropriate planning permission) for his vehicles.
- That the operating centre specified for the vehicles is environmentally suitable.

The TC has the power to call an operator to public inquiry so he can:

- Consider the application for an operator's licence in public.
- Question an operator about offences which have been committed in contravention of the 'O' licence requirements. This is referred to as a Section 69 Inquiry in recognition of the powers given to TCs in this respect under Section 69 of the Transport Act 1968.
- Listen to environmental representations by local residents about the suitability of the vehicle operating centre and the use of vehicles at the centre.
- Listen to statutory objections to the granting of a licence by specified objectors (see page 191).

Under provisions contained in the Transport Act 1982, TCs have powers to impose conditions on 'O' licences relating to vehicle operating centres, in terms of the number of vehicles parked there, how they are parked, their size, the times when they arrive and depart, the route they must follow in going in and out, and on other related activities there such as maintenance and vehicle loading and unloading.

Licence penalties

The TC also has powers under Section 69 of the Transport Act 1968 to impose penalties on the holder of an operator's licence as follows:

- Revocation, whereby the complete licence can be revoked for a stipulated period. In extreme circumstances the TC can recommend that the person concerned should never be permitted to hold another operator's licence.
- Suspension, where the TC can suspend the complete 'O' licence or a number of vehicles from the licence temporarily.
- Curtailment, where the TC reduces the number of vehicles that may be operated under the licence.

In the case of curtailment or suspension the TC can rule that the vehicles concerned must not be used under any other 'O' licence for a period of up to six months.

Objections to an 'O' licence application

The bodies listed below may object – not to be confused with environmental representations mentioned above – within 21 days of publication of the application in the booklet *Applications and Decisions* (commonly referred to as 'As and Ds'), to the granting of an 'O' licence on the grounds that the applicant does not meet the necessary qualifications, because:

- the applicant is not of good repute;
- he is not of appropriate financial standing;
- he does not meet the requirements of professional competence;
- he is not likely to comply with the law regarding drivers' hours and records and the overloading of vehicles;
- there are not satisfactory arrangements or facilities for maintaining the vehicles;
- the applicant does not have suitable facilities for parking vehicles when they are not in use.

The bodies are:

- A chief officer of police.
- A local authority.
- A planning authority.
- The Freight Transport Association (FTA).
- The Road Haulage Association (RHA).
- The British Association of Removers (BAR).
- The General and Municipal Workers' Union (GMWU).
- The National Union of Railwaymen (NUR).
- The Transport and General Workers' Union (TGWU).
- The Union of Shop, Distributive and Allied Workers (USDAW).
- The United Road Transport Union (URTU).

If an objection is to be raised by any of the listed bodies against an application, the objector is required to provide the applicant with a copy of the objection.

Appeals to the Transport Tribunal

An applicant for an operator's licence whose application is refused, or an existing operator whose licence is revoked, suspended or curtailed, has the right of appeal to the Transport Tribunal, which will consider his appeal and rule for or against him in the light of information provided at the appeal. An operator may also appeal against the decision of a TC following representations on environmental grounds or against conditions placed on a licence in such circumstances.

An objector can appeal against a TC's decision but people making environmental representations have no such rights of appeal.

Appeals must be made within one month of the TC's decision being published in *Applications and Decisions*.

The Tribunal has three members: the chairman, who is a QC, plus two other eminent and experienced people from industry.

Admission to the occupation – professional competence

Applications for a standard operator's licence must be supported by the name of a person (the applicant himself or one partner or a director of the applicant's company or a full-time employee) who is professionally competent in either national or international transport operations (depending on whether a standard national or international 'O' licence is required), in accordance with The Goods Vehicles (Operators Licences Qualifications and Fees) Regulations 1984 (as amended).

Methods of acquiring competence
There are various methods by which a person can or could have become professionally competent.

Grandfather Rights
Any person who was employed by an 'O' licence holder in responsible road transport employment or who held an 'O' licence in his own name prior to 1975 could obtain a Certificate of Professional Competence based on past experience (known as 'Grandfather Rights') by applying to the TC for the traffic area in which he lived by 30 November 1979.

Temporary Grandfather Rights
Any person who took up a position of responsibility for the operation of goods vehicles on an 'O' licence between 1 January 1975 and 31 December 1977 or who became the holder of an 'O' licence during that time was considered to be professionally competent until 31 December 1979. After that date professional competence had to be confirmed either by passing the appropriate examination or by gaining exemption.

Definition of responsible road transport employment
The legal definition of the 'responsible road transport employment' an applicant for a Certificate of Professional Competence under the Grandfather Rights scheme had to have was as follows:

> employment in the service of a person or a company who has held an 'O' licence where that employment was such that the person had responsibility for the operation of goods vehicles under that 'O' licence and where that employment was prior to 1 January 1975.

NB: It should be understood that it is no longer possible to qualify for professional competence under the Grandfather Rights scheme. All certificate issues under this scheme have now ceased. This item is included here for information only.

Exemption

Certain members of professional transport institutes in specified grades qualify for professional competence by exemption by virtue of their continuing valid membership, and therefore do not need to meet the experience requirement mentioned above or pass the official examination. The institutes and membership grades are as follows:

For both international and national operations:

- Membership of the Chartered Institute of Transport (CIT) in the grade of Fellow or Member (in the road transport sector). *NB:* The CIT is now the Institute of Logistics and Transport (ILT).
- Membership of the Institute of Transport Administration (IoTA) in the grade of Fellow, Member or Associate Member (in the road transport sector).
- Membership of the Institute of Road Transport Engineers (IRTE) in the grade of Member or Associate Member.
- Membership of the Institute of Furniture Warehousing and Removing Industry (IFWRI) in the grade of Fellow or Associate.

For national operations only:

- Membership of the Chartered Institute of Transport (CIT) in the grade of Associate (in the road transport sector).
- Membership of the Institute of Road Transport Engineers (IRTE) in the grade of Associate (by examination).
- Membership of the Institute of Transport Administration (IoTA) in the grade of Graduate or Associate (must be a holder of the NEBSS Certificate, road transport sector), must be at least 21 years of age and have 3 years' practical experience.
- Holder of the General Certificate in Removals Management issued by the Institute of Furniture Warehousing and Removing Industry (IFWRI).
- Holders of the RSA Certificate in Road Goods Transport gained by examination since May 1984.

Examination

Those people who do not qualify for professional competence by other means can do so by examination. The official examination is conducted at various centres throughout the country four or more times per year on behalf of the official examining body (OCR). Copies of the examination syllabus can be obtained from OCR. For further details see page 18 of this manual.

Fees and validity

Certificates of Professional Competence were granted on a once-only basis with no renewal, and they were free of charge. Similarly, gaining or holding the professional competence qualification costs nothing beyond the price of studying for and sitting the examination or payment of Institute annual subscriptions. Once acquired, the professional competence qualification will remain valid, without renewal, so long as the scheme remains in existence.

Issue of Certificates of Professional Competence

Certificates of Professional Competence were issued *only* to those persons who qualified under the Grandfather Rights scheme. Where the qualification is achieved under the exemption arrangements through membership of the professional institutes a valid membership is sufficient indication that the person is professionally competent, although the institutes listed will issue a confirmatory certificate if required.

Where professional competence is obtained by passing the official RSA examinations a pass certificate from the examination board will indicate that the person is professionally competent. This certificate will *not* be exchanged for a Certificate of Professional Competence of the type issued to those people who qualified under the Grandfather Rights.

F2. SETTING UP A ROAD TRANSPORT UNDERTAKING

Applications for 'O' licences

Applicants for 'O' licences are required to complete form GV 79, which should be sent to the Traffic Area Office in which the vehicles to be specified on the licence are based, at least nine weeks in advance of the date when operation of the vehicles is required to commence.

In addition, form GV 79A (the list of vehicles to be specified on the licence) must be completed. A TC also usually requires further information about the applicant's financial standing, which must be provided initially by the submission of accounts, accountant's letter, bank statements or other evidence of resources. Applicants are sometimes required to complete form GV 79F giving details of their projected expenditure and earnings.

If there are environmental representations against a licence application following publication of the newspaper advertisement, form GV 79E (dealing with environmental matters) must be completed.

Form GV 79

Form GV 79 is the basic application for an 'O' licence – it requires the name, trading name, address, telephone and telex numbers of the applicant together with the following information:

- Details of any subsidiary companies whose vehicles are to be included on the licence.
- Details of the previous experience of the applicant, his partners or fellow directors in operating or driving goods vehicles.
- Details of any other operator's licence held or previously held.
- Details of the operating centres for the vehicles to be included on the licence and the number of vehicles and trailers in possession or to be acquired.
- Details of any previous convictions which the applicant, his partners or fellow directors may have had during the past five years relating to the roadworthiness of vehicles, overloading offences or drivers' hours and records offences which have resulted in a fine or imprisonment.
- Details about the financial status of the business proprietor, his partners or the directors of the business, and whether any of them have been made bankrupt in the past three years.
- Details about the professionally competent person in the case of applications for standard operator's licences.

Declaration of intent: in addition to these basic questions form GV 79 requires the applicant to make a declaration of intent regarding his ability and willingness to comply with the law. The points included in the declaration are as follows:

'I declare that the statements made in this application are true. I understand that the licence may be revoked if the licensed operator does not comply with the undertakings made below and that it is an offence to make a false declaration.

'I, or the licensed operator, undertake to make proper arrangements so that:

- the rules on drivers' hours are observed and proper records are kept;
- motor vehicles and trailers are not overloaded;
- vehicles will operate within speed limits;
- motor vehicles and trailers, including hired vehicles and trailers, are kept fit and serviceable;
- drivers report promptly any defects or symptoms of defects that could prevent the safe operation of vehicles and/or trailers, and that any defects are promptly recorded in writing;
- records are kept (for 15 months) of all driver defect reports, all safety inspections, routine maintenance and repairs to vehicles and trailers, and these are made available on request; and that in respect of each operating centre specified, that the number of authorized motor vehicles and the number of authorized trailers kept there will not exceed the maximum

numbers recorded against the operating centre (ie named in section 14 of Form GV 79).

'If the licence is granted these undertakings may be recorded in the licence.

'I, or the licensed operator, understand that failure to comply with the conditions or undertakings recorded on a licence can result in disciplinary action being taken against the licence holder and that failure to comply with the conditions is a criminal offence.'

Form GV 79E (environmental information)

Form GV 79E is sent to licence applicants if the Licensing Authority receives representations from local residents following publication of details of the applicant's operating centres in local papers. The form requires details of the applicant and his proposed operating centre, the vehicles normally to be kept there and the number and types of trailer to be kept there. Information must be given of any other parking place in the vicinity of the centre used for parking vehicles specified on the licence. If the licence applicant is not the owner of the premises he must send evidence to show that he has permission or authority to use the place for parking vehicles.

Questions must be answered about the operating times of authorized vehicles (ie those on the licence or licence application – *not* others). In particular, what time will lorries arrive at and leave the centre, will they use the centre on Saturdays or Sundays, what times will they arrive and leave on these days, will maintenance work be carried out there and between what hours, and will any of this work take place on Saturdays or Sundays and, if so, between what hours? Information must be given about any covered buildings at the centre in which this work is carried out.

A plan must be sent showing the parking positions for authorized vehicles, entry and exit points, main buildings, and surrounding roads with names. Details must be given of any application for or any planning permission granted for use of the site as a vehicle operating centre.

Form GV 79F (financial information)

Form GV 79F may be sent to new standard licence applicants when the TC requires additional financial information to enable him to consider whether the applicant meets the extra financial requirements for this type of licence (ie to run a professional haulage business and not be dependent on any other trading activity). An application will be refused unless the TC is satisfied that the applicant has sufficient financial resources to set up and run the business.

Answers have to be given on the form about the vehicles to be included on the licence, their average annual mileage and the estimated running cost for each individual type of vehicle.

Details must be given about the funds available to start up the business and where these are held (eg in a bank as savings, or overdraft or loan facilities, or share capital, or a deposit elsewhere) and about the start-up costs for the business including the purchase price or down payment on the vehicles and on the premises (advance rents, etc, or purchase of the freehold or leasehold) and the sum to be held in reserve as working capital. The applicant is required to give a forecast of the annual expenditure and income for his road haulage operations for a financial year. The TC expects this information to give a clear indication of the business finances for the year ahead.

Form GV 79A

Form GV 79A is a supplementary sheet to form GV 79, requiring the applicant to provide details of every vehicle currently in possession to be included on the licence as follows:

- Registration number.
- The official (ie Vehicle Inspectorate) plated maximum permissible weight or gross train weight.
- Body type (van, tipper, tanker, platform, etc) and whether articulated.

This document will eventually become part of the operator's licence, if granted, and the Traffic Area Office will place its stamp in the right-hand column of the form alongside authorized vehicles. This stamp will be cancelled when the vehicles are removed from the licence. In some instances a new style of computerized form is being used.

Form GV 80

Application to make changes within the total number of vehicles already authorized on an existing 'O' licence should be made on form GV 80. The form requires details of the applicant and of the vehicles to be added to or removed from the licence. A period of one month is allowed in which to notify the Traffic Area Office of details of vehicles added to a licence within the margin (ie the total number authorized).

Form GV 81

Application to vary an 'O' licence by increasing the total number of vehicles authorized on the licence should be made on form GV 81. It is also used to make other variations of the licence such as a change of operating centre, a change of maintenance arrangement, to add or delete other operating centres, to change the type of licence (eg from restricted to standard or vice versa), to request a change or removal of conditions from the licence. This form requires details of the applicant and any convictions against him, his partners or co-directors. It also requires the applicant to repeat the declaration of intent made on the original application form GV 79 and place an advertisement in a local newspaper as previously described.

Advertising of applications

Applicants for new, varied or renewed 'O' licences must place an advertisement in a local newspaper, to appear up to 21 days before or no more than 21 days after their application is received by the TC, giving the address of the proposed operating centre or centres for vehicles covered by the licence. The advertisement gives local residents the opportunity to make representations (which must not be vexatious, frivolous or irrelevant) to the TC against the grant of a licence (or variation of a licence) on environmental (but no other) grounds, in that it would prejudicially affect their enjoyment of the land they own or occupy. Such representors must write to the TC within 21 days of the advertisement appearing, setting out their complaint, and a copy must be sent to the licence applicant, otherwise the representation becomes invalid.

Publication of applications

Applications for new 'O' licences or for variations of existing licences are published by the TC in the booklet *Applications and Decisions*, so that potential objectors can see details of the applications and, if they wish, make objection within 21 days (see also page 191). Similarly, decisions to grant licences or variations of licences or refusal to grant applications may also be published in this document, copies of which are obtainable from Traffic Area Offices.

Subsidiary/associate companies

The vehicles of any subsidiary company (ie one in which more than a 50 per cent shareholding is held) may be included in the application for an 'O' licence by a holding/parent company, but those of an associate company (ie where there is less than 50 per cent share holding) may not.

Transfer of vehicles

If vehicles are transferred to another traffic area for more than three months they must be specified on an 'O' licence in that area. If a licence is not held in that area then a new application must be made at least nine weeks before the vehicles are to start operating. It is illegal to operate goods vehicles (ie over 3.5 tonnes maximum permissible weight) from a base in a Traffic Area in which *no* 'O' licence is held.

Licence margin

Application may be made and granted for more vehicles than are initially required in order to provide a 'margin' of surplus vehicles on the licence in case needed at any time during the currency of the licence (normally five years) to cover for maintenance, vehicles off the road for other reasons and to cater for peaks of trade.

Adding vehicles

Additional vehicles within the total number authorized on an 'O' licence may be added at any time. The TC must be advised of details of the vehicles added within one month by submission of form GV 80.

Notification of changes

Licence holders must notify the TC of any changes in the legal entity of their business (eg change of name, partners, or if a limited company is formed) because the existing licence will no longer be valid and application will have to be made for a new one. Any change of business address must be notified within three weeks. Other changes which must be notified are those affecting a nominated professionally competent person or where such a person dies or becomes physically disabled or mentally disordered and unable to work, or where the licence holder or a partner or director is declared bankrupt or the company goes into insolvent liquidation. Failure to notify the TC can result in a fine and he can revoke, suspend or curtail the 'O' licence.

Fees and validity

The fee for an 'O' licence is calculated on a per vehicle per quarter basis plus a licence fee. Licences run continuously but are subject to review by the TC at five-year intervals when payment of the appropriate fees is due. Failure to pay the fee on request will result in automatic termination of the licence.

Interim licences

A TC may grant an interim 'O' licence pending consideration of an application for a full licence. Issue of an interim licence does not guarantee that a full licence will be granted.

Temporary derogation

Holders of a standard 'O' licence may operate without a professionally competent person if the person dies or becomes physically or mentally incapacitated (the TC must be notified in writing) for no more than 12 months, after which time the licence will be revoked unless the TC accepts that there are exceptional circumstances and permits an extension of this period (the maximum is 18 months).

F3. DOCUMENTS AND ADMINISTRATION

'O' licence documents

Following the grant of an 'O' licence the applicant will be sent Form GV 82 'Fee Request' in accordance with the number of vehicles requested on the licence. On payment of the relevant fee the applicant will receive the following documents:

- Form GVOL 1 – Goods Vehicle Operator's Licence (Restricted or Standard depending on application).
- Form GVOL N – Notes about the licence.
- Form GVOL 2 – Operating Centres (specified centres and the number of vehicles authorized at each).
- Form GVOL 2R – General Conditions Attached to a Standard/ Restricted Operator's Licence.
- Form GVOL V – Details of Goods Vehicles.

Production of 'O' licences
The TC, a certifying officer, examiner, police constable or other person authorized by the TC can demand production of an 'O' licence for examination within 14 days either at an operating centre covered by the licence or at the main place of business of the holder or, in the case of a demand by a police constable, at a police station selected by the holder.

Windscreen discs
A windscreen disc will be supplied for each vehicle listed on the licence (identified by vehicle registration number) in one of the following colours:

Restricted licence	– orange
Standard licence, national	– blue
Standard licence, international	– green
Interim licence	– yellow
Copy disc	– bearing the word COPY in red

The discs show the type of licence, the operator's name, the 'O' licence number, the licence expiry date and the vehicle registration number.

Community authorizations

Applicants who are granted a standard national and international licence will also receive an EEC Community Authorization document (form GV 274) comprising an original document to be kept at the address of the licence holder, and a certified copy for each vehicle listed on the licence – to be carried in the vehicle at all times when undertaking international journeys within the territory of one or more of the 15 current member states of the European Union.

Tachograph records

The subject of tachographs and tachograph records has been dealt with extensively in section C4. However, it is useful to emphasize here the legal requirement for the operator to check tachograph records and to take appropriate action should he find any contravention of the law by his drivers. In particular he should check that:

- each driver produces a tachograph record (chart) for each day on which he drives a relevant vehicle;
- the chart is fully completed with the date, the driver's name, the vehicle registration number, beginning and end odometer readings, and the starting and finishing points of the journey;
- a continuous record has been made (ie with no unexplained interruptions in the recording);
- that any non-recordable events have been manually entered on the chart;
- that the legal requirements regarding driving limits and break and rest periods have been complied with.

The legal requirement is for tachograph (and/or manual records – log books) to be retained, available for inspection by the enforcement authorities if required, for at least 12 months.

Waybills/consignment notes

Waybills and consignment notes are the usual form of documentation by which goods vehicle drivers are instructed to collect and deliver loads. They specify relevant details such as collection and delivery locations/addresses and times; a description of the goods and their quantity and/or weight; and any special instructions regarding safe handling/securing of the load.

In international transport operations CMR consignment notes are key documents. These are described fully in section A4.

Driving entitlements

Driving entitlements are described fully in section H1. However, here it is important to stress the need for goods vehicle operators to establish a system whereby they regularly check the driving licences of those whom they employ, whether on a permanent basis or only temporarily, to drive their vehicles. These checks should ideally be carried out at six-monthly intervals, the purpose being to determine that drivers still hold a valid licence to drive and that the licence covers the category of vehicle being driven. It is not unknown for unqualified drivers to claim that they are covered to drive particular vehicles (eg driving a category C+E vehicle with only a category C or C1+E driving entitlement) or for disqualified drivers to continue driving because they do not want to lose their job.

Maintenance documents

There is a legal requirement under the Road Traffic Act 1988 for goods vehicle operators to keep records of maintenance work carried out on their vehicles. When completing form GV 79, 'O' licence application, operators have to make the statutory 'declaration of intent' in which they promise to fulfil undertakings made at that time throughout the duration of the 'O' licence. A number of items in the declaration of intent relate to maintenance records. From this can be determined what records are needed by law.

In the declaration of intent the operator promises to ensure that records will be kept of safety inspections, routine maintenance and repairs to vehicles.

A promise is also made that drivers will report defects in their vehicles; the TCs insist that these reports should be in writing and therefore they become part of the vehicle record-keeping system. The operator promises to keep all these records for a minimum period of 15 months and to make them available on request by Vehicle Inspectorate (VI) examiners or the TC.

Additionally, operators are frequently asked by vehicle examiners and the TCs to keep a wall chart showing vehicles in the fleet and when they are due for inspection, service and annual test. The VI Code of Practice on vehicle maintenance (see page 281) recommends annual flow charts showing vehicle inspection-due dates.

Driver defect reports

It is a specific requirement (and part of the declaration of intent on an 'O' licence application form) that arrangements must be made for drivers to have a proper means of reporting 'safety faults' (ie defects) in the vehicle they are driving as soon as possible. As already mentioned, the TCs expect these defect reports to be made in writing, not verbally. Ideally, the report should be made either on an individual form which is completed and handed in by the driver, or in a defect book reserved for recording defects found on a vehicle, which is kept in a convenient place where all drivers have easy access to it, as well as whoever is responsible for ensuring that repair work is carried out. To reiterate, it has been made abundantly clear that verbal reporting of defects is not in itself a system acceptable to the TCs.

Whichever method is used it is important that the repair of the defects is recorded on the form or in the book by a note of the work done and the signature of the person who has done it (see also under repair records). It is also important for the operator to make regular checks on drivers and repair staff to see that the procedure adopted is being followed correctly. This requirement has been pointed out by the TCs on a number of occasions. Using separate pads of defect sheets is the best alternative and where these can be made out in duplicate they provide the driver with his own copy of the report for future reference.

Systems of defect reporting which rely on a centrally located defect book or on verbal reports by drivers are open to the risk of drivers forgetting to report defects when they return to base. If a driver's attention is distracted by his manager who wants to talk to him, for example, just as he is about to report a defect, another driver may take the vehicle out next day with a defect which could result in a prohibition notice being issued in a roadside check. A driver may also forget to report a defect when he returns late from a journey and is in a rush to get home or if he cannot find the defect book.

It is the operator's responsibility to make sure that the system used is infallible in all these circumstances, first because it is an offence to fail to cause the defect to be reported, and second because the vehicle could be found on the road subsequently with a safety fault not reported and not repaired.

Inspection reports

The Road Traffic Act 1988 requires that records of regular safety inspections of vehicles must be made. For this purpose the vehicle inspector should have a sheet on which are listed all the items to be inspected, preferably in accordance with the contents of *The Heavy Goods Vehicle Inspection Manual*.

The inspection sheet should identify the necessary items for inspection with a cross-check reference number to the *Inspection Manual* to enable, if necessary, full details of the method of inspection of that item – and the reason for its rejection as not being within acceptable limits – to be determined. The sheet should have provision for the inspector to mark against each item whether it is 'serviceable' or 'needs attention' and space to comment on defects for immediate rectification and other items for attention at a future date or on which a watch should be kept if attention is not required immediately. The form should contain space for the inspector to sign his name and add the date.

Repair sheets

Besides ensuring that proper records are kept of vehicle safety fault reports made by drivers and of regular safety inspections, the operator must also keep a record showing that any defects reported or found on inspection are rectified in order to keep the vehicle in a fit, serviceable and safe condition. Records of such repairs may be added to the driver defect report or the inspection report to provide combined records, or a separate repair or job sheet may be used.

The important points about repair records are, first, that they should show comprehensive details of the actual repair work carried out, identifying components which were repaired or replaced and new parts added, and, second, that there should be a matching repair sheet for every defect reported or found on inspection so that the vehicle examiners, when they visit to examine records, can see the report of the defect and a subsequent report of the repair work carried out to rectify it. Reports of defects which do not have a corresponding repair record can arouse suspicion in the examiner's mind that perhaps the necessary repair has not been carried out and that the defect still exists. This is a good reason for him then to consider examining that vehicle, or perhaps the whole fleet.

Service records

In addition to the records of defects and vehicle inspections that have to be kept, a record should also be kept of all other work carried out on the vehicle, whether it is repair or replacement of working parts or normal servicing (oil changes and greasing, etc).

Retention of records

It is a legal requirement that records of maintenance must be retained by operators. The original inspection report, or a photocopy of it, with the inspector's comments, the date and the mileage at which the inspection was carried out, must be retained and kept available for inspection if required by the VI examiners for 15 months from the date of the inspection. Work sheets showing the repair work carried out following the inspection and all other work done on the vehicle, including repairs following defect reports by drivers, as well as defect reports themselves, must be kept for 15 months, available for inspection by VI examiners or the TC, if requested.

Repair records from garages

When vehicle safety inspections, servicing and repair work are carried out for the operator by repair garages, the operator should obtain from the garage comprehensive documentation to enable him to meet the legal requirements detailed above. In many cases the VI examiners are quite happy if the garage retains the records of inspection and repair, so long as they can be made available for examination when required. The operator must be certain, in these instances, that the garage is keeping proper records (for a period of 15 months) which satisfy the legal requirements and that they are being kept available for inspection, not bundled away out of easy reach in a store with thousands of others.

In the event of failure of the garage to keep records as required, the operator's licence would be at risk but there would be no penalty imposed on the garage. On the GV 79 declaration of intent the operator promised that he would 'make proper arrangements so that records are kept for (15 months) of all driver defect reports, safety inspections, routine maintenance and repairs to vehicles and trailers and these are made available on request'.

It is important to note that in this respect, invoices, or copies of invoices from garages, for repair work are not in themselves sufficient to satisfy the record-keeping requirement. It is the actual inspection sheet and repair sheets, or photocopies of them, which are needed because of the greater and more precise detail which they contain. Similarly, maintenance records in computer printout form are unlikely to satisfy the requirement of enforcement staff to examine actual records – they will still want to see the original inspection sheets. This is an important point to consider with the increasing application of computers to transport operations and vehicle maintenance functions.

Location of records

Where companies hold operators' licences in a number of separate Traffic Areas the maintenance records for the vehicles under each licence should be kept in the area covered by the individual licence (preferably at the vehicle operating centre). With the sanction of the local TC, records may be kept centrally at a head office or central vehicle workshop, although the vehicle examiners may ask for them to be produced for inspection at the operating centre of the vehicles in the Traffic Area – probably giving three days' to one week's notice to enable the records to be obtained from the central files.

Wall planning charts

While it is not strictly a legal requirement, many vehicle examiners (and the current West Midland TC) like to see operators using wall planning charts (see note above about use of flow charts in accordance with new

VI Code of Practice on vehicle maintenance) to provide a visual reminder of important dates such as:

- vehicle/trailer due for inspection;
- vehicle/trailer due for service;
- vehicle/trailer due for annual test;
- excise duty due.

Such charts usually provide facilities for a whole year's recording of these items for the fleet, either shown by vehicle registration number or by fleet number.

Vehicle history files
For efficiency in record keeping, a system of vehicle history files – one for each vehicle and trailer in the fleet – is most useful. This provides the facility for keeping all relevant records relating to individual vehicles and trailers together and in one place. Individual files can have all the important details of the vehicle/trailer on the front cover for easy reference, as follows:

- registration number/fleet number;
- make/type;
- date of original registration;
- price new plus extras/options;
- annual test date;
- taxation (ie VED) date;
- base/location;
- model designation;
- wheelbase (in/mm);
- body type;
- special equipment;
- chassis number;
- engine number;
- gearbox type/number;
- rear axle type;
- electrical system – 12V/24V;
- plated weights – gross/axle;
- supplier's name and address;
- insurance documents.

Certificates of insurance
A policy of motor insurance does not provide the cover required by the Act until the insured person or organization has in their possession a certificate of insurance. Possession meaning, in this context, exactly what it

says: 'promised' or 'in the post' is not sufficient to satisfy the law. The policy itself is not *proof* of insurance cover, it only sets out the terms and conditions for the cover and the exclusion and invalidation clauses.

The certificate (or a temporary cover note proving cover until the certificate is issued) which is *proof* (or evidence) of cover must show the dates between which the cover is valid, give particulars of any conditions subject to which the policy is issued (eg the permitted purposes for which the vehicle may be used and those which are not permitted) and must relate to the vehicles covered, either individually by registration number or by specification, and to the persons who are authorized to drive them.

Production of insurance certificate
It is necessary to produce a current certificate of insurance when making application for an excise licence (road tax) for a vehicle. Alternatively, a temporary cover note may be produced and this will be accepted, but the insurance policy document itself is not acceptable.

The owner (ie registered keeper) of a motor vehicle must produce a certificate of insurance relating to the vehicle if required to do so by a police officer. If he is not able to produce the certificate on the spot, or if an employed driver is required to produce a certificate of insurance for the vehicle he is driving, it may be produced for inspection no later than seven days from the date of the request by the police officer, at any police station that the owner or driver chooses. The person to whom the request is made does not have to produce the certificate personally, but may have somebody else take it to the nominated police station for him. A valid temporary cover note would suffice instead of the certificate if this has not yet been issued.

Document checking and control procedures

It is incumbent upon transport operators to ensure they have properly established systems for the control of relevant documents. Many of these documents are required by law, for example those relating to vehicle and goods licensing, tachograph records, vehicle maintenance records and so on, which must be kept for specified minimum periods of time (eg tachograph records – 12 months; maintenance records – 15 months) and which must be produced for inspection at the request of the appropriate authorities.

Accounting records, including wage records and records relating to the deduction and payment of income tax and National Insurance contributions, VAT records and a host of records required under employment legislation must also be kept for specified periods of time and produced for inspection on request – the former for at least six years.

Busy though the operator may be, he should not neglect compliance with all these varying but nevertheless important requirements. In most cases, the legal minima for record keeping, document checking and control procedures are explained in the relevant parts of this study manual.

F4. MARKET ORGANIZATION

The market in road haulage is divided initially into two main sectors: professional (ie hire or reward) road haulage; and own-account operation.

These sectors may be further subdivided in a variety of ways. Road hauliers, for example, may be general or specialist hauliers, or may offer logistics services on a contract basis. The sector also divides between those firms which provide only national (or domestic) haulage services and those which offer international services.

The differences mentioned above are reflected in the types of operator licence required as follows and described in detail elsewhere; for professional haulage: standard licence (national) and standard licence (national and international); for own-account operations: restricted licence.

Regulatory authority and bodies

The UK road haulage market is substantially regulated by relevant Acts of Parliament and associated regulations set out in the form of Statutory Instruments and Orders. Account has also to be taken of European Union Directives and regulations issued by the European Commission (EC), too numerous to list here.

Two key Acts to take note of are the Transport Act 1968, in which the current UK system of operators' licensing is founded, and the Transport Act 1985, which was introduced to amend the law relating to road passenger transport, including the abolition of road service licensing and to make provision for:

- the transfer of operations of the National Bus Company (NBC) to the private sector;
- the reorganization of passenger transport in the private sector;
- local and central government financial support for certain passenger transport services and travel concessions;
- further powers for London Regional Transport;
- new powers and proceedings for the Transport Tribunal;
- grants payable under s92 of Finance Act 1965; and
- establishing a Disabled Persons Transport Advisory Committee.

In reconstituting the Transport Tribunal, the Act removed the previous restriction on the number of members and the requirement to sit in two divisions.

Powers of the Secretary of State
The Secretary of State (SoS) is a prime-ministerial appointee who heads a government department and sits in the Cabinet. Basically, the role is similar to that of a Minister of State, but in a more senior capacity – an SoS may have a number of ministers in charge of individual branches (portfolios) within the ministry that he or she heads.

Acts of Parliament (statutes) give the SoS discretionary powers to issue regulations (Statutory Instruments) and implement Orders which bring into force legal provisions outlined in an Act and set out the detailed aspects of such provisions. The duty of the SoS is to make the law, not interpret its meaning, which is the role of the courts.

The Office of Fair Trading
The Office of Fair Trading (OFT) was founded to promote and safeguard the interests of consumers by administering competition and consumer affairs legislation. It investigates:

- agreements that restrict the freedom of individual companies;
- companies that unfairly exploit their dominant position in any market; and
- traders who persistently neglect their obligations to consumers.

The Monopolies and Mergers Commission
The Monopolies and Mergers Commission (MMC) is a statutory body set up to inquire into matters referred to it relating to mergers, monopolies, anti-competitive practices and the performance of public sector bodies. It is independent of government in its conduct of inquiries and in its conclusions.

International movements

Border controls
The Single European Market has brought with it significant change in the hitherto bureaucratic, time-consuming and costly administrative procedures that were a necessity when transporting goods across national boundaries. Fundamental to the whole concept of the Single European Market is that EU citizens, goods, money and services should be able to pass (or be transacted) freely across internal borders between member states. However, it is still a legal requirement that EU citizens carry their national passports when travelling abroad (even within the Union). This applies equally to transport drivers whose passports also provide suitable identification for other purposes (eg to substantiate travellers' or Eurocheque encashments and other payments). However, within the Union

most travellers find that frontier crossing authorities take only a cursory glance at the cover of the document.

Community Road Haulage Authorizations

One of the most important legislative steps taken to allow freedom of movement for goods between member states directly affects road transport. The complex and restrictive system of Union and bilateral permits and quota allocations necessary for international road haulage journeys within the EU, which also applied to transit traffic to and from non-EU member countries, have been abolished. From 1 January 1993 a new system of Community Authorizations was implemented to enable EU hauliers to operate freely (ie to undertake as many journeys as they wish) *between* member states – not to be confused with the quite separate Cabotage Authorizations which are necessary to operate *within* member states other than their own (see below).

However, it is important to note the continuing requirement for certain permit authorizations when operating road haulage journeys *outside* the EU (see page 201).

EU Regulation 881/92 – Community Authorization

EU Regulation 881/92 is the regulation providing for the new system of Community Authorizations for intra-Union international road haulage. It amends earlier legislation (EU Regulations 1841/88 and 3164/76 on access to the market in the international carriage of goods by road) by effectively introducing qualitative criteria in place of the previous system of quantitative restriction. The qualitative criteria are as specified in EU Regulation 561/74 as amended by 438/89, namely a requirement for the operator to be of good repute, of adequate financial standing and professionally competent in road haulage operations.

International carriage

For the purposes of this regulation, 'international carriage' means:

1. where a goods vehicle departs from one and arrives in another member state (whether transiting other member states or non-member countries en route); or
2. where a vehicle departs from a non-member country and arrives in a member state or vice versa (with or without transit through one or more member states or non-member countries en-route); or
3. where a vehicle departs from and arrives in a non-member country but travels via a member state en route.

This definition also includes all unladen journeys undertaken in conjunction with the carriage of goods on the defined journeys.

UK Issue of Community Authorizations

The UK issues these Authorizations (under the provisions of EU Regulation 881/92) via Traffic Area Offices on an automatic basis to all existing operators holding a standard international licence (ie there will be no need for existing operators to apply for these Authorizations) and to new operators, as a matter of course, with the issue of their new licence documents.

The Authorization comprises an original document to be retained safely at the licence holder's main place of business, and a number of certified copies equalling the total number of vehicles authorized on the operator's licence. One of the certified copies of the Authorization must be carried in each vehicle undertaking international journeys within the EU.

Penalties for infringement of Authorizations

An international haulier who jeopardizes his 'O' licence by reason of failing to meet the requirements of good repute, financial standing or professional competence will also jeopardize his Community Authorization. In other words, where circumstances arise which require suspension or revocation of an 'O' licence, the Community Authorization will also be automatically suspended or withdrawn (ie revoked). Where curtailment of an 'O' licence is deemed to be necessary, the certified true copies of the Community Authorization will be temporarily or partially suspended according to the seriousness of the infringement of relevant regulations.

In member states where no 'O' licence or its equivalent is issued, failure to meet (or maintain) standards of good repute, financial standing and professional competence will result in direct jeopardy of the Community Authorization.

It is a specific requirement that where one member state becomes aware of infringement of Community Authorization legislation by a haulier from another member state, it shall inform the authorities in that member state and may ask that state to impose sanctions on the haulier in accordance with the regulations (ie for temporary or partial suspension of certified copies or withdrawal of the Community Authorization).

Community Authorizations and the certified copies carried on vehicles must be produced for inspection on request. Failure to do so, and not to carry the certified copy on a vehicle while on an international journey within the EU, is an offence.

Validity and duration of Authorizations

Community Authorizations are to be made out in the original licence holder's name and are not transferable to any third party. They are valid for five years. Certified copies as mentioned above, must be carried on the relevant vehicle when on an international journey and must be produced by the driver for examination whenever he is required to do so by an authorized inspecting officer.

On the expiry of a Community Authorization, it is a requirement that the issuing authority (in the UK the TCs on behalf of the Department of Environment, Transport and the Regions) must verify whether the operator still satisfies the legal conditions for its issue. Since these conditions are identical to those on which renewal of the haulier's 'O' licence depends, namely good repute, financial standing and professional competence, UK operators whose 'O' licences are renewed will have their Community Authorization automatically re-supplied at the same time.

Authorization document

Annex I to the EU Regulation (EU 881/92) illustrates a model for the Community Authorization, the front page of which contains details of the haulier, date and authority for its issue and dates of its validity; on the back are the general provisions for the use of such Authorizations, in particular that while within the territory of any member state the holder (ie operator and driver) must comply with the 'laws, regulations and administrative provisions in force in that state', especially in regard to transport and traffic.

Exemptions from requirement for Community Authorization

Certain transport operations are specifically exempt from the requirement for Community Authorizations in accordance with Annex II to the regulations, as follows:

- Carriage of mail as a public service.
- Carriage of vehicles which have suffered damage or breakdown.
- Carriage of goods in vehicles with a permissible laden weight (including that of any trailer drawn) which does not exceed 6 tonnes or the maximum permitted payload of which does not exceed 3.5 tonnes.
- Carriage of goods in vehicles owned (including hired) by an own-account firm solely for its own purposes, plus where the transport is no more than ancillary to its overall activities and where the vehicle is driven only by an employee of the firm.
- Carriage of medicinal products, appliances, equipment and other articles required for medicinal care in emergency relief, in particular for natural disasters.

Bilateral road haulage permits

Certain road haulage operations from the UK and other EU member states to non-EU member states still require the issue of a bilateral road haulage permit (see Table 6.1). At the present time road haulage journeys to or through Belarus, Estonia, Georgia, Kazakhstan, Moldova, Morocco, Russia, Turkey, Tunisia, Ukraine and Uzbekistan require such permits or authorizations for specified transport operations. Third country permits are required for journeys from either Germany or Romania.

Bilateral road haulage permits are not required for transport operations within the EU or for journeys to or through Bulgaria, Croatia, Czech Republic, Hungary, Latvia, Lithuania, Macedonia, Moldova, Norway, Poland, Romania, Slovakia, Slovenia and Switzerland. However, hauliers on transit journeys across Community territory to such destinations must be in possession of a Community Authorization.

Validity of permits

Where bilateral road haulage permits are required as described above (see also Table 6.1), such permits are available covering single journeys only, allowing just *one* return journey to be undertaken between the dates shown on the permit. Outside of these dates the permit is invalid and it would be illegal to commence or continue the journey.

In the case of Turkey, single journey permits as described above are available as well as multiple journey permits authorizing four journeys.

For Austria, normal termination permits are available for journeys destined for that country, but for transit traffic the Eco-points system applies whereby the haulier has to obtain stamps to affix to an Eco card (see below).

Single journey permits are valid only between the dates shown, as mentioned above. Permits for Austria are valid for two months from the date of issue, while those for Turkey, Russia, Estonia, Ukraine and Belarus are valid from the date of issue until 31 December.

Return of used permits

Used and expired permits must be returned to the issuing authority not later than 15 days after the relevant journey has been completed or the permit expiry date, whichever is earlier.

Journey record sheets issued with period permits (eg the four-journey permit for Turkey) must be returned within the same timescale.

Lost or stolen permits

Road haulage permits are valuable transit documents and as such should be treated with care and appropriate security. They are not transferable to another operator and such misuse is illegal throughout the Union, with harsh penalties imposed on offenders (see also below). Replacement of lost or stolen permits is not normally automatic, and in any case a full written explanation of the circumstances surrounding the loss or theft is required, together with a copy of the police report.

Third country traffic

Third country traffic, which is the carriage of goods between two countries other than the one in which the vehicle is registered, is permissible in certain cases. For UK hauliers, journeys are permissible between any two EU countries, and the following applies when goods are carried between any EU country and a non-EU country:

- It is permissible with Austria, Bulgaria, Belarus,* Czech Republic, Denmark, Estonia, Finland, France, Germany,* Hungary, Latvia, Luxembourg, Netherlands, Norway, Poland, Republic of Ireland, Romania,* Russia, Slovak Republic, Sweden, Turkey* and Ukraine.
- It is permissible with Portugal, Spain and Switzerland only where in the course of its journey the vehicle passes in transit through the UK.
- It is permissible with Croatia, and Greece (except for UK vehicles carrying goods to that country from the Republic of Ireland), subject to special permission first being obtained from the competent authorities of those countries.
- It is not permissible with Belgium and Italy.

* Permits valid for third country traffic are available and full details can be obtained from the IRFO.

Issue of permits

Road haulage permits where necessary as described above are issued by the relevant authority in each member state. Normally, this involves completion of application forms, advance payment of the relevant fee and submission by the applicant of a copy of his authority to operate (eg his Community Authorization).

Journeys to or through non-agreement countries

If vehicles are to travel to or through a country with which an EU member state has no agreement, permission to operate in that country has to be sought direct from its transport authority. Application should be made well before the journey is due and full details of the vehicle, the load and the route should be given.

ECMT permits for non-EU journeys

A number of ECMT (European Conference of Ministers of Transport) permits are allocated to the UK each year for haulage journeys between ECMT member countries (all EU member states plus Albania, Armenia, Azerbajan, Belarus, Bulgaria, Bosnia Herzegovina, Croatia, Czech Republic, Estonia, Georgia, Hungary, Iceland, Latvia, Lithuania, Macedonia, Moldova, Norway, Poland, Romania, Slovakia, Slovenia, Switzerland and Turkey). However, the validity of some permits is limited in certain countries, particularly Austria.

These ECMT permits allow journeys between member countries, including laden or empty transit journeys and third country journeys to other ECMT countries, which are prohibited by certain bilateral agreements. However, they cannot be used for transit of ECMT countries on journeys to non-ECMT states or for cabotage. They are for hire or reward journeys only and may not be used by unaccompanied trailers or semi-trailers. They are valid for one calendar year and allow an unlimited number of journeys within that period, but they may be used with only one vehicle at a time. The quota for their issue is limited, so these permits are allocated before the beginning of the year in which they are issued. Usually no further supplies are available during the course of the year, but should the quota be increased an announcement is made in the trade press.

ECMT removals permits
These permits are quota-free and can be used for international removals between, or crossing, ECMT member countries. They are available only to firms employing the specialized equipment and staff needed to undertake such operations and are valid for one year from the date of issue.

Permit checks

As a result of the exposure of a number of cases of permit frauds, stringent regulations have been made to prevent vehicles on international journeys travelling without valid permits (see above) and checks are made on vehicles to ensure that these regulations are complied with. A vehicle will be prevented from continuing its journey if it does not carry a valid permit.

In the UK the International Road Haulage Permits Act 1975 makes it an offence to forge or alter permits, to make a false statement to obtain a permit, or to allow one to be used by another person.

Eco-points system for transit journeys through Austria
Transit permits previously required for authorizing journeys through Austria have been abolished but have been replaced by a new system involving the issue of Eco-point stamps. This scheme is intended to reduce the effects of air pollution created by exhaust emissions from heavy lorries in transit through the country, hence Eco- (ecology) points. It is intended to benefit operators who use 'less polluting' vehicles. The number of Eco-points available (both to the UK and other EU member states) will decrease annually, thereby reducing the total number of transit journeys permitted unless greater use is made of ecologically-friendly vehicles.

Table 6.1 Permit requirements

Type of operation
1. Own-account carriage
2. Unaccompanied trailer/semi-trailer
3. Unladen in transit
4. Unladen relief vehicle
5. Unladen entry to collect goods
6. Airports – re-routed goods
7. Airports – carriage of luggage
8. Carriage of broken-down vehicles
9. Funeral transport
10. Works of art for fairs/exhibitions
11. Works of art for commercial purposes
12. Carriage of antiques
13. Goods for publicity or information purposes
14. Sports/theatre/media
15. Fairs and exhibitions
16. Animal carcasses *not* for human consumption
17. Animal carcasses *for* human consumption
18. Household removals
19. Carriage of mails
20. Refuse and sewage
21. Bees and fish fry
22. Valuable goods
23. Medical emergencies
24. Vehicles with plw* not over 3.5 tonnes
25. Vehicles with ulw** not over 6 tonnes
26. Payload not over 3.5 tonnes
27. Abnormal loads
28. Spare parts for sea-going vessels
39. Ships provisions
30. Transit traffic

plw = permissible laden weight
**ulw = unladen weight

	EU States	Austria	Belarus*	Estonia	Morocco	Russia	Tunisia	Turkey	Ukraine
1.	–	O	P	P	P	P	P	P	–
2.	C	–	P	P	P	P	P	P	P
3.	C	E	P	P	P	P	P	P	P
4.	C	–	P	P	P	P	P	P	P
5.	C	P	P	P	P	P	P	P	P
6.	C	–	P	P	–	P	P	–	P
7.	C	–	P	P	P	P	–	–	P
8.	–	–	–	–	P	–	–	–	–

Table 6.1 *continued*

	EU States	Austria	Belarus*	Estonia	Morocco	Russia	Tunisia	Turkey	Ukraine
9.	C	–	–	P	P	–	P	–	P
10.	C	–	–	–	P	–	–	P	–
11.	C	–	P	–	P	P	–	P	–
12.	C	–	P	P	P	P	–	P	P
13.	C	–	P	–	P	P	P	P	–
14.	C	–	–	–	P	–	–	–	–
15.	C	–	–	–	P	–	–	–	–
16.	C	–	P	P	P	P	P	–	P
17.	C	–	P	P	P	P	P	P	P
18.	C	–	–	P	P	P	–	P	P
19.	–	–	–	–	P	–	P	–	–
20.	C	–	P	P	P	P	P	–	P
21.	C	–	P	P	P	P	P	–	
22.	C	P	P	P	–				
23.	–	–		–	–		–	–	
24.	–	–	–	–	P	P	–	P	–
25.	–	–	–	–	P	P	P	P	–
26.	–	–	–	–	P	P	P	P	–
27.	S	S	S	S	S	S	S	S	S
28.	C	–	P	P	P	P	–	P	P
29.	C	–	P	P	P	P	P	P	P
30.	C	E	P	P	P	P	P	P	P

– = no permit needed
C = Community Authorization
E = Ecopoint system
O = own-account document
P = bilateral permit required
S = special permit required

*bilateral agreement not signed yet (informal arrangement at present)

Source: A Guide to Taking Your Lorry Abroad, International Road Freight Office. Newcastle upon Tyne

The broad principle of the system is that the greater the potential exhaust emission, the greater the number of Eco-point stamps the haulier will have to submit to fulfil his journey. Conversely, the lower the potential exhaust emission, the fewer the number of stamps required.

Verification of vehicle exhaust emissions will be by means of a CoP (Conformity of Production) document issued to vehicle operators and required to be produced at the border on entry to Austria.

It is emphasized that for journeys terminating in Austria existing permit requirements continue to apply (see above) but Eco-point stamps are *not* required. They are not required either for operations carried out under an ECMT permit.

Eco-point exemptions
Certain transport operations are exempt from the Eco-points system as follows:

- Occasional freight movements by road to and from airports in the event of diversion of air services.
- Transport of baggage in the trailers of vehicles intended for the carriage of passengers and baggage transport using vehicles of any kind to and from airports.
- Transport of post.
- Transport of damaged vehicles or vehicles requiring repair.
- Transport of refuse and faecal matter.
- Transport of animal carcasses intended for disposal.
- Transport of bees and fish fry.
- Funeral transport.
- Transport of objects d'art and works of art for exhibitions and for professional purposes.
- Occasional freight transport for reasons exclusively relating to publicity and education.
- Removals transport (ie household removals) carried out by companies employing qualified workers and having the necessary equipment.
- Transport of instruments, accessories and animals to and from theatrical, musical, cinema, sport and circus performances, exhibitions or fairs, and to or from radio recordings, filming sessions or television recordings.
- Transport of spare parts intended for ships and aeroplanes.
- An unladen journey by a freight transport vehicle intended to replace a vehicle which has broken down en route and the subsequent transport operation carried out by this replacement vehicle under cover of the authorization allocated to the defective vehicle.
- Transport of emergency medical aid (in particular during natural disasters).
- Transport of securities (for example precious metals) in specialized vehicles, accompanied by the police or other security services.

The Eco-points system
The Eco-points system comprises Eco-point stamps and Eco cards (plus the issue of the CoP document for relevant vehicles as described below). To undertake international road haulage journeys which involve a transit crossing of Austria, operators need a supply of Eco-point stamps and an Eco card on which to stick them for each leg of the journey (ie one each for the outward and homeward bound transit of Austria).

Eco cards

These cards are readily available on application to national transport authorities (in the UK, the International Road Freight Office – IRFO), usually free with the issue of Eco-points stamps (see below), or they may be purchased from the Austrian authorities on reaching the border.

The Eco card comprises three pages, which have to be completed by the haulage operator or the driver prior to entering Austria:

- Page one has space for affixing the Eco-points stamps, which must be cancelled by the driver signing across their face before crossing into the country. This page will be detached and retained by the Austrian authorities.
- Page two (with carbon copies) requires details to be completed of the vehicle, load and journey (including, where possible, the postcode of both loading and unloading locations – but an offence is not committed if this information is omitted). This page will be stamped by the authorities at the border, confirming the number of Eco-points stamps used, and a copy will be given to the driver to be carried for the rest of the journey as proof that Eco-points stamps have been paid.*
- Page three lists the appropriate codes for the Austrian border controls and international distinguishing signs to be used when completing page two of the document.

* It is important to note that this copy (page two of the Eco card) must be returned to the issuing authority, complete with operator's name, address and reference number within seven days of use (ie of completing the journey) – future issues of Eco-points stamps will depend on it.

Eco-points stamps

Eco-points stamps (each worth one Eco-point) are issued solely by national transport authorities in connection with international road haulage journeys involving transit through Austria. For this purpose, the Austrian authorities 'charge' vehicles with Eco-points in accordance with the following rules: for vehicles first registered prior to 1 October 1990 and those not carrying a CoP document (see below) – 16 Eco-points (16 Eco-points stamps); for vehicles carrying a CoP document – the number of Eco-points equal to the rounded (up or down) CoP value shown on the CoP document.

Conformity of Production (CoP) documents

CoP documents are issued by the relevant transport authority (in the UK, the IRFO) on application by road hauliers for vehicles first registered from 1 October 1990 whose engines have a lower Nox emission than older vehicles.

Operators are required to supply the following information in respect of each vehicle (ie those to be used for journeys involving transit through Austria):

- vehicle registration number;
- the date of first registration;
- the type approval number;
- the chassis number.

The CoP document (each vehicle will carry an individual one that is non-transferable) shows the Nox emission value and the CoP value (the Nox emission value plus 10 per cent) for the vehicle. It also indicates the corresponding number of Eco-points stamps that will be needed for each single-leg journey by that vehicle.

The document must be carried on the vehicle to verify its so-called 'greener' performance. When shown at the Austrian border, the authorities will charge fewer Eco-points stamps to permit the transit journey through the country (see above).

Own-account transport operations

Own-account transport operations within Community territory are now free from all road haulage permit requirements (under the provisions of EC Regulation 881/92 Annex II) provided that goods are carried solely in connection with the trade or business of the vehicle user and are not carried for hire or reward, and that the following conditions are also met:

1. The goods carried must be the property of the business (of the vehicle user) or must have been sold, bought, let out or hired, produced, extracted, processed or repaired by the business.
2. The purpose of the journey must be to carry the goods to or from the business or to move them, either within the business or outside, for its own needs.
3. Motor vehicles used for the carriage must be driven by employees of the business.
4. The vehicles carrying the goods must be owned by the business or have been bought by it on deferred terms or hire (this does not apply where a replacement vehicle is used during a short breakdown of the vehicle normally used).
5. Road haulage must not be the major activity of the business.

Own-account operations between the UK, Austria, Cyprus and Hungary are free from permit requirements, but in the case of such journeys, drivers should carry on the vehicle a document containing the following information to confirm that the operation is solely for own-account purposes:

- The name and address of the vehicle operator (ie user).
- The nature of the operator's trade or business.
- The nature of the goods being carried.
- The location of the loading and unloading points.
- The registration number of the vehicle on which the goods are carried.
- Details of the route to be followed.

In all cases, own-account vehicle operators (and their drivers) should be aware that they may be asked to provide satisfactory evidence to help the authorities to determine the ownership of the goods, and also prove that the goods are being carried solely for own-account purposes.

Road haulage cabotage

Cabotage operation is provided for under the Treaty of Rome. A UK transport minister was reported as saying that, 'the liberalization of cabotage is essential to the creation of a true single market in road haulage', and furthermore, 'it would help to reduce the wasteful costs associated with empty running, bringing both economic and environmental benefits, and would open up exciting new markets for hauliers'.

Cabotage is quite simply internal haulage by foreign transport operators – the collection and delivery of goods by road within a country by a road haulier whose business is established in another country. The significance of cabotage, of course, is that it protects internal haulage markets against incursion – or in this case the abstraction of domestic traffics – by outsiders (see below). Hence the reason why, hitherto, it has always been an illegal practice, but now with the liberalization policies of the Single European Market in force, such restrictive practices have been swept away and road freight cabotage within EU member states is permitted by regulation.

Cabotage by EU own-account road transport operators is permitted, but only on the same basis as defined above (ie item 4 under exemptions from Community Authorization requirements).

Distortion of domestic haulage markets

Provision is included in the EU regulation for safeguard measures to be implemented – on the authority of the Commission of the EU – where cabotage operations cause or lead to serious disturbance of the national transport market in a given geographical area.

In practice, the operation of road haulage cabotage in the early days of the liberalization process appears to have had negligible impact on domestic haulage markets – no more than 0.25 per cent, according to EU Transport Commissioner, Neil Kinnock – and most of that probably within Germany by Dutch and Belgian hauliers.

The permanent cabotage regime

Council Regulation (EEC) 3118/93 (of 25 October 1993) initially limited access to cabotage within the EU on the basis of a quota system only, with specified annually increasing numbers of cabotage permits being available for member states. These permits were obtainable by road hauliers who wished to operate internally within other member states so long as they held a valid Community Authorization permitting international road haulage operations. The total allocation of cabotage permits throughout the EU (acknowledged by the issuing authorities to be more than adequate to meet current demand) increased by some 30 per cent or more annually until the quota system was legally abolished and replaced by the so-called 'permanent cabotage regime' (ie total liberalization of the European Union road haulage market) from 1 July 1998.

With the permanent cabotage regime, all international road hauliers holding Community Authorizations are entitled to operate temporary road haulage services in member states other than their own without any restriction as to quantitative limits or any requirement for a registered office or any other establishment in that state. There is no longer any requirement for transport operators to obtain cabotage authorization or for goods vehicles to carry cabotage permits. However, they have to comply with the laws, regulations and administrative provisions in force in the 'host' country including those concerning:

- rates and conditions incorporated in haulage contracts;
- weights and dimensions of road vehicles – which may, in fact, exceed those of the home country, but must not in any case exceed the vehicle's design standards;
- dangerous goods, perishable foodstuffs and live animals;
- goods vehicle drivers' hours and rest periods;
- VAT on transport services (see also below).

The word 'temporary' used in the context above means that cabotage permit holders may enter a member state (temporarily) and carry out internal road haulage journeys as required. It does not mean that they have the right to establish a permanent haulage operation in that country. If a haulier is established on a permanent basis within a member state, or wishes to be so, so that he can operate domestic haulage, then he must conform to the relevant national legislation of that state relating to internal haulage.

VAT on cabotage operations
Internal transport operations under cabotage authorization requires operators to comply with national VAT regulations. For this purpose, operators may need to register in the member states in which they are operating or appoint a suitable VAT agent or fiscal representative to handle these matters on their behalf.

Prohibited operations, offences and penalties
Cabotage by hauliers and own-account operators in non-EU states is prohibited.

Non-resident hauliers who infringe either the cabotage rules when operating in a state other than that in which their business is established, or who otherwise offend against Community or national transport legislation while in such states, may be penalized by the host nation, on a non-discriminatory basis. Penalties may comprise an official warning or, in the case of more serious or repeated infringements, a temporary ban on cabotage. Where falsified cabotage documents are found these will be confiscated immediately and returned to the appropriate authority in the haulier's own country.

Member states are required to cooperate in applying the cabotage rules and may ask another member state to impose penalties on its own hauliers who are found to have breached these rules – even to the point of withdrawing an offending haulier's right to operate (in the case of a UK haulier this could mean loss of his 'O' licence). Additionally, the haulier may be prosecuted for relevant offences and brought before a court in his home country for offences committed in another EU member state.

Documentation to be carried on the vehicle

International haulage operations largely depend for their efficiency on having the correct documentation. Incorrectly completed or missing documents cause problems for drivers at points of entry to and exit from national states (within the EU and beyond) and can result in extensive delays for vehicles and, consequently, considerable extra cost.

The following documents should be carried on a vehicle making an international journey:

For the driver:

- his national (ie new EU-type) driving licence;
- an international driving licence (where appropriate – see below);
- a translation of the driving licence (where appropriate – eg for Italy);
- his passport (current and valid to cover the period away from the UK);

- an entry visa (where appropriate – see list of countries below);
- a letter of authority to have charge of the vehicle (on company letter-heading);
- a bail bond (for Spain only – usually issued with the insurance green card);
- tachograph charts (where applicable – ie for vehicles over 3.5 tonnes);
- ADR training certificate (if applicable).

For the vehicle:

- the registration document (original form V5 – log book for NI vehicles);
- a current tax disc displayed in the windscreen (showing full duty paid);
- the current 'O' licence disc displayed in the windscreen;
- the certificate of insurance;
- insurance green card (not compulsory but advisable);
- copies of the vehicle annual test and plating certificate;
- road haulage/cabotage authorization permit (as appropriate);
- *Carnet de passage en douane* for certain countries (see also page 23)
  - France (no longer required for plated trailers and semi-trailers),
  - Gibraltar,
  - Greece (if staying longer than 10 days),
  - Italy (for vehicles remaining more than three months),
  - Portugal (triptype for spare parts);
- nationality plate (in the UK, a GB plate);
- Eco-points card and stamps (for Austria).

For the load:

- road haulage/cabotage permit/Community Authorization (where applicable);
- CMR consignment note (for haulage operations or own-account certificate);
- carnet (as appropriate)
  - TIR,
  - ATA (for temporary importation of goods);
- copies of invoices for the goods;
- certificate of origin/health/consular certificates (where appropriate);
- certificates issued under the following conventions (as appropriate)
  - ADR (for dangerous goods – see page 290),
  - ATP (for perishable foodstuffs – see page 317).

Full details of the requirements for documents in respect of individual countries may be obtained from the International Road Freight Office. It should be noted that when on an international journey, certain documents may be required only in particular circumstances, whereas others are required at all times.

A *national identification plate* should always be fixed to the vehicle when it is travelling in a country other than that of its registration.

The driver should carry his *passport* (and visa, which is usually stamped in the passport – see also below) with him at *all* times, when in the vehicle and when away from it (eg when out for a meal in the evening). The passport provides a means of identification and carrying it everywhere helps to prevent it being stolen, which could then result in difficulties when crossing borders.

The driver should have with him in the vehicle the *original* of the *vehicle registration document* and a *letter of authorization* from the vehicle owners, confirming that he is authorized to be in possession of the vehicle.

In some countries a British/Euro driving licence is not sufficient to meet national requirements. In these circumstances the driver should have an *international driving permit (IDP)* which is obtainable from the AA, RAC or RSAC and the National Breakdown Recovery Club. Spain and Italy are two examples of countries where the old British green-type licences are not generally acceptable. An applicant for an IDP must be a UK resident and aged 18 years or over.

A *visa* is required by the driver for visiting certain countries (not EU member states). Employers should obtain the visas from the relevant country's embassy in Britain or from the British embassy in countries to be visited. Among the countries for which visas are required are Bulgaria, CIS, Romania and Turkey.

F5. CUSTOMS PROCEDURES

The opening of the Single European Market in 1993 brought significant changes in Customs procedures and documentation requirements. All Customs barriers to trade within the European Union were effectively abolished and international transport operators no longer have to comply with the complex and burdensome task of completing, and producing for inspection and stamping, a whole range of hitherto required paperwork.

Goods shipped to EU destinations are no longer classified as exports provided they are of EU origin and in free circulation, in which case they do not require Customs control documentation of any kind. However, where goods are not in free circulation within the EU, certain Community Transit (CT) procedures remain in force. Where vehicles travel within the EU on a non-regular ferry service (ie one that has visited a port of call outside the EU or in an EU Freezone port area), Form T2L will be required on disembarkation to satisfy T2 status requirements.

Where goods are exported to or imported from non-EU destinations then other Customs procedures apply (eg export/import declarations) and must be explicitly followed if additional costs and delays en route are to be avoided.

Customs and Excise authorities in the UK and elsewhere have an interest in all international goods vehicle movements for a number of reasons:

- it is their duty to ensure that where imported or exported goods are subject to duty or tariff those duties or tariffs are collected;
- their role is to control the import/export of restricted and prohibited goods – this could be anything from arms and other weapons to drugs, pornographic literature and other contraband;
- they fulfil a role in gathering trade statistics for governments.

In carrying out these duties, of necessity to ensure that nothing slips through their net, a range of disciplined procedures and official documentation has been established for dealing with both imported and exported traffics.

Despatches within the EU

As stated above, goods which originate in or are in free circulation within the EU (ie that have 'Community status') and which are transported from the UK to destinations within the EU (or vice versa), or between EU member states, are not subject to Customs procedure. The only documentation required is that necessary to prove 'Community status', namely an Intrastat invoice (see Customs Notice 750) showing a valid VAT number, a transport document (Form T1) and, where appropriate, a completed Copy 4 of the Single Administrative Document (SAD).

Customs entry for exports outside the EU

When goods are exported to non-EU countries an 'entry' or declaration must be made to Customs and Excise (with certain exceptions). A number of different procedures are used for export clearance as follows:

- Pre-entry.
- Non-statistical procedure.
- Low value goods procedure.
- Simplified Clearance Procedure (SCP).
- Local Export Control (LEC).
- Period entry (exports).

Pre-entry or pre-shipment declaration

This is the normal method for making full export declarations for Customs clearance of goods using the SAD – Form C88 (available from local offices of HM Customs and Excise) which is presented with the goods at the office of export. The following details may be omitted from pre-entry declarations if not available in advance:

- date of shipment;
- ship name/flight number;
- dock/station;
- port or airport of export;
- flag code;
- port code.

Non-statistical procedure
The export of certain goods is of no statistical interest to Customs and may therefore follow the non-statistical procedure. Mainly this scheme applies to household and personal effects being sent abroad, goods for the Channel Islands and certain temporary exports. If the goods are not dutiable or restricted an export declaration can be made with an approved commercial document or a partly completed Copy 2 of the SAD. For dutiable and restricted goods a full export declaration must be made.

Low value goods procedure
For single consignments of certain low value goods not exceeding £600 in total value and with a net weight not exceeding 1000kg, the low value procedure can be used where the goods are not dutiable or restricted. Such goods may be presented for export with either a copy of an approved commercial document or a partially completed Copy 2 of the SAD.

Simplified Clearance Procedure (SCP)
This is an alternative to pre-entry and involves the use of either an approved commercial document or a partly completed Copy 2 of the SAD. Conditions for using the procedure are that exporters must be registered with Customs as an SCP user, the goods concerned must not be dutiable or restricted, and the shipper does not have enough information available to complete the full SAD (C88) at the time of export. Once the consignment has been despatched, the Customs Tariff and Statistical Office must, within 14 days, be provided with a fully completed SAD.

Local Export Control (LEC)
Where an exporter has large or regular consignments for Customs pre-entry application can be made to HM Customs and Excise for clearance at the exporter's (or carrier's) premises, subject to certain conditions, under what is known as the local export control (LEC) procedure.

Period entry (exports)

Regular exporters of large quantities of goods whose systems are computerized may use the period entry (exports) system under which simplified pre-shipment documents are used at the time of export, with full statistical information about the exported goods being supplied via computer media (tape, disk, etc) later – usually returns are made twice a month.

Customs entry for non-EU imports

Goods imported into the UK which have not originated in or are not in free circulation within the EU must comply with Customs' import entry procedure. In some cases such loads are cleared on arrival in the UK and are moved inland by domestic hauliers so, in the main, there is not the same requirement for the driver to have to deal with specialized documentation. Where loads are not been cleared at first port of arrival, the driver is responsible for producing the goods and the T-form (see below) to a valid Office of Destination within the UK.

Goods in free circulation within the EU and covered by a T2 declaration do not require an import entry unless they are from one of the so-called 'special territories' such as the Channel Islands, the Canaries, Andorra and San Marino.

Goods not in free circulation within the EU (eg T1 status goods) require an import entry providing all the necessary details required by Customs.

T-forms

T-forms or declarations are known as 'movement documents' (ie T1s and T2s which travel with the goods) or 'status' documents (T2Ls which do not travel with the goods) and indicate the Customs status of the goods to which they relate, as follows:

T1 used where the goods are not in 'free circulation' within the Community.

T2 used where the goods are in 'free circulation' within the Community.

T2L used when the goods are in 'free circulation' within the Community, but where the transit arrangements of the Community Transit (CT) system are not required.

SAD copies

For T1 and T2 declarations copies numbered 1, 4, 5 and 7 of the Single Administrative Document (SAD) are required. For T2L declarations copies numbered 1 and 4 only of the SAD are required.

Procedure when import documents are unavailable or unsatisfactory
Under the full Community transit procedure, the T-forms must accompany the goods and are therefore not available if import entry is made
prior to the arrival of the goods. In such instances the importer or his
agent should give the following undertaking on the entry: 'Transit documents will be produced to the import office'. However, it is important to
note that the T1 and the goods must still be presented to the Office of
Destination on arrival.

Goods removed for clearance elsewhere than place of importation
Where goods, other than spirits and tobacco, are removed for clearance
to an Office of Destination away from the place of importation (which
must be an approved Office of Destination), for instance to an Inland
Clearance Depot (ie a depot inland from the port of entry/exit, where
Customs have facilities to process and clear import/export consignments), they must move forward under existing documents unless the
guarantee is not valid for the UK. If the guarantee is in the form of a cash
deposit, a fresh cash deposit or bond will be required to cover the removal
of the goods within the UK.

Goods in transit through the UK
The normal UK transit documentation (SAD) and procedures apply to
goods imported under the full Community Transit procedure which are
in transit through this country for a destination elsewhere. If the goods
are moving in circumstances where the Community guarantee requirement is waived, security in the form of a guarantee is still required.

Customs documentation – Single Administrative Document
The Single Administrative Document (SAD – Form C88) was introduced
on 1 January 1988 to replace a large number of existing export, import
and transit documents. Its purpose is to simplify documentation, facili-
tate trade and computerize communication of Customs data throughout
the whole of the European Community. The SAD form is also used for
declarations for exports to and imports from non-Community countries.
   The SAD (Form C88) comprises an eight-part set:

Copy 1   Copy for the Customs Office of Departure.
Copy 2   Statistical copy (remains in country of despatch).
Copy 3   Consignor/exporter's copy (travels with the goods to the point
         of exit from the EU).
Copy 4   For Customs Office of Destination, or Community status
         (T2L) declaration (this copy is required for presentation to

Customs on arrival in an EFTA or VISEGRAD country where goods are to be cleared inland).

Copy 5   Return copy from Customs Office of Destination to prove that the goods arrived intact under Community Transit.

Copy 6   Copy for the country of destination (should be retained in case it is required).

Copy 7   Statistical copy for Customs in the country of destination.

Copy 8   Copy for the consignee.

Copies 1 and 3 remain in the country of origination (ie export) and copies 4, 5 and 7 travel forward with the goods, copy 5 eventually being returned to the office of departure.

TIR

Under the Customs Convention on the International Transport of Goods by Road (TIR Carnets) 1959, to which the UK is a party, goods in Customs-sealed vehicles or containers may travel through intermediate countries with the minimum of Customs formalities provided a TIR carnet has been issued in respect of the journey.

The carnet is a recognized international Customs document intended purely to simplify Customs procedures; it is not a substitute for other documents, nor is it mandatory for any operator to use it. It does not give any operator the right to run vehicles in any European country. Use of a carnet frees the operator from the need to place a deposit of duty in respect of the load he is carrying in each country through which the vehicle is to pass.

The issuing authorities for the carnets (in this country the FTA and the RHA) act as guarantors on behalf of the IRU (International Road Transport Union – the international guarantor), and for this reason carnets are only issued to bona fide members of these two associations.

Goods may only be carried under a TIR carnet provided the vehicle in which they are carried complies with special requirements and has been approved for this purpose by the Vehicle Inspectorate (an agency of the Department of the Environment, Transport and the Regions).

Approval for vehicles is only given if they are constructed so that the load-carrying space can be sealed by Customs, after which it must not be possible for any goods to be removed from or added to the load without the seals being broken, and there must be no concealed spaces where goods may be hidden.

Detailed requirements are laid down concerning the structure of the body, particularly regarding the manner in which it is assembled, so that there is no possibility of panels being removed by releasing nuts and bolts and so on. The manner in which doors and roller shutters are secured must also meet stringent specifications. Sheeted vehicles or containers may be used provided conditions relating to the construction of the sheet are observed and as long as when the closing device has been secured it becomes impossible to gain access to the load without leaving obvious traces.

The VI examines vehicles to ensure that they meet the technical requirements for operation under the TIR Convention and issues a certificate of approval, which must be renewed every two years and must be carried on the vehicle when it is operating under a TIR carnet. This latter point is particularly important as Customs authorities make random checks on vehicles leaving the UK to ensure that this certificate is being carried where necessary.

Application for the examination of vehicles or containers must be made to the VI, now VOSA, in the Traffic Area in which they are available for inspection (ie at a local goods vehicle testing station). The GVTS will provide the application form GV 62, and a leaflet setting out the technical conditions that have to be met. If a TIR-approved vehicle is sold to another operator, the TIR certificate (form GV 60) is not transferable and the new owner must have the vehicle re-certified if he wishes to use it for TIR operations.

TIR plates

When a vehicle has been approved it must display at the front and the rear a plate showing the letters 'TIR' in white on a blue background. Such plates are obtainable from the FTA and RHA. They should be removed or covered when the vehicle is no longer operating under TIR.

TIR carnets

TIR carnets are internationally recognized Customs' documents. They are in four parts and contain 6, 14 or 20 pages (*volets* in French). A 6-page carnet is valid only for a journey between the UK and one other country. Journeys to more than one other country require 14- or 20-page carnets which are valid for two months and three months respectively. A carnet covers only one load and if a return load is to be collected, a separate carnet is needed (each individual voucher covers one frontier crossing) and the driver should take this with him on the outward journey. Careful attention must be paid to the completion of the carnet if delays and difficulties are to be avoided.

Carnets are in pairs and have counterfoils in a bound cover. At each Customs point en route a voucher is detached and the counterfoil is stamped. Therefore a 14-page carnet may be used to cross six frontiers, the other pair of vouchers being required at the Customs Office of Departure.

The four parts of the carnet comprise the following:

Part 1   Details of the issuing authority, the carnet holder, the country of departure, the country of destination, the vehicle, the weight and the value of the goods as shown in the manifest.

Part 2   A declaration that the goods specified have been loaded for the country stated, that they will be carried to their destination with the Customs seals intact and that the Customs regulations of the countries through which the goods are to be carried will be observed.

Part 3   A goods manifest giving precise details of the goods, the way in which they are packed (the number of parcels or cartons) and their value.

Part 4   Vouchers which Customs officials at frontier posts will remove, stamping the counterfoil section which remains in the carnet.

Before obtaining a carnet the member must sign a form of contract with the issuing authority, agreeing to abide by all the necessary legal and administrative requirements. A financial guarantee is required to ensure that the member meets any claims that may be made against him.

Carnets are valid for limited periods only (see above), and if not used they must be returned to the issuing authority for cancellation. Those which are used and which bear all the official stampings acquired en route must also be returned within 10 days of the vehicle's return.

Strict instructions regarding the use of carnets are supplied by the issuing authorities, both for the operator and the driver. For example, the driver should never leave the carnet with any Customs authority without first obtaining a signed, stamped and dated declaration quoting the carnet number and certifying that the goods on the vehicle conform with the details contained in the carnet. Drivers should also ensure that the Customs officials at each departure office, transit office and arrival office take out a voucher from the carnet and stamp and sign the counterfoil accordingly.

If a Customs seal on a TIR vehicle is broken during transit for any reason, Customs officials or the police must be contacted immediately to endorse the carnet to this effect.

Carnets

Carnets de passage
Most European countries permit the temporary importation of foreign vehicles and containers (not to be confused with the loads they carry) free of duty or deposit and without guaranteed Customs documents. However, a *carnet de passage en douane pour l'admission temporaire* is required for vehicles and trailers entering Gibraltar, Iran, Iraq, Jordan,

Kuwait, Lebanon, Saudi Arabia, Syria, Turkey and other Middle East countries. It is also required for vehicles remaining in Greece for more than 10 days, in Italy for more than three months, and those remaining in Portugal for more than one month.

A deposit of duty in lieu of a *carnet de passage* is required for unaccompanied trailers entering Norway and Denmark. Vehicles entering the Benelux countries (The Netherlands, Belgium and Luxembourg) do not require carnets provided they show signs of use (ie they are not new imports).

Carnets de passage are issued by the Automobile Association, the Royal Automobile Club and the Royal Scottish Automobile Club.

ATA carnets

Goods that are only being imported temporarily can be moved under an ATA carnet (an international Customs clearance document – valid for 12 months). Normally these documents are used in connection with the movement of samples for demonstration, display material for exhibitions and trade fairs and equipment for use by service or maintenance personnel fulfilling overseas contracts. They are issued by Chambers of Commerce or by the RHA to members without the need for payments of, or deposits against, duty. Holding an ATA carnet, however, does not relieve the transport operator from observing Customs requirements in each individual country.

Other Customs/transit documentation

Bills of Lading

A Bill of Lading is a legal document of title. It acts as a receipt for goods delivered to a carrier and as evidence of a contract of carriage for such goods. A bill comes in two forms: the traditional 'long' form and the new shortened form. The shortened bill was devised by the General Council for British Shipping and SITPRO (Simplification of International Trade Procedures) in order to reduce the costs of export documentation and to simplify completion procedures.

House bill

This is an alternative to a bill of lading in that it is used by shipping and forwarding agents and groupage operators when making up consolidated loads or arranging through-transit of goods by land and sea. Therefore, whereas a bill of lading normally covers only a sea journey (between two ports), the house bill covers both the sea journey and the inland journeys at either end. This document is also referred to as a 'combined transport document'.

Invoice

An invoice is a document giving details of a sale of goods showing the supplier, the purchaser and any other parties involved. It identifies the goods, the quantity, the price and any other charges to be paid to the supplier, the terms or arrangements for payment, and details of the origin of the goods. Some countries insist on details of invoices being certified by suitable authorities (eg Chambers of Commerce).

Consular invoice

This is an invoice document similar to that described above, but prepared on a special form and given legal status (ie legalized) by the Consul of the importing country. Consular invoices are required by some countries to confirm the specific details of the goods and the transaction, as well as the origin of the goods – this conforms to the Customs requirements of the country concerned. Forms can usually be obtained from the Consul of the appropriate country and when completed, they normally have to be lodged with the country for visa purposes.

Certificates of insurance

These certificates of insurance are issued as confirmation and evidence that a policy of insurance exists to cover risks involved in the movement of goods for export. The certificate indicates the type of risks covered, eg all risks, with average (WA) or free from particular average (FPA).

ECGD certificates

Insurance for British exporters against the risks of export movement is provided by the Export Credits Guarantee Department. Guarantees are given in respect of goods manufactured in this country for sale abroad and the risks covered include loss or damage in transit plus the risk of non-payment by the overseas customer. The ECGD certificate provides evidence of the cover against specified risks.

Guarantee vouchers

To avoid having to make individual guarantees or deposits of duty in respect of individual consignments when moving goods under the full Community Transit documentation system, operators can obtain guarantee vouchers against possible Customs claims for duty. Vouchers are obtainable from the FTA, RHA on payment of the appropriate fee. Guarantee vouchers are valid in all EU member states plus Switzerland.

Bail bonds

When vehicles travel to Spain, an additional insurance requirement is a Spanish bail bond which should be taken out to protect the driver in the event of his being involved in an accident or infringing local regulations.

It is the practice of the Spanish police, in the event of an accident or incident, to hold all the parties involved until the blame has been clearly established. The purpose of the bond is to secure the release of the driver and the vehicle, pending the outcome of any investigation into the event.

The bonds are supplied by insurance companies, usually equivalent in value to approximately £1,000–£1,500.

SITPRO

The UK Committee for the Simplification of International Trade Procedures was set up in 1968 by the National Economic Development Council, to 'study documentation in international trade and the commercial and governmental procedures associated with it and to make recommendations to assist the more efficient flow of trade'. Its purpose was to establish simplified procedures and forms of documentation to ease trade between countries, thereby reducing costs and improving efficiency in the administration of export and import trade. The documentation is referred to as 'aligned documentation'.

With the 'aligned' method, the size of essential documents is standardized and their layout is designed in such a way that they can be produced in a unified set from a single master document. By typing the details on the master the aligned forms can be prepared by the 'one-run' system. Various methods can be used – spirit duplicating, dyeline and electrostatic are examples. Items of information that are not required can be omitted by the use of plastic masks or other techniques. This system reduces the cost and time taken to prepare documents and, once the master is checked, ensures that the information on all forms is accurate. The most up-to-date example of aligned documentation is the Single Administrative Document (SAD) used for inter-EU movements since January 1988.

PART 7

Technical standards and aspects of operation

G1. WEIGHTS AND DIMENSIONS OF VEHICLES AND LOADS

Definition of vehicle weights

Vehicle weights are specified by different means for different purposes. The following definitions generally apply.

Unladen weight (ULW)
The weight of the vehicle inclusive of body and parts normally used in operation (the heavier of any alternative body being counted), but exclusive of weight of water, fuel, loose tools and equipment and batteries where these are used for propelling the vehicle.

Kerb weight
The weight of a vehicle in road-going condition inclusive of oil, water and fuel but without its load and without the driver and any passengers on board.

Tare weight
The weight of a vehicle in road-going condition including the weight of the driver and any passenger carried, prior to loading. This is the weight deducted from the gross weight to determine the actual or potential 'payload'.

Maximum laden weight (MLW)
The actual total weight of a vehicle and its load including the weight of fuel, driver and passenger, if carried. This weight should not exceed the limits specified by law for the vehicle – see below.

Gross vehicle weight (GVW)
The maximum weight at which a rigid vehicle is designed and permitted to operate as indicated on the vehicle plate (ie manufacturer's plate showing the design weight) or the 'Ministry' (ie VOSA) plate and plating certificate (showing the permitted maximum weight to be transmitted to the road by *all* the wheels of the vehicle in Great Britain). This is sometimes called the gross plated weight (gpw) – or gross mass – but, more correctly, is the permissible maximum weight (pmw).

Gross train weight (GTW)
The total weight of a drawbar combination (eg a rigid vehicle and drawbar trailer) including its load, fuel and driver and as defined above for gross vehicle weight.

Gross combination weight (GCW)
The total weight of an articulated vehicle with its load, fuel and driver and as defined above for gross vehicle weight.

Permissible maximum weight (pmw)

Permissible maximum weights (ie the total weight allowed on the road in the UK for the vehicle and load, including fuel and driver, plus passenger if carried) for goods vehicles and trailers depend on their wheelbase, the number of axles, the outer axle spread (the distance between the centre of the wheels on the front and rear axles) or the relevant axle spacing in the case of articulated vehicles. All goods vehicles over 3,500kg gross weight (and trailers over 1,020kg ulw) should be fitted with a 'Ministry' plate showing the permissible maximum axle and gross weight (or for articulated vehicles, the gross train weight) for that vehicle in Great Britain. These weights must not be exceeded.

The current permissible maximum weights for different types of vehicle are specified in both Construction and Use regulations and the Authorized Weight regulations, as shown in Table 7.1.

Combined transport vehicles
Rules introduced in March 1994 by the Government to boost rail freight prior to rail privatization permit swap-body and container-carrying lorries running to and from rail terminals to operate at up to 44 tonnes gross

Table 7.1

Vehicle type	Permissible maximum weight (kg)	
	C&U	AW
Two-axled rigid	17,000	18,000
Three-axled rigid	26,000*	26,000*
Rigid with four or more axles	32,000*	32,000*
Articulated		
– with three axles	26,000*	26,000*
– with four axles	35,000*	38,000 ^
– with five axles	38,000	40,000
(in road-rail opns)	44,000	
– with six axles	44,000**	41,000 ^

(NB: A general weight increase to 44 tonnes will be permitted for all six-axle vehicles in 2001)

Lorry and trailer (ie draw-bar or roadtrain) combinations		
– with four axles	35,000*	36,000 ^
– with five axles	38,000*	40,000 ^
– with six axles	44,000**	41,000 ^

(NB: See note above about general weight increase in 2001)

Maximum drive axle weight	10,500	11,500
Maximum weight on tandem-axle bogie	20,000	20,000
Maximum weight on tri-axle bogie	24,000	24,000

All the above maximum weights are dependent upon the vehicle/trailer meeting relevant plated weights.
* Dependent upon the fitment of road-friendly suspensions.
^ Dependent upon meeting certain specified conditions
** Operation permitted at up to 44 tonnes pmw in combined transport operations only – subject to meeting all relevant conditions

weight. This increased weight limit applies only to articulated vehicles and drawbar combinations equipped with at least six axles and road-friendly suspensions (or those that have no axle exceeding 8.5 tonnes), and to articulated vehicles comprising specially built bi-modal semi-trailers (ie capable of running on road or rail), used in combined road-rail transport operations.

When operating at this weight (ie above normal weight limits) the driver must carry with him documentary evidence to show that the swap-body or container load is on its way to a rail terminal (the document must show the name of the rail terminal, the date of the contract and the parties to it), or is on its way back from a rail terminal (in which case the document must show the terminal and the date and time that the unit load was collected). There is no restriction on the distance that may be travelled to or from a rail terminal for the purposes of complying with this legislation.

Gross weight calculation

The gross weight of a goods vehicle is the unladen weight of that vehicle plus the weight of its driver, any passengers carried, fuel (ie the tare weight) plus the load and load-securing devices – in other words, when the vehicle is laden and 'ready for the road'.

The permissible maximum weight is that shown on the VI plate and plating certificate. Vehicles may only be operated up to the maximum legal limit as shown on this plate, which is not necessarily that which is shown on the manufacturer's plate.

Axle weight calculation

In order to calculate front or rear axle weights for vehicles when given certain information, the following formula is used:

1. Determine the vehicle wheelbase.
2. Determine the weight of the load (ie payload).
3. Calculate the front loadbase (ie centreline of front axle to centre of gravity of load); or calculate the rear loadbase (ie centreline of rear axle to centre of gravity of load).
4. Apply the formula as follows:

$$\frac{\text{Payload (P) x Loadbase Distance (D)}}{\text{Wheelbase (W)}} = \text{(see items 1 and 2 below)}$$

ie for simplicity, remember the formula: $\dfrac{P \times D}{W}$

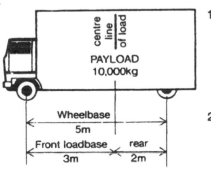

1. If *front* loadbase distance is used the answer will be the weight on the *rear axle*.

2. If the *rear* loadbase distance is used the answer will be the weight on the *front axle*.

Figure 7.1

1. Rear axle weight calculation:

$$\frac{\text{payload x front loadbase}}{\text{wheelbase}} = \text{payload weight on rear axle}$$

$$\frac{10,000 \text{ x } 3}{5} = 6000\text{kg}$$

2. Front axle weight calculation:

$$\frac{\text{payload x rear loadbase}}{\text{wheelbase}} = \text{payload weight on front axle}$$

$$\frac{10,000 \text{ x } 2}{5} = 4000\text{kg}$$

Overloading and GV 160 procedure

It is an offence to overload a goods vehicle. A police constable, VI examiner or trading standards officer may require a goods vehicle to be driven to a weighbridge to determine whether or not the vehicle is overloaded. In the event of an overloading offence being detected, both the vehicle driver and the 'user' (ie the driver's employer) are liable for prosecution and penalty on conviction.

When weighed, a certificate will be issued which shows the weight and which exempts the vehicle from further weighing on that journey with that load – whether the vehicle is overloaded or not. If the weight of the vehicle and load exceeds legal limits and appears unsafe or to be a danger a prohibition notice (Form GV 160) will be issued. This requires the excess weight to be off-loaded and reduced to within the legal limit before the vehicle proceeds. The driver may be directed to take the vehicle to a specific place to remove the excess load.

A vehicle may be sent up to five miles to a weighbridge without the owner being able to claim compensation for the costs incurred should the weight prove to be within legal limits. If sent beyond this distance, and the vehicle is found to be within legal limits, a claim for any losses incurred can be made to the Highway Authority on whose behalf the direction for weighing would have been made.

Dynamic weighing

Under the Weighing of Motor Vehicles (Use of Dynamic Axle Weighing Machines) Regulations 1978, vehicles can be weighed at roadside checks on dynamic weighing machines. Vehicles are driven slowly across the machine allowing each axle to be separately weighed and the weight printed out, or manually recorded by an authorized examiner. The weights shown by a dynamic weighing machine are presumed to be accurate to within plus or minus 150kg per axle (unless proved otherwise).

Overall length and width of vehicles

The overall length and width of a motor vehicle is the total distance between two vertical planes passing through its extreme projecting points but exclusive of the following items of equipment:

- driving mirror;
- starting handle;
- hood;
- fire escape or turntable;
- snow plough;
- container for Customs seal.

Maximum overall lengths and widths for vehicles/trailers
These are shown in Table 7.2.

Table 7.2   Maximum overall lengths and widths for vehicles/trailers

Vehicle/trailer	Dimensions (metres)
LENGTHS	
1. Rigid goods vehicles	12
2. Articulated vehicles (except those constructed to carry indivisible loads of exceptional length, low loaders and those with semi-trailers complying with the items below)	15.5
3. Articulated vehicles with semi-trailers complying with item below and satisfying conditions as to turning circles*	16.5
4. Articulated low-loader type vehicles	18
5. Lorry and drawbar trailer combinations	18.75~
6. Drawbar trailers (with four wheels and over 3500kg gross weight)	12
7. Composite trailers (comprising towing dolly plus semi-trailer)	14.04
8. Other trailers not exceeding 3500kg gross weight	7
9. Semi-trailers built since 1 May 1983 (not of a type in item below and not a low-loader) (internal load space dimension)	12.2 ^
10. Semi-trailers used in combinations up to 16.5m (see item 3 above):	
– kingpin to rear	12
– kingpin to rear (car transporters)	12.5
– kingpin to front*	2.04
– kingpin to front* (car transporters)	4.19

WIDTHS

1. Locomotives (see page 238 for definition)	2.75
2. Motor tractors (see page 238 for definition)	2.55
3. Heavy motor cars	2.55
4. Motor cars	2.55
5. Trailers	2.55
6. Trailers when drawn by a vehicle not exceeding 3500kg gross weight	2.3
7. Specially designed refrigerated vehicles with insulated side walls at least 45mm thick	2.6

*Articulated vehicles exceeding 15.5 metres overall length must be capable of turning within minimum and maximum swept circles with radii of 5.3 metres and 12.5 metres respectively (ie no part of the vehicle must pass outside concentric circles of these radii). This does not apply to articulated vehicles which are car transporters, low loaders or step-frame low-loaders and those constructed and used for the carriage of indivisible loads of exceptional length.

~This dimension must comprise a minimum driving-cab length of 2.35m and a minimum coupling distance of 0.75m. This leaves a potential load space of 15.65m within a 16.4m 'envelope' measured from the back of the cab to the rear of the trailer.

^ This dimension does not apply when such semi-trailers are used in international operations.

'Front' in this context means the dimension is measured to the furthest point of the semi-trailer forward of the kingpin (ie the front corners).

Overhang
The overhang of a vehicle is the distance measured between the centreline of the rear axle and the extreme rear projection of the body or chassis. The overhang distance must not exceed 60 per cent of the vehicle wheelbase.

In the case of vehicles with twin rear axles, the overhang distance to the extreme rear projection is measured from a point 110mm to the rear of the centre of the two rear axles (see Figure 7.2).

There is no overhang limit for trailers and the overhang limit does not apply to tipping vehicles if the distance from the centre of the rear axle to the rearmost point of the vehicle does not exceed 1.15 metres.

Dimensions of vehicles and loads

Apart from the actual maximum length and width limitations on vehicles and trailers already covered, additional regulations specify the maximum dimensions for vehicles and the loads they are carrying. These apply to:

- vehicles operating under the Construction & Use (C&U) Regulations;

OVERHANG

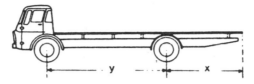

Four-wheeled vehicles: overhang 'x' must not exceed 60 per cent of length 'y'

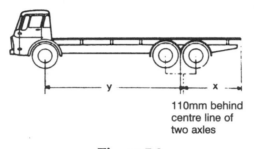

110mm behind centre line of two axles

Figure 7.2

- vehicles which comply with the Regulations but which are constructed and normally used for carrying indivisible loads of exceptional length;
- vehicles operating under the provision of the Special Types General Order (STGO) carrying abnormal indivisible loads.

The relevant dimensions together with the requirements that must be met, such as police notification and carrying statutory attendants, are shown in Table 7.3. Where notification of the police is required, this means notification of the police for every district through which the vehicle and load is to pass. The notification must be given at least two clear working days (ie excluding weekends and bank holidays) in advance of the movement. In the interests of road safety, the police have power to delay the movement or direct that particular routes should or should not be used. Where three or more vehicles and loads requiring statutory attendants travel in convoy, attendants are only required on the first and last vehicles in the convoy.

Projecting loads

A projecting load is one which extends beyond the foremost and/or rearmost points of a vehicle. Depending on the length of the projection, certain requirements (such as police notification, carrying attendants and displaying side and/or end marker boards – see Highway Code for coloured illustration of these) have to be met.

Table 7.3

Vehicle type	Two days' police notification	Attendant to be carried
LENGTH		
Rigid vehicle and load		
over 18.3m	yes	yes
Articulated vehicle and load		
over 18.3m	yes	yes
Articulated vehicle for carrying long loads		
over 18.3m (excluding length of tractive unit)	yes	yes
Combination of vehicles and load (excluding the length of the drawing vehicle) over 25.9m	yes	yes
over 27.4m (excl length of drawing unit)	*only by special order (from Secretary of State for Transport)*	
WIDTH		
Vehicles and trailers		
over 2.9m	yes	no
over 3.5m	yes	yes
over 4.3m (on C&U vehicle but operating under STGO*)	yes	yes
over 5.1m up to 6.1m (under STGO*)	*only by special order (from Secretary of State for Transport)*	

See note above about attendants on vehicles travelling in convoy.
*See module B 4/4 for details of operation under STGO

Forward projections
If a vehicle carries a load which projects to the front:

1. more than 2m – side and end markers and attendant required;
2. more than 3.05m – side and end markers, attendant and two days' notice to the police;
3. more than 4.5m – as in 2 above plus additional side markers within 2.5m of first and subsequent sets.

Rearward projections
If a vehicle carries a load which projects to the rear:

1. more than 1m – it must be made clearly visible;
2. more than 2m – end marker boards required;

3. more than 3m – side and end markers, attendant and two days' notice to the police;
4. more than 5m – as in 3 above plus additional side markers within 3.5m of the first and subsequent sets.

Side projections
If a vehicle carries a load which projects to the side:

1. more than 400mm beyond the existing front or rear position lamps – extra position lamps must be carried within 400mm of the outer edges of the load (this is a requirement of The Road Vehicles Lighting Regulations 1989 as amended);
2. more than 305mm on either side or more than 2.9m overall – two days' notice to the police;
3. more than 3.5m – two days' notice to the police and an attendant is needed;
4. more than 5m – see note above about need for approval from Secretary of State for Transport.

For these purposes, unless the load comprises loose agricultural produce or is indivisible, it must not be carried if the side projection exceeds the dimensions given in item 2 above.

Vehicle weights and dimensions in EU member states

The maximum articulated vehicle and road train weights and dimensions (lengths and widths) within individual EU member states are shown in Table 7.4.

Height
There is a height limit of 4 metres on goods vehicles entering Austria, Belgium, Denmark, Germany, Greece, Italy, Luxembourg, Netherlands, Portugal, Spain and Switzerland. Where vehicles registered in EU member states enter other states this limit is not usually enforced.

Carriage of abnormal indivisible loads

The provisions of the C&U Regulations regarding length, width and weight do not apply to vehicles specially designed, constructed and used solely for the carriage of abnormal indivisible loads (these are known as 'special types vehicles'). Such vehicles come within the scope of The Motor Vehicles (Authorization of Special Types) General Order.

Table 7.4

Member State	Nationality Sign	Max Width (metres)	Max Length (metres)	Max Weight (tonnes)	Rigid/Artic/ RT Axle*	Rigid Artic/ RT/CT
Austria	(A)	2.55	12/16.5/18.75	10/11.5	18/26	38/38/42
Belgium	(B)	2.55	12/16.5/18.75	10/12/27	19/26/32	44/44
Denmark	(DK)	2.55	12/16.5/18.75	10/11.5/24	18/26/32	48/48
Republic of Ireland	(IRL)	2.5	12/16.5/18.35	10/10.5/24	17/26/32	40/40/44
Finland	(FIN)	2.55	12/16.5/18.75	10/11.5/24	18/26/32	48/60
France	(F)	2.55	12/16.5/18.75	13/13/19	19/26/32	40/40/44
Germany	(D)	2.55	12/16.5/18.75	10/11.5/24	18/26/32	40/40/44
Greece	(GR)	2.55	12/16.5/18.75	10/11.5/24	18/26/32	40/40/44
Italy	(I)	2.55	12/16.5/18.75	12/12/19	18/26/32	44/44/44
Luxembourg	(L)	2.6	12/16.5/18.35	10/12/27	19/26/32	44/44
Netherlands	(NL)	2.55	12/16.5/18.75	10/11.5/27	21.5/33/43	50/50
Portugal	(P)	2.55	12/16.5/18.75	10/12/24	19/26/32	40/40/44
Spain	(E)	2.55	12/16.5/18.75	10/11.5/24	18/26/32	40/40/44
Sweden	(S)	2.6	24/25.25	10/11.5/24	18/26/32	up to 60
United Kingdom	(GB)	2.55	12/16.5/18.75	10/11.5/24	18/26/32	41/41/44
Non-EU country						
Switzerland	(CH)	2.55	12/16.5/18.75	10/11.5/24	18/26	28/28/40

Source: *IRU Handbook of International Road Transport – 1998* (15th edition)

*Axle = axle/drive axle/multi-axle Rigid = 2, 3 or 4 axles Artic/RT = 5 or 6 axles. Most member states permit a 2.6-metre width limit for refrigerated vehicles.

CT = vehicles used exclusively for combined transport operations or container carrying.

An abnormal load is defined as one which cannot, without undue expense or risk of damage, be divided into two or more loads for a journey by road and which cannot be legally carried by a vehicle complying with the C&U Regulations (ie one having a permissible maximum weight not exceeding 38,000kg and complying with the dimensional limitations and all other requirements for such vehicles).

Certain conditions apply to these vehicles when abnormal indivisible loads are carried. To ensure the safe carriage of large loads, such vehicles (locomotives and trailers) may if necessary be up to a maximum of 6.1m wide (including the width of the load). The overall length of a special types vehicle and its load or a combination of vehicles/ trailers and the load must not exceed 27.4m.

Special types vehicles
Special types vehicles used for carrying abnormal indivisible loads are divided into three categories according to their total laden weight. Such vehicles must observe varying speed limits. Details of categories, weights and speed limits are shown in Table 7.5. Vehicles operating under this order must display an identification sign at the front with white letters on a black background reading as follows:

STGO   Letters 105mm high
CAT   Letters and figures 70mm high

A figure 1, 2 or 3 must follow the word 'CAT' as appropriate.

Additionally, such vehicles falling in categories 2 and 3 must display 'special types plates' (under the provisions of the Road Vehicles (Marking of Special Weights) Regulations 1983) showing the maximum operational weights recommended by the manufacturer when travelling on a road at varying speeds as follows: 12, 20, 25, 30, 35, 40mph. The weights to be shown are the maximum gross and train weights and weights for each axle. Plates on trailers (including semi-trailers) will show maximum gross weight and the maximum weights for each axle.

Table 7.5

Cat.	Laden weight	Speed limits not exceeding		
		Motorways	Dual carriageways	Other roads
1	50,000kg	60	50	40
2	80,000kg	40	35	30
3	150,000kg	40	35	30

Attendants

An attendant must travel on special types vehicles where:

- the vehicle or its load is more that 3.5m wide;
- it is more than 18.3m long (excluding the drawing vehicle), or in combination with other vehicles is more than 25.9m long;
- the load projects more than 1.83m to the front or more than 3.05m to the rear of the vehicle.

If three or more vehicles carrying abnormal loads or other loads of dimensions requiring statutory attendants to be carried travel in convoy, attendants are only necessary on the first and last vehicles in the convoy.

Police notification

The police of every district through which a special types vehicle combination is to be moved must be given two clear working days' notice (ie excluding Saturdays, Sundays and bank holidays):

- if the vehicle or its load is more than 2.9m wide; or
- if it is more than 18.3m long (excluding the drawing vehicle), or in combination with other vehicles is more than 25.9m long; or
- if the load projects more than 3.05m to the front or rear; or
- if the weight of the vehicle combination and the load is more than 80,000kg.

When notice has been given to the police of the movement of an abnormal load, they have the power to delay the vehicle during its journey if it is holding up other traffic or in the interests of road safety.

Extra-wide loads

Application for approval must be made to the Secretary of State for Transport when the width of a vehicle and its load exceeds 5 metres. Form VR1 (movement order) is used for the application and must be carried on the vehicle at all times during the authorized movement.

Notification to Highway and Bridge Authorities

If a vehicle and its load weighs more than 80,000kg or in other ways does not comply with C&U Regulations, five clear days' notice must be given to the highway and bridge authorities for the areas through which the vehicle is to pass. The operator of such a vehicle is also required to indemnify the authorities against damage to any road or bridge over which it passes. An appropriate form for this purpose is set out in Schedule 2 to the Special Types General Order. Two days' notice must be given to these authorities in any case where a vehicle exceeds the overall C&U weight limit (ie 38,000kg) or a maximum axle weight.

A special types vehicle must not knowingly be driven on to a bridge at the same time as any other such vehicle or parked on a bridge (apart from in circumstances outside the driver's control). If such a vehicle, weighing more than 38,000kg, has to stop on a bridge for any reason it must be moved off as soon as possible. If it has broken down, the advice of the bridge authority (usually the highways department of the local authority) must be sought before the vehicle is jacked up on the bridge.

Movement of abnormal loads abroad

Where it is necessary to move an abnormal load either through EU member states or other European countries it is necessary to seek authorization from the national transport authority (eg as with the Department for Transport in the UK) of the country or countries concerned. There are no standard rules as to vehicle/load weights and dimensions or the manner of conducting such loads while in transit – each country has its own legal requirements and in the case of France for example, authorization is needed from the police for each individual regional *départment*.

G2. VEHICLE SPECIFICATIONS

Definition of vehicle types

Motor vehicles of various types have specific legal definitions laid down in regulations. The Road Traffic Act 1988 defines vehicles as follows

- *Goods vehicle: A vehicle (or trailer) constructed or adapted for use in the carriage of goods.*
- *Motor car:* A vehicle constructed to carry goods or passengers with an unladen weight not exceeding 3,050kg. (*NB: 3,050kg* not 3,500kg). Otherwise any other vehicle with an unladen weight not exceeding 2,540kg.
- *Heavy motor car:* A vehicle constructed to carry goods or passengers with an unladen weight exceeding 2,540kg.
- *Motor tractor:* A vehicle which is not constructed to carry a load and which has an unladen weight not exceeding 7,370kg.
- *Light locomotive:* A vehicle which is not constructed to carry a load and which has an unladen weight of more than 7,370kg but not exceeding 11,690kg.
- *Heavy locomotive:* A vehicle which is not constructed to carry a load and which has an unladen weight exceeding 11,690kg.

- *Articulated vehicle:* (As defined in the C&U Regulations) a motor car or heavy motor car with a trailer so attached that when the semi-trailer is uniformly loaded at least 20 per cent of the weight of the load is imposed on the drawing vehicle.

Definition of other relevant vehicles (defined elsewhere in legislation):

- *Small vehicles* (for 'O' licensing purposes):
  - *rigid vehicles* which have plated weight of not more than 3.5 tonnes;
  - *vehicle and trailer outfits* which have a total combined plated weight of not more than 3.5 tonnes *(Note:* for 'O' licensing purposes only trailers with an unladen weight of less than 1,020kg should not be included);
  - *articulated vehicles* which do not exceed 3.5 tonnes. The weight is calculated as follows: 'the plated weight of the semi-trailer plus the unladen weight of the tractive unit'.
- *Medium-sized goods vehicle:* A vehicle constructed or adapted for the carriage of goods, which has a maximum gross weight between 3.5 and 7.5 tonnes.
- *Heavy goods vehicle:* A vehicle constructed or adapted for the carriage or haulage of goods, which is an articulated vehicle or has a maximum gross plated weight exceeding 7.5 tonnes (this definition is used in determining whether or not an LGV driving entitlement is required).
- *Rigid vehicle:* Under C&U Regulations – a vehicle not constructed or adapted to form part of an articulated vehicle. In practical terms, a vehicle where the driving cab and the load-carrying space are mounted on a rigid chassis.
- *Tractive unit:* A motor vehicle which forms the towing unit of an articulated vehicle with a semi-trailer attached by a coupling in such a way that when the semi-trailer is uniformly loaded, at least 20 per cent of the weight of the load is borne by the tractive unit. It is *not* designed to carry a load other than when a semi-trailer is attached and should not be confused with a 'tractor' as described below.
- *Tractor:* See motor tractor. A towing unit which does *not* have part of the weight of the trailer superimposed upon it (as described above for articulated tractive units). Usually tractors are employed in heavy haulage operations and carry ballast to give them sufficient traction for pulling very heavy loads at low speeds.
- *Semi-trailer:* A trailer drawn by a tractive unit in a manner where at least a proportion of its weight is superimposed on the tractive unit (ie at least 20 per cent of the weight of the load when uniformly loaded – see also above) and connected by means of a kingpin and fifth wheel mounting plate or by an automatic-type coupling.

- *Drawbar trailer:* One which has axles on both the front and the rear and the steerable front axle is connected to the rear of the rigid towing vehicle by means of a solid drawbar with flexible brake and electrical connections between the vehicle and the trailer. No part of the weight of the trailer is imposed on the towing vehicle.
- *Composite trailer:* A semi-trailer connected to a towing dolly to comprise a drawbar trailer.

Choice of vehicle

An operator's choice of vehicle is governed by many factors but the initial consideration will relate to the weight and volume of loads to be carried and the nature of the loads which will determine the size of the vehicle and its type (for example platform truck, box van, refrigerated vehicle, tipping vehicle). The choice will also be significantly affected by the need for the vehicle to be specified on an operator's licence (ie 3.5 tonnes gross weight threshold) and to employ LGV-licensed drivers (currently 7.5 tonnes gross weight threshold).

Selection for operational needs
Efficient operation of goods vehicles starts with the selection of the right vehicle for the job. A badly chosen vehicle which is unsuited to its work will prove costly in terms of:

1. inefficient use;
2. under use;
3. repeated breakdowns;
4. excessive downtime;
5. driver discontent;
6. disruption of delivery schedules;
7. customer discontent;
8. reduced vehicle life.

The operator needs to take account of operational and economic factors such as that savings in initial capital cost are frequently more than offset by higher operating costs and shorter life, so the ideal approach is to buy on the basis of likely 'total life cost' (ie purchase price plus operating costs throughout the vehicle life, less its residual value).

Selection to achieve environmental objectives
Increasing attention is being given to the adverse environmental impact of large vehicles, particularly fuel consumption, excessive noise and air pollution from exhaust systems. Great strides have been made in heavy vehicle technology to reduce these impacts and the transport operator

seeking more environmentally friendly vehicles has many choices when specifying new trucks. He can select:

- road-friendly suspensions (usually air) which will give him greater permissible axle and vehicle gross weights and provide reduced drive-by noise levels;
- vehicles with Euro II and Euro III reduced pollution engines allowing reduced rates of vehicle excise duty to be claimed (ie up to £1000 per year currently);
- a catalyser fitment for existing vehicle exhaust systems to gain a Reduced Pollution Certificate that will also give him the reduced rate of vehicle excise duty;
- gas-powered trucks which provide cleaner emissions and reduced operating costs (up to 20 per cent cost per mile savings are claimed).

G3. VEHICLE CONDITION AND FITNESS

Goods vehicle type approval

The Motor Vehicles (Type Approval) Regulations 1980 (as amended) make provision for vehicles and their components to be 'type approved'. This means that manufacturers of vehicles and components can submit examples of their products, which conform to an established specification, for 'Ministry' approval and if such products meet all the necessary requirements a Type Approval Certificate (Certificate of Conformity) will be issued. Once such a certificate is issued all subsequent identical products meeting the same specification are therefore of the same 'type' and as such are legally approved for sale and for use. The manufacturer issues a certificate to purchasers confirming that the product conforms to that approved type – this is required for production when first registering a type-approved vehicle.

Once a new vehicle is first registered, the operator has no legal obligations under type approval but must conform to the detailed requirements of the C&U Regulations in respect of the vehicle and all its component parts.

Goods vehicle plating and testing

Goods vehicles are required to display (in a conspicuous position where they can be readily seen) plates showing the permissible maximum weight at which they may be operated and the respective maximum weights for any axle. The statutory provisions for these requirements are to be found in The Road Traffic Act 1988 and the Goods Vehicles (Plating and Testing) Regulations 1988 (as amended).

These regulations also require that goods vehicles must be tested annually at a Vehicle Inspectorate (VI) goods vehicle test station, with the first test being due no later than 12 months from the date of original registration. Trailers are due for test no later than 12 months from the date on which they were first supplied or sold retail. Because trailers have no identification by registration, they are given a serial number indicating when they are due to be tested. This number must be permanently fixed to the trailer – usually by welding it on to the chassis side frame on the nearside.

Vehicles covered – plating

The following vehicles are required to be plated:

- By the manufacturer (showing the vehicle design weights or legal weights, whichever are the lower):
  - all goods vehicles;
  - trailers over 1,020kg unladen.
- By the VI ('Ministry plating' showing permissible – ie legal – maximum weights):
  - articulated vehicles;
  - rigid goods vehicles over 3,500kg gross weight;
  - trailers over 1,020kg unladen.

Vehicles covered – annual testing

The following vehicles are required to be tested:

- At MoT-approved garages (by the third anniversary of the date of their original registration and annually thereafter):
  - private cars and dual-purpose vehicles;
  - goods vehicles up to 3,500kg gross weight .
- At VI goods vehicle test stations (annually from the first year):
  - articulated vehicles;
  - rigid goods vehicles over 3,500kg gross weight;
  - trailers over 1,020kg unladen.

Manufacturers' plates

Manufacturers of all goods vehicles, and trailers over 1,020kg unladen, must, by law, fit a plate on the vehicle or trailer showing the maximum weights at which the vehicle or trailer is designed to operate. Where such weights exceed current legal limits in Great Britain, the legal maxima will normally be shown (see also below).

The information to be shown on the plate is as follows:

- Manufacturer's name.
- Date of manufacture.

- Vehicle type.
- Engine type and power rating.
- Chassis or serial number.
- Number of axles.
- Maximum weight allowed on each axle.
- Maximum gross weight for the vehicle (including the weight imposed on the tractive unit by a semi-trailer in the case of articulated vehicles).
- Maximum train weight.

In the case of a trailer, the following information is required:

- Manufacturer's name.
- Date of manufacture.
- Chassis or serial number.
- Number of axles.
- Maximum weight allowed on each axle.
- Maximum weight imposed on the drawing vehicle if it is a semi-trailer.
- Maximum gross weight for the trailer.

'Ministry' plates

When a goods vehicle or trailer is first registered it is issued with a plate and plating certificate showing the maximum weights at which it is legally permitted to operate in Great Britain.

The gross weight and axle weight figures shown on the 'Ministry' plate and certificate may coincide with those shown on the manufacturer's plate or they may be lower if the maximum legal limit for the class in which that vehicle falls is lower than the weight at which the particular vehicle is designed to operate (eg where a 44 tonnes gtw articulated vehicle is permitted to operate at only 38 tonnes gtw in Great Britain under current legal weight limits) – see also above.

The plate will show the following information:

- Registration/identification mark.
- Chassis/serial number.
- Year of original registration.
- Make.
- Model.
- Axle weights (not to be exceeded in Great Britain).
- Gross weight (not to be exceeded in Great Britain).
- Train weight (not to be exceeded in Great Britain).
- Design weights (where these are greater than those indicated above).

It is an offence to use a vehicle on a road loaded to a weight in excess of the gross, train and axle weights shown on the plate or, if the vehicle is not plated, in excess of the maximum legal limits for that class of vehicle.

Standard lists

In determining the relevant plated weight for vehicles or trailers, VI testing stations use information contained in published 'standard lists' which identify by type, code and serial number every make and model of vehicle/trailer produced and the appropriate gross and axle weights in accordance with the vehicle specification. Copies of standard lists can be obtained from The Stationery Office.

Notifiable alterations

If the structure of a vehicle is altered, the Goods Vehicle Centre, Swansea, must be advised (on form VTG 10) before the vehicle is used on the road. The items which constitute alterations for this purpose are:

- Alterations to the structure or fixed equipment of a vehicle which vary its carrying capacity, including
  - chassis frame or structure;
  - steering, suspension, wheels and axles (including stub axles and wheel hubs);
  - fitting an alternative body of a different design, construction or type.
- Alterations to the braking system.
- Other alterations to the structure or fixed equipment.

Annual testing

Operators of vehicles subject to testing must apply to the Goods Vehicle Centre, Swansea, on the following forms:

- VTG 1L: first test of vehicle.
- VTG 2L: first test of trailer.
- VTG 40L: subsequent annual tests of vehicles and trailers.

Application should be made not less than one month but not more than three months before the last date when the vehicle can operate without a test certificate. An appointment for the test will generally be made at the testing station of the operator's choice unless that station is over-booked.

The test

Goods vehicle annual tests are categorized as follows:

- First test (first annual test of a goods vehicle or trailer).
- Part 2 re-test (examination of a vehicle/trailer which fails its first test).
- Periodical test (the annual test applicable to all vehicles/trailers after the first test).
- Part 3 re-test (examination of a vehicle/trailer which fails its periodical – annual test).

- Part 4 test (examination of a vehicle/trailer following a notifiable alteration).
- Re-test following appeal (examination of vehicle/trailer after an appeal to the VI).

NB: Additionally, the reader should be aware that goods vehicle test stations carry out the 'Group V' test, which is the light vehicle MoT test for large passenger vehicles that cannot get into normal MoT test garages because of their size.

On arrival at the test station, the vehicle will be subjected to a rigorous inspection covering all the points listed in the *HGV Inspection Manual* (copies available from The Stationery Office). The inspections are carried out in four main areas: outside, where the external aspects of the vehicle cab and bodywork, lights, equipment and fittings are examined and the engine is tested for smoke emission; inside the station, over the pit, where the underside is inspected including the vehicle's steering, suspension, transmission, wheels and tyres, wiring and pipework; in the next area, where headlamp beam settings are checked; and finally on the roller brake tester, where the vehicle's braking efficiency is checked.

Test certificate

If the vehicle or trailer is found to be in a satisfactory mechanical condition a test certificate (form VTG 5), valid for one year, will be issued. Test certificates must be produced to a police constable on request.

A vehicle must not be operated on the road unless it has a valid and current test certificate except where it is being driven to a place to be tested by prior appointment. The certificate is required in order to re-tax the vehicle when its excise licence expires.

Refusal to test

The test station may refuse to test a vehicle on the following grounds, in which case they will issue form VTG 12 (Refusal to Test):

- Arrival after the appointed time.
- If the appointment card or vehicle registration document is not produced.
- If it is found that the vehicle brought to the test station does not conform to the details given on the application form.
- If the vehicle was booked for the test with a trailer but the trailer is not taken to the test station.
- If the chassis number cannot be found by the examiners or if the serial number given for the vehicle by the VI is not stamped on it.
- If the vehicle is in a dirty or dangerous condition.

- If the vehicle does not have sufficient fuel or oil to enable the test to be carried out.
- If the test appointment card specifies that the vehicle should be loaded for the test and it is taken to the test station *without* a load (normally, the decision as to whether the vehicle is to be tested loaded or empty is left to the operator but in some circumstances the Goods Vehicle Centre may ask for the vehicle to be submitted with a load or part load to enable the brakes to be accurately checked).
- With a trailer, if the vehicle submitted with it is not suitable to draw it.
- If a vehicle breaks down during the test.
- If the vehicle is submitted for its annual test (not the first test) or a re-test and the previous test and plating certificates are not produced.

Test failure and re-test

If a vehicle undergoing a test is found to have defects it will not pass the test; the necessary repairs need to be carried out and the vehicle submitted for re-test.

If the re-test is booked at the same test station within 14 days of the failure, a reduced test fee will be charged.

Temporary exemption

Temporary exemption from the test for up to three months can be granted by the test station manager if for special reasons the test cannot be conducted (eg because of bad weather, fire, epidemic, industrial dispute). A Temporary Exemption Certificate (form VTG 33) is issued. The three months' exemption can be extended by the Secretary of State for Transport for up to 12 months.

Appeals against test decisions

An appeals procedure is laid down for operators not satisfied with a test station decision.

Appeals must be made to the Goods Vehicle Centre at Swansea within 14 days of the test. If no satisfaction is achieved with this appeal, a further appeal to the Secretary of State for Transport may be made.

Northern Ireland certification of vehicles

The UK system of goods vehicle plating and annual testing does not apply in Northern Ireland. The province has its own Goods Vehicle Certification scheme (commonly known and referred to in the province as the PSV test) which requires heavy goods vehicles to be submitted to the Department of the Environment (NI) for an annual mechanical examination. Under The Goods Vehicles (Certification) Regulations (Northern Ireland) 1982, owners of goods vehicles (other than those specifically exempted – see page 249) must obtain a test certificate for each vehicle no later than one year from the date of first registration and annually thereafter.

Application for a certificate must be made to the Department of the Environment, Vehicle and Driving Test Centre in Belfast at least one month before the date on which the certificate is to take effect.

Re-test fees apply where application is made within 21 days from the date of service of the notice and the vehicle is presented for re-examination within 28 days.

Applications by non-NI based bodies

Where an application is made by a corporate body with its principal or registered office outside Northern Ireland or by a person residing outside Northern Ireland the following conditions must be observed:

- During the currency of the certificate a place of business must be retained in NI.
- They must be prepared to accept, at such a place of business, any summons or other document relating to any matter or offence arising in NI in connection with the vehicle for which the certificate is applied for.
- They must undertake to appear at any court as required by such a summons or by any other document.
- They must admit and submit to the jurisdiction of the court relative to the subject matter of such summons or other document.

Failure to comply with any of the above requirements will involve immediate revocation of the certificate.

Examination of vehicle

When notified by the Department the applicant must present the vehicle for examination, in a reasonably clean condition, together with the registration book and previous certificate, if any, at the time and at the centre specified in the notice.

Issue of certificate

If, after examining the vehicle, the Department is satisfied that it complies in all respects with the regulations in respect of the construction, use, lighting and rear marking of vehicles, a certificate will be issued.

Refusal of certificate

If the vehicle does not meet the requirements of the regulations a certificate will be refused and the applicant will be notified of the reasons why.

Re-examination of vehicles

When a certificate has been refused and the defects specified in the notice have been put right, an application may be made for a further examination of the vehicle. A reduced re-test fee will be payable if the re-test is conducted within 21 days of the original test.

Refund of fees

Prepaid test fees may be refunded in the following circumstances:

- if an appointment for an examination of a vehicle is cancelled by the Department;
- if the applicant cancels the appointment by giving the Department (at the centre where the appointment is made) three clear working days' notice;
- if the vehicle is presented to meet the appointment but the examination does not take place for reasons not attributable to the applicant or the vehicle;
- if the applicant satisfies the Department that the vehicle could not be presented for examination on the day of the appointment because of exceptional circumstances which occurred no more than seven days before the day of the appointment, and provided notice is given to the centre where the examination was to take place within three days of the occurrence.

Duplicate certificates

Duplicate certificates may be issued in replacement of those that have been accidentally lost, defaced or destroyed. A fee is payable for replacement certificates. If subsequently the original certificate is found, it must be returned to the nearest examining centre or to any police station.

Display of certificates

The certificate issued on satisfying the examiners must be attached to the vehicle in a secure, weather-proof holder and must be displayed on the nearside windscreen or on the nearside of the vehicle not less than 610mm and not more than 1830mm above the road surface so that the particulars of the certificate are clearly visible (ie at eye level) to a person standing at the nearside of the vehicle.

Conditions of certificate

It is a condition of the certificate that the vehicle owner:

- must not permit the vehicle to be used for any illegal purpose;
- must not deface or mutilate the certificate or permit anybody else to do so;
- must, at all reasonable times, for the purpose of inspection, examination or testing of the vehicle to which the certificate relates:

- produce the vehicle at such a time and place as may be specified by any Inspector of Vehicles;
- afford to any Inspector of Vehicles full facilities for such inspection, examination or testing including access to his premises for that purpose;
- must ensure that the vehicle and all its fittings are maintained and kept in good order and repair and must take all practical steps to ensure that all parts of the mechanism, including the brakes, are free from defects and are in efficient working order;
- must immediately notify the nearest examination centre of any alteration in design or construction of the vehicle since a certificate was issued.

Transfer of certificates

If a vehicle owner sells or changes the ownership of a vehicle, he must return the certificate for the vehicle to the nearest examination centre and notify the Department of the name and address of the transferee. The Department may then transfer the certificate on request by the new owner.

If a vehicle owner dies or becomes infirm of mind or body the Department may transfer the certificate to another person, on application.

Change of address

If a certificate holder changes his address during the currency of a certificate, he must notify details of such changes to the nearest examination centre.

Markings on vehicles

When certificates have been issued for vehicles, those vehicles must be marked with the name and address of the owner in legible writing and in a conspicuous position on the nearside of the vehicle; and where the unladen weight of the vehicle exceeds 1,020kg, the unladen weight should be painted, or otherwise clearly marked, in a conspicuous position on the offside of the vehicle. In the case of articulated vehicles the unladen weight of the tractive unit and the trailer must be marked on the respective unit and trailer.

Offences

It is an offence to operate when a certificate has expired, to alter, deface, mutilate or fail to display a certificate. Failure to observe such rules will result in the certificate being declared invalid. It is also an offence to assign or to transfer a certificate to another person with the same resultant penalty. Fines or six months' imprisonment may be imposed on summary conviction for such offences or up to two years' imprisonment upon any further conviction or indictment.

Renewal of certificates

At least one month before the expiry date of a certificate the holder should apply for a new one using an application form obtainable from any examination centre or Local Vehicle Licensing Office of the Department.

Exemptions from certification

The following vehicles are exempt from the requirements of NI certification:

- vehicles constructed or adapted for the sole purpose of spreading material on roads or used to deal with frost, ice or snow;
- a land tractor, land locomotive or land implement;
- an agricultural trailer drawn on a road only by a land tractor;
- a vehicle exempted from duty under section 7(i) of the Vehicles (Excise) Act (Northern Ireland) 1972 and any trailer drawn by such a vehicle;
- a motor vehicle for the time being licensed under the Vehicles (Excise) Act 1971, paragraph (a);
- a trailer brought into NI from a base outside the province if a period of 12 months has elapsed since it was last brought in;
- a pedestrian-controlled vehicle;
- a track-laying vehicle;
- a steam-propelled vehicle;
- a vehicle used within a period of 12 months prior to the date of it being registered for the first time in NI or the UK. Where a vehicle has been used on roads in NI or elsewhere before being registered, the exemption applies for the period of 12 months from the date of manufacture rather than from the date of registration. For this purpose any use before the vehicle is sold or supplied retail is disregarded.

Fleet inspections and roadside checks

Authorized examiners of the Vehicle Inspectorate (VI) conduct regular mechanical inspections on vehicles both at roadside checkpoints set up specially for the purpose (where the police are in attendance to stop moving vehicles and often enforcement officers of the VOSA who check drivers' records – tachographs), and on operator's premises where they have certain legal rights of entry (see below).

These examiners have statutory powers to impose prohibition notices on goods vehicles found to be defective, overloaded or unsafely loaded in the circumstances mentioned above, or when a vehicle is presented for its annual test, to prevent them from being driven on roads until the specified defects have been rectified. The prohibition notices take account of the severity of the defects found and may give the operator a specified time in which to carry out the necessary repairs (delayed prohibition) or they may have instant effect (immediate prohibition – plus the prospect of prosecution for an offence under the C&U Regulations).

When a prohibition notice has been received, the operator must arrange to effect the repairs and must then submit the vehicle for further inspection by VOSA examiners, at a goods vehicle test station, who may give a clearance notice, or if the defect has not been satisfactorily rectified, may issue a further notice (see below).

It is a serious offence to use a goods vehicle on a road contrary to the provisions of a prohibition notice. However, it is permissible to drive the vehicle (unladen) to a testing station, by appointment, for re-examination after repair. It may also be road tested after repair but only within three miles of the repair location.

Prohibition notices

A number of official forms as described below are used by VOSA examiners in the process of inspecting vehicles, recording defects and prohibiting the use of vehicles that are defective.

Form GV 3

This form is authorization for the VOSA examiners to direct a vehicle to proceed to a specified place to be inspected (normally not more than five miles away).

Form PGDN (35) (Vehicle Inspection Notice)

Following an inspection of a vehicle, this form may be issued to indicate to the user one or more defects which it is in his interest and the interests of other road users to have rectified at an early date – it is not actually a prohibition.

Form PG 9

When an inspection by a VOSA examiner reveals defects of a serious nature, form PG 9 will be issued, specifying the defects and stating the precise time at which the prohibition preventing further use of the vehicle comes into force (which could be when the notice is written out – ie with immediate effect – or later).

When form PG 9 has been issued, a copy is given to the driver and this must be carried on the vehicle until the prohibition is removed. A further copy of the notice is sent to the vehicle operator (the 'O' licence holder) as well.

If the PG 9 has immediate effect, this means that the vehicle cannot be driven or towed away at least until it has been unloaded (see below).

Form PG 9A

This form (Variation in the Terms of a Prohibition...) is issued if the VOSA examiner wishes to vary the terms of a PG 9 notice by either suspending the PG 9 until a future time (eg midnight on the day of issue), altering the time (which is effectively the same thing as suspending the notice as mentioned above) or altering the list of defects shown on the PG 9 notice.

Form PG 9B

A VOSA examiner may, after issuing a PG 9, exempt the vehicle (Exemption from a Prohibition...) from the terms of the prohibition and permit its movement on certain conditions, as follows:

1. that the vehicle is unladen;
2. that the vehicle proceeds at a speed not in excess of a specified figure;
3. that the vehicle does not tow a trailer;
4. that the vehicle is towed on a rigid tow-bar;
5. that the vehicle is towed on a suspended tow;
6. that the vehicle is not used after lighting up time (if it has lighting defects);
7. that the vehicle proceeds only between two specified points.

Form PG 9C

When a vehicle which is subject to a PG 9 notice is presented to a VOSA examiner for clearance of the defect and the examiner is not satisfied that it is fit for service, he may issue form PG 9C (Refusal to Remove a Prohibition...), which means that the original PG 9 notice remains in force until the defects are satisfactorily rectified.

Form PG 10

If the defects specified in a PG 9 notice have been repaired to the satisfaction of the VOSA examiner to whom the vehicle is presented for clearance and the examiner is satisfied that the whole vehicle is in a satisfactory condition for use on the road, he will issue a PG 10 notice (Removal of Prohibition...) which removes the prohibition.

Form GV 160

This notice relates to prohibition on the use of overweight vehicles. It effectively requires the driver of the vehicle to take it to a weighbridge and, if found to be overloaded, reduce the gross weight to legal limits before proceeding on his journey.

NB: It is a defence to a charge of overloading that the vehicle was on its way to the nearest practicable weighbridge or that at the time of loading the weight was within legal limits and was subsequently not more than 5 per cent heavier despite not having any additions to the load en route.

Appeals against the issue of prohibition notices

There is no appeal against the imposition of a PG 9 prohibition notice, but there is a right of appeal against refusal to remove a prohibition after repair.

Powers of police and VOSA examiners and certifying officers

The Road Traffic Act 1988 gives authorized examiners – specifically, Department of Transport (VOSA) examiners, London taxi examiners, authorized police officers and persons appointed for the purpose by a chief officer of police, and certifying officers appointed under the Public Passenger Vehicles Act 1981 – powers to test and inspect vehicles and examine vehicle records, on production of their authority, as follows:

- They can test any motor or trailer on a road to check that legal requirements regarding brakes, silencer, steering, tyres, lights and reflectors, smoke and fumes are complied with, and may drive the vehicle for this purpose.
- They can test a vehicle for the same purposes on premises if the owner of the premises consents or has been given at least 48 hours' notice, except where the vehicle has been involved in a notifiable accident, when there is no requirement to give notice. If the notice is given in writing it must be sent by recorded post and the time limit is extended to 72 hours.
- They may at any time enter and inspect any goods vehicle and goods vehicle records, and may at a reasonable time enter premises on which they believe a goods vehicle or goods vehicle records are kept.
- They can request a driver of a stationary goods vehicle to take the vehicle to a place for inspection up to five miles away.
- They can at any reasonable time enter premises where used vehicles are sold, supplied or offered for sale or supply or exposed or kept for sale or supply to ensure that such vehicles can be used on a road without contravening the appropriate regulations. They may drive a vehicle on the road for this purpose.
- They may enter at any reasonable time premises where vehicles or vehicle parts are sold, supplied, offered for sale or supply, exposed or kept for sale or supply.
- They may require the person in charge of any vehicle to take it to a weighbridge to be weighed. If the vehicle is more than five miles from

the place where the request is made and the vehicle is found not to be overloaded the operator can claim against the highway authority for any loss sustained.

- When a goods vehicle has been weighed and found to exceed its weight limit and its use on a road would be a risk to public safety, they can prohibit its road use by the issue of form GV 160 until the weight is reduced to within the legal limit.
- If they find that a goods vehicle is unfit or likely to become unfit for service they can prohibit the driving of the vehicle on the road either immediately or from a later date and time by the issue of a prohibition notice (form PG 9 – see above).
- Where a prohibition order has been placed on a vehicle for various reasons, they are empowered to remove the prohibition (by the issue of form PG 10) when they consider the vehicle is fit for use.
- They can ask the driver of a goods vehicle registered in an EU member state, fitted with a tachograph, to produce the tachograph record of the vehicle when it is used in this country and ask to examine the official calibration plaque in the instrument. They can at any reasonable time enter premises where they believe such a vehicle is to be found or that tachograph records are kept and may inspect the vehicle and records (ie tachograph charts).

Police constables

A police constable *in uniform* or an approved VOSA examiner can stop a moving vehicle on a road ('constable' includes any rank of uniformed police officer). In Northern Ireland DoE examiners in plain clothes may also stop a moving vehicle. They can test any motor vehicle or trailer on a road to check that legal requirements regarding brakes, silencer, steering, tyres, lights and reflectors, smoke and fumes are complied with. They may drive the vehicle for this purpose.

They can test a vehicle for the same purposes on premises if the owner of the premises consents or has been given at least 48 hours' notice (or 72 hours if given by recorded post) except that consent is not necessary where the vehicle has been involved in a notifiable accident.

NB: This authority applies to all constables even if not specially authorized under the Road Traffic Act 1988 as mentioned above.

Trading standards officers

Trading standards officers employed by local authorities can request the driver of a vehicle which is carrying goods that need an official conveyance note (ie ballast which includes sand, gravel, shingle, ashes, clinker, chippings, including coated material, hardcore and aggregates) to take that vehicle to a weighbridge to be weighed. Goods may have to be unloaded if necessary.

G4. CONSTRUCTION AND USE OF VEHICLES

The Road Vehicle (Construction & Use) Regulations 1986 and their subsequent amendments regulate the manner in which motor vehicles and their components, accessories and equipment are constructed, adapted and used, to ensure the safety of vehicles/trailers on roads, and the legal standards regarding the weights, dimensions, design and construction of vehicles/trailers.

The C&U Regulations for motor vehicles specify many aspects of vehicle construction and use in considerable detail, of which the following requirements are the important items as identified in the CPC examination syllabus. In general terms it is illegal to use any vehicle or trailer on a road when these specific conditions, and indeed any of the requirements, are not complied with. Conviction for such offences can result in heavy fines, the endorsement of driving licence penalty points (for both the driver and his employer – but not if a company), and penalty against LGV driving licences and 'O' licences.

Brakes

Goods vehicles must be fitted with efficient braking systems that provide specified braking efficiencies on the primary (ie service) and the secondary braking systems; a parking brake meeting specified efficiency standards must also be provided. Goods vehicles first used since 1 April 1983 must meet technical requirements laid down in EU Directive 489/1979. Vehicles first used prior to this date can comply with the EU requirements or with the requirements of the C&U Regulations broadly as described in the following text.

Where a vehicle has dual-circuit brakes (ie a split-braking system), the system must provide emergency braking in the event of one part of the system failing. If one part of a split-braking system fails, the rest of the system must provide a minimum braking efficiency of not less than that specified for the secondary brake – namely 25 per cent.

Braking efficiency
The specified braking efficiencies are as follows:

Vehicles first used on or after 1 January 1968

Service brake	50 per cent.
Secondary brake	25 per cent.
Parking brake	must be capable of holding the vehicle on a gradient of at least 1 in 6.25 (ie 16 per cent) without the assistance of stored energy (eg compressed air in a reservoir – air tank).

Trailers constructed before 1 January 1968 must have an efficient braking system on half the number of wheels. Trailers constructed after 1 January 1968 must be fitted with brakes operating on all wheels which can be applied by the driver of the drawing vehicle, having maximum efficiencies matching the braking requirements for the drawing vehicle, emergency brakes operating on at least two wheels and a parking brake capable of holding the trailer on a gradient of at least 1 in 6.25 (ie 16 per cent).

Post-1977 trailers which have a gross weight of not more than 3,500kg can be fitted with over-run brakes.

Trailers weighing less than 102kg unladen, agricultural trailers and broken-down vehicles being towed are exempt from the braking requirements.

Vehicle combinations in which either the vehicle or the trailer conforms to EU braking requirements are exempt from the C&U braking provisions.

Speedometers

Motor vehicles must be fitted with a speedometer which indicates to the driver the speed of the vehicle in miles per hour and kilometres per hour simultaneously or by operating a switch.

Speedometers are not required on vehicles with a maximum speed not exceeding 25mph or which it is unlawful to drive in excess of this speed. On vehicles to which the relevant law applies (ie EU 3821/85), a tachograph instrument replaces the speedometer.

It is a good defence to a charge of having a defective speedometer to show that the defect occurred during the course of the journey in which the offence was detected, or to show that at the time when the contravention was detected steps had been taken to have the defect repaired 'with all reasonable expedition'.

Speed limiters

UK legislation requires certain heavy vehicles to be fitted with speed limiter devices restricting their top speed to 60mph (96.5kph). Separate EU legislation also requires certain vehicles to be fitted with speed limiters restricting top speed to a maximum of 90kph (56mph).

UK Regulations
The UK regulations limiting relevant vehicles to a maximum speed of 60mph (96.5kph) apply:

- from 1 August 1992 to newly registered goods vehicles over 7.5 tonnes gross weight and capable of more than 60mph on the flat when unladen;

- from 1 August 1993, to existing vehicles over 16 tonnes gross weight capable of more than 60mph on the flat when unladen, first registered on or after 1 January 1988 and which are:
  - rigid vehicles constructed to draw trailers, having a difference between the plated gross weight and gross train weight of at least 5 tonnes,
  - articulated tractive units.

Vehicles which cannot exceed 60mph (eg refuse collection and certain highway maintenance vehicles) are exempt from the regulations, as are vehicles:

- being taken to a place to have a speed limiter device fitted or calibrated;
- owned and being used by the navy, army or airforce;
- being used for military purposes or while under military orders;
- being used for fire brigade, ambulance or police purposes;
- exempt from excise duty under the Vehicles Excise and Registration Act 1994.

Speed limiter equipment must comply with BS AU 217 Part 1 1987 (or an acceptable equivalent), be calibrated to a set speed not exceeding 60mph and be sealed by an 'authorized sealer'. A speed limiter plate must be fitted (see below).

Existing speed limiters, fitted to vehicles on a voluntary basis prior to 1 August 1992, are permitted and do not have to be sealed by an 'authorized sealer'. In this case no speed limiter plate is required.

Speed limiters must be maintained in good working order, but it is a defence to show that where a vehicle is driven with a defective limiter the defect occurred during that journey, or that at the time it was being driven to a place for it to be repaired.

Speed limiter plates
Vehicles required to have speed limiter equipment must also carry a plate (fitted in a conspicuous and readily accessible position in the vehicle cab) showing the words SPEED LIMITER FITTED, the standard with which the installation complies, the speed setting in mph/kph and the name/trade mark of the calibration firm. Normally these plates are provided by the authorized sealer.

EU requirements
The speed limiter requirements of EU Directive 6/92 (which came into force from 1 January 1994) apply to newly registered goods vehicles over 12 tonnes gross weight, which must have speed limiter devices set to a maximum of 90kph (56mph). Vehicles over 12 tonnes first registered between 1 January 1988 and 1 January 1994 should have been fitted by 1

January 1995, but those used exclusively in national transport operations have until 1 January 1996 to comply.

Mirrors

Goods vehicles and dual-purpose vehicles must be fitted with at least two mirrors; one of these must be fitted externally on the offside and the other may be fitted either in the driver's cab or driving compartment, if it can provide an adequate view to the rear or, otherwise, externally on the nearside. Mirrors must show traffic to the rear or on both sides rearwards.

Goods vehicles exceeding 12 tonnes pmw and first used since 1 October 1988 must be fitted with additional mirrors which provide close proximity and wide angle vision in accordance with EU Directive 562/1986

Safety glass

Goods vehicles must be fitted with safety glass (ie toughened or laminated) for windscreens and windows in front and on either side of the driver's seat. The windscreen and all windows of dual-purpose vehicles must be fitted with safety glass. Glass should be maintained in good condition and should be clean; it is an offence for the driver's vision to be obscured while driving on a road.

Windscreen wipers and washers

All vehicles must be fitted with one or more efficient automatic windscreen wipers capable of clearing the windscreen to provide the driver with an adequate view of the road. The wipers must be maintained in good and efficient working order and must be properly adjusted. Windscreen washers must also be fitted which are capable of cleaning the area of the windscreen swept by the wipers of mud or dirt. Vehicles *must not* be driven on the road with defective windscreen washers or wipers.

Audible warning devices

All vehicles must be equipped with an audible warning device (ie a horn). Gongs, bells, sirens and two-tone horns are prohibited on all vehicles except emergency vehicles and those from which goods are sold (eg mobile shops and ice-cream vans). Such devices must not be sounded in built-up areas between the times of 11.30 pm and 7.00 am. Reversing alarms (see also page 274) come within the same restriction.

Fuel tanks

Vehicles first used since 1 July 1973 which are propelled by petrol engines must have metal fuel tanks fitted in a position to avoid damage and prevent leakage. This requirement does not apply if the petrol tank complies with EU Directive 221/70.

Silencers

Adequate means of silencing exhaust noise must be fitted to all vehicles. Silencers must be maintained in good condition at all times when a vehicle is on a road.

Tyres

Most goods vehicles must be fitted with pneumatic tyres and they must be maintained in good condition at all times when on the road. In particular:

- They must be inflated to the vehicle or tyre manufacturer's recommended pressure to be fit for the use to which the vehicle is being put.
- No tyre must have a break in its fabric or a cut which is deep enough to reach the body cords or is more than 25mm or 10 per cent of its section width in length, whichever is the greater.
- There must be no lumps or bulges caused by separation or partial fracture of the tyre structure, nor must any portion of the ply or cord structure be exposed.
- All tyres on goods vehicles (over 3.5 tonnes gross weight*) must have a tread depth (excluding any tie bars or tread wear indicators) of at least 1mm across three-quarters of the breadth and around the entire circumference of the tyre. Across the remaining section width, the base of the original tread pattern grooves must still be visible.

*For light goods vehicles not exceeding this weight and for cars, the relevant minimum tread depth is 1.6mm. NB: Exemptions apply to vehicles used solely on rough ground.

Recut tyres may be fitted to goods vehicles of over 2,540kg unladen weight which have wheels of at least 405mm rim diameter. The use of a mixture of cross-ply tyres on the rear axle and radial-ply tyres on the front axle is prohibited on goods vehicles which have single rear wheels (ie light/medium vans/trucks) but such mixtures are permitted where the vehicle has twin rear wheels. It is an offence to have tyres of different structure (ie cross-ply and radial-ply) fitted to opposite wheels of the vehicle or on the same axle.

Seat belts

Seat belts for the driver and one front seat passenger must be fitted to goods vehicles of not more than 1,525kg unladen weight registered since 1 April 1967 and goods vehicles of not more than 3,500kg gross weight registered since 1 April 1980. The belts must be maintained in good condition, must be secured so they do not lie on the floor, and must be worn by the driver and the front-seat passenger for whom they are provided. Where, for example, a van has a dual passenger seat, the requirement is for a belt to be fitted only for the occupant of the outer part of the seat (ie furthest from the driver) so a person sitting in the middle section need have no belt. However, where only one person occupies such a seat he must sit in the part for which a belt is provided – he cannot choose to sit in the middle and not wear the belt, as this is illegal.

Wings

Vehicles and trailers must be fitted with wings capable of catching mud or water thrown up by the wheels of the vehicle unless adequate protection is provided by the vehicle bodywork. See also details of anti-spray requirements on page 274.

Noise

It is an offence to use, cause or permit to be used a motor vehicle or trailer which emits excessive noise due to a defect, lack of repair or faulty adjustment of its components or of its load, or which could have been reasonably avoided by the driver.

Maximum permissible noise levels for vehicles in use, first used since 1 October 1983, are as follows:

Vehicles not exceeding 3,500kg gross plated weight	81dB(A).
Vehicles exceeding 3,500kg gross plated weight	86dB(A).
Vehicles over 12,000kg gross weight with engine power of 200hp (DIN) or more	88dB(A).

Smoke

Vehicles must not emit smoke, visible vapour, grit, sparks, ashes, cinders or oily substances which may cause damage to property or injury or danger to any person.

Excess fuel devices must not be used on diesel-engined vehicles while they are in motion.

Diesel-engined vehicles first used since 1 April 1973 must comply with smoke opacity limits specified in BS AU 141a/1971.

Towing

Goods vehicles (ie motor cars and heavy motor cars as defined in law) may draw only one trailer. Motor tractors may draw one laden or two unladen trailers; locomotives (both light and heavy) may draw three trailers.

A rigid goods vehicle (which is a heavy motor car) can legally tow a trailer which comprises a towing dolly and an articulated semi-trailer supported on that dolly because under the regulations this is defined as a composite trailer and counts as one trailer only.

Similarly, a rigid goods vehicle (in this case either a motor car or a heavy motor car) is permitted to tow a broken-down rigid vehicle partially raised on a towing dolly, although this would normally be considered to be two trailers. Also, a heavy motor car can tow a broken-down articulated vehicle provided it is *unladen* because it counts as one trailer only; if the broken-down articulated vehicle is *laden* it counts as two trailers and can only be towed by a light locomotive or heavy locomotive (see page 249 for definitions of these vehicles).

When one vehicle is towing another with the aid of a rope or chain (or with a modern-style webbing towing strap) the distance between the two vehicles must not exceed 4.5m. If the distance exceeds 1.5m the tow rope/chain/strap must be made clearly visible from both sides of the vehicles. If a rigid towbar is used no minimum distance limit or marking requirements are specified.

When a vehicle is on tow the registration number of the towing vehicle must be clearly displayed to the rear and additional lights must be provided if the towed vehicle's rear lights are not working.

Rear underrun bumpers

Rear underrun bumpers (referred to in legislation as 'rear underrun protection') must be fitted to most rigid vehicles over 3.5 tonnes gross weight which are manufactured from 1 October 1983 and first used from 1 April 1984.

Trailers, including semi-trailers, over 1,020kg unladen weight manufactured since 1 May 1983 must also be fitted with bumpers.

Certain specialized vehicles and trailers are exempt from the fitting requirements.

Strength of bumpers

Rear underrun bumpers must be capable of withstanding a force equivalent to half the gross weight of the vehicle or trailer or a maximum of 10 tonnes, whichever is the lesser, without deflecting more than 400mm from the rearmost point of the vehicle or trailer.

Fitment of bumpers

Usually only one bumper will be fitted but, where a tail-lift is fitted or the bodywork or other parts of the vehicle make this impracticable, two or more bumpers may be fitted.

Bumpers must be fitted as near as possible to the rear of the vehicle and the lower edge must not be more than 500mm from the ground.

Sideguards

Sideguards must be fitted to goods vehicles exceeding 3.5 tonnes maximum gross weight manufactured from 1 October 1983 and first used from 1 April 1984; and to trailers exceeding 1,020kg unladen weight manufactured from 1 May 1983 and which, in the case of semitrailers, have a distance between the foremost axle and the centreline of the kingpin (or rearmost kingpin if there is more than one) exceeding 4.5 metres.

Sideguards are *not* required on vehicles and trailers, other than semitrailers, where the distance between any two consecutive axles is less than 3 metres.

Strength of sideguards

Sideguards must be capable of withstanding a force of 200kg (two kilonewtons) over their length, apart from the last (or rear) 250mm of their length, without deflecting more than 150mm. Over the last 250mm of their length the deflection must not be more than 30mm under such force.

Ground clearance for trailers

Minimum ground clearances are specified for goods-carrying trailers manufactured from 1 April 1984. They must have a minimum ground clearance of 160mm if the trailer has an axle interspace of more than 6 metres and not more than 11.5 metres. If the interspace is more than 11.5 metres the minimum clearance is 190mm.

Measurement of the axle interspace is taken from the point of support on the tractive unit in the case of semi-trailers, or the centreline of the front axle in other cases, to the centreline of the rear axle or the centre point between rear axles if there is more than one.

In determining the minimum ground clearance no account should be taken of any part of the suspension, steering or braking system attached to any axle, any wheel and any air skirt. Measurement of the ground clearance is taken in the area formed by the width of the trailer and the middle 70 per cent of the axle interspace.

Reversing alarms

Voluntary fitment of reversing alarms (bleepers) to certain goods and passenger vehicles is permitted. It is a condition that the sound emitted must not be capable of being confused with the 'sound emitted in the operation of a pedestrian crossing' and such alarm sounds must not be emitted in a built-up area between the hours of 11.30 pm and 7.00 am (the same as with audible warning instruments).

The only vehicles legally permitted to use such alarms on the road are:

- Goods vehicles over 2 tonnes permissible maximum weight.
- Large passenger-carrying vehicles.
- Engineering plant.
- Works trucks.

Anti-spray

Certain heavy goods vehicles and goods-carrying trailers are required to be fitted with anti-spray equipment which conforms to British Standard Specification BS AU 200 Parts 1 and 2 1984 and 1986. The vehicles and trailers to be fitted and the relevant dates are: motor vehicles over 12 tonnes gross weight made on or after 1 October 1985 and first used on or after 1 April 1986; and trailers over 3.5 tonnes gross weight made on or after 1 May 1985.

In order to comply with the legislation, relevant vehicles and trailers must be fitted with anti-spray systems which fall into one or other of two main categories:

- A straight valance across the top of the wheel and a flap hanging vertically behind the wheel all made from approved spray suppressant material; or
- a semi-circular valance following the curvature of the wheel with either:
  - air/water separator material round the edge, or
  - a flap of spray suppressant material hanging from the rear edge.

All devices fitted to comply with the legal requirement (and every part of such device) must be maintained, when the vehicle/trailer is on the road, so that they are free from 'any obvious defect which would be likely to affect adversely the effectiveness of the device'.

Maintenance of parts

It is a general condition of the C&U Regulations that all parts and equipment required to be fitted to vehicles (brakes, lights, wipers, safety glass, etc) must be maintained in clean, fit and serviceable condition and must be correctly adjusted where appropriate. It is illegal to use (ie drive) a vehicle on a road if any of these requirements are not met.

Safety

All vehicles and trailers, their parts and components and the weight distribution, packing and adjustment of their load must be such that no danger is caused or is likely to be caused to any person in or on the vehicle or the road. A vehicle must not be used for any purpose for which it is so unsuited as to be likely to cause danger to persons in or on the vehicle or the road.

Lighting and marking of goods vehicles

Between sunset and sunrise vehicles used on a public road must display obligatory lights shown with an asterisk in the list below. Other lights and reflectors should also be shown:

- Two dipped-beam headlamps showing white (or yellow) lights to the front (when driven on unlit roads between the hours of darkness – defined as being from half and hour after sunset to half an hour before sunrise).
- Two front position lamps* (ie sidelights) showing white (or yellow if part of a yellow headlamp) lights to the front.
- Two rear position lamps* showing red lights to the rear.
- Two rear red reflex retro reflectors.
- The rear registration plate must be indirectly illuminated.*
- One or two red rear fog lights (on post-1 April 1980 vehicles).
- Certain goods vehicles and trailers must be fitted with side and end marker lights.*

*Vehicles must not show red lights to the front or white lights to the rear (with the exception of reversing lights when reverse gear is engaged).

Lights in poor visibility conditions
Vehicles must display front and rear position lights and headlamps during daylight hours if visibility is poor due to fog, mist, rain, spray, hail, snow and similar conditions. Rear fog lamps, if fitted, should also be used under these conditions.

Headlamps
Vehicles must be fitted with two headlamps showing white or yellow lights to the front which are permanently dipped or fitted with dipping devices.

Further, vehicles must also be fitted with main-beam headlamps (any number so long as they comply with the regulations) capable of illuminating the road a long distance ahead. They must be mounted so as not to cause dazzle and be capable of being dipped. Main-beam headlamps on pre-1 April 1986 vehicles must have a light intensity of at least 30 watts.

When driving on roads where there are no street lamps or the street lamps are more than 200 yards apart (the definition of unlit roads), headlamps must be illuminated. When stationary, except at traffic stops (ie when parked) the headlamps must be switched off.

Front fog lamps

Front fog lamps (any number for pre-1 April 1991 vehicles but only two for vehicles first used after this date) should be fitted and used in pairs (ie symmetrically mounted and emitting light of substantially the same colour and intensity). They may be used only in conditions of poor visibility, without headlamps, provided the vehicle front and rear position lights are also illuminated. If such lamps are used singly (and then only in seriously reduced visibility conditions), the vehicle headlamps must also be switched on. In any case they should not cause dazzle or discomfort to other road users.

Such lamps should be fitted not more than 1,200mm from the ground (with certain exceptions) and not more than 400mm from the outer edge of the vehicle.

Stop lamps

Vehicles registered since January 1971 must be fitted with two red stop lamps. Vehicles registered before that date need only one stop lamp, which should be fitted in the centre or on the offside of the vehicle.

Number plate lamps

Rear registration number plates on vehicles must be indirectly illuminated by a white light which must be shielded so it does not show to the rear.

Reversing lamps

One or two white reversing lamps may be fitted to a vehicle provided that:

- they are only used when the vehicle is reversing;
- they operate automatically when the reverse gear is selected or they may be operated manually provided they are on a separate switch and the driver has a warning light showing when they are in use;
- they do not dazzle other road users.

Rear fog lamps

Vehicles and trailers manufactured on or after 1 October 1979 and first used after 1 April 1980 must be fitted with rear fog lamps as follows:

- one lamp on the offside or two lamps (maximum) fitted as an equal pair;
- fitted not less than 250mm and not more than 1m from the ground except certain special vehicles (ie agricultural vehicles, engineering plant and motor tractors) when the maximum height may be 1.9m – or if the body shape makes this impossible, 2.1m;
- the lights must only operate when the other lights of the vehicle are switched on;
- they must not be connected to the brake light circuit;
- the driver must be provided with an indication that the lights are switched on;
- the lights must be used only in poor visibility conditions (fog, rain, snow, smoke, spray, etc) when the vehicle is moving or during a traffic stop;
- the lights must not dazzle other road users.

Vehicles first used before 1 October 1979 which have such lights fitted voluntarily must comply with the above requirements and the lights must be fitted so that no part of the illuminating surface is within 100mm of the illuminating surface of the vehicle stop lamps.

Direction indicators

All goods vehicles must be fitted with direction indicators positioned between 350mm and 1500mm from the ground.

The following indicators are required:

- one front and one flashing amber rear indicator on each side; or
- one shoulder and one flashing amber rear indicator on each side; or
- one flashing amber side indicator on each side.

Where front and rear indicators are more than 6m apart an additional flank indicator must be fitted on each side of the vehicle, within one third of the vehicle's length from the front.

Indicators must flash between 60 and 120 times a minute. A visible or audible warning must indicate to the driver when they are in operation.

Emergency (ie hazard) warning

Direction indicators operating on both sides of the vehicle simultaneously may be used in hazardous situations and emergencies, if a vehicle is stationary on a road due to a breakdown or if the vehicle is causing a temporary obstruction while loading or unloading. A telltale in the cab must indicate to the driver when the lights are in use.

Roof-mounted lamps

Amber rotating lamps (called 'beacons' in legislation) mounted on vehicle roofs or cab tops may be used on vehicles used in connection with road clearance, breakdowns, road maintenance, special types operation and Customs & Excise for fuel testing.

White swivelling spot lamps may be used on vehicles at the scene of an accident or breakdown, provided the vehicle carrying the lamp also has an amber rotating lamp and this is in use.

Blue rotating lamps may only be used on the following vehicles:

- Fire, police or ambulance service vehicles.
- Vehicles carrying human tissue for transplanting.
- Forestry Commission vehicles.
- Bomb disposal vehicles.
- Blood transfusion vehicles.
- HM Coastguard and Coast Lifesaving Corps vehicles.
- National Coal Board vehicles used for mines rescue.
- RAF mountain rescue vehicles.
- Royal National Lifeboat Institution vehicles used for launching lifeboats.

Green rotating lamps (beacons) may be used on vehicles in an emergency by a medical practitioner registered by the General Medical Council (GMC).

Side marker lamps
Side marker lamps (on each side) must be fitted on long vehicles and trailers as follows:

- Vehicles (including a combination of vehicles) exceeding 18.3m long (including the length of the load):
  a) one lamp within 9.15m of the front (of the vehicle or load);
  b) one lamp within 3.05m of the rear (of the vehicle or load);
  c) additional lamps at 3.05m intervals between front and rear side marker lamps – see items a) and b) above).
- Vehicles in combination between 12.2m and 18.3m long carrying a supported load:
  a) one lamp within 1,530mm of the rear of the rearmost vehicle in the combination;
  b) one lamp within 1,530mm of the centre (ie midway point) of the load, if the load extends further than 9.15m to the rear of the drawing vehicle.
- Trailers more than 9.15m long (excluding the length of the drawbar):
  a) one lamp within 1,530mm of the centre (ie midway point) of the trailer length.

For vehicles first used from 1 April 1991 side marker lamps are required if they have a maximum speed exceeding 25mph and are more than 6 metres long. Trailers built since 1 October 1990 must also be fitted with such lamps if they exceed 6 metres overall length. The lamps must be positioned no more than 4 metres from the front and no more than one metre from the rear and at not more than 3 metre intervals in between.

Side marker lamps may show a white light to the front and a red light to the rear on pre-1 October 1990 trailers but on all other vehicles and trailers they must show an amber light (unless fitted within one metre of the rear of the vehicle/trailer when they must be red). They must be positioned not more than 2300mm from the ground.

End-outline marker lamps

Vehicles first used from 1 April 1991 and exceeding 2.1 metres overall width and trailers built from 1 October 1990 and exceeding this width must be fitted with at least two end-outline marker lamps visible from the front (showing white lights) and at least two visible from the rear (showing red lights). Additional such lights may be fitted as required so long as they show only white lights to the front and red lights to the rear. They must be positioned not more than 400mm in from the outer edges of the vehicle/trailer and mounted at the front at least level with the top of the windscreen.

Rear reflectors

Vehicles and trailers must be fitted with two red reflex retro reflectors facing squarely to the rear.

Side-facing reflectors

Vehicles more than 8 metres long (6 metres if first used since 1 April 1986) and trailers more than 5m long must be fitted with two or more amber* side-facing reflectors on each side. One must be fitted not more than one metre from the extreme rear end of the vehicle (*this one can be red instead of amber) and the other not more than 4 metres from the front with further reflectors on each side at 3 metre intervals. The reflectors must be mounted between 350mm and 1,500mm from the ground.

Vehicle marking

The unladen weight of goods vehicles over 3 tons unladen must be marked on the nearside of the vehicle where it can be easily seen. This is not necessary where the vehicle is fitted with a 'Ministry' plate showing the *unladen* weight of the vehicle.

Height marking

Goods vehicles and trailers carrying containers constructed mostly of metal and greater than 8 cubic metres capacity (including demountable bodies) and engineering equipment or which itself is engineering plant must have the overall travelling height marked in the cab for the driver to see to within plus or minus 1 inch if such height exceeds 12ft (3.66m). The figures must not be less than 40mm tall.

The overall travelling height is defined as the distance from the ground to the highest point of the vehicle or its load measured when the vehicle is standing on a reasonably flat surface, and is in normal road-going condition (ie with tyres complying with legal requirements, etc).

Plates

A 'Ministry' plate must be displayed on goods vehicles over 1,525kg unladen (unless the vehicle is exempt from plating and annual testing) after the end of the first anniversary month of the date of their original registration. Other vehicles must be fitted with a manufacturer's plate (see page 253).

Number plates

Motor vehicles must be fitted with registration plates which can be clearly read. On vehicles first registered after 1 January 1973 (except goods vehicles fitted with rear reflective markers – see below) the plates must be made of reflecting material, white at the front and yellow at the rear, with black letters and numerals.

Rear reflective markings

The following goods vehicles and trailers must be fitted with rear reflective markers:

- Goods vehicles first used *before* 1 August 1982 which are over 3,000kg *unladen* weight.
- Goods vehicles first used *from* 1 August 1982 which are over 7,500kg *gross* weight.
- Trailers first used *before* 1 August 1982 which are over 1,020kg *unladen* weight.
- Trailers first used *from* 1 August 1982 which are over 3,500kg *gross* weight.

The rear reflective markers are described as follows (see also illustration in colour in the Highway Code):

- Vehicles not exceeding 13m in length and trailers in combinations not exceeding 11m in length – a single or pair of diagonally striped markers – the long one mounted horizontally or the pair mounted horizontally or vertically.

- Trailers in combinations between 11m and 13m in length – markers as above or a single or pair of 'long vehicle' markers.
- Vehicles more than 13m in length and trailers in combination more than 13m in length – a single or pair of 'long vehicle' markers.

Markers must be fitted so that the lower edge is between 400mm and 1700mm from the ground. They must be parallel to the ground and facing square to the rear.

Environmental legislation

The principal piece of UK environmental legislation is the Environmental Protection Act 1990 while vehicle emissions are largely controlled by EU Directive 91/441/EEC.

The need for legislation to control emissions is paramount because of their effect on human health. Vehicles emit a variety of pollutants including carbon dioxide and other products of combustion such as carbon monoxide, volatile organic compounds (VOCs) and, from diesel engines, particulate matter, which is especially injurious to health.

Measures to combat air pollution include:

- specifying new vehicles with low-emission engines (eg Euro II, III and IV);
- the fitment of catalytic converters to existing vehicles;
- the use of low-sulphur fuels;
- ensuring that engines and exhaust systems are properly maintained and are operating effectively.

G5. VEHICLE MAINTENANCE

An important aspect of vehicle operation is the need for a comprehensive system of preventive maintenance to ensure that vehicles are kept fully serviceable and do not suffer unexpected mechanical problems between regular safety inspections or manufacturer's recommended scheduled services. Also, it is vital to ensure that the mechanical condition of vehicles complies at all times with the C&U Regulations so they are both legally sound and safe to operate on the road.

Breakdowns on the road are costly in terms of the use of breakdown services and of lost time, plus the annoyance suffered by customers awaiting delivery of their goods. Further, being found on the road with a legally defective vehicle can result in the issue of a prohibition notice, possibly followed by prosecution for contravention of the C&U Regulations. This can lead to the vehicle being off the road for a period until repairs are satisfactorily carried out and cleared with the enforcement authorities (VOSA), a costly business on its own without the fines which could be imposed when the prosecution is brought to court, plus the further risk of penalty to the firm's 'O' licence.

For these reasons every care should be taken when a vehicle is being inspected and serviced to ensure that all visible and potential defects are identified and remedied. It is much cheaper to deal with these items in the workshop (even replacing certain parts prematurely) than to have a failure when the vehicle is perhaps on a motorway many miles from base or for it to be found defective in a roadside check.

Systems of preventive maintenance

It is useful for examination candidates to read a copy of the VOSA booklet on preventive maintenance systems called, *Guide To Maintaining Roadworthiness* (available from The Stationery Office).

Vehicle maintenance operations may be carried out by the owner in his own workshop or he may contract the work out to a garage or repair specialist.

Responsibility for contracting out
In the latter circumstances, the TC will expect the vehicle owner, as the 'O' licence holder, to have a proper arrangement with the repairer for regular inspection and repair of his vehicles to an established timetable or schedule of time or mileage. Further, although the repair work may be carried out by a contractor, the vehicle owner or operator (ie the 'user') is still responsible for ensuring that the work is properly carried out and that the vehicles comply fully with the law regarding their mechanical condition. Copies of all documents which relate to the regular inspection and repair of vehicles, including drivers' defect reports and details of action taken in response to drivers reporting defects, must be obtained from the repairer.

Safety inspections
It is a requirement, as a condition upon which the 'O' licence is issued, that vehicles and trailers are inspected at regular intervals of time or mileage (some Traffic Commissioners prefer a time-based inspection system). These inspections are intended to ensure that they meet all legal requirements and are safe to operate on the road. A written report of the inspection (usually in the form of a pre-printed checklist of all relevant components to be inspected) and any defects found should be made and a written record kept of the action taken to rectify any defects found.

Driver defect reporting

It is a further requirement of 'O' licensing (again a condition of the licence) that goods vehicle operators must provide drivers with a means of reporting defects in their vehicles. This is best done by issuing pads of defect reports so that any problem can easily be noted during the day while the driver has it in his mind. Ideally (and preferred by some TCs), if there is nothing wrong with the vehicle, the driver should write 'nil' so that the operator knows there were no defects in that vehicle on that day.

Once a driver has reported a defect, positive action should be taken to have it rectified and a note of the action, when it was taken and by whom, should be made either on the defect report or on another record filed with the defect report.

Regular servicing

Regular manufacturers' recommended services, such as oil changes and other lubrication tasks, and regular replacement of certain components such as diesel fuel injectors, should also be carried out. These may coincide with safety inspections, which will reduce vehicle downtime.

Maintenance records

It is a condition upon which 'O' licences are issued that records of inspections, defects, repairs and other maintenance work on vehicles should be kept for at least 15 months. To comply with this requirement record systems should ideally consist of the following:

- *Wall charts:* To indicate 'at a glance' when vehicles/trailers are due for safety inspections, service or annual test, etc and, subsequently, when the work was done.
- Vehicle history files: To contain all relevant details of the vehicle – date of purchase, price, specification, engine/chassis numbers, supplier, body manufacturer, etc. All other records such as those relating to regular inspections, driver defect reports, servicing and repair should be kept in this file.
- *Safety inspection reports:* As described above, these should be completed at regular intervals of time or mileage in accordance with promises made to obtain the 'O' licence. Ideally, the checklist used should cover all the items shown in the *HGV Inspection Manual* (available from The Stationery Office).
- *Driver defect reports:* As described above, these are important records which the TCs are very anxious for operators to keep as promised when obtaining their 'O' licences. They should be made by drivers in writing, ideally with a 'nil' report when no defects are found, and should be acted upon immediately.

- *Repair sheets:* These are a record of the work carried out to rectify defects identified on safety inspection reports and as reported by drivers on their defect reports as well as other necessary repairs.
- *Service records:* A record should be kept of manufacturers' recommended services carried out – lubrication, adjustments, replacements, etc.
- *Tyre records:* A separate record may be kept of tyres on the vehicle, tyre repairs and changes.
- *Repair invoices:* When work is carried out by outside repair garages a copy of the repair invoice should be kept in the vehicle history file as evidence of maintenance work done, together with a record of the replacement components fitted and the cost. The garage should also provide copies of their safety inspection, servicing and defect repair reports to accompany the invoice – the invoice alone does not satisfy the legal requirement relating to maintenance record keeping (see above).

G6. SAFE LOADING OF VEHICLES AND TRANSIT OF GOODS

Risk assessment

Employers have a statutory duty under health and safety legislation to carry out risk assessments of their work activities and this obviously includes the activities surrounding the operation of goods vehicles, namely the loading and transit of goods.

Loading and unloading procedures should be examined and assessed as to the potential hazards and likely risks to the health and safety of employees and others. In particular, account should be taken of the need for special measures to be taken for handling non-standard loads such as:

- dangerous goods;
- refrigerated loads;
- livestock;
- loose loads;
- large, wide or long loads;
- machinery, etc.

Safe procedures should be established and strictly followed with regular monitoring to ensure compliance.

The Department for Transport *Code of Practice on Safe Loading* provides advice on the correct and safe methods to be followed when dealing with a variety of loads, especially those which present particular hazards or difficulties in stowage and securing (see also below).

Legislation on safe loading and carriage of goods

The C&U Regulations 1986 state that every motor vehicle and trailer and all parts and accessories of the vehicle and trailer and the weight, distribution, packing and adjustment of the load on the vehicle or trailer shall, at all times, be such that no danger is caused or is likely to be caused to any person in or on the vehicle or trailer or on the road.

Further, the Regulations state that the load carried by a vehicle or trailer shall at all times be so secured, or be in such a position, that danger or nuisance is not likely to be caused to any person by reason of the load or any part of it falling or being blown from the vehicle or as a result of movement of the load on the vehicle. The load must be secured by physical restraint if necessary.

It is an offence under these regulations to use a vehicle that is so unsuitable as to cause, or be likely to cause, danger. Further, it is an offence to load a vehicle so that the permitted maximum individual axle or gross vehicle weights are exceeded.

Liability

Both the driver and his employer as 'users' of the vehicle are liable for prosecution in the event of a load or part of it falling from a vehicle or otherwise causing danger, and for overloading offences. If such an occurrence results in injuries to another road user claims for compensation could be made against both the driver and the employer. Conviction for offences under these provisions can result in very heavy fines, imposed by the courts, and to further penalty by the Traffic Commissioner against the driver's LGV driving entitlement and the vehicle operator's 'O' licence.

Code of Practice – safety of loads

The Department for Transport (DfT) Code of Practice 'Safety of Loads on Vehicles' (available from The Stationery Office) explains the legal requirements for the safe loading of vehicles and identifies the problems concerned with the safety of loads on vehicles. It describes methods of load restraint and load distribution and covers the strength requirements of restraint systems and load-securing equipment. The Code identifies a variety of particular types of load and shows how they should ideally be secured to the vehicle and the restraining equipment which should be used. It mentions the possible hazards connected with carrying certain types of load and lists the precautions to be taken to reduce them.

The basic principle upon which the Code of Practice is based is that the combined strength of the load restraint system must be sufficient (under normal road-going circumstances – not accident situations) to withstand a force, 'not less than the total weight of the load forward and half the weight of the load backwards and sideways'.

Dos and don'ts
The Code lists some advisory dos and don'ts for drivers as follows:

Dos

- Do make sure your vehicle's load space and the condition of its load platform are suitable for the type and size of the load.
- Do make use of load anchorage points.
- Do make sure you have enough lashings and that they are in good condition and strong enough to secure your load.
- Do tighten up the lashings or other restraining devices.
- Do make sure that the front of the load is abutted against the headboard, or other fixed restraint.
- Do use wedges, scotches, etc, so that your load cannot move.
- Do make sure that loose bulk loads cannot fall or be blown off your vehicle.

Don'ts

- Don't overload your vehicle or its individual axles.
- Don't load your vehicle too high.
- Don't use rope hooks to restrain heavy loads.
- Don't forget that the size, nature and position of your load will affect the handling of your vehicle.
- Don't forget to check your load:
  - before moving off;
  - after you have travelled a few miles;
  - if you remove or add items to your load during your journey.
- Don't take risks.

Handling and loading devices

A wide variety of mechanical devises are used in load handling and vehicle loading. These include:

- fork-lift trucks;
- pallet trucks;
- lorry-mounted cranes;
- dockside cranes;
- overhead cranes;
- straddle-carriers;
- reach trucks;
- stackers (for container stacking);
- pallets;

- stillages;
- roll-cages;
- containers.

The CPC student should ensure that he is familiar with the general appearance and mode of operation of these various items of equipment and the particular type of loading operations to which they are best suited.

Safe operations

Under legal provisions set out in the Management of Health and Safety at Work Regulations 1999 employers are charged with a statutory duty to make a detailed assessment of any risks present in their workplace (ie identify any hazards present) that could put the health and safety of workers, or other persons at the workplace, in jeopardy. Where five or more persons are employed, the employer must record the findings of his risk assessment and take relevant action to protect the health and safety of workers. This includes establishing systems for ensuring that the staff complies with safety regulations; that suitable emergency procedures are in place and that training is provided in safe procedures. Where appropriate, health surveillance must be provided for employees as relevant to the risks to their health and safety as identified by the risk assessment. Additionally, employers must appoint one or more competent persons to assist them in undertaking the measures necessary to comply with the requirements and prohibitions of this legislation.

This legislation also places a duty on employers to ensure that all operations are conducted in a safe manner with suitable control procedures being put in place to avoid any risk of injury to or impact upon the health of employees. See also page 284.

G7. TRANSPORT OPERATING SYSTEMS

A wide variety of transport modes and systems may be used by exporters, and frequently movements require the use of a combination of such modes. Although the principal forms of transportation require special study, brief outlines are given here with their relative advantages and some sources of information.

Freight forwarders

Exporters who do not wish to make their own arrangements with carriers and agents and deal directly with Customs can use the services of freight forwarders who will make all the necessary arrangements for them, negotiating the carriage, completing documentation, clearing Customs, etc. As an alternative, the services of freight forwarders may be used for only specific aspects of the whole export operation.

The principal advantages of using freight forwarders are relief from the need to coordinate all the activities of exporting, and the availability of special expertise in this field. Information on freight forwarders and their services may be obtained from BIFA (the British International Freight Association).

Roll-on/roll-off

The development of roll-on/roll-off (ro/ro) short sea-ferry ships has been one of the significant advances in modern transportation. On these ships, goods vehicles and trailers can make journeys abroad without their cargo having to be unloaded or the vehicle lifted aboard the ship. They offer speed and efficiency in loading and unloading and reduce the risks of loss or damage to goods through transhipment.

Progressively, the original Channel-crossing ro/ro services have developed to a point where an enormous variety of services and cross-Channel routes are available to international transport operators.

The Channel Tunnel

The Channel Tunnel, which opened in 1994, provides yet another alternative mode for international transport. Freight may travel through the Tunnel on a driver-accompanied basis, with complete road vehicles using Eurotunnel's Freight Shuttle rolling motorway system whereby the vehicles are driven on at Folkestone and off at Calais (or vice versa) with only an 80-minute transit time from motorway to motorway. Other freight is carried on an intermodal basis by container or swap body on through train services from inland terminals in the UK to destinations in Europe. Conventional rail freight is also carried through the Tunnel.

Containerization and swap bodies

This is another aspect of transport that has changed the face of the industry in recent years. With the benefits of providing exporters with a means of transport, conforming to very rigid dimensions, being easily handled with the right equipment, being sufficiently strong to protect the goods inside in all the circumstances which may be met on overland journeys and sea crossings, and being capable of being sealed to provide security for the goods, the container has a special place among transport modes.

Swap bodies fulfil many of the roles of containers with the principal exception that they cannot be stacked. Extensive use of this form of transport exists in Europe and with the opening of the Channel Tunnel (see above) the potential exists for a significant increase in this form of loading for UK-international intermodal freight traffic. It is worth pointing out that the term 'combined' or 'road-rail' transport has come to the fore. Indeed, as we have seen earlier in this manual, legislative provision has been made in the UK and Europe for vehicles used in this traffic to be permitted to run at 44 tonnes gross weight.

Information on the use of containers and swap bodies may be obtained from many sources, including the Inter-Governmental Maritime Consultative Organization (IMCO).

Other methods of unitization

Besides containers/swap bodies which provide shippers with a means of packing their export consignments in a safe and secure way, there are other methods of unitization used in international transport, as follows:

- Sealed TIR vehicles and trailers.
- On pallets with goods secured by:
  - netting;
  - banding;
  - shrink wrapping.
- In airfreight-type igloos (small, specially shaped containers).
- For liquids, in tanks.

Unitization of loads ensures more efficient handling, reduced risk of consignments becoming dispersed and lost, and reduced risk of damage.

Groupage

For shippers and exporters who do not have consignments sufficiently large to fully occupy TIR vehicles or trailers or containers, the services of groupage companies are useful.

These firms combine the shipper's consignments with those of other similar small-scale shippers to fill vehicles and containers, thereby providing an economical means of sending 'less-than-container-load' (LCL) shipments.

Road/rail

In some European countries, national rail networks provide a system whereby road vehicles can be carried by rail. For example, the French Kangourou system is available for the transit of unaccompanied trailers and semi-trailers, and German railways operate the 'piggy-back' service for semi-trailers. The advantage of such systems is that the rail rate may be less than the vehicle operating cost over the route, but more significantly the systems provide a means of reducing heavy lorry use of congested road networks and pollution from vehicle exhausts.

In the UK, interest in piggy-back operations has led to the development of limited services, between southern England and Glasgow for example, but the major expansion of such services is inhibited by restricted rail gauge clearances through bridges and tunnels on key routes, which prevents the carriage of full-height road semi-trailers.

Intermodalism

Since the previous edition of this Study Manual was published in 2001 there has been increasing interest in the concept of intermodalism. While by no means a new technique (even in 2001), it is a fact that the relatively recent publication of such key governmental policy documents as the UK's White Paper, *A New Deal for Transport: Better for Everyone*, followed by the *Transport Ten Year Plan 2000: Delivering Better Transport – progress report*, published in December 2002 and the EU's own 10-year transport plan, *European Transport Policy for 2010: Time to Decide* published in September 2001, promoted intermodalism as an effective means of reducing the adverse effects of road congestion – namely, exhaust pollution, road traffic accidents, noise and vibration – by encouraging a switch of long-haul freight traffic to rail and waterway freight systems.

G8. CARRIAGE OF DANGEROUS GOODS AND WASTE

Readers please note:

A complete restructuring of UK dangerous goods legislation as described in this section is due to take effect from 10 May 2004 under new regulations currently before Parliament. These are entitled The Carriage of Dangerous Goods and Use of Transportable Pressure Equipment Regulations 2004 and will replace the majority of existing legislation on this subject. A set of Guidance Notes should also be issued when the regulations are published.

Relevant information and copies of the documents will be available on the Health and Safety Executive (HSE) Web site: http://www.hse.gov.uk

In the meantime the pre-existing text on this subject is retained because it is likely to remain the basis for OCR examination questions on dangerous goods carriage for some months to come.

UK national legislation on the carriage of dangerous goods by road is now aligned with the European Agreement Concerning the International Carriage of Dangerous Goods by Road (ADR) under Council Directive 94/55/EC which harmonizes the law throughout the European Union.

So far as road transport is concerned, three sets of regulations cover, respectively, the classification, packaging and labelling of dangerous goods, their transport by road in containers, tanks and vehicles, and the training and certification of dangerous goods drivers. New regulations introduced in 1999 to implement EU Council Directive 96/35/EC require those who load, unload and transport dangerous goods by road to appoint a dangerous goods safety adviser (DGSA) with effect from 31 December 1999 – to continue the loading, unloading or transporting of dangerous goods after this date without a DGSA appointed is an offence with substantial penalties likely on conviction.

Dangerous goods legislation is both extensive and complex and it should be studied in detail by those responsible for such operations. Failure to comply with the strict provisions of the law can lead to harsh penalties as already mentioned above. It could also result in risk to health and human life and cause serious environmental pollution.

The legislation

The following principal regulations apply:

- The Carriage of Dangerous Goods (Classification, Packaging and Labelling) and Use of Transportable Pressure Receptacles Regulations 1996 (SI 2092/1996) – abbreviated to CDGCPL2.
- The Carriage of Dangerous Goods by Road Regulations 1996 (SI 2095/1996) – abbreviated to CDGRoad.
- The Carriage of Dangerous Goods by Road (Driver Training) Regulations 1996 (SI 2094/1996) – abbreviated to DTR2.
- The Transport of Dangerous Goods (Safety Advisers) Regulations 1999 (SI 1999/257).

These regulations are supported by the following Health and Safety Commission (HSC) 'approved documents':

- Approved Carriage List.
- Approved Requirements and Test Methods for the Classification and Packaging of Dangerous Goods for Carriage.

- Approved Vehicle Requirements.
- Approved Tank Requirements.

Besides conforming with the actual regulations, operators whose vehicles carry dangerous goods, and those who design, build or maintain vehicles and/or tanks for such use, must also comply with these 'approved documents'.

Packaging and labelling

The CDGCPL2 regulations cover the classification, packaging and labelling of dangerous goods (other than explosives and radioactive materials) for carriage by road or rail. There are some specified exceptions: for example, for international journeys by road or rail under, respectively, ADR or COTIF/RID (which deals with the international carriage of dangerous goods by rail) or a sea journey under the IMDG Code (International Maritime Dangerous Goods Code, which deals with carriage of dangerous goods by sea) or in emergency situations.

Classification of dangerous goods

The carriage of dangerous goods is prohibited unless their classification, packing group and any subsidiary hazards have been determined from the Approved Carriage List, along with their proper shipping name, their UN number and the relevant danger sign and subsidiary hazard sign.

Schedule 1 to the regulations lists the relevant classifications plus the packing group number, the class number and any optional lettering (see Table 7.6) and illustrates the danger sign for each (see Table 7.7).

Packaging

Packaged dangerous goods must not be transported unless the packages are suitable; in particular being:

- designed, constructed, maintained, filled and closed so the contents cannot escape;
- made of materials unlikely to be adversely affected by the contents or, when combined with the contents, unlikely to form substances which cause risk to health and safety;
- in the case of replaceable closures, designed for repeated use without leakage.

Packagings, generally, must be of approved type except where, for example, they have a capacity over three cubic metres, or a nominal capacity of 25 litres

Table 7.6

Classification	Packing Group	Class No	Optional lettering
Non-flammable, non-toxic gas		2.2	Compressed gas
Toxic gas		2.3	Toxic gas
Flammable gas		2.1	Flammable gas
Flammable liquid	I, II or III*	3	Flammable liquid
Flammable solid	I, II or III*	4.1	Flammable solid
Spontaneously combustible substance	I, II or III*	4.2	Spontaneously
Combustible substance which in contact with water emits flammable gas	I, II or III*	4.3	Dangerous when wet
Oxidizing substance	I, II or III*	5.1	Oxidizing agent
Organic peroxide	II	5.2	Organic peroxide
Toxic substance	I, II or III*	6.1	Toxic
Infectious substance		6.2	
Corrosive substance	I, II or III*	8	Corrosive
Miscellaneous dangerous goods		9	

*Depending on its relevant properties

Table 7.7

Description of sign	Symbol	Lettering	Background
Non-flammable, non-toxic gas	Black gas cylinder	Black or white	Green
Toxic gas	Black skull & crossbones	Black	White
Flammable gas	Black flame	Black or white	Red
Flammable liquid	Black flame	Black or white	Red
Flammable solid	Black flame	Black	Vertical white/red stripes
Spontaneously combustible substance	Black flame	Black or white	White top/red bottom
Substance which in contact with water emits flammable gas	Black flame	Black or white	Blue
Oxidizing substance	Black 'O' and flame	Black (5.1)	Yellow
Organic peroxide	Black 'O' and flame	Black (5.2)	Yellow
Toxic substance	Black skull & crossbones	Black	White
Infectious substances	Black symbol	Black	White
Corrosive substance	Black symbol	White	White top/black bottom
Miscellaneous			Vertical white/black stripes at top

or less and are empty and uncleaned en route for cleaning or disposal. There are other circumstances in which individual receptacles need not comply with these packaging requirements – these are listed in the regulations.

Marking

Dangerous goods packages must not show any unauthorized mark that could be confused with an ADR/RID/UN mark. Conversely, they must be marked with their designation, the UN number (preceded by the letters 'UN'), the danger sign and any relevant subsidiary hazard signs. Markings must be clear (being indelibly marked on the package or printed on a label securely fixed to the package), in English or the official language of another EU member state if being supplied to that state, so they can be read easily, and so they stand out from the background to enable them to be readily noticeable.

Pressure receptacles

Designers, manufacturers, importers or suppliers of transportable pressure receptacles (gas receptacles, tank containers and other forms of gas storage vessel) must ensure they are safe and suitable for their purpose and comply fully with the 'Approved Requirements'. (Receptacles are defined in the regulations as a vessel or the innermost layer of packaging that is in contact with any dangerous goods therein, and includes any closure or fastener). The same applies to those who repair or modify such receptacles. No repaired, modified or damaged gas receptacle must be used until it has been examined and tested in accordance with the 'Approved Requirements'.

It is illegal to import, supply or own a transportable pressure receptacle containing dangerous goods unless an approval certificate is held, or unless it has a quality assurance stamp on it. Owners of such tanks must ensure they are marked by a competent authority or approved person following initial examination and test, and that any periodic examination is not overdue.

Employers of those who fill gas receptacles must ensure that, before filling, the receptacle is appropriately marked, that the marks are checked to verify that the receptacle is suitable for the gas and that other safety checks are made. Receptacles must be filled in accordance with the 'Approved Requirements' and after filling they must be checked to ensure they are within their safe operating limits and are not overfilled – any excess gas must be removed safely.

Carriage by road

The carriage by road regulations (CDGRoad) deal with the actual road transport of dangerous goods, other than explosives and radioactive material, in bulk or in packages, in any container, tank or vehicle. They also include measures on the control of volatile organic compound (VOC) emissions – ie vapours that result from the storage and distribution of petrol.

There are certain exemptions to the regulations, such as for very small quantities of specified dangerous goods in packages, for vehicles on international dangerous goods journeys under ADR, and for vehicles owned or operated by the armed forces.

Definitions

For these purposes, 'the operator' of a container or vehicle is either the person responsible for its management or the driver; and in the case of a tank (other than the carrying tank of a road tanker) either the person who owns the tank, his agent, the person managing the tank, or the driver of the vehicle carrying it. A container is one which has an internal volume of not less than one cubic metre, is designed for repeated use and can be readily handled and transferred between transport modes.

Bulk carriage

Only goods shown with the letter Y in the Approved Carriage List may be carried in bulk or in a tank.

Suitability of vehicles and tanks

All containers, tanks and dangerous goods vehicles must be suitable for the purpose, in particular for the journey to be undertaken and the hazardous properties of the goods, and must be adequately maintained. Packaged dangerous goods must, if the packaging is sensitive to moisture, be sheeted, or carried in a closed vehicle.

Road vehicle tanks and tank containers must be of certified design conforming with constructional and equipment requirements, must be suitable for the purpose and have been examined and tested and a signed certificate to this effect issued by the competent authority. Such certificates must be kept by the operator at his place of business in Great Britain, at the place from which a tank is deployed or a road tanker is operated or, when the operator does not have a place of business in Great Britain, on the vehicle; or the certificate must be readily available from the owner of the tank.

Carriage requirements

Dangerous goods must not be carried unless a consignor's declaration has been received and the operator has ensured that the goods are fit for carriage. Drivers must not carry unauthorized passengers on vehicles carrying dangerous goods and must not open any package containing dangerous goods unless authorized to do so. No matches or lighters (or anything else capable of producing a flame or sparks) must be carried on vehicles carrying dangerous goods (except where the only goods on the vehicle are infectious substances). Food must not be carried in vehicles carrying (or which have carried) toxic or infectious substances unless it is effectively separated from such goods.

Information

Consignors of dangerous goods must provide the transport operator with a document showing:

- the designation, classification code and UN number for the goods;
- any additional information needed to determine their transport category* and their control and emergency temperatures;
- for packaged goods – the number and weight or volume of individual packages, or the total mass or volume in each transport category;*
- for bulk loads – the weight or volume in each tank or container and the number of tanks/containers;
- the name and address of both consignor and consignee;
- any other information which the operator must give to the driver;
- a 'consignor's declaration' that the goods may be carried as presented, that they, their packaging and any container or tank in which they are contained is fit for carriage and is properly labelled.

*Transport categories for these purposes are listed in Schedule 1 to the regulations.

It is an offence to provide false or misleading information and where one operator subcontracts a dangerous goods consignment to another operator he must pass on the information provided by the consignor.

Documentation to be carried during carriage

Drivers of vehicles carrying dangerous goods must be provided with the following 'Transport Documentation', in writing:

- The information provided by the consignor.
- The weight or volume of the load.
- The emergency action code (where appropriate) and the prescribed temperature for the goods.
- Emergency information comprising
  - the dangers inherent in the goods and safety measures;
  - what to do and the treatment to be given should any person come into contact with the goods;
  - what to do in the event of fire and what fire-fighting appliances or equipment must not be used;
  - what to do in case of breakage or deterioration of packagings or of the goods, particularly where this results in a spillage on to the road;

  – what to do to avoid or minimize damage in the event of spillage of goods likely to pollute water supplies.
- Any relevant additional information about the particular type of dangerous goods being carried.

It is an offence to provide false or misleading information to drivers about the particular type of dangerous goods being carried.

The emergency information described above may be carried in a variety of forms. The consignor may transmit the information to the vehicle operator by letter, fax or e-mail, or it may be entered on the consignment note for the load. The operator may in turn provide the driver with such information in written form or by means of a Tremcard, which is a formalized system using pre-printed documents – usually laminated cards suitable for repeated use. These cards are prepared by CEFIC (the European Council of Chemical Manufacturers' Federation). Tremcards are now available electronically from the National Chemical Emergency Centre on CD ROM.

Drivers must keep the transport documentation readily available during dangerous goods journeys and produce it on request by the police or a goods vehicle examiner. Where a dangerous goods-carrying trailer is detached from the towing vehicle, the transport documentation (or an authenticated copy) must be given to the owner/manager of the premises where it is parked, or attached to the trailer in a readily visible position.

Documentation relating to dangerous goods no longer on a vehicle must be either removed completely, or placed in a securely closed container clearly marked to show that it does not relate to dangerous goods still on the vehicle.

Operators must keep a record of journey transport documentation (apart from the emergency information) for at least three months.

Information to be displayed on containers, tanks and vehicles
Containers, tanks and vehicles used for carrying dangerous goods must display information as described below. All panels and danger signs must be kept clean and free from obstruction.

It is an offence to display information when the container, tank or vehicle is not carrying dangerous goods, and to cause or permit the display of any information likely to confuse the emergency services.

Signs and panels relating to dangerous goods no longer being carried must be covered or removed. Where an orange-coloured panel is covered, the covering material must remain effective after 15 minutes engulfment in fire. Danger signs, hazard warning panels, orange-coloured panels or subsidiary hazard signs need not be covered or removed if the mass or volume of dangerous goods in packages falls below the limits shown in Table 7.8.

Table 7.8

Transport category	Total mass/volume (kg/litres)
0	0
1	20
2	200
3	500
4	unlimited

It is an offence to remove panels or signs from a container, tank or vehicle carrying dangerous goods (except for updating the information) and to falsify information on any panel or sign.

Danger signs and panels

A reflectorized orange-coloured, black-bordered panel (plain with no letters or figures) must be displayed at the front of vehicles carrying dangerous goods. A similar panel must be attached to the rear of vehicles carrying dangerous goods in packages.

Single load labelling

Where a single load of dangerous goods is carried in a container, tank or vehicle an orange-coloured panel showing the appropriate UN number and emergency action code must be displayed:

- one at the rear of the vehicle;
- one on each side of the vehicle, the container or the tank; and,
- in the case of a tank, one on each side of the frame of the tank, or on the vehicle positioned immediately below the tank.

Multi-load labelling

Where a vehicle is carrying a multi-load in tanks, or in bulk in separate compartments of the vehicle, or in separate containers, an orange-coloured panel showing the appropriate emergency action code only (see below) must be displayed at the rear of the vehicle.

Additionally, orange-coloured panels are required on both sides of each tank (or, if it has multiple compartments, on each compartment), on each compartment of the vehicle or on each container on the vehicle – at least one on each side showing the appropriate UN number and emergency action code; and the remainder showing only the appropriate UN number.

Alternatively, for dangerous goods carried in a tank, the panels may be displayed on both sides of the frame of each tank, or on the vehicle positioned immediately below the tank or tank compartment concerned.

Where diesel fuel or gas oil or heating oil (UN 1202), petrol, motor spirit or gasoline (UN 1203), or kerosene (UN 1223) is carried in a multi-compartment road tanker it may be labelled as a single load only, showing the UN number and emergency action code for the most hazardous of the products carried.

Detail of panels

The orange-coloured panels must be either a rigid plate fitted as near vertical as possible; or, in the case of a vehicle carrying dangerous goods in a tank container or in bulk in a container, orange-coloured self-adhesive sheets, or orange-coloured paint (or equivalent), provided the material is weather resistant and ensures durable marking.

UN numbers and emergency action codes must be shown in black, at least 100mm high and 15mm wide – but where the emergency action code is white on a black background, it must appear as orange on a black rectangle at least 10mm greater than the height and width of the letter. Except where panels comprise self-adhesive sheets or are applied by paint, UN numbers and emergency action codes must be indelible and remain legible after 15 minutes' engulfment in fire (not applicable to tanks constructed before 1 January 1999).

Where there is insufficient space for full-sized panels, these may be reduced to 300mm wide by 120mm high with a 10mm black border.

Emergency action codes

The emergency action codes are as follows.

By numbers 1 to 4 indicating the equipment suitable for fire fighting and for dispersing spillages, ie:

1 = water jets
2 = water fog
3 = foam
4 = dry agent.

By letters indicating the appropriate precautions to take, as shown in Table 7.9.

Where a letter 'E' is shown at the end of an emergency action code this means that consideration should be given to evacuating people from the neighbourhood of an incident.

Display of telephone number

A contact telephone number, comprising black digits at least 30mm high on an orange background, must be shown on vehicles carrying single or multi-loads of dangerous goods in tanks, positioned:

Table 7.9

Letter	Danger of violent reaction	Protective clothing and breathing apparatus	Measures to be taken
P	Yes	Full protective clothing	Dilute
R	No	Full protective clothing	Dilute
S	Yes	Breathing apparatus	Dilute
S*	Yes	Breathing apparatus for fire	Dilute
T	No	Breathing apparatus	Dilute
T*	No	Breathing apparatus for fire	Dilute
W	Yes	Full protective clothing	Contain
X	No	Full protective clothing	Contain
Y	Yes	Breathing apparatus	Contain
Y*	Yes	Breathing apparatus for fire	Contain
Z	No	Breathing apparatus	Contain
Z*	No	Breathing apparatus for fire	Contain

*These symbols are shown as orange (or can be white) letters reversed out of a black background.

- at the rear of the vehicle;
- on both sides of the tank (or each tank if more than one), the frame of each tank, or the vehicle; and
- in the immediate vicinity of the orange-coloured panels.

Instead of a telephone number, the words 'consult local depot' or 'contact local depot' may be substituted, but only if the name of the operator is clearly marked on the tank or the vehicle, and the fire chief for every area in which the vehicle will operate has been notified in writing of the address and telephone number of that local depot, and has confirmed in writing that he is satisfied with the arrangements.

Display of danger signs and subsidiary hazard signs
Where a vehicle is carrying:

- packaged dangerous goods in a container – any danger sign or subsidiary hazard sign required on the packages must also be displayed on at least one side of the container;
- dangerous goods in a tank container or in bulk in a container – any danger sign or subsidiary hazard sign required on the packages containing such goods must be displayed on each side of the tank container or container, and where such signs are not visible from outside the carrying vehicle, the same signs must also be shown on each side of and at the rear of the vehicle;

- dangerous goods in a tank, other than a tank container, or in bulk in a vehicle, but not in bulk in a container on a vehicle – any danger sign or subsidiary hazard sign required on the packages containing such goods must be displayed on each side of and at the rear of the vehicle.

Danger signs for a particular classification, or subsidiary hazard signs, need not be shown more than once on the sides or rear of any container, tank or vehicle.

Danger signs and subsidiary hazard signs must have sides at least 250mm long; have a line the same colour as the symbol 12.5mm inside the edge and running parallel to it; and be displayed adjacent to one another and in the same horizontal plane.

Display of hazard warning panels
Despite the requirements described above for the display of orange-coloured panels the regulations permit, wherever such a panel is required on the sides or rear of a container, tank or vehicle, the alternative use of existing-type combined hazard warning panels.

These are mainly orange with black borders and lettering – except for the white background where a reduced size (ie 200mm sides) danger sign is located and any subsidiary hazard sign must be the same size and displayed adjacent to it and in the same horizontal plane.

All danger panels and signs required on the front or rear of a vehicle must be positioned at right angles across its width, and those on the sides of a container, tank or vehicle at right angles along its length. All signs must be clearly visible.

Loading and unloading

A number of provisions deal with loading and unloading, in particular:

- requiring the cleaning of vehicles before reloading, unless the next load is of the same designation;
- prohibiting smoking in or near the vehicle during loading/unloading;
- requiring an earth connection before loading/unloading where dangerous goods have a flash point of 61°C or below;
- limiting the rate of filling tanks to prevent electrostatic discharge;
- requiring vehicle engines to be stopped during loading/unloading unless needed to drive a pump;
- giving the driver responsibility for ensuring that all openings and valves are securely closed before and during the journey.

Emergency provisions
Vehicles carrying dangerous goods must be equipped so the driver can take emergency measures and, where toxic gases are carried, must carry respiratory equipment to enable the crew to escape safely.

In accident or emergency situations drivers must comply with the emergency information given to them. Where an incident cannot be immediately controlled the emergency services must be notified by the quickest practical means.

Vehicles must carry at least one portable fire extinguisher with a minimum capacity of 2kg of dry powder (or other extinguishant with an equivalent test fire rating of at least 5A and 34B – defined in British Standard BS EN 3–1:1996), suitable for fighting a fire in the engine (unless the vehicle has an automatic extinguisher system) or cab, and not likely to aggravate a fire in the load. *NB:* Such an extinguisher is not required on a detached trailer; at least one portable fire extinguisher with a minimum capacity of 6kg of dry powder (or other extinguishant with an equivalent test fire rating of at least 21A and 183B – defined as above)* suitable for fighting a tyre or brake fire, or a fire in the load, and not likely to aggravate a fire in the engine or cab. (* Where the vehicle has a gross weight under 3.5 tonnes, a 2kg dry powder extinguisher, or another suitable extinguishant with a test fire rating of at least 5A and 34B, will suffice.)

A fire extinguisher is not needed where only infectious substances are carried.

Portable fire extinguishers must not be liable to release toxic gases into the driver's cab, or under the heat of a fire. They must be marked in compliance with a recognized standard, fitted with a seal verifying they have not been used and, where manufactured after 31 December 1996, be inscribed with the date for their next inspection – it is an offence to carry an extinguisher with an overdue inspection date.

Supervision and parking of vehicles

Vehicles carrying dangerous goods when parked must be supervised at all times by a competent person over the age of 18 years, or a member of the armed forces. Otherwise they must be parked (with the parking brake applied and properly secured) in one of the following places:

- In an isolated position unsupervised in the open in a secure depot or factory premises.
- In a vehicle park supervised by an appropriate person who knows the nature of the load and the whereabouts of the driver.
- In a public or private vehicle park where they are not likely to suffer damage from other vehicles.
- In a suitable open space separated from the public highway and from dwellings, where the public does not normally pass or assemble.

None of these requirements applies when the vehicle has been damaged or has broken down on the road and the driver has left to seek assistance, provided he has taken all reasonable steps to secure it and its contents before leaving it unattended.

Defence

A person charged under these regulations can, in his own defence, prove that the offence was due to the act or default of another person (other than his own employees), and that he had tried to avoid committing the offence, but he must give the prosecutor, in writing, at least seven days before the court hearing and to the best of his knowledge, information identifying or assisting in the identification of that other person.

Carriage of explosives

Regulations which mainly came into force on 3 July 1989 control the movement of explosives by road. The Road Traffic (Carriage of Explosives) Regulations 1989 were made under the Health and Safety at Work, etc Act 1974 and replace parts of the requirements of the Explosives Act 1875, as do the Packaging of Explosives for Carriage Regulations 1991 which require that explosives in packages being transported should be tested, certified and labelled in a specified manner.

For the purposes of the regulations the term 'explosives' means explosive articles or substances which have been classified under the Classification and Labelling of Explosives Regulations 1983 as being in Class 1, or those which are unclassified. An 'explosive article' is an article which contains one or more explosive substances and an 'explosive substance' is a solid or liquid substance or a mixture of solid or liquid substances, or both,

> which is capable by chemical reaction in itself of producing gas at such a temperature and pressure and at such speed as could cause damage to surroundings or which is designed to produce an effect by heat, light, sound, gas or smoke or a combination of these as a result of non-detonative self-sustaining exothermic chemical reactions.

The term 'Compatibility Group' also has a meaning assigned to it by the 1983 regulations referred to above. The term 'carriage' means from the commencement of loading explosives into a vehicle or trailer until they have all been unloaded, whether or not the vehicle is on a road at the time. However, the term carriage is not applied where explosives are loaded on an unattached trailer or semi-trailer; carriage begins and ends when the trailer is attached to and later is detached from the towing vehicle or when the explosives have been unloaded, whichever is the sooner.

The regulations prohibit the carriage of any explosive in Compatibility Group K in a vehicle and any unclassified explosive except where it is being carried in connection with an application for their classification and in accordance with conditions approved in writing by the Health and Safety Executive (or, in the case of military explosives, by the Secretary of State for Defence).

Explosives must not be carried in any vehicle being used to carry passengers for hire or reward except that a passenger in such a vehicle may carry explosives under the following conditions:

- the substance carried is an explosive listed in Schedule 1 to the regulations (eg certain cartridges, fireworks, distress-type and other signals, certain flares, fuses, igniters, primers and other pyrotechnic articles), gunpowder, smokeless powder or any mixture of them;
- the total quantity of such explosive carried does not exceed 2kg;
- the explosives are kept by that person and are kept properly packed;
- all reasonable precautions are taken by the person to prevent accidents arising from the explosives.

The person carrying the explosives on the vehicle remains totally responsible for them and no responsibility is legally attached to the driver or the vehicle operator.

Suitability of vehicles and containers

It is the vehicle operator's duty under the regulations to ensure that any vehicle or any freight container used for the carriage of explosives is 'suitable' to ensure the safety and security of the explosives carried, bearing in mind their type and quantity. The operator is also responsible for ensuring that the specified maximum quantities of any particular class of explosive carried on a vehicle or in a freight container are not exceeded and that no greater quantity of explosive is carried than that for which the vehicle or container is 'suitable'.

The limits on quantities of explosives permitted to be carried are shown in Table 7.10.

The operator must ensure that explosives in different Compatibility Groups are not carried unless permitted as shown in Schedule 3 to the regulations.

Table 7.10

Type of explosives		Maximum quantity
Division	*Compatibility Group*	
1.1	A	500kg
1.1	B, F, G or I	5 tonnes
1.1	C, D, E or J	16 tonnes
1.2	Any	16 tonnes
1.3	Any	16 tonnes
Unclassified explosives carried solely in connection with an application for their classification		500kg

Marking of vehicles

Vehicles used for the carriage of explosives must be marked at the front and rear with a 400mm x 300mm rectangular reflectorized orange plate with black border (max 15mm wide). Additionally a square placard set at an angle of 45 degrees must be displayed on each side of the vehicle container or trailer containing the explosives. The placard must conform to the minimum dimensions specified and have an orange-coloured background with a black border and with a 'bomb blast' pictograph and any figures or letters denoting classification and Compatibility Group shown in black.

Certain exemptions apply to the display of markings as described above where the quantities of explosives of particular categories carried are below limits set out in Schedule 4 to the regulations.

Markings on vehicles and containers must be clearly visible, be kept clean and free from obstruction and must be completely covered or completely removed when all explosives have been removed from the vehicle or container. Both the vehicle driver and operator are responsible for ensuring these marking provisions are complied with.

Duty to obtain information

Operators must obtain information in writing from consignors of explosives which enable them to comply with the regulations. The consignor's duty is to ensure the information given is both accurate and sufficient to allow the operator to comply.

Information to be given to drivers

The operator must give the driver or the vehicle attendant the following information in writing:

- The Division and Compatibility Group for classified explosives.
- The net mass (in tonnes or kg) of each type of explosive carried (or the gross mass if the net mass figure is not available).
- Whether the explosives carried are explosive articles or explosive substances (in the case of Group C, D or G explosives).
- The name and address of the consignor, the operator of the vehicle and the consignee.
- Such other information as necessary to enable the driver to know the dangers which may arise and the emergency action to be taken.

This information must be carried on the vehicle at all times during the carriage from the start of the journey and must be shown on request to a police officer or goods vehicle traffic examiner. It must also be shown to a fire brigade officer or inspector if required. Information must not be carried on a vehicle when the explosives it refers to are no longer on that vehicle. It must be removed, destroyed or placed in a securely closed container marked to show that the contents do not relate to explosives then being carried. If the necessary information is not available to the driver or vehicle attendant the explosives must not be carried.

Safe and secure carriage

The vehicle operator and the driver and any other person involved in the carriage of explosives must take all reasonable steps to prevent accidents and minimize the harmful effects of any accident. They must also prevent unauthorized access to, or removal of, all or part of the load. The operator and driver must ensure that a competent person is constantly in attendance with the vehicle whenever the driver is not present, except during stops in a safe and secure place as defined in the regulations – namely within a factory or magazine licensed under the Explosives Act 1875 or at a place with an exemption certificate granted under the Explosives Act 1875 (Exemptions) Regulations 1979 and when the vehicle is on a site where adequate security precautions are taken.

The operator and driver of a vehicle used to carry more than 5 tonnes of explosives in Division 1.1 must follow a route agreed with the chief officers of police for each area through which it is to pass.

Procedure in the event of accident

The driver or vehicle attendant must contact the police, fire brigade and vehicle operator as quickly as possible in the event of the following circumstances:

- Spillage of explosives such as to constitute a safety risk.
- Damage to the explosives or their packaging such as to constitute a safety risk.
- If the vehicle overturns.
- If a fire or explosion takes place on the vehicle.

When such circumstances arise the driver, vehicle attendant and the operator must take all proper precautions to ensure the security of the explosives and the safety of persons likely to be affected, and the vehicle operator must immediately notify the Health and Safety Executive.

Duration of carriage and delivery

Both the vehicle operator and the driver are responsible for ensuring that the carriage of explosives is completed within a reasonable period of time having regard to the distance involved, that explosives are unloaded as soon as reasonably practicable on arrival, that the explosives are delivered to the consignee or his agent or to another person who accepts them in custody for onward despatch provided they are delivered to a safe and secure place or a designated parking area in an airport, a railway transhipment depot or siding, a harbour or harbour area. If they cannot be delivered as required they must be returned to the consignor or his agent. If loaded in a trailer the trailer must not be detached except in a safe place or in an emergency.

Training of drivers and attendants

Vehicle operators must ensure that drivers and vehicle attendants have received adequate training and instruction to enable them to understand the nature of the dangers which may arise from the carriage of the explosives, the action to be taken in an emergency and their duties under these regulations and under the Health and Safety at Work etc Act 1974.

Vocational training certificates are required by drivers of explosives vehicles in accordance with the requirements of the Road Traffic (Training of Drivers of Vehicles Carrying Dangerous Goods) Regulations 1992 and EU legislation.

Minimum ages

The regulations specify a minimum age of 18 years for those engaged in the carriage of explosives as a driver or vehicle attendant, for being made responsible for the security of explosives, or for travelling in a vehicle carrying explosives unless in the presence of and supervised by a competent person over 18 years of age.

Radioactive substances

Complex legislation controls the carriage of radioactive substances. In particular, the Radioactive Material (Road Transport) (Great Britain) Regulations 1996 made under the provisions of the Radioactive Material (Road Transport) Act 1991 apply to the carriage of such materials, while the Ionising Radiations Regulations 1985 and the Ionising Radiations (Outside Workers) Regulations 1993 cover controls on radiation doses received by persons working with such materials. Further, *A Code of Practice for the Carriage of Radioactive Materials by Road* is available from The Stationery Office, which sets out the law and gives advice on all aspects of transporting these materials.

Driver training

Drivers of vehicles carrying dangerous goods must be instructed and trained so they understand the dangers of the particular goods being carried and the emergency action to be taken, as well as their duties under the Health and Safety at Work etc. Act 1974, and current dangerous goods legislation. Operators must keep training records and give copies to the drivers concerned.

The driver training regulations (DTR2) apply (from the time of loading until the goods have been unloaded and, where appropriate, the compartment has been cleaned or purged) to drivers of the following dangerous goods vehicles:

- road tankers exceeding 1,000 litres capacity;
- those carrying tank containers exceeding 3,000 litres capacity;
- those exceeding 3.5 tonnes permissible maximum weight when carrying dangerous goods
  - in bulk
  - as a road tanker with a capacity not exceeding 1,000 litres,
  - in a tank container with a capacity not exceeding 3,000 litres,
  - where any of the goods are in transport category 0,
  - comprising more than 20kg/litres* of category 1 goods in packages,
  - comprising more than 200kg/litres* of category 2 goods in packages,
  - comprising more than 500kg/litres* of category 3 goods in packages;
- those carrying explosives,
- those carrying radioactive materials.

* The regulations refer to 'total mass or volume' (as measured in kg or litres).

Vocational training certificates

Transport operators must ensure their drivers hold valid vocational training certificates appropriate to the dangerous goods work they are employed in.

These certificates are granted to drivers on successful completion of an approved course of theoretical study and practical exercises and passing an approved examination. Certificates are valid for five years and may be extended for further five-year periods if in the 12 months preceding their expiry the holder has successfully completed a refresher course and passed the examination.

Current driver ADR certificates (if valid for the type of operation engaged in) are accepted as vocational training certificates for these purposes.

Certificates to be carried and produced to the police

Drivers must carry their vocational training certificates on all dangerous goods journeys and produce them on request by the police or a goods vehicle examiner.

Minimum training requirements for issue of vocational training certificates

Approved training for drivers must cover at least:

- general requirements on dangerous goods carriage;
- main types of hazard;
- environmental protection in the control of the transfer of wastes;
- preventive and safety measures appropriate to various types of hazard;
- what to do after an accident (first aid, road safety, the use of protective equipment, etc);
- labelling and marking to indicate danger;
- what to do and not do when carrying dangerous goods;
- the purpose and operation of technical equipment on vehicles used for carrying dangerous goods;
- prohibitions on mixed loading in the same vehicle or container;
- precautions during loading and unloading of dangerous goods;
- civil liability;
- multi-modal transport operations.

For drivers of vehicles carrying packaged dangerous goods, training must also cover the handling and stowage of packages, and for road tanker or tank container drivers training must cover the behaviour of such vehicles on the road, including load movement during transit.

Dangerous Goods Safety Advisers

From 31 December 1999, firms which load, unload or carry dangerous goods by road (and by rail and inland waterway) must appoint a qualified Dangerous Goods Safety Adviser (DGSA). This also applies to self-employed persons who must become qualified and appoint themselves. The person appointed must hold a valid vocational training certificate confirming he has passed the official DGSA examination conducted by the Scottish Qualifications Agency (SQA – appointed by the DETR to conduct all UK DGSA examinations). Details of the examination system and a copy of the syllabus may be obtained from the SQA, Testing Services Section, Hanover House, 24 Douglas Street, Glasgow G2 7NQ, or it may be downloaded from the SQA's website – http://www.sqa.org.uk/dgsa/

To qualify as a DGSA it is necessary to study the subject material contained in the official syllabus, sit the relevant examinations and pass in at least three of the following subjects: the core examination which is compulsory for all candidates; one modal paper covering either road, rail or inland waterways; and at least one dangerous goods class paper covering either Class 1, Class 2, Class 3 (specifically UN 1202, 1203 and 1223 – ie mineral oils), Class 7, General Chemical Classes (3, 4.1, 4.2, 4.3, 5.1, 5.2, 6.1, 6.2, 8 and 9), or all classes.

It is illegal to carry on a business in which dangerous goods are loaded, unloaded or transported after 31 December 1999 unless a qualified DGSA has been appointed and taken up his duties as outlined below.

Tasks and functions of DGSAs

Appointed DGSAs must effectively carry out the legal duties and bear the responsibilities set out in law as follows:

- Monitor compliance with the law on the transport of dangerous goods.
- Advise their employer on the transport of dangerous goods.
- Prepare an annual report to their employer on the firm's activities in transporting dangerous goods (to be kept for five years and made available to the authorities on request).

The DGSA must also monitor:

- procedures for identifying dangerous goods being transported;
- practices for taking account of any special requirements in connection with dangerous goods being transported;
- procedures for checking equipment used in the transport, loading or unloading of dangerous goods;
- employee training and maintenance of training records;
- emergency procedures to be taken in the event of accidents that may affect safety during the transport, loading or unloading of dangerous goods;
- investigation and preparation of reports on serious accidents or legal infringements during the transport, loading or unloading of dangerous goods;
- implementation of steps to avoid the recurrence of accidents, incidents or serious legal infringements;
- account taken of the legal requirements in the choice and use of sub-contractors;
- operational procedures and instructions that employees must follow;
- introduction of measures to increase awareness of the risks inherent in the transport, loading and unloading of dangerous goods;
- verification procedures to ensure that vehicles carry the documents and safety equipment required and that they comply with the law;
- verification procedures to ensure that the law on loading and unloading is complied with.

Controlled and hazardous waste

Many transport operators (and skip-hire firms) are concerned with the disposal of 'waste' and, as such, they are affected by newly imposed and strictly enforced legislation. For these purposes waste may be considered in two forms: 1) controlled waste which comprises 'household, industrial and commercial waste or any such waste' (including waste paper, scrap metal and recyclable scrap); 2) hazardous waste, which is material defined as 'special waste' in the controlled waste legislation, or material which falls within the classification of dangerous substances for the purposes of the road tanker or packaged dangerous goods legislation described above.

A range of legislation applies in this area of activity including the Disposal of Poisonous Waste Act 1972 (which makes it an offence to dispose of poisonous waste in an irresponsible way), the Criminal Justice Act 1988 (which provides powers for the authorities to impound vehicles engaged in illegal fly-tipping) and the Control of Pollution (Amendment) Act 1989, the Controlled Waste (Registration of Carriers and Seizure of Vehicles) Regulations 1991 and the Controlled Waste Regulations 1992. Two other sets of regulations are important, The Waste Management Licensing Regulations 1994 and the Special Waste Regulations 1996. Offences against the regulations can result in fines of £2000 on conviction.

Controlled waste
Controlled waste should not be disposed of, to, or transported away by, a person or firm not legally authorized for this purpose.

Registration of operators
The law (see above) requires operators who transport controlled waste within Great Britain to register with the appropriate waste regulation authority (ie in the area in which they have their business). It is an offence to fail to register or to carry controlled waste when not registered. Besides fines following prosecution and conviction for such offences, legislation provides powers for the seizure and disposal of vehicles used for such illegal purposes.

Exemptions are provided for charities, voluntary organizations, domestic householders disposing of their own waste, waste collection authorities and producers of controlled waste. Builders and demolition companies are not exempt and must register and otherwise comply with the legislation.

Registration costs £95 initially and, currently, £65 at each three-yearly renewal period. Registration may be refused to operators (ie companies or individuals) convicted of relevant offences as set out in the regulations.

Duty of care
Under the Environmental Protection Act 1990 firms and individuals who produce, import, store, treat, process, recycle, dispose of or transport controlled waste (see above for definition) have a statutory 'duty of care'. This places responsibility on such firms and individuals for the completion of paperwork (ie 'waste transfer notes') and for taking all reasonable steps to stop waste escaping and ensuring its safety and security.

Waste transfer notes

Waste transfer notes comprise written descriptions of waste handed over to other persons to transport and/or dispose of, and a transfer note signed by both parties (allowable as a single document) containing the following details:

- What the waste is and the quantity.
- The type of container in which it is carried.
- The time and date of transfer.
- The place where the transfer took place.
- The names and addresses of both parties (ie consignor and recipient).
- Detail as to which category each falls into (eg producer and registered waste carrier).
- A certificate number if either or both parties hold waste licences and the name of the issuing authority.
- Reasons for any exemption from registration or waste licensing.

Copies of documents (ie descriptions of waste and/or transfer notes) given and received must be retained for at least two years. Both or either party may be required to produce these and prove in court where particular consignments of controlled waste originated.

Seizure of vehicles

The seizure of vehicles aspects of the legislation are a new method of penalty in the UK – and, incidentally, are also being sought in regard to 'O' licence offenders. The law gives powers to waste regulation authorities to seize the vehicles of offenders, remove and separately store or dispose of loads as necessary, and dispose of (or destroy) vehicles following set procedures to publicize details of the seizure in local newspapers. Attempts will be made to seek out legitimate owners who may reclaim their vehicles on satisfactory proof of entitlement and identification.

Hazardous/poisonous waste disposal

Broadly, the law on hazardous waste requires that waste which is poisonous, noxious or polluting is not deposited on land where its presence is liable to give rise to an environmental hazard. It is necessary for anyone removing or depositing poisonous material to notify both the local authority and the river authority before doing so.

An environmental hazard is defined as waste that is deposited in a manner or in such quantity that it would subject persons or animals to material risk of death, injury or impairment of health, or threaten the pollution or contamination of any water supply. A booklet, *Guidelines on the Responsible Disposal of Wastes*, is available from the Confederation of British Industry. The European Commission has also produced a booklet on this subject for local authorities in EU member states.

There are additional controls over the carriage and disposal of particularly hazardous waste. The Control of Pollution (Special Waste) Regulations 1980 were introduced in order to comply with EU directives. The main requirements of these regulations are outlined below:

- Certain types of waste are to be regarded as special waste and subject to additional controls. These are wastes that are regarded as dangerous to life as set out in the regulations.
- Waste producers have to give not less than three days' and not more than one month's prior notice to waste disposal authorities of their intention to dispose of a consignment of special waste.
- A set of consignment notes must be completed when special wastes are transported. This means that a consignment of special waste can be transported from the producer to the disposal site only if each person has signed for it and taken on responsibility for it. This is to ensure that waste disposal authorities know who is carrying the waste and they have to be informed within 24 hours of when it reaches the disposal site. Waste producers should take particular note of the requirement that all notices must be made on the statutory forms. Each form contains a unique reference number to assist the Authority in making sure that waste is safely disposed of.
- A record of the location of the point of disposal on site of all special wastes must be kept in perpetuity. This is to ensure that proper arrangements can be made to bring the site back into use after the waste disposal operation has ceased.
- Proper registers of consignments must be kept by the producers, carriers and disposers.
- There will be a 'season ticket' arrangement for regular consignments of special wastes of similar composition disposed of at the same site. The waste disposal authorities will decide which producers and disposers in their areas qualify.
- The Secretary of State will have emergency powers to direct receipt of special wastes at a particular site. This is likely to be used rarely.
- Radioactive waste which also has the characteristics of special waste will be subject to the new controls.

Failure to comply with any of the requirements of the regulations is an offence.

Advice on particular problems can be obtained from waste regulation authorities (usually the district or county council).

Waste site licensing

The site licensing provisions of the Control of Pollution Act 1974 require all commercial, industrial or domestic wastes to be disposed of at a site licensed for that purpose and nowhere else. The licences are issued by the waste disposal authorities (these are the county councils in England and the district councils in Wales and Scotland). These licences, which are a matter of public record, set conditions for the operation of each site including the types of waste which can be disposed of there, the manner of disposal, site supervision, boundary fences, noticeboards, etc. waste disposal authorities must inspect sites regularly and make sure the operators are following the conditions of the licence. Failure to comply with licence conditions is a criminal offence. In addition to prosecution, the authority can amend or even revoke the licence.

Packaging waste
The Producer Responsibility Obligations (Packaging Waste) Regulations 1997 made under the Environment Act 1995 are designed to encourage businesses to recover value from products at the end of their life with the aim of:

- achieving a more sustainable approach to dealing with packaging waste;
- reducing the amount of packaging waste going to landfill;
- implementing the recovery and recycling targets in the EC Directive 94/621EC on packaging and packaging waste.

Businesses affected by the regulations are those with an annual turnover in excess of £5 million (reducing to a threshold of £1 million annually from 1 January 2000) and which handle more than 50 tonnes of packaging or packaging material annually. If one or other of the thresholds are not met the business is excluded form the regulations.

The regulations impose three main obligations on relevant businesses, namely: registration, recovery and recycling, and certifying.

Registration
Registration requires producers to register with the Environment Agency in England or Wales, or with the Scottish Environment Protection Agency (SEPA) if their principal place of business or registered office is in Scotland. A registration fee must be paid and packaging data must be provided on a data form (set out in Schedule 4 to the regulations) which will be provided by the Agency. The deadline for businesses continuing their registration or registering for the first time is 1 April each year.

Recovery and recycling
Recovery and recycling obligations started in 1998 and require producers to take reasonable steps to recover and recycle specific tonnages of packaging waste calculated on the basis of three factors:

1. the tonnage of packaging handled by the producer in the previous year;

2. the 'activities' that the producer performs and the percentage obligation attached to each activity, ie
   - manufacturing packaging raw materials,
   - converting materials into packaging,
   - packing and filling packaging,
   - selling packaging to the final user;
3. the national recovery and recycling targets (as set out in the regulations).

Certifying

Producers must write to the Agency by 31 January following the end of the calendar year in which they fall within scope of the regulations (ie by virtue of turnover and the tonnage of packaging waste handled) certifying that they have recovered and recycled the necessary tonnages of packaging waste. The person writing must be an 'approved person' (ie a director of a company, a partner in a partnership business or a sole trader).

European waste regulation

European Community Regulation 259/93/EC specifies that international shipments of waste must be notified to the competent authorities in the countries of origin, destination and transit, unless they are destined for recovery and are classified as non-hazardous by being specified on the so-called 'green list'. Export of hazardous waste to developing countries is prohibited.

Regulation 259/93 applies to all international shipments of waste to or from EU countries. Its aims are to prevent the export of hazardous waste to developing countries, and to ensure that international shipments of waste are properly monitored and are acceptable to the national regulatory authorities of the importing and exporting countries.

Waste for disposal

Where waste is destined for final disposal the exporter must notify the relevant authorities in the exporting country, the importing country and any other countries through which the waste consignment will pass; and the shipment can take place only when all relevant authorities have given their written consent – authorities have the right to refuse such shipments.

Waste for recovery

Depending on the severity of the hazards they present, wastes destined for recovery are divided into three lists as follows:

1. red list wastes (the most hazardous) are subject to the same prior informed consent procedure as wastes destined for disposal (see above);
2. amber list wastes must be notified to the competent authorities, but their consent is assumed provided no objections are made;

3. green list wastes (the least hazardous) are not normally subject to the EC regulation, although shipments should be accompanied by a transfer note.

All shipments of hazardous waste to non-OECD countries are banned, and the governments of individual developing countries also have the option of banning shipments of green list wastes.

G9. CARRIAGE OF PERISHABLE FOODSTUFFS

The ATP Agreement

This is an international agreement on the transport of perishable food-stuffs and on the special equipment to be used for such carriage (in its full French title – *L'Accord relatif aux Transports internationaux de denrees Perissables et aux engins speciaux a utilizer pour ces transports*) to which Britain acceded from 1 October 1979 by implementation of the International Carriage of Perishable Foodstuffs Act 1976 and The International Carriage of Perishable Foodstuffs Regulations 1985.

Its purpose is to improve the conditions of preservation of perishable foodstuffs during their carriage, particularly in international trade. It applies on journeys by road or rail (or a combination of both), and where sea crossings (eg by ferry ship) are involved provided these do not exceed 150 kilometres (see item 3 in the list below). It does not apply to national transport of such goods within the UK.

The principal terms of the Agreement are as follows:

1. The use of the following terms is prohibited unless the equipment (ie vehicles and containers) in question complies with the standards set out in the Agreement:
   (a) insulated
   (b) refrigerated
   (c) mechanically refrigerated
   (d) heated.
2. The equipment (ie vehicles and containers) referred to in point 1 must be inspected and tested for compliance at six-yearly intervals. Certificates of compliance, which must be carried on the vehicle and produced for inspection on request by an authorized inspecting officer, will be recognized by contracting parties to the Agreement. When a certificate has been issued, vehicles/containers must be fitted with a 'designated mark' showing the month and year of the inspection expiry (blue figures on white background).
3. The Agreement applies to carriage, if the carriage is between two different states, on own-account or for hire and reward by rail or road of:

(a) quick (deep) frozen and frozen foodstuffs
(b) other foodstuffs (including meats, offal, game, milk, fish, poultry and rabbits and dairy products) which are not quick frozen or frozen.

This condition applies if the original vehicle containing the goods having travelled by road or rail is subsequently carried on a sea crossing of less than 150km between one or more land journeys.

4. The equipment referred to in point 1 must be used in movements covered by the Agreement unless the temperatures to be anticipated during the carriage make this unnecessary; otherwise the equipment must be used to maintain temperatures laid down in the Agreement.
5. The Agreement does not apply to carriage in containers by land where this is preceded by or followed by a sea crossing other than as described in point 3 above (ie if it is more than 150km).
6. Parties to the Agreement must ensure observance of its conditions.

Countries which are party to the ATP Agreement include all EU member states plus Bosnia-Herzegovina, Bulgaria, Croatia, Czech Republic, Estonia, Georgia, Hungary, Kazakhstan, Macedonia, Morocco, Norway, Poland, Romania, Russia, Serbia and Montenegro, Slovakia, Slovenia plus Switzerland (signed but not ratified).

Vehicles (including trailers and containers) used on ATP operations must be examined at an approved establishment of which there are currently five in Great Britain. On satisfactory completion of the test a certificate (or a metal certification plate for affixing to the vehicle/trailer/container) is issued which is valid for six years. This certificate is transferable to a new owner on request.

Transport of perishables to Italy
Vehicles used for the transport of frozen and deep frozen foodstuffs to Italy during the period from 1 April to 31 October each year must be tested to ensure that they comply with specific regulations relating to carriage in vehicles with thin side walls – The International Carriage of Perishable Foodstuffs (Vehicles with Thin Side Walls) Regulations 1987.

G10. CARRIAGE OF LIVE ANIMALS

The Welfare of Animals (Transport) Order 1997 which became effective from 1 July 1997 signified an important step forward in strengthening animal welfare legislation in Great Britain. It revoked and re-enacted with modifications the Welfare of Animals during Transport Order 1994, as amended, and other British animal welfare legislation, which together with that Order implemented EU Council Directive 91/628/EEC on the protection of animals during transport. It also implemented the amending Council Directive 95/29/EEC.

Two further items of legislation have recently been introduced. The Welfare of Animals (Staging Points) Order 1998 (SI 1998/2537) implements in the UK the provisions of EU Council Regulation 1255/97/EC on the provision of staging points for animals in transit. It specifies the approval authority and the powers of veterinary inspectors in relation to such premises and identifies the offences that may be committed for breach of the Order.

The Welfare of Animals (Transport)(Amendment) Order 1999 (SI 1999/1622) which came into effect on 1 July 1999 implements in the UK the requirements of EU Council Regulation 411/98/EC on animal protection standards applicable to road vehicles used for the carriage of livestock on journeys exceeding eight hours, by creating an offence for any person to use a road vehicle for the transport of animals in contravention of the regulation.

Most recently, in August 1999, The Ministry of Agriculture, Fisheries and Food (MAFF) issued a consultation document with the intention of reviewing (after two years in operation) current rules on the transport of animals.

General rules

As a general rule it is illegal to transport any animal in a way which is likely to cause injury or unnecessary suffering and which is in contravention of the new Order. The person in charge of animals in transit must ensure that they are not injured or suffer unnecessarily while waiting to be loaded or after being unloaded. On journeys over 50 kilometres animals must be given sufficient space having regard to their weight, size and physical condition, to weather conditions and the likely journey time. They must be fed and watered before and during a journey at specified intervals and must be transported to their destination without delay.

Fitness of animals to travel

It is illegal to transport any animal unless it is fit for the intended journey, and suitable provision has been made for its care during the journey and on arrival at its destination. Animals are not considered fit for an intended journey if they are ill, injured, infirm or fatigued, unless the intended journey is not likely to cause them unnecessary suffering.

Animals may be transported to the nearest available place for veterinary treatment or diagnosis, or to the nearest available place of slaughter, provided they are not likely to suffer unnecessarily. When transported under this provision they must not be dragged or pushed by any means, or lifted by a mechanical device, except under the supervision of a veterinary surgeon. Animals which fall ill or are injured during transport must be given first aid or veterinary treatment as soon as possible, or be slaughtered without unnecessary suffering.

Journey times, feeding and watering

Normally, journey times for cattle, sheep, pigs, goats and horses must not exceed eight hours. However, where the transporting vehicle meets the following additional requirements, journey times may be extended:

- where there is sufficient bedding on the floor of the vehicle;
- provided appropriate feed is carried for the animals concerned and for the length of the journey;
- where there is direct access to the animals;
- where adequate ventilation is provided which can be adjusted depending on both inside and outside temperatures;
- where movable panels are provided for creating separate compartments;
- if it is equipped for connection to a water supply during stops;
- if, when transporting pigs, sufficient liquid is carried for drinking during the journey.

Provided the above requirements are met, watering and feeding intervals, journey times and rest periods may be extended as follows:

- Unweaned calves, lambs, kids and foals which are still on a milk diet and unweaned piglets must be rested for at least one hour (ie sufficient for them to be given liquid and fed) after nine hours of travel. After this they may be transported for a further nine hours.
- Pigs may be transported for a maximum of 24 hours but they must have continuous access to liquid during the journey.
- Horses may be transported for a maximum of 24 hours but they must be given liquid during the journey and, if necessary, be fed every eight hours.
- All other cattle, sheep and goats must be rested for at least one hour (ie sufficient for them to be given liquid and fed) after 14 hours of travel. After this they may be transported for a further 14 hours.

When the maximum journey times specified have been reached, animals must be unloaded, fed and watered and be rested for at least 24 hours. Where it is solely in the interests of the animals, the maximum journey times mentioned above may be extended by two hours, depending on the proximity to the final destination (ie it would not be expected that journeys would be curtailed when within close proximity of their final destination).

Unweaned calves, lambs, kids and foals which are still on a milk diet and unweaned piglets may be transported for nine hours from a market if the journey to the market took not more than four hours (or nine hours if it was in a vehicle as described above). Pigs or horses may be transported for nine hours from a market if the journey to market took not more than four hours (or eight hours if it was in a vehicle complying with items one to four listed above). All other cattle, sheep and goats may be transported for 14 hours from a market if the journey to market took not more than four hours (or 14 hours if it was in a vehicle as described above).

Accompaniment by competent persons

Hauliers carrying animals on journeys of over 50 km in length, or a person who accompanies the animals on the journey, must have had specific training or equivalent practical training to enable them to handle the animals properly and administer care where necessary.

A system for establishing competence in the handling and care for animals in transport is to be instituted (the Order sets out a framework for competence – see below). Those with practical experience (as opposed to specific training) must be assessed as to their ability, competence and knowledge and have a record to this effect, which must be kept by the transporter while the person concerned is engaged on livestock journeys and for six months after such time. The record must be produced on request by an inspector.

The Order specifies the 'framework of competences' – the knowledge which people responsible for the welfare of animals during transport must have. They must have:

- an understanding of
  - when to seek veterinary help and knowledge,
  - which body or organization to contact with general questions (eg about transport conditions),
  - matters of law or documentation;
- knowledge of the powers of enforcement authorities to inspect animals, documentation and vehicles before, during and after a journey;
- basic knowledge of authorization requirements for transporters and when such authorization is necessary;
- knowledge of how to plan a journey (taking account of such factors as maximum travelling times, required rest periods, and the time taken to load and unload), and the ability to anticipate changing conditions and make contingencies for unforeseen circumstances;
- understanding of when route plans or documentation are required and how to complete these documents;

- knowledge of vehicle construction and use requirements in current welfare legislation;
- the ability to load, operate and control a vehicle safely, efficiently and effectively so as to ensure the welfare of the animals;
- knowledge of the appropriate methods for handling animals during loading and unloading, including the use of visual fields and flight zones, lighting and the appropriate use of such things as sticks, boards, blindfolds and electric goads – and know which handling methods are prohibited;
- knowledge of the specific requirements of the Order relating to different animal species for the provision of rest, feed and liquid;
- knowledge of stocking densities (ie the effects of overcrowding and understocking) and headroom and segregation requirements, taking account of the species being transported, methods of transport, sex, condition, age, length of journey and ambient conditions;
- an understanding of the importance, for animal welfare, of temperatures both inside and outside the vehicle, including the effect on different species and the need for the adjustment of ventilation;
- an ability to clean and disinfect vehicles and a knowledge of when it is necessary to do so before and after the journey;
- elementary knowledge of the causes of stress in animals, ability to recognize the signs of stress and ill-health, and basic knowledge of how to reduce such symptoms;
- an ability to care for animals which become unfit or injured during transport, including an understanding of when to seek veterinary advice;
- knowledge of the limited circumstances when it is permissible to transport unfit animals for veterinary treatment or for slaughter.

Tighter rules on competence for persons in charge of animals during transportation were introduced from 1 July 1998 after which date such persons must have demonstrated that they are qualified to handle, transport, care for and safeguard the welfare of animals.

The Ministry of Agriculture, Fisheries and Food (MAFF) has produced a guidance booklet on the subject for employers, *Assessment of Practical Experience in the Handling, Transport and Care of Animals*.

Authorizations and registration

Authorizations, issued in writing by the appropriate authority, are required by livestock transporters who carry animals on journeys over 50 kilometres. Authorizations may be either 'general' or 'specific' and may be made subject to conditions.

Applicants for authorizations must be persons fit to transport animals (ie persons who have not committed any offences relating to animal welfare or contravened provisions of the Animal Welfare Act of 1981). Authorizations may be suspended or revoked for breach of the Order or of Council Directive 91/628/EEC whether this results in conviction or not.

Specific authorizations are issued by the Minister only to a named transporter and cover activities described in the authorization. General authorizations do not name individual transporters but cover individual transporters resident in Great Britain or transporter companies incorporated in Great Britain undertaking activities described in the authorization.

Since 1 October 1997 a specific authorization has been required for transporting cattle, sheep, pigs, goats and horses in a road vehicle on journeys exceeding eight hours' duration. For journeys of less than eight hours only a general authorization is needed

Although a transporter may be covered by a general authorization for certain activities, this does not prevent him also holding a specific authorization for the same activities. However, where a specific authorization has been issued the general authorization no longer applies to animals covered by the specific authorization, and the transporter must not carry out any transport of those particular animals except under the terms of the specific authorization. Furthermore, if the specific authorization is revoked, or limited in any way (see below), then the transporter may not transport the animals concerned under the general authorization

Both specific and general authorizations may be amended or revoked by the Minister, the former by notice in writing served on the transporter to whom the specific authorization was granted, and the latter by publication in a manner determined by the Minister. In the case of general authorizations the Minister may give notice in writing to a transporter, either excluding him from transport operations under a general authorization, or imposing on him additional conditions differing from the conditions in the general authorization.

Revocation or suspension of a specific authorization, or removal of a transporter from a general authorization, either temporarily or permanently, would occur if the transporter or any associate, employee or agent of the transporter:

- repeatedly infringes this Order in Great Britain (or any other Order implementing Council Directive 91/628/EEC);
- commits a single act resulting in serious suffering to animals (whether or not such an act leads to a criminal conviction);
- in the case of a journey taking place partly within and partly outside Great Britain, breaches the rules relating to route plans or repeatedly

infringes national legislation implementing Council Directive 91/628/EEC, or a single such infringement involving serious suffering to animals (whether or not this leads to a criminal conviction).

The Minister must notify an offending transporter in writing that he is minded to revoke the authorization, or suspend it until a specified date or indefinitely.

Route plans

Where horses, cattle, sheep, pigs and goats are traded between member states or exported to third countries on journeys exceeding eight hours, the transporter must draw up and sign a route plan. This route plan must be submitted along with an application for an export health certificate for approval by the Ministry. It will be returned with an authorization stamping and with the appropriate health certificates. Where more than one transporter is involved in such a journey the route plan requirements must be met by the person consigning the animals for the whole of the journey.

It is an offence to transport animals on such journeys unless an approved route plan is in force. The original of the route plan and the attached health certificates must accompany the consignment throughout the journey. All reasonable steps must be taken to comply with the route plan.

Feeding and watering times during the journey must be endorsed on the route plan (at the time they take place) by the person in charge of the animals.

When a route plan journey is completed, the person who signed it when it was originally submitted must certify in writing on the route plan that it was complied with or, if not, must describe the actual journey together with the reasons for the route plan not being followed.

Within 15 days of completion of the journey the route plan must be returned to the issuing office and the sender must keep (for six months) proof that it was sent and of the date on which it was sent. The transporter must also keep a second copy of the route plan for six months from completion of the journey, and produce it on demand at the request of an inspector and allow copies to be taken.

The information to be provided on the route plan is as follows.

Section 1 – information to be completed before the journey:

- Name, full address, business name, telephone number and fax number of the transporter.
- Number and species of animals to be transported.
- Health certificate number(s).
- Number of the transporter's authorization (if any).

- Registration number of the vehicles to be used, and the trailers if different.
- Name of the person(s) in charge of the transport during the journey.
- Place where the animals are to be first loaded, and full address.
- Planned date and time of departure.
- Full itemized itinerary of the journey.
- Full address of the final destination.
- Estimated date and time of arrival at the final destination (local time).

Section 2 – information to be completed during the journey:

- Actual date and time of loading the first animal.
- Actual time of departure from the place of loading.
- Full itemized itinerary of the journey.
- Actual date and time of arrival at the final destination (local time).

Animal transport certificates

Where animals are transported other than under a route plan they must be accompanied by documentation which shows:

- The name and address of the transporter.
- The name and address of the owner of the animals.
- Where the animals were loaded and their final destination.
- The date and time the first animal was loaded.
- The date and time of departure.
- The time and place where rest period requirements were met.

This documentary requirement does not apply where poultry and domestic birds are transported for distances of not more than 50 kilometres and where the number of such poultry and domestic birds is less than 50, or the entire journey is on land occupied by the owner of the poultry and domestic birds.

In the case of animals which are not cattle, sheep, pigs, goats, horses or poultry and domestic birds, the documentary requirement mentioned above does not apply to journeys of 50 kilometres or less.

Transporters are required to retain a copy of the documentation for a period of six months from the completion of the journey, and must produce it to an inspector on demand and allow a copy to be taken. Where such copy is kept in electronic or magnetic form, the inspector may request its production in written form and for copies to be taken in writing.

Powers of livestock inspectors

Where they consider that animals are being transported, or are about to be transported, in a manner likely to cause injury or unnecessary suffering, or in any other way in contravention of the Order, inspectors appointed for the purposes of the Animal Health Act 1981 by the Minister or by a local authority* may serve notice on the person in charge of the animals requiring them to take any action necessary to ensure compliance with the Order and giving reasons for the requirements.

*In practice these inspectors will be veterinary inspectors from the State Veterinary Service, a local veterinary inspector of MAFF, or an officer from the trading standards department of a local authority.

In particular the inspector may:

- prohibit that movement of the animals, either indefinitely or for a specified period;
- specify conditions under which the animals may be transported;
- require the journey to be completed or the animals to be returned to their place of departure by the most direct route, provided this would not cause unnecessary suffering to the animals;
- require the animals to be held in suitable accommodation with appropriate care until the problem is solved;
- require the humane slaughter of the animals.

Inspectors may, where necessary for identification purposes, mark an animal. It is an offence for any person to remove, deface, obliterate or alter such marks.

Construction of vehicles

The Order specifies general requirements for the construction and maintenance of vehicles and receptacles. In particular they must:

- be safe and not cause injury or suffering during transport, or while loading or unloading;
- be weatherproof;
- allow space for animals to lie down;
- have strong, non-slip floors which are free of protrusions;
- protect animals from the weather and from excessive humidity, heat and cold;
- be free of sharp edges;
- allow appropriate cleaning and disinfection;
- be escape-proof;
- prevent animals from undue exposure to noise or vibration;

- provide sufficient natural or artificial light to enable animals to be properly cared for;
- have partitions if necessary which
  - provide adequate support and prevent animals being thrown about during transport,
  - are of rigid construction and strong enough to bear the weight of any animal,
  - do not obstruct ventilation.

When transporting animals (ie all mammals and birds):

- they must not be subject to severe jolting or shaking;
- they must not be injured during loading or unloading;
- they must be driven without excessive use of prods and such like;
- the vehicle must carry means for emergency unloading;
- they must be segregated from goods carried on the same vehicle;
- carcasses must not be carried on the same vehicle except those of animals which die on the journey;
- the vehicle or receptacle must have been thoroughly cleaned and, where appropriate, disinfected;
- dead animals, soiled litter and droppings must be removed as soon as possible;
- vehicle/receptacle floors must be covered with sufficient litter, unless alternative arrangements are made or urine and droppings are regularly removed;
- receptacles must be marked/labelled to indicate
  - they contain live animals of a named species,
  - the upright position;
- receptacles must be kept upright and secured during transport;
- at least one attendant must accompany the animals unless
  - receptacles are secure,
  - adequately ventilated,
  - contain sufficient food and liquid, in dispensers which cannot tip over, for a journey of twice the anticipated time,
  - the transporter (driver) acts as the attendant,
  - the consignor has appointed an agent to care for the animals at stopping or transfer points.

Additional provisions relating to the construction and maintenance of vehicles and receptacles and for the transport of animals are as follows:

- There must be sufficient space for animals to stand normally.
- They must allow adequate ventilation and provide space above the animals to enable air to circulate properly.

- They must allow for the inspection of animals and their feeding and watering.
- Road vehicles must have a roof to protect against the weather.
- Have barriers (for horse-carrying vehicles, straps) to prevent animals falling out when doors are opened.
- Ramps on vehicles must (so as not to cause injury)
  - prevent slipping,
  - not be too steep for the animals being carried,
  - not have a top or bottom step which is too high,
  - not have gaps at the top or bottom which are too wide.
- Road vehicles must enable inspection of the animals from the outside (and must have suitable footholds).
- For animals which are normally tied, tying facilities must be provided and ties must be
  - strong enough not to break during normal transport conditions,
  - designed to eliminate any danger of strangulation or injury,
  - long enough to allow animals to lie down and to eat and drink.
  NB: Animals must not be tied by their horns or by a nose ring.
- On multi-deck vehicles, suitable ramps or lifting gear of sufficient strength must be provided.
- Certain animals must be segregated during transport as follows:
  - a cow with a suckling calf,
  - a sow with unweaned piglets,
  - a mare with a foal at foot,
  - a bull over 10 months old,
  - a breeding boar over 6 months old,
  - a stallion.
  NB: Bulls, boars and stallions may be carried with others of the same species/sex if they have been raised in compatible groups or are accustomed to one another – other animals of mixed species may be carried together if separation from their companions would cause them distress.
- Animals must not be carried together if, due to differences in their age and size, injury or unnecessary suffering may be caused. Also, animals which are hostile to each other or fractious must not be carried together.
- Other animals which must not be carried together are:
  - uncastrated male adults with female animals (unless accustomed to each other),
  - horned cattle with unhorned cattle,
  - broken horses with unbroken horses (unless they are all secured).
- Animals must not be suspended by mechanical means, lifted or dragged by the head, horns, legs, tail or fleece.
- Excessive force must not be used to control animals including no use of:
  - electric shock instruments,
  - stick, goad or other instrument (to hit cattle under 6 months old),

– stick, non-electric goad or other instrument (to hit or prod pigs).
NB: Use of such items is allowed on the hindquarters of cattle over 6 months old and on adult pigs which are refusing to move forward when there is space to do so – but such action must be avoided as far as possible.

- Attendants must look after animals including, if necessary, feeding and watering them.
- Animals in milk must be milked at appropriate intervals – in the case of cows in milk this must be at intervals of about 12 hours but not exceeding 15 hours.
- Horses being transported in groups must wear halters unless they are unbroken and have their hind feet unshod.
- Horses must not be transported in vehicles with more than one deck in operation.

When poultry and domestic birds and domestic rabbits are carried, further requirements are specified for the construction and maintenance of vehicles and receptacles:

- Adequate ventilation and air space must be provided.
- Receptacles must allow inspection of and care for the animals.
- Receptacles must be of such size as to protect the animals from injury or unnecessary suffering during transport.
- Receptacles for carrying birds must prevent the protrusion of heads, legs or wings.
- Birds must not be carried in a sack or bag.
- Birds must not be lifted or carried by the head, neck, wing or tail except:
  – ducks which may be lifted or carried by the neck,
  – geese which may be lifted or carried by the base of both wings.
- Birds must not be tied by the neck, leg or wing.
- Rabbits must not be carried in the same undivided pen, receptacle or road vehicle as an animal of any other species.
- Birds must be segregated according to sex and species except that:
  – female birds may be transported with their broods,
  – male and female chicks may be transported together,
  – male and female birds which are familiar with one another may be transported together,
  – chicks must be segregated from all other poultry except their mother or other chicks.
- Birds must not be transported next to any animal which is hostile to them or in the presence of any animal likely to cause them unnecessary suffering.

NB: The term 'birds' as used above means poultry and domestic birds.

Additional standards for road vehicles

A new EU Council regulation, 411/98/EC, which came into force on 1 July 1999, requires additional standards to be applied to road vehicles used from that date for the carriage of animals on journeys of over eight hours' duration. In particular, the new standards concern access to the vehicle, separation of animals by moveable partitions, detailed arrangements concerning feeding and watering, and the provision of adequate ventilation either by a forced system or a system which will ensure compliance with a prescribed temperature range.

PART 8

Road safety

H1. DRIVER LICENSING

Any person wishing to drive a motor (ie mechanically propelled) vehicle on a public road in the UK or within Europe must hold a licence showing a driving entitlement (either full or provisional) for the relevant category of vehicle. Specifically in the case of goods vehicles, drivers must hold a current licence showing a relevant LGV (large goods vehicle) vocational driving entitlement (either full or provisional). This is the legal responsibility of the individual concerned and heavy penalties are imposed on any person found to be driving either without a licence, without a licence covering the correct category of vehicle, or while disqualified by a court from driving.

Furthermore, it is the responsibility of the employer of any person required to drive for business purposes to ensure that such employee drivers, irrespective of their function, status or seniority, are correctly licensed to drive company vehicles. The fact that a driver may be disqualified or has allowed his licence to lapse without the employer knowing is no defence for the employer against prosecution on a charge of allowing an unlicensed person to drive a vehicle.

Offences

The law states that it is an offence to drive, or to cause or permit another person to drive, a vehicle on the road without a current and valid driving licence. In the case of LGVs, it is an offence to drive, or to cause another person to drive, without a valid licence (ie full or provisional) giving entitlement to drive vehicles in categories C or C+E.

Checking licences

Haulage employers are advised by the police to check their drivers' licences on a regular basis – always initially when giving a driver a job and then at least once every three to six months – otherwise they leave themselves wide open to prosecution for a range of licensing offences and for the vehicle insurance to be invalidated. When checking licences only an original licence should be accepted, never a photocopy, check that all of a driver's first names shown match those in the company record, and that the date of birth also coincides with that recorded at the time of employment.

Invalidation of insurance

Driving without a current and valid driving licence covering the category of vehicle being driven can invalidate insurance cover (which is itself an offence and is usually included among the charges for an unlicensed person driving) and could result in any accident or damage claim being refused by the insurance company under the terms of its policy contract – which is invariably conditional upon the law being complied with in full.

Legislative changes since 1990

Major changes to Britain's ordinary and HGV driving licence schemes were introduced in 1990/1 as the UK harmonized with EU requirements. Since 1 April 1991 the pink and green European 'unified' driving licence (Euro-licence), which shows all of an individual's entitlements to drive (ie for motorcycle, car, light and large goods vehicles, and passenger carrying vehicles as appropriate), has been issued from the DVLA, Swansea. Traffic Commissioners (TCs) no longer have responsibility for issuing large goods and passenger vehicle licences. The Euro-licence carries the words 'European Communities Model' and has 'Driving Licence' printed in the 11 languages of the EU (besides the language of the country of issue), including Greek and Gaelic, on the front. British-issued Euro-licences also show, where appropriate, provisional driving entitlements and any endorsements of penalty points or licence disqualification made by the courts. This part of the document is called the 'counterpart' and is coloured green.

Existing UK licence holders

For a large proportion of British ordinary driving licence holders (ie those who have no vocational – LGV or PCV – entitlements) who currently hold 'licences-for-life', the changes mentioned above will not be noticed unless or until they apply to change the details on their licence (eg to record a new address or, in the case of a woman, applying for a new licence to show her married name), when they will be issued with the new style Euro-licence.

The licensing provisions described in this section are principally contained in the:

- Road Traffic Act 1988;
- Road Traffic (Driver Licensing and Information Systems) Act 1989;
- Road Traffic (New Drivers) Act 1995;
- Motor Vehicles (Driving Licences) Regulations 1996 as amended; and
- Motor Vehicles (Driving Licences)(Large Goods and Passenger Carrying Vehicles) Regulations 1990 (which deal with entitlements to drive large goods vehicles over 7.5 tonnes gross weight and passenger carrying vehicles which are used for hire and reward operations) plus a number of subsequent amendments.

The licence scheme changes brought about by this legislation involved significant change in vocational (ie HGV/PSV) licensing. Particularly, the terminology changed so that heavy goods vehicles (HGV) and public service vehicles (PSV) are now called large goods vehicles (LGV) and passenger carrying vehicles (PCV) respectively, and goods vehicles are no longer classified by the number of axles.

Definitions
For driver licensing purposes:

- a 'large goods vehicle' is 'a motor vehicle (not being a medium-sized goods vehicle) which is constructed or adapted to carry or haul goods and the permissible maximum weight of which exceeds 7.5 tonnes';
- a medium-sized goods vehicle is defined as one having a permissible maximum weight exceeding 3.5 tonnes but not exceeding 7.5 tonnes.
- a large passenger carrying vehicle is a vehicle constructed or adapted to carry more than 16 passengers;
- a small passenger carrying vehicle is a vehicle which carries passengers for hire or reward and which is constructed or adapted to carry more than 8 but not more than 16 passengers.

Unified licences
Where previously drivers had separate licences to drive large vehicles, their qualification to drive them now are referred to as 'entitlements' within the unified licence scheme and are shown in the single combined (ie unified) licence document along with their ordinary (ie car, light goods vehicle and any motorcycle) driving entitlements.

The previous British system of vehicle groups (shown on ordinary licences) and classes (shown on HGV licences) has been changed to the

EU system of vehicle 'categories' (see Table 8.1). Applicants for new or renewed HGV/PSV licences are issued with a 'unified' licence showing their goods (LGV) and/or passenger vehicle (PCV) driving entitlements under these new categories.

Photographs on licences

New British-issued driving licences now carry a photograph of the holder as part of a campaign to eliminate misuse and fraud. Northern Ireland-issued driving licences already carry a photograph of the holder. Plastic photocard driving licences for British licence holders were launched on 23 July 1998. These will eventually replace the current licence, although existing paper licences will remain valid until their expiry or revocation.

Standard information is shown on the licence, such as the individual's name, address and date of birth, the vehicles they are entitled to drive, and the date of issue and expiry of the licence. All this is against a pink background in one of the EU's 11 official languages (plus one other language if required, eg Welsh or Gaelic). The nationality symbol for the country of issue is shown (in the case of UK issued licences, 'UK' will be used rather than 'GB' as shown on vehicle nationality plates) on a blue background and surrounded by the EU's 12 gold stars, together with the holder's photograph.

The new-type licence will be issued to new licence applicants and to existing licence holders who apply for replacements or who wish to change the details on their licence – existing licences will not be recalled for change.

The issuing authority

Responsibility for the issue of vocational driving entitlements rests with the Driver and Vehicle Licensing Agency (the DETR's Executive Agency – DVLA), Swansea. However, it should be noted that the TCs still retain a disciplinary role in regard to vocational entitlements.

Age limits for drivers

Certain minimum ages are specified by law for drivers of various categories of motor vehicle as follows:

Invalid carriage or moped*	16 years
Motor cycle other than a moped* (ie over 50cc engine capacity)	17 years
Small passenger vehicle or small goods vehicle (ie not exceeding 3.5 tonnes gross weight and not adapted to carry more than nine people including the driver)	17 years

Agricultural tractor	17 years
Medium-size goods vehicle (ie exceeding 3.5 tonnes but not exceeding 7.5 tonnes gross weight)	18 years
Other goods vehicles (ie over 7.5 tonnes gross weight) and passenger vehicles with more than nine passenger seats	21 years

*The definition of moped is as follows: in the case of a vehicle first registered before 1 August 1977, a motorcycle with an engine cylinder capacity not exceeding 50cc which is equipped with pedals by means of which it can be propelled. In the case of a vehicle first registered on or after 1 August 1977, a motorcycle which does not exceed the following limits: kerbside weight 250kg; cylinder capacity (if applicable) 50cc.

If a goods vehicle and trailer combination exceeds 3.5 tonnes permissible maximum weight the driver must be at least 18 years of age; if such a combination exceeds 7.5 tonnes the driver must be at least 21 years of age (and will also need to hold an LGV driving entitlement).

Members of the armed forces are exempt from the 21 years age limit for driving heavy goods vehicles when such driving is in aid of the civil community; the limit is reduced to 17 years. Similarly, exemption from the 21-year minimum age limit applies to learner LGV drivers of vehicles over 7.5 tonnes gross weight if they are undergoing registered training by their employer or by a registered training establishment. In this case the minimum age is reduced to 18 years.

Vehicle categories/groups for driver licensing

For driver licensing purposes vehicles are defined according to specified categories which are shown on licences by means of capital letters as indicated in Table 8.1.

Restricted categories for post-1997 drivers

Since 1 January 1997, new drivers passing the car and light vehicle test (ie with vehicles up to 3.5 tonnes permissible maximum weight) for the first time are not permitted to drive vehicles above this weight without securing additional driving categories on their licence. This restriction to 3.5 tonne driving applies *only* to those who first pass their test since this date – it is not applied retrospectively to existing licence holders.

Drivers who pass their car test (ie category B) are not permitted to drive minibuses (in category D1), medium-sized goods vehicles (in category C1), or tow large (over 750kg) trailers (in categories B+E, C1+E and D1+E). They must take a further test if they wish to drive such vehicles or vehicle combinations.

Any driver wishing to drive a vehicle towing a heavy trailer (ie one with a gross weight over 750kg) must first pass a test in the associated rigid vehicle. Learner drivers in categories B, C1, C, D1 and D cannot drive a vehicle towing a trailer of any size.

Towed and pushed vehicles

It has been ruled that a person who steers a vehicle being towed (whether it has broken down or even has vital parts missing, such as the engine) is 'driving' the vehicle for licensing purposes and therefore needs to hold current and valid driving entitlement covering that category of vehicle. Conversely, it has been held that a person pushing a vehicle from the outside (with both feet on the ground) is not 'driving' a vehicle, nor are they 'using' the vehicle.

Learner drivers

Learner drivers must hold a provisional driving entitlement to cover them while driving under tuition. This provisional driving entitlement is shown on the green 'counterpart' of the licence.

Full category C LGV entitlement holders can use this entitlement in place of a provisional entitlement for learning to drive vehicles in category C+E (ie drawbar combinations and articulated vehicles). But it should be noted that full entitlements in categories B and C1 *cannot* be used as a provisional entitlement for learning to drive vehicles in categories C or C+E. A proper provisional entitlement for these classes is required.

Learner drivers must be accompanied, when driving on public roads, by the holder of a full entitlement covering the category of vehicle being driven (see also below) and must not drive a vehicle drawing a trailer, except in the case of articulated vehicles or agricultural trailers.

An 'L' plate of the approved dimensions must be displayed on the front and rear of a vehicle being driven by a learner driver . Learners driving in Wales may alternatively display a 'D' plate.

Learner drivers (of category B and C1 vehicles) are not allowed to drive on motorways. However, learner LGV drivers seeking a licence for category C and C+E vehicles and who hold full entitlements in licence categories B and C1, may drive such vehicles on motorways while under tuition.

Compulsory re-tests for offending new drivers
Newly qualified drivers who tot up six or more penalty points on their licence within two years of passing the test will revert to learner status (ie with the display of 'L' plates and the need to be accompanied by a

Table 8.1

Category	Vehicle type

Motorcycles

A   Motorcycles (with or without sidecar) and scooters but excluding vehicles in category K.
        Additional categories covered: *B1, K, P*

A1   Light motorcycles not over 125cc and 11kW (14.6bhp).
        Additional category covered: *P*

Cars and light vans

B   Motor vehicles up to 3.5 tonnes mass and with not more than eight seats (excluding the driver's seat) including drawing a trailer of up to 750kg mass. Including combinations of category B vehicles and a trailer where the combined weight does not exceed 3.5 tonnes and the weight of the trailer does not exceed the unladen weight of the towing vehicle.
        Additional categories covered: *F, K, P*

B1   Motor tricycles and three/four-wheeled cars and vans up to 550kg unladen with a design speed not exceeding 50kph and, if fitted with an internal combustion engine, a cubic capacity not exceeding 50cc.
        Additional categories covered: *K, P*

B+E   Motor vehicles in category B drawing a trailer over 750kg where the combination does not come within category B.
        Medium goods vehicles

C1   Medium goods vehicles between 3.5 tonnes and 7.5 tonnes (including drawing trailer of up to 750kg – maximum weight of the combination must not exceed 8.25 tonnes).

C1+E   Medium goods vehicles between 3.5 tonnes and 7.5 tonnes and drawing a trailer over 750kg but which does not exceed the unladen weight of the towing vehicle – maximum weight of the combination must not exceed 12 tonnes.
        Additional category covered: B+E

Large goods vehicles

C   Large goods vehicles over 3.5 tonnes (but excluding vehicles in categories D, F, G and H) including those drawing a trailer of up to 750kg.

C+E   Large goods vehicles in category C drawing a trailer exceeding 750kg. *Some C+E licences, where the holder was previously qualified to drive vehicles in old HGV class 2 or 3, show a restriction limiting driving to drawbar combinations only.*
        Additional category covered: *B+E*

Minibuses

D1   Passenger vehicles with between 9 and 16 seats including drawing trailer up to 750kg.

D1+E   Motor vehicles in category D1 drawing a trailer over 750kg – the weight of the trailer must not exceed the unladen weight of the

towing vehicle and the maximum weight of the combination must not exceed 12 tonnes.
Additional category covered: *B+E*

Passenger vehicles

D	Passenger vehicles with more than eight seats including drawing a trailer up to 750kg.
D+E	Passenger vehicles in category D drawing a trailer over 750kg. Additional category covered: *B+E*

Other vehicles

F	Agricultural or forestry tractors but excluding any vehicle in category H.
G	Road rollers.
H	Track-laying vehicles steered by their tracks.
K	Mowing machine or pedestrian-controlled vehicle (with up to three wheels and not over 410kg).
L	Electrically propelled vehicles.
P	Mopeds.

NB: In this table, vehicle/trailer weights, unless otherwise specified, are to be taken as the maximum authorized mass (mam) which is the same as the permissible maximum weight (pmw) for the vehicle/trailer – commonly referred to as the 'gross weight'.

qualified driver) and have to re-pass both the theory test and the practical driving test before regaining a full licence.

Supervision of 'L' drivers

Qualified drivers who supervise learner drivers in cars, and in light, medium and large goods vehicles, must be at least 21 years old, have held a full driving entitlement for a continuous period of at least three years (excluding any periods of disqualification), and for accompanying learner LGV drivers, have held a relevant entitlement (ie for the type of vehicle on which they are supervising) continuously since 6 April 1998.

Exemptions from vocational licensing

Exemptions from the need to hold an LGV driving entitlement (ie in categories C or C+E) apply when driving certain vehicles as follows (in most cases such vehicles may be driven by the holder of a category B licence):

- Steam-propelled vehicles.
- Road construction vehicles used or kept on the road solely for the conveyance of built-in construction machinery.

- Engineering plant, but *not* mobile cranes.
- Works trucks.
- Industrial tractors.
- Agricultural motor vehicles which are not agricultural or forestry tractors.
- Digging machines.
- Vehicles used on public roads only when passing between land occupied by the vehicles' registered keeper and which do not exceed an aggregate of 9.7 kilometres in a calendar week.
- Vehicles, other than agricultural vehicles, used only for the purposes of agriculture, horticulture or forestry, between areas of land occupied by the same person and which do not travel more than 1.5 kilometres on public roads.
- Vehicles used for no purpose other than the haulage of lifeboats and the conveyance of the necessary gear of the lifeboats which are being hauled.
- Vehicles manufactured before 1 January 1960 used unladen and not drawing a laden trailer.
- Articulated goods vehicles with an unladen weight not exceeding 3.05 tonnes.
- Vehicles in the service of a visiting military force or headquarters as defined in the Visiting Forces and International Headquarters (Application of Law) Order 1965.
- Any vehicle being driven by a police constable for the purpose of removing it to avoid obstruction to other road users or danger to other road users or members of the public, for the purpose of safeguarding life or property, including the vehicle and its load, or for other similar purposes.
- Breakdown vehicles which weigh less than 3.05 tonnes unladen, provided they are fitted with apparatus for raising a disabled vehicle partly from the ground and for drawing a vehicle when so raised, are used solely for the purpose of dealing with disabled vehicles, and carry no load other than a disabled vehicle and articles used in connection with dealing with disabled vehicles.
- A passenger-carrying vehicle recovery vehicle other than an articulated vehicle with an unladen weight of not more than 10.2 tonnes which belongs to the holder of a PSV 'O' licence when such a vehicle is going to or returning from a place where it is to give assistance to a damaged or disabled passenger-carrying vehicle or giving assistance to or moving a disabled passenger-carrying vehicle or moving a damaged vehicle.
- A mobile project vehicle, which is defined as a vehicle exceeding 3.5 tonnes pmw constructed or adapted to carry not more than eight

persons in addition to the driver and which carries mainly goods or burden comprising play or educational equipment for children or articles used for display or exhibition purposes.

Application for licences and vocational entitlements

Applications for all driving licences have to be made to Swansea on Form D1 (obtainable from main post offices, direct from Swansea or from Local Vehicle Registration Offices).

Questions on the form are concerned with personal details of the applicant, the type of licence required, any previous licence held and whether the applicant is currently disqualified. LGV/PCV entitlement applicants are asked about any convictions they may have recorded against them.

Health declaration

Applicants are asked to declare information about their health, particularly as to whether they have:

- had an epileptic event (ie seizure or fit);
- sudden attacks of disabling giddiness, fainting or blackouts;
- severe mental handicap;
- had a pacemaker, defibrillator or anti-ventricular tachycardia device fitted;
- diabetes controlled by insulin;
- angina (heart pain) while driving;
- a major or minor stroke;
- Parkinson's disease;
- any other chronic neurological condition;
- a serious problem with memory;
- serious episodes of confusion;
- any type of brain surgery, brain tumour or severe head injury involving hospital in-patient treatment;
- any severe psychiatric illness or mental disorder;
- continuing or permanent difficulty in the use of arms or legs which affects the ability to control a vehicle safely;
- been dependent on or misused alcohol, illicit drugs or chemical substances in the previous three years (excluding drink/driving offences);
- any visual disability which affects both eyes (short/long sight and colour blindness do not have to be declared).

Applicants for LGV/PCV entitlements (unless submitting a medical report – Form D4 – see below) are required to state whether they have:

- sight in only one eye;
- any visual problems affecting either eye;
- angina;
- any heart condition or had a heart operation.

Where a licence applicant has previously declared a medical condition they are required to state what the condition is, whether it has worsened since it was previously declared, and whether any special controls have been fitted to the applicant's vehicle since the last licence was issued.

The DVLA's considerations for vocational entitlements

Applicants for vocational driving entitlements must meet specified conditions:

- they must be fit and proper persons;
- they must meet laid-down eyesight requirements;
- they must satisfy a medical examination and specifically must not have had an epileptic attack in the previous 10 years (see below), or suffer from insulin dependent diabetes.

The decision as to whether or not an applicant will be granted an LGV driving entitlement rests entirely with the DVLA and in making this decision it will take into account any driving convictions for motoring offences, drivers' hours and record offences, and offences relating to the roadworthiness or loading of vehicles, against the applicant in the four years prior to the application, and any offence connected with driving under the influence of drink or drugs during the 11 years prior to the application. The applicant has to declare such convictions on the licence application form (D1) but the DVLA has means of checking to ensure that applicants have declared any such convictions against them.

TCs' powers in respect of vocational entitlements

Although the issue of vocational (LGV/PCV) entitlements is the prerogative of the DVLA, TCs still have powers to consider the fitness of persons applying for or holding such entitlements. This disciplinary role allows a TC to call upon applicants or entitlement holders to provide information as to their conduct (and if necessary to appear before him to answer in person), to refuse the grant of an entitlement, and to suspend or disqualify a person from holding such an entitlement. The TC's decision must be communicated to the person concerned, upon whom it is binding, and to the Secretary of State for Transport (effectively the DVLA).

Date for vocational applications
Application for an LGV driving entitlement should be made not more than three months before the date from which it is required to run. Reminders will be sent out by the DVLA to existing licence/entitlement holders two months prior to the expiry date of their existing licence/entitlement.

Medical requirements for vocational entitlements

Strict medical standards for vocational entitlement holders are legally established to ensure that those wishing to drive large goods or passenger carrying vehicles are safe to do so and are not suffering from any disease or disability (especially cardiovascular disease, diabetes mellitus, epilepsy, neurosurgical disorders, excessive sleepiness, nervous or mental disorders, vision problems, or the excessive use of prescribed medicines or illicit drugs, for example) which would prevent them from driving safely.

UK applicants for LGV driving entitlements must satisfy such medical standards on first application and subsequently. To do so, they must undergo a medical examination and have their doctor complete the medical certificate portion of the application Form D4 not more than four months before the date when the entitlement is needed to commence.

A further examination and completed medical certificate is required for each five-yearly renewal of the entitlement after reaching age 45 years. After reaching the age of 65 years a medical examination is required for each annual renewal of the entitlement. Further medical examinations may be called for at any time if there is any doubt as to a driver's fitness to drive.

The form D4 requests the applicant's consent to allow the DVLA's medical adviser to obtain reports from his own doctor and any specialist consulted if this helps to establish his medical condition.

Medicals for new category C1 drivers
Since 1 January 1997 new drivers of vehicles over 3.5 tonnes gross weight (ie covered by driving licence category C1) require the same medical examination that previously applied only to over 7.5 tonne vocational licence holders and must follow the same regime as described above for subsequent medical examinations (ie five-yearly after age 45 years and annually after age 65 years).

Diabetes
Normally, insulin-dependent diabetes sufferers are barred from holding an LGV entitlement but if they held an HGV driving licence, and the TC was aware of their condition prior to 1 January 1991, an entitlement may be granted. However, new regulations enable some insulin-treated diabetic

drivers to renew their licences to drive medium-sized goods vehicles. This concession applies only to those drivers who already held a category C1 and C1+E driving entitlements covering vehicles up to 7.5 tonnes and goods vehicle and trailer combinations up to 8.25 tonnes on 31 December 1996, and who can show sufficient recent experience of driving such vehicles in the course of their employment to enable a practical assessment of the risk posed to be made.

To renew their entitlement these C1 drivers must:

- have experienced no hypoglycaemic episodes while driving;
- undergo an annual health check by a diabetes specialist;
- show (by a report from the specialist) that they have a history of responsible diabetic control with minimum risk of incapacity due to hypoglycaemia during normal working hours;
- regularly monitor their condition while employed as a driver of such vehicles; and
- satisfy the TC that their driving is not likely to be a source of danger to the public.

Epilepsy

A person will now be prevented from holding an LGV/PCV entitlement *only* if they have a 'liability to epileptic seizures'. Applicants must satisfy the DVLA that:

- they have not suffered an epileptic seizure during the 10 years prior to the date when the entitlement is to take effect;
- no epilepsy treatment has been administered during the 10 years prior to the starting date for the entitlement; and
- a consultant nominated by the DVLA has examined their medical history and is satisfied that there is no continuing liability to seizures.

Car, light vehicle and certain other drivers (ie in licence categories A, B, B+E, F, G, H, K, L and P), but not LGV/PCV drivers, who suffer from epilepsy can obtain a licence provided they have been free from an epileptic attack during the period of one year from the date the licence is granted; or, if not free from such an attack, had an asleep-attack more than three years before the date on which the licence is granted and have had attacks only while asleep between the date of that attack and the date when the licence is granted. The DVLA must be satisfied that their driving will not cause danger.

Coronary health problems

Drivers who have suspected coronary health problems are permitted (since April 1992) to retain their LGV driving entitlements while medical enquiries are made. (Previously the rule was to revoke the licence pending enquiries into the holder's health.) Such drivers no longer have to submit to coronary angiography (ie angiogram testing). The DVLA says that ECG exercise tests will be undertaken no earlier than three months after a coronary event and provided the driver displays no signs of angina or other significant symptoms, he is allowed to keep his driving entitlement while investigations are made, but subject to the approval of his own doctor.

Drivers who have suffered, or are suffering from, the following heart-related conditions must notify the DVLA:

- heart attack (myocardial infarction, coronary thrombosis);
- coronary angioplasty;
- heart valve disease/surgery;
- coronary artery bypass surgery;
- angina (heart pain);
- heart operation (other than a heart transplant).

The DVLA's Drivers Medical Branch will give the following advice to heart sufferers. Following a heart attack or heart operation driving should not be recommended for at least one month following the attack or operation. Driving may be resumed after this time if recovery has been uncomplicated and the patient's own doctor has given his approval.

A driver suffering from angina may continue to drive (whether he is receiving treatment or not) unless attacks occur while driving, in which case he must notify the DVLA immediately (see below) and *stop driving*.

A driver who suffers sudden attacks of disabling giddiness, fainting, falling, loss of awareness or confusion must notify the DVLA immediately (see below) and *stop driving*.

Any driver who has doubts about his ability to continue to drive safely is advised to discuss the matter with his own doctor who has access to medical advice from the DVLA.

Alcohol problems

A person with repeated convictions for drink-driving offences may be required to satisfy the DVLA (with certification from his own doctor) that he does not have an 'alcohol problem' before his licence is restored to him.

Other medical conditions

Other disabilities which may cause failure of the driver's medical examination include:

- sudden attacks of vertigo ('dizziness');

- heart disease which causes disabling weakness or pain;
- a history of coronary thrombosis;
- the use of hypertensive drugs for blood pressure treatment;
- serious arrhythmia;
- severe mental disorder;
- severe behavioural problems;
- alcohol dependency;
- inability to refrain from drinking and driving;
- drug abuse and dependency;
- psychotrophic medicines taken in quantities likely to impair fitness to drive safely.

A licence will be refused to a driver who is liable to sudden attacks of disabling giddiness or fainting unless these can be controlled.

Those who have had a cardiac pacemaker fitted are advised to discontinue LGV driving, although driving vehicles below the 7.5 tonne LGV threshold is permitted if a person who has disabling attacks which are controlled by a pacemaker has made arrangements for regular review from a cardiologist and will not be likely to endanger the public.

Notification of new or worsening medical conditions
Once a licence has been granted (whether ordinary or covering vocational entitlements), the holder is required to notify the Drivers Medical Group, DVLA at Swansea, of the onset, *or worsening*, of any medical condition likely to cause him to be a danger when driving – *failure to do so is an offence*. Examples of what must be reported are:

- giddiness;
- fainting;
- blackouts;
- epilepsy;
- diabetes;
- strokes;
- multiple sclerosis;
- Parkinson's disease;
- heart disease;
- angina;
- 'coronaries';
- high blood pressure;
- arthritis;
- disorders of vision;
- mental illness;
- alcoholism;

- drug-taking; and
- the loss or loss of use of any limb.

In many cases the person's own doctor will either advise him to report his condition to the DVLA himself, or the doctor (or hospital) may advise the DVLA direct. In either case the driving licence will have to be surrendered until the condition clears.

There is no requirement to notify the DVLA of temporary illnesses or disabilities such as sprained or broken limbs where a full recovery is expected within three months.

Enquiries about medical conditions can be raised with the Drivers Medical Group at the DVLA.

Medical appeals and information

The final decision on any medical matter concerning driving licences rests with the Drivers Medical Group of the DVLA. However, there is the opportunity of appeal, within six months in England and Wales to a magistrate's court, and within 21 days in Scotland to a sheriff's court. In other cases the refused driver may be given the opportunity to present further medical evidence which the medical adviser will consider.

Drugs and driving

Official sources say that drugs are a major cause of one in five fatal road accidents. Another source says that driving after smoking cannabis could be a greater danger than drink-driving, and that as many as 3 million people could be driving under the influence of this drug. Yet another report has highlighted the fact that drivers who use tranquillizers are involved in 1,600 road accidents every year – 110 of them fatal.

Illegal drugs

Among the illegal drugs which may be detected and which can adversely affect driving are:

- Cannabis – produces slow reaction times.
- Cocaine – may increase reaction times, but severely affects accuracy and judgement. Has potential to cause hallucination.
- Amphetamines – may increase reaction times in the short term, but severely affects accuracy and judgement.
- Ecstasy – may increase reaction times, but severely affects accuracy and judgement.
- Heroin – produces reduced reaction times and causes drowsiness and sleep.

Prescribed drugs

Prescribed tranquillizers, sedatives and anti-depressants, as well as diabetes and epilepsy drugs, may have an adverse effect on a driver's judgement and reactions and therefore increase the risk of an accident. These include a number of anti-anxiolytic benzodiazepines (prescribed to reduce stress and anxiety) including Valium, Librium and Ativan.

The sedatory effect of these drugs is substantially compounded by the addition of alcohol, even when taken in relatively small quantities, resulting in a potentially significant loss of coordination. Similarly, sleeping tablets (eg Diazepam, Temazepam and Nitrazepam) including the new drug Zopiclone may also have a continuing sedatory effect on a driver the following morning. Furthermore, a whole range of other proprietary medicines such as painkillers, antihistamines, cold and flu remedies, eyedrops, cough medicines and common painkillers taken in sufficient quantities may have similar effects.

If a driver feels drowsy, dizzy, confused, or suffers other side effects that could affect his reaction times or judgement, he should not drive.

Eyesight requirement

The statutory eyesight requirement mentioned above for ordinary (ie car and light goods vehicle) licence holders is for the driver to be able to read, in good daylight (with glasses or contact lenses if worn), a standard motor vehicle number plate from 20.5 metres (67 feet). It is an offence to drive with impaired eyesight and the police can require a driver to take an eyesight test on the roadside. If glasses or contact lenses are needed to reach these vision standards they must be worn at all times while driving. It is an offence to drive with impaired eyesight. There are proposal for drivers to undergo regular eye tests.

Eyesight standards for vocational licence holders

Tougher eyesight standards for LGV and PCV drivers were introduced from 1 January 1997. Specifically, drivers of vehicles in categories C, C1, C+E, C1+E, D, D1, D+E and D1+E – effectively trucks over 3.5 tonnes and passenger vehicles with more than nine seats – must have eyesight which is at least:

- 6/9 on the Snellen scale in the better eye;* and
- 6/12 on the Snellen scale in the other eye;* and
- 3/60 in each eye without glasses or contact lenses.

*These standards may be met with glasses or contact lenses if worn.

To achieve these standards means being able to read the top line of an optician's chart (ie Snellen chart) with each eye from a distance of *at least*

3m without the aid of glasses or contact lenses – if it can only be read from, say, 2.5m or less the test is failed. Wearers of spectacles or contact lenses must have vision of at least 6/9 in the better eye and at least 6/12 in the weaker eye, which means being able to read the sixth line of an optician's chart at 6 metres. Besides these requirements, all drivers must meet existing eyesight standards, which includes having a field of vision of at least 120° (horizontal) and 20° (vertical) in each eye with no double vision.

Licence validity

Full driving entitlements are valid from the date of issue until the applicant's 70th birthday (unlike vocational entitlements – categories C, C+E, D and D+E – see below). After reaching their 70th birthday ordinary entitlement holders must make a new application and, if this is granted, each subsequent licence will be valid for three years.

A provisional HGV licence holder or a provisional (category C or C+E) LGV entitlement holder who passes the LGV driving test will be issued with a test pass certificate which is valid for two years during which time the holder may continue to drive, although the DVLA advice is to convert this to a full entitlement as soon as possible – there is no additional fee for this change. Failure to apply for a full licence within two years of passing the driving test will result in the need to take and pass the test again to obtain a full licence. This time limit applies irrespective of the category of test taken (ie motorcycle, car, LGV or PCV).

An LGV/PCV driving entitlement is normally valid for five years or until the holder reaches the age of 45 years, whichever is the longer. After the age of 45 years, five-year entitlements are granted subject to medical fitness, but may be for lesser periods where the holder suffers from a relevant or prospective relevant disability. From the age of 65 years, vocational entitlements are granted on an annual basis only.

Production of driving licences

Both the police and enforcement officers of the Vehicle Inspectorate (VI) can request a driver – and a person accompanying a provisional entitlement holder – to produce his licence showing his ordinary and vocational entitlements to drive. If he is unable to do so at the time, he may produce them without penalty if the request was by a police officer, at a police station of his choice within seven days, or if the request was by an enforcement officer, at the Traffic Area Office within 10 days.

In either case, if the licence cannot be produced within the 7 or 10 days it can be produced as soon as reasonably practicable thereafter. A TC can also require the holder of an LGV/PCV driving entitlement to produce his licence at a Traffic Area Office for examination within 10 days. Failure to produce a licence on request is an offence.

A police officer can ask a driver to state his or her date of birth – British ordinary driving licences carry a coded number which indicates the holder's surname and their date of birth. The name and address of the vehicle owner can also be requested.

When required by a VI examiner to produce his licence, an LGV entitlement holder may be required to give his date of birth and to sign the examiner's record sheet to verify the fact of the licence examination. This should not be refused.

Licence holders apprehended for endorsable fixed penalty (ie yellow ticket) offences are required to produce their driving licence to the police officer at that time or later (ie within seven days) to a police station and surrender the licence for which they will be given a receipt. Failure to produce a licence in these circumstances means that the fixed penalty procedure will not be followed and a summons for the offence will be issued requiring a court appearance. Drivers summoned to appear in court for driving and road traffic offences must produce their driving licence to the court on, at least, the day before the hearing.

International Driving Permits (IDPs)

Certain foreign countries do not accept British ordinary driving licences – eg Albania, Bulgaria, CIS, Estonia, Hungary, Latvia, Lithuania, Poland, Slovenia and the Ukraine – in which case an IDP will be required by British licence holders wishing to drive in those countries. These permits are obtainable from the RAC, RSAC, AA or Green Flag. A passport-type photograph is required for attachment to the permit. Applicants must be UK residents, over 18 years of age and hold full driving entitlements for the category of vehicle which the IDP is required to cover.

Driving licence penalty points and disqualification

Driving licence holders may be penalized following conviction by a court for offences committed on the road with a motor vehicle. These penalties range from the issue of fixed penalty notices for non-endorsable offences, which do not require a court appearance unless the charge is to be contested, and incur no driving licence penalty points although the relevant fixed penalty has to be paid; to those for endorsable offences when penalty points are added on the licence counterpart and the fixed penalty is incurred or a heavy fine imposed on conviction if a court appearance is made.

In other cases, licence disqualification for a period (extending to a number of years in serious cases – especially for drink-driving related offences), and in very serious instances imprisonment of the offender, may follow conviction in a magistrates' court or indictment for the offence in a higher court. Holders of vocational driving entitlements may be separately penalized for relevant offences, which could result in such entitlements being suspended or revoked and in serious circumstances the holder being disqualified from holding a vocational entitlement – see below.

The penalty points system on conviction and disqualification

Driving licence endorsement of penalty points following conviction for motoring offences is prescribed by the Road Traffic Offenders Act 1988 with further provisions relating to driving offences being contained in the Road Traffic Act 1991.

The penalty points system grades road traffic offences according to their seriousness by a number or range of penalty points, between 2 and 10 points, imposed on the driving licence of the convicted offender. Once a maximum of 12 penalty points has been accumulated within a three-year period counting from the date of the first offence to the current offence (not from the date of conviction), disqualification of the licence for at least six months will follow automatically.

Most offences rate a fixed number of penalty points to ensure consistency and to simplify the administration, but a discretionary range applies to a few offences where the gravity may vary considerably from one case to another. For example, failing to stop after an accident which only involved minor vehicle damage is obviously less serious than a case where an accident results in injury.

Unless the court decides otherwise, when a driver is convicted of more than one offence at the same hearing, only the points relative to the most serious of the offences will normally be endorsed on the licence. Once sufficient points (ie 12) have been endorsed on the driving licence and a period of disqualification has been imposed (six months for the first totting-up of points), the driver will have his 'slate' wiped clean and those points will not be counted again. Twelve more points would have to be accumulated before a further disqualification would follow, but to discourage repeated offences the courts will impose progressively longer disqualification periods in further instances (minimum 12 months for subsequent disqualifications within three years and 24 months for a third disqualification within three years).

Licence endorsement codes and penalty points

Following conviction for an offence, the driver's licence (ie the green counterpart) will be endorsed by the convicting court with a code, to which employers and prospective employers should refer so they can assess the offences drivers have committed, and with the number of penalty points imposed.

Disqualification

The endorsing of penalty points will also arise on conviction for offences where disqualification is discretionary and where the court has decided that immediate disqualification is not appropriate (for example if acceptable 'exceptional' reasons are put forward – see also below). In this case the offender's driving licence will be endorsed with four points. The courts are still free to disqualify immediately if the circumstances justify this.

Offences (Road Traffic Offenders Act 1988, Sch 2) carrying obligatory disqualification are:

- Causing death by dangerous driving and manslaughter.
- Dangerous driving within three years of a similar conviction.
- Driving or attempting to drive while unfit through drink or drugs.
- Driving or attempting to drive with more than the permitted breath-alcohol level.
- Failure to provide a breath, blood or urine specimen.
- Racing and speed trials on the highway.

Driving while disqualified is a serious offence that can result in a fine at level five on the standard scale (see below), or six months' imprisonment, or both.

Special reasons for non-disqualification

The courts have discretion in exceptional mitigating circumstances (ie when there are 'special reasons') not to impose a disqualification. The mitigating circumstance must not be one which attempts to make the offence appear less serious and no account will be taken of hardship other than exceptional hardship. Pleading that you have a wife and children to support or that you will lose your job is not generally considered to be exceptional hardship for the purposes of determining whether or not disqualification should be imposed.

If account has previously been taken of circumstances in mitigation of a disqualification, the same circumstances cannot be considered again within three years.

Where a court decides, in exceptional circumstances as described above, not to disqualify a convicted driver, four penalty points will be added to the driver's licence in lieu of the disqualification.

Driving offences

Dangerous driving

The previous charge of reckless driving was replaced from 1 July 1992, by a charge of 'dangerous' driving. A person is to be regarded as driving dangerously if the way he drives 'falls far short of what would be expected of a competent and careful driver, and it would be obvious to a competent and careful driver that driving in that way would be dangerous'. Driving would be regarded as dangerous 'if it was obvious to a competent and careful driver that driving the vehicle in its current state would be dangerous' – this obviously applies to the vehicle's mechanical condition or the way it is loaded. Also, 'dangerous' refers to danger either of injury to any person or of serious damage to property. The principal offences to which this relates are dangerous driving and causing death by dangerous driving.

Interfering with vehicles, etc

It is an offence for any person to cause danger to road users by way of intentionally and without lawful authority placing objects on a road, interfering with motor vehicles, or directly or indirectly interfering with traffic equipment (road signs, etc).

Penalties

Penalties for these offences are heavy. For example, causing death by careless driving while under the influence of drink or drugs carries a maximum penalty of up to five years in prison and/or a fine. For causing a danger to road users the maximum penalty is up to seven years' imprisonment and/or a fine.

In addition to disqualification and the endorsement of penalty points on driving licences, courts may impose fines and, for certain offences, imprisonment. The maximum fine for most offences is determined by reference to a scale set out in the Criminal Justice Act 1991 (ie Level 1 to Level 5).

Offences such as dangerous driving, failing to stop after an accident or failure to report an accident, and drink-driving offences, carry the maximum fine, as do certain vehicle construction and use offences (eg overloading, insecure loads, using a vehicle in a dangerous condition) and using a vehicle without insurance.

New driver penalties

The Road Traffic (New Drivers) Act 1995 concerns new drivers who first passed their driving test on or after 1 June 1997. Where such drivers acquire six or more penalty points on their licence within two years of passing that test (the so-called 'probationary period') the DVLA will automatically revoke the licence on notification by a court or fixed penalty office. Such drivers have to surrender their full licence and obtain a provisional licence to start driving again as a learner. They will have to pass both the theory and practical tests again in order to regain their full driving licence.

Penalty points counting towards the total of six include any incurred before passing the test, if this was not more than three years before the latest penalty point offence. Points imposed after the probationary period will also count if the offence was committed during that period.

Passing the retest will not remove the penalty points from the licence; these will remain and if the total reaches 12, the driver will be liable to disqualification by a court.

Short period disqualification (SPD)

If a driver is disqualified for less than 56 days, the court will stamp the counterpart of his driving licence and return it to him. The stamp will show how long disqualification is to last. The licence does not have to be renewed when the SPD ends – it becomes valid again the day following expiry of the disqualification.

Removal of penalty points and disqualifications

Penalty points endorsed on driving licences can be removed after a specified waiting period. The waiting period before which no such application would be accepted are four years from the date of the offence, except in the case of reckless/dangerous driving convictions when the four years is taken from the date of conviction. Endorsements for alcohol-related offences must remain on a licence for 11 years.

Licences returned after disqualification will show no penalty points but previous disqualifications (within four years) will remain and if a previous alcohol/drugs driving offence disqualification has been incurred, this will remain on the licence for 11 years.

Application may be made by disqualified drivers for reinstatement of their licence after varying periods of time depending on the duration of the disqualifying period as follows:

- Less than two years – no prior application time.
- Less than four years – after two years have elapsed.
- Between four years and ten years – after half the time has elapsed.
- In other cases – after five years have elapsed.

The courts are empowered to require a disqualified driver to retake the driving test before restoring a driving licence, and following the introduction of provisions contained in the Road Traffic Act 1991, it is now mandatory for them to impose 'extended' re-tests following disqualification for the most serious of driving offences, namely, dangerous driving, causing death by dangerous driving and manslaughter by the driver of a motor vehicle (in Scotland, the charge is culpable homicide).

Re-tests for offending drivers

Where drivers are convicted of the offences of manslaughter, causing death by dangerous driving or dangerous driving and mandatory disqualification is imposed, an 'extended' re-test (involving at least one hour's driving) must be taken before the driving licence is restored. This also applies to drivers disqualified under the penalty points totting-up procedure. Courts may also order drivers disqualified for lesser offences to take an appropriate (ie ordinary) driving test.

Drink-driving and breath tests

It is an offence to drive or attempt to drive a motor vehicle when the level of alcohol in the breath is more than 35 micrograms per 100 millilitres of breath. This is determined by means of an initial breath test, conducted on the spot when the driver is stopped, and later substantiated by a test on a breath-testing machine (eg Lion Intoximeter) at a police station. The breath/alcohol limit mentioned above equates to the blood/alcohol limit of 80 milligrams of alcohol in 100 millilitres of blood or the urine/alcohol limit of 107 milligrams of alcohol in 100 millilitres of urine.

Failure to produce a breath sample and low breath-test readings

If the person suspected of an alcohol-related offence cannot, due to health reasons, produce a breath sample, or if a breath test shows a reading of not more than 50 micrograms of alcohol per 100 millilitres of breath, he is given the opportunity of an alternative test, either blood or urine, for laboratory analysis. This test can only be carried out at a police station or a hospital and the decision as to which alternative is chosen rests with the police (unless a doctor present determines that for medical reasons a blood test cannot or should not be taken). Similarly, if a breath test of a driver shows the proportion of alcohol to be no more than 50 micrograms in 100 millilitres of breath, the driver can request an alternative test (ie blood or urine) as described above for those who cannot provide a breath sample for analysis.

Prosecution for drink-driving offences

Prosecution will follow a failure to pass the test, which will result in a fine or imprisonment and automatic disqualification from driving. Failure to submit to a breath test and to a blood or urine test are serious offences, and drivers will find themselves liable to heavy penalties on conviction and potentially long-term disqualification or driving licence endorsement (endorsements for such offences remain on a driving licence for 11 years).

The police *do not* have powers to carry out breath tests at random but they *do have* powers to enter premises to require a breath test from a person suspected of driving while impaired through drink or drugs, or who has been driving or been in charge of a vehicle that has been involved in an accident in which another person has been injured.

Drink-driving disqualification

Conviction for a first drink-driving offence will result in a minimum one year period of disqualification, and for a second or subsequent offence of driving or attempting to drive under the influence of drink or drugs longer periods of disqualification will be imposed. If the previous such conviction took place within 10 years of the current offence the disqualification must be for at least three years.

Drivers convicted twice for drink-driving offences may have their driving licence revoked altogether. Offenders who are disqualified twice within a 10-year period for any drink-driving offences, and those found to have an exceptionally high level of alcohol in the body (ie more than two and a half times over the limit), or those who twice refuse to provide a specimen, will be classified as high-risk offenders (HROs) by the Driver and Vehicle Licensing Agency. They will be required to show that they no longer have an 'alcohol problem' by means of a medical examination (including blood analysis of liver enzymes) by a DVLA-approved doctor before their licence will be restored to them.

Penalties against vocational entitlements

Where a licence holder is disqualified from driving following conviction for offences committed with cars or other light vehicles, or as a result of penalty point totting-up, any vocational entitlement which that person holds is automatically lost until the licence is reinstated. Additionally, the holder of an LGV/PCV vocational entitlement may have this revoked or suspended by the DVLA without reference to the TC – see below – and be disqualified from holding such entitlement, for a fixed or an indefinite period, at any time, on the grounds of misconduct or physical disability. Furthermore, a person can be refused a new LGV/PCV driving entitlement following licence revocation, again either indefinitely or for some other period of time which the Secretary of State (via the DVLA) specifies. A new vocational test may be ordered before the entitlement is restored – see further below.

Disqualification from holding an LGV vocational entitlement as described above does not prevent a licence holder from continuing to drive vehicles within the category B and C1 entitlements that he holds.

The TCs continue to play a disciplinary role under the new licensing scheme in regard to driver conduct, but only at the request of the DVLA. They have powers under the new provisions to call drivers to a public inquiry (PI) to give information and answer questions as to their conduct. Their duty is to report back to the DVLA if they consider that an LGV/PCV entitlement should be revoked or the holder disqualified from holding an entitlement – the DVLA must follow the TC's recommendation in these matters.

Failure to attend a PI when requested to do so (unless a reasonable excuse is given) means that the DVLA will automatically refuse a new vocational entitlement or suspend or revoke an existing entitlement.

Large goods vehicle drivers who have been off the road for a period of time after being disqualified are having to prove themselves capable of driving small goods vehicles legally and safely for a period of time before their LGV driving entitlement may be restored by the TCs.

Rules on disciplining LGV entitlement holders require TCs to follow a set of recommended guidelines in imposing penalties against such entitlements. Under these rules, and where there are no aggravating circumstances, a driver being disqualified for 12 months or less should be sent a warning letter with no further disqualification of the LGV entitlement. Where a driving disqualification is for more than one year, the offender should be called to appear before the TC and he should incur an additional suspension of his LGV entitlement, amounting to between one and three months. The intention here is to allow the person to regain his driving skills and road sense in a car before driving a heavy vehicle again. Where two or more driving disqualifications of more than eight weeks have been incurred within the past five years, and the combined total of disqualification exceeds 12 months, the driver should be called to a PI and a further period of LGV driving disqualification imposed amounting to between three and six months.

In the case of new LGV entitlements, for applicants who already have nine or more penalty points on their ordinary licence, the guidelines recommend that the TC should issue a warning as to future conduct or suggest that the applicant tries again when the penalty points total on his licence has been reduced.

Removal of LGV driving licence disqualification

Drivers disqualified from holding an LGV/PCV entitlement, as described above, may apply to have the disqualification removed after two years if it was for less than four years, or after half the period if the disqualification was for more than four years but less than 10 years. In any other case including disqualification for an indefinite period an application for its removal cannot be made until five years have elapsed. If an application for the removal of a disqualification fails, another application cannot be made for three months.

The DVLA will not necessarily readily restore LGV/PCV driving entitlements on application following disqualification of a driving licence. An applicant may be called to a PI by a TC who will inquire into the events which led to the disqualification and who may also decide that the applicant must wait a further period before applying again, must spend a period driving small (ie up to 7.5 tonne) vehicles, or must take a new LGV/PCV driving test in order to regain the vocational entitlement.

Appeals

If the DVLA refuses to grant an application for an LGV/PCV driving entitlement or revokes, suspends or limits an existing entitlement, the applicant or entitlement holder may appeal against the decision under the Road Traffic Act 1988. The first step is for him to notify the DVLA, and any TC involved in consideration of the applicant's conduct, of his intention to appeal. The appeal can then be made to a magistrates' court acting for the petty sessions in England or Wales, or in Scotland to the local sheriff.

Road traffic offences and legal action

When road traffic-related offences are committed alternative procedures may be followed by the police (or traffic wardens where appropriate) in the way of legal action. Depending on the nature of the offence, the offender may be issued with a fixed-penalty notice or reported for prosecution and required to answer directly to the court. These various procedures are described here.

Fixed-penalty system

Fixed-penalty notices (tickets) may be issued for a very large number of traffic, motoring and vehicle offences. Generally these will be issued by the police but traffic wardens are empowered to issue them for some offences. When offences are committed, the driver of the vehicle is given a notice which specifies the offence, an indication as to whether it is a driving licence endorsable or non-endorsable offence (ie by the colour and wording on the notice), and the penalty which has to be paid. If the driver is not available the ticket may be attached to the vehicle windscreen, but the driver is still responsible for paying the penalty. Should the driver of a vehicle fail to pay, responsibility for payment will rest with the registered vehicle keeper (ie the person/company whose name is on the registration document).

Fixed-penalty procedure

The fixed-penalty system for dealing with road traffic and related offences is operated by the police and, to a certain extent, by traffic wardens. Some 250 motoring offences are included in the scheme, divided into driving licence endorsable offences and non-endorsable offences. The former involves the police issuing a yellow penalty ticket for which a penalty is payable and the driving licence being confiscated and returned with the appropriate penalty points added when the penalty is paid.

If the offender does not have his driving licence with him at the time a penalty notice will not be issued on the spot but will be issued at the police station when the driving licence is produced there within seven days. For non-endorsable offences a white ticket (involving a lesser penalty) is issued either to the driver, if present, or is fixed to the vehicle.

Any driver who receives a fixed-penalty notice (yellow or white) can elect to have the matter dealt with by a court so he can defend himself or put forward mitigating circumstances. Alternatively he can accept that he was guilty of the offence and pay the penalty. However, failure to pay the penalty within the requisite period (28 days) will result in the penalties being increased by 50 per cent. In this case the increased amount becomes a fine and non-payment will lead to arrest and a court appearance. Among the offences covered by the scheme are the following.

Yellow ticket (endorsable):

- Speeding.
- Contravention of motorway regulations.
- Defective vehicle components (brakes, steering, tyres, etc) and vehicle in a dangerous condition.
- Contravention of traffic signs.
- Insecure and dangerous loads.
- Leaving vehicles in dangerous positions.
- Contravention of pedestrian rights.

White ticket (non-endorsable):

- Not wearing seat belt.
- Driving and stopping offences (reversing, parking, towing, etc).
- Contravention of traffic signs, box junctions, bus lanes, etc.
- Contravening driving prohibitions.

- Vehicle defects (brakes, steering, speedometer, wipers, etc).
- Contravening exhaust and noise regulations.
- Exceeding weight limits (overloading, etc).
- Contravention of vehicle lighting requirements.
- Contravention of vehicle excise requirements.

This is only a summary of a very extensive list of offences included within the scheme.

Failure to pay a fixed penalty within the prescribed period can result in a fine unless a statutory statement of ownership or of fact (to the effect that he was not the legal owner of the vehicle at the time the alleged offence was committed or that, if he was the owner at the relevant time, the vehicle was being used at that time without his permission) has been given to the police in whose area the original offence was committed.

Prosecution

Where one of the following road traffic offences is committed, the offender must be warned of possible prosecution at the time of the offence (unless an accident occurred at that time or immediately afterwards) or alternatively, within 14 days of the offence, must be served with either a Notice of Intended Prosecution or a summons for the offence:

- Dangerous, careless, inconsiderate driving.
- Failure to comply with traffic signs or the directions of a police constable on traffic duty.
- Leaving a vehicle in a dangerous position.

Notice of Intended Prosecution

The Notice of Intended Prosecution must be in writing and must specify the offence and the time and place where it was committed. It must be served on the driver who committed the offence or the registered keeper of the vehicle. If, after due diligence, the police are unable to trace the vehicle driver or registered keeper within 14 days, action can still be taken to bring about a prosecution. If, as a result of the offence (or immediately after the offence was committed), an accident occurs, there is no requirement to serve a Notice of Intended Prosecution.

The summons

In the case of offences other than those listed above, such as those committed immediately before or at the time of an accident, a summons (to answer the charges before the court) should normally be issued within six months of the date of the offence but in the case of certain offences (ie obtaining a driving licence while disqualified; driving while disqualified; using an uninsured vehicle; forging a driving licence or test and insurance certificates or making false statements in connection with driving licences, test and insurance certificates) proceedings may be brought to court up to three years from the date of the offence.

The summons will give details of the offence including when and where it took place. The court at which the case is to be heard will be named within six months (see also above). The recipient of a summons must respond as follows:

- appear in court in person on the appointed day and make a plea of guilty or not guilty; or
- appoint a legal representative to appear in court and make a plea on his behalf; or
- plead guilty in writing to the court and allow the case to be heard in his absence (in certain cases the court may adjourn the hearing and summon the defendant to appear in person). *NB:* A not guilty plea will not (ie cannot) be accepted in writing.

The offender must surrender his driving licence when required to do so to the court, either by delivering it in person or by sending it by post to arrive on the day prior to the hearing or by having it with him at the time of the hearing. If he fails to do this an offence is committed, and the licence will be suspended from the time its production was required and until it is produced (thus to continue driving with it is a further offence). Where a person fails to produce his licence to the court as required the police will request its production and will seize it and hand it over to the court.

Court hearing

Depending on the nature of the offence, the court may hear the case in the absence of the offender and accept a written plea of guilty with a statement of mitigating circumstances. Alternatively, the hearing may be suspended pending the personal appearance of the offender. Following the hearing, a verdict will be reached. If the offender is judged not guilty, there will be no conviction and the matter is ended.

If the offender is found guilty, a summary conviction is made. If the case concerns an indictable offence (ie one which must be tried before a jury) the accused may be bailed or remanded for the case to be heard by the Crown Court. On conviction (indictment) by the court, a penalty will be imposed (a fine or imprisonment or both) as appropriate to the offence. The driver may be disqualified from driving or have his licence endorsed with an appropriate number of penalty points.

Where an offence requires obligatory disqualification under the Road Traffic Offenders Act 1988, 34{1} (see page 351) but for special reasons the court decides not to impose that penalty it must, as an alternative, endorse a penalty of four points (see below for description of penalty points system) on the offender's driving licence (ie on the counterpart under the new 'unified' licence scheme). Further offences under the Road Traffic Act 1988 allow the courts a discretionary power of disqualification with the alternative of the obligatory endorsement of a specified number of penalty points on the offender's licence (see below).

12-point disqualification

The penalty points system described below does not alter the mandatory disqualification procedure on conviction for serious offences. Also, disqualification of the driving licence will automatically follow, for a minimum of six months, when 12 or more penalty points are endorsed on the licence in a period of three years counting from the date of the *first offence* to the *current offence* and *not* from the date of conviction (but see also below).

Subsequent disqualifications

When a driver has been disqualified once, any subsequent disqualifications within three years (preceding the date of the latest offence – *not conviction*) will be for progressively longer periods (minimum of 12 months for two disqualifications and 24 months for three disqualifications).

The court has discretion to disqualify for a period of less than the normal six-month minimum or not to disqualify when 12 points are endorsed on a licence in exceptional circumstances (see below) but in such cases it is required to endorse the driving licence with four penalty points.

Special reasons for non-disqualification

As already mentioned, the court has discretion in exceptional mitigating circumstances not to impose an obligatory disqualification as described above. However, the mitigating circumstances must not be of a nature which appears to make the offence not serious, and no account must be taken of hardship other than exceptional hardship. Furthermore, if account has previously been taken of circumstances in mitigation of a disqualification, the same circumstance cannot be considered again within three years.

Other reasons for non-disqualification

Where a person is convicted of an offence requiring obligatory disqualification and he can prove to the court that he did not know and had no reasonable cause to suspect that his actions would result in an offence being committed, the court must not disqualify him or order any penalty points to be endorsed on his driving licence.

Removal of disqualification
Disqualifications may be removed from a driving licence after the following periods of time:

- If disqualification for less than four years – after two years.
- If disqualification for four years to ten years – after half the period.
- If disqualification for more than ten years – after five years.

Penalty points system (not applicable in Northern Ireland)

When drivers are convicted of driving and other road traffic offences where the court has discretion about imposing a disqualification but is obliged to endorse a licence, the endorsement takes the form of a number of penalty points entered on the driving licence. The number of points endorsed varies according to a scale ranging from 2 points to 10 points depending on the seriousness of the offence (as specified in Schedule 2 of the Road Traffic Offenders Act 1988). When the court convicts a driver of more than one offence at the same hearing, only the points relative to the most serious of the offences will be endorsed on the licence – the points relative to each individual offence will *not* be aggregated. The main penalty points offences are listed in Table 8.3.

Removal of penalty points
If a driver is convicted for an offence and is disqualified from driving, any existing penalty points on the licence will be erased. The driver will then start again with a 'clean slate' after each disqualification except that, as already mentioned, subsequent disqualifications will be for a longer period.

When the time interval between one offence and the endorsement on a licence of one lot of penalty points and a subsequent offence resulting in endorsement of penalty points is greater than three years (from the date of offence to the date of offence), the earlier points no longer count towards disqualification.

Penalty-point endorsements (and disqualifications) shown on driving licences can be removed by applying for the issue of a new licence after the following periods of time:

- For disqualifications and offences other than those below – after four years from the date of the offence (from the date of conviction in the case of a disqualification).
- For reckless driving offences – after four years from the date of conviction.
- For drink-driving offences – after 11 years.

Table 8.3

Section of Road Traffic Act 1988 creating offence	Description	Number of penalty points
2	Reckless driving (1st offence in 3 years) (now	
3	replaced by a dangerous driving offence under the RTA 1991 {s 1})	4
3	Careless or inconsiderate driving	3–9
5(2)	Being in charge of motor vehicle when unfit through drink or drugs	10
5(1)(b)	Being in charge of motor vehicle with excess alcohol in breath/blood/urine	10
6	Failing to provide specimen for breath test	4
7	Failing to provide specimen for analysis	10
22	Leaving vehicle in dangerous position	3
35/36	Failing to comply with traffic directions and signs	3
42	Contravention of construction and use regulations	3
87(1)	Driving without licence	2
96	Driving with uncorrected defective eyesight or refusing eyesight test	2
97	Failing to comply with conditions of licence	2
103(1)	Driving while disqualified (by order of court)	6
143	Using motor vehicle uninsured and unsecured against third-party risks	6–8
170(4)	Failing to stop after accident	8–10
178	Taking in Scotland a motor vehicle without consent or lawful authority or driving, or allowing oneself to be carried in, a motor vehicle so taken	8

Other penalties

The courts may also impose fines and, for certain offences, imprisonment, or in serious cases both penalties may be imposed. Drivers convicted twice for drink/driving-related offences may have their licences revoked altogether. Offenders found with exceptionally high levels of alcohol in their breath/blood will be classed by the DVLA as being of 'special risk' and will have to show that they no longer have an 'alcohol problem' before their licences are restored to them.

Drinking and driving

It is an offence to drive or attempt to drive or to be in charge of a motor vehicle when unfit because of the effects of drink or drugs. The maximum permitted level of alcohol in the breath is 35 micrograms per 100 millilitres of breath. This breath/alcohol limit equates to a blood/alcohol limit of 80 milligrams of alcohol in 100 millilitres of blood and the urine limit of 107 milligrams of alcohol in 100 millilitres of urine.

Breath tests

A police constable in uniform may arrest any person who is in charge of, driving or attempting to drive a vehicle on a public road (or other public place) while unfit through drink or drugs. A constable may request any person driving or attempting to drive a motor vehicle on a road or other public place to take a breath test if he has reasonable cause to suspect the person of having alcohol in his body or of having committed a traffic offence while the vehicle was in motion or if the person was driving or attempting to drive a vehicle at the time of an accident.

If a breath test proves positive, the person will be requested to provide a further breath sample at a police station (or may be taken there under arrest if appropriate) and may be held there until fit to drive or only released if there is no likelihood of him driving while still unfit to do so. If the second sample exceeds the limit, prosecution will follow and on the basis of evidence provided by the breath analysis a conviction may be made by the court, resulting in mandatory disqualification (see above) from driving plus a possible fine or imprisonment or both.

A person who for health reasons cannot provide a breath sample may request a blood test. So, too, may persons whose breath analyses show not more than 50 micrograms of alcohol per 100 millilitres of breath.

It is an offence (resulting in arrest and prosecution) to refuse to provide a breath test or a sample of blood or urine.

Drink-driving disqualification

Conviction for a drink-driving offence will result in a driving licence disqualification (see obligatory disqualification above) for at least one year.

Conviction for a second or subsequent offence of driving or attempting to drive under the influence of drink or drugs will result in longer periods of disqualification. If the previous conviction took place within 10 years of the current offence the driver *must* be disqualified for at least three years.

Use of duty-free fuel

It is an offence to use diesel fuel on which the full applicable rate of duty has not been paid for road vehicles powered by diesel engines (ie heavy oil engines). Fuel used for other non-road-going vehicles (ie contractors' plant) may be that which is known as rebated heavy oil, or commonly referred to as gas oil or red diesel, on which no duty is payable. This fuel must not be used in road-going diesel vehicles. Road fuel testing units staffed by Customs and Excise officers may, at any time, examine a vehicle. Such officers may also enter premises and inspect, test or sample any oil held there whether in vehicles or not. Powers for this purpose are conferred by the Hydrocarbon Oil Regulations 1973.

Powers of the police, traffic wardens and others

Traffic law enforcement

Enforcement of road traffic regulations is carried out by the police and traffic wardens. The latter are concerned mainly with stationary traffic offences and with assisting in traffic control and direction. Most moving vehicle offences are dealt with by the police. The respective legal powers of each are outlined here.

Police constables

So far as the law is concerned all policemen are 'constables' irrespective of rank. The police have wide powers to control road traffic and can, in general, direct drivers to follow particular directions, prevent them from following certain routes, can stop them, request the removal of parked vehicles, request the production of driving licences and other documents and so on. Their main powers in this regard are listed below; however, it should be noted that space here permits only a summary. Failure to comply with any of these requirements is an offence which could lead to prosecution on a variety of charges including obstructing the police in their duties:

- A police constable *in uniform* can stop a moving vehicle on a road.
- Where a vehicle has been left on a road causing an obstruction or danger or is in contravention of a parking restriction or has broken down, the police can ask the driver or owner to remove the vehicle. If it appears to have been abandoned they may remove it themselves (even without holding a driving licence covering that category of vehicle) or may arrange for it to be removed. *Note:* The local authority is also empowered to remove vehicles that appear to be abandoned.
- The police can require the driver of a vehicle on a road to produce his driving licence and/or to state his date of birth if he fails to provide the licence at the time.
- They can request an 'L' driver of a vehicle or the person accompanying him to produce his licence.
- They can request a person believed to have been the driver in an accident or when a traffic offence was committed to produce his driving

licence. In both of these cases the licence may be produced immediately or within seven days at a police station nominated by him.

- They can request a driver to perform the driving test eyesight requirement if they suspect that his vision is deficient.
- Police constables in uniform can arrest any person driving or attempting to drive a motor vehicle on a road who is suspected of being a disqualified driver.
- They can arrest a person who takes a breathalyser test indicating that he has an excess of alcohol in the blood, and can also arrest a person who refuses to take a breath test.
- They can arrest a person driving or attempting to drive a motor vehicle on a road or other public place if he is unfit to drive through the effects of drink or drugs.
- They can arrest a driver of a motor vehicle who commits an offence of dangerous, careless or inconsiderate driving if he will not give his name and address or provide his driving licence for examination.

Traffic wardens

Traffic wardens, appointed by the police authority, have powers to enforce the law in respect of vehicles parking without lights and reflectors; vehicles obstructing a road; vehicles waiting; vehicles parked; vehicles loading or unloading on a road or contravening the Vehicles (Excise) Act; vehicles parked without paying meter charges. They may fulfil duties at street parking places and car pounds, act as school crossing patrols, and have the power to direct and regulate traffic. They can be empowered to make enquiries about the identity of a driver and, when on duty at a car pound only, can demand to see driving licences. They can request a driver to give his name and address if he is believed to have committed an offence in the list below and can request the name and address of a pedestrian who ignores a traffic direction. Traffic wardens may also issue fixed penalty tickets for the following non-endorsable driving licence offences:

- Leaving a vehicle parked at night without lights or reflectors.
- Waiting, loading or parking in prohibited areas.
- Unauthorized parking in controlled parking zone areas.
- Contravention of the Vehicles (Excise) Act 1971 by not displaying a current licence disc.
- Making U-turns in unauthorized places.
- Lighting offences with moving vehicles.
- Driving the wrong way in a one-way street.
- Over-staying on parking meters or feeding meters to obtain longer parking time than that permitted in the meter zone.

Vehicle owner liability

When a fixed-penalty offence has been committed the vehicle owner (ie the registered keeper) is assumed to be the driver unless the actual driver was given the ticket at the time the offence was committed. Vehicle owners must give information to the police on request about details of the driver of a vehicle at the time an offence was committed. The vehicle owner is liable to pay any penalty imposed if the driver fails to do so within 28 days. In the case of hired vehicles the hirer becomes the owner for these purposes. Alternatively, a statutory statement of ownership may be given (within the same period – 28 days) certifying that at the time of the alleged offence the vehicle was owned by somebody else (in which case the name of the previous or subsequent owner must be given) or, that the vehicle was at the time being used without the owner's knowledge or permission.

Forgery and false statements

Forgery

Forgery means to make an imitation in writing or to produce information in writing to appear (or be passed off) as though it was made by another person (eg by signing somebody else's name) and was genuine. It is an offence to deceive intentionally by means of forgery, alteration or misuse (ie by lending or allowing another person to use) of any document or licence; vehicle test, plating or manufacturer's certificate; maintenance record, driving licence, certificate of insurance or security. Documents altered or obtained by these means are invalid. It is also an offence to have in your possession (with intent to deceive) a forged or false document even if you did not personally perpetrate the forgery or false statement.

False statements

A false statement is one which is made when it is known to be untrue – in other words it is a lie – and intended to deceive. It is an offence to make false statements knowingly for the purpose of obtaining or preventing the grant of any licence, to produce false evidence or to make false statements knowingly or to make a false entry in any record, or to withhold any material information for the purpose of obtaining a certificate of insurance (Road Traffic Act 1988). Any document, record, licence or certificate obtained as a result of a false statement is invalid (see also above about possession of such documents).

Driving tests

The main purpose of driver testing is to ensure that all drivers taking a vehicle on the road are safe and competent to do so, know the rules of the road and the significance of traffic signs and signals, and appreciate the dangers arising from moving vehicles.

The purpose of the additional tests for LGV/PCV entitlements is to ensure that such drivers are competent to drive these large vehicles on the roads in safety – especially when carrying heavy loads or passengers. Vocational testing also provides a measure of professionalism among goods and passenger vehicle drivers – it is more comprehensive and more complex than the ordinary (ie car and light goods) driving test and, consequently, demands greater skill and knowledge from the driver who wishes to pass.

Proof of identity

Candidates for both ordinary and vocational (ie LGV and PCV) driving tests must produce satisfactory photographic evidence of identity when arriving for a test. Acceptable identity documents for this purpose include existing driving licences (ordinary, LGV or PCV or an overseas driving licence), a passport or an employer-issued identity card bearing the holder's name, signature and photograph. If a test candidate cannot produce satisfactory means of identification the test will not be conducted and the fee will be forfeited.

This measure is necessary to combat a rising incidence of persons with false identities taking multiple LGV driving tests on behalf of others, who cannot themselves pass the test, but who are prepared to pay large sums to acquire a test pass certificate.

Ordinary driving test

Before a person can be granted a licence to drive a motor vehicle on the road he must pass both a written theory test and a practical driving test on the class of vehicle for which he requires the licence. An entitlement will not be gained until both parts of the test are passed – the theory test having to be passed before the practical driving test can be taken.

The theory test

Driving test candidates must take and pass a written theory test – which replaces the old, verbal questioning to test the candidate's knowledge of the *Highway Code* – carried out by DriveSafe Ltd (a private company) on behalf of the Driving Standards Agency (DSA – an Executive Agency of the DETR) at a nationwide network of dedicated theory test centres.

The test comprises 35 multiple-choice questions of which the candidate must get at least 26 correct to achieve a pass certificate. The questions concern such matters as driver attitude, traffic signs and regulations, the effects of alcohol and drugs, driver fatigue, and safety and environmental aspects of vehicles. All these topics are covered in the *Highway Code* and the DSA's *Driving Manual*. The DSA has also published *The Complete Theory Test for Cars and Motorcycles* which explains the test and lists the bank of questions from which test papers are set, together with the correct answers. These publications are available from The Stationery Office or main booksellers.

Practical driving tests
The practical driving test, lasting 30 minutes, is carried out by examiners from the DSA. Candidates must present a theory test pass certificate – practical driving tests will not be carried out without the candidate having first passed the theory test.

Test candidates have to meet the following requirements:

- They must show that they are fully conversant with the contents of the *Highway Code*.
- They must prove that they are able to read in good daylight (with the aid of spectacles, if worn) a motor vehicle's registration number in accordance with the vision requirements (see page 334).
- They must show that they are competent to drive without danger to and with due consideration of other users of the road, including being able to:

  - start the engine of the vehicle;
  - move away straight ahead or at an angle;
  - overtake, meet or cross the path of other vehicles and take an appropriate course;
  - turn right-hand and left-hand corners correctly;
  - stop the vehicle in an emergency and in a normal situation, and in the latter case bring it to rest at an appropriate part of the road;
  - drive the vehicle backwards and while doing so enter a limited opening either to the left or to the right;
  - cause the vehicle to face the opposite direction by the use of forward and reverse gears;
  - carry out a reverse parking manoeuvre which involves stopping the vehicle next to and parallel with a parked vehicle, then reversing to position and park the vehicle in front of or behind the other vehicle, level with and reasonably close to the kerb;
  - indicate their intended actions at appropriate times by giving appropriate signals in a clear and unmistakable manner (in the case of a left-hand drive vehicle, or a disabled driver for whom it is impracticable or undesirable to give hand signals, there is no requirement to provide any signals other than mechanical ones);
  - act correctly and promptly on all signals given by traffic signs and traffic controllers and take appropriate action on signs given by other road users.

New test requirements

Besides extending the duration of the test by some five to seven minutes (as mentioned above) and including, where possible, de-restricted dual carriageway driving, a more stringent marking system is now applied under which the candidate is permitted a maximum of 15 minor (non-hazardous) faults after which the test is terminated, as well as termination in the event of a serious driving error. Previously it required only a serious driving error for a test to be prematurely terminated.

Cars used for the ordinary (category B) driving test must be fitted with a seatbelt and a head restraint for the front seat passenger and an additional rear view mirror for use by the examiner.

Candidates who fail the driving test are given an oral explanation of the reasons for their failure.

Driving instruction

Only approved instructors (ADIs – approved by the DSA) are permitted to give driving instruction for payment on vehicles legally defined as 'motor cars', which basically means private cars and goods vehicles not exceeding 3,050kg unladen weight. More stringent standards have been introduced for driving instructors; in particular, extended training periods are necessary before they can become qualified.

Tuition given for payment on heavy goods vehicles does not come within the scope of this legislation despite a certain amount of transport industry opinion that it should do so. However, to ensure that the level of driving instruction available to learner LGV drivers is of a consistently high standard, a new scheme for the voluntary registration of LGV driving instructors has been established. Entry to the register is currently via a two-part examination of both driving and instructional abilities.

LGV driver testing

In order to drive a large vehicle (goods or passenger) it is necessary to pass both the large vehicle theory test and a practical driving test on a large goods or passenger vehicle of the appropriate category for which a licence is required.

Theory testing

Since 1 January 1997 LGV/PCV driving test candidates must take and pass a 40 minute touch-screen theory test – which has replaced the old, verbal questioning to test the candidate's knowledge of technical and safety matters and the *Highway Code*. This test includes a wide range of topics such as fuel economy, environmentally sensitive driving and safety issues.

Theory tests comprise 35 multiple-choice questions – a pass is achieved with 30 or more correct answers.

The LGV driving test

In order to undertake an LGV/PCV driving test, candidates must, since 1 January 1997, produce a large vehicle theory test pass certificate – without this the examiner will not conduct the practical driving test.

The LGV practical driving test is conducted by DSA examiners and booking has to be made through the local offices of the DSA.

The staged system of testing means that:

- Applicants for LGV tests must already hold a full category B (car and light vehicle) driving entitlement before taking a test to obtain a category C entitlement.
- Category B entitlement holders have to pass a test on a rigid goods vehicle in category C before being able to take a test to qualify for driving articulated vehicles and drawbar combinations in category C+E.
- Category C1 entitlement holders wishing to drive vehicles in category C1+E must take a further test for this type of vehicle combination.
- In each case the driver must hold a provisional entitlement for the category of vehicle on which he wants to be tested.

Identification

Test candidates must be able to produce satisfactory identification on arrival at the test centre otherwise the examiner may refuse to conduct the test and the fee will be forfeited.

Vehicles for the LGV driving test

The candidate has to provide the vehicle (or arrange for the loan of a suitable vehicle) on which he wishes to be tested and it must comply with the following requirements:

- it must be unladen and of the category (ie a 'minimum test vehicle') for which an LGV driving entitlement is required – see below;
- it must display ordinary 'L' plates front and rear (learner drivers in Wales may display a 'D' plate instead);
- it must be in a thoroughly roadworthy condition;
- seating accommodation in the cab must be provided for the examiner;
- it must have sufficient fuel for a test lasting up to two hours.

Minimum test vehicles

LGV driving test candidates must supply vehicles which meet the following requirements as regards their minimum weight and speed capability (known as minimum test vehicles – MTVs):

- Vehicles for category B tests must have at least four wheels and be capable of a speed of at least 100kph.
- For category B+E tests the vehicle itself must comply with category B requirements (see above) and must be drawing a trailer of at least 1 tonne gross weight (ie 1 tonne maximum authorized mass – mam).
- For category C1 tests the vehicle must be of at least 4 tonnes mam and capable of a speed of at least 80kph.
- For category C1+E tests the vehicle must comply with the requirements for category C tests (see above) and must be drawing a trailer of at least 2 tonnes mam – the combined length of the combination must be at least 8 metres.
- For category C tests (ie rigid goods vehicles exceeding 3.5 tonnes pmw) the vehicle must be of at least 10 tonnes pmw (or mam), at least 7 metres long and capable of at least 80kph.
- For a category C+E test (articulated vehicles) the vehicle must be articulated and have a permissible maximum weight (mam) of at least 18 tonnes, be at least 12 metres long and capable of at least 80kph.
- For a category C+E test (restricted to drawbar vehicle combinations only) the rigid towing vehicle should meet the requirements for a category C test and the trailer should be at least 4 metres long. The combination must have a minimum total weight of at least 18 tonnes, a minimum overall length of 12 metres, and the 80kph minimum speed capability also applies.

The LGV driving test syllabus

The recommended syllabus to be studied by candidates preparing for the LGV driving test is to be found in the DSA publication, *The Goods Vehicle Driving Manual* (available from The Stationery Office).

The syllabus comprises 10 main sections containing advice and detailing specific requirements for the test as well as an introductory section outlining the prior 'thorough' knowledge that a candidate should acquire before attempting the test.

LGV test passes and failures

A driver who passes the LGV/PCV driving test is issued with a certificate to that effect, valid for a period of two years, and the holder can apply for an LGV driving entitlement of the appropriate category to be added to his unified driving licence.

A driver who fails the LGV/PCV driving test is given a written statement of failure and an oral explanation of the reasons for his failure. He may apply for an immediate re-test.

H2. TRAFFIC REGULATIONS

Speed limits

Speed limits in Great Britain are applied to various types of vehicle on various types of road.

The current UK (ie national) maximum speed limits on different classes of road (those for vehicles are to be found below) are shown in Table 8.4. Where speed limits for different classes of vehicle and road vary, *the lower limit always applies.*

A 'restricted' road is one which has street lights placed not more than 200 yards apart and with the 30mph (or other indicated speed) limit shown on a circular sign at the beginning of the restricted section of road. On other roads where lower limits are indicated these must be observed (eg 30mph, 40mph and 50mph areas).

Advisory/mandatory speed limits on motorways

Advisory speed limits on motorways should be observed. These are shown by illuminated signs and indicate hazardous situations and roadworks ahead. The amber flashing warning lights located on the nearside of motorways indicate danger ahead – you should slow down until the road is clear. Failure to observe these signs can lead to prosecution for offences such as 'driving without due care'.

Mandatory limits may also be found on motorways at roadworks sites (indicated by a white sign with black letters and red border). Failure to comply with these particular signs can result in speeding prosecutions.

The national limits applicable to goods vehicles are shown in Table 8.5.

Exemptions from speed limits

Fire, police or ambulance service vehicles, when necessary in the performance of their duty, may exceed speed limits if they can do so in safety.

Table 8.4

Type of road	Maximum speed, any vehicle
Motorways	70mph
Dual carriageway roads	70mph
Single carriageway roads	60mph
Restricted roads	30mph

Table 8.5 Speed limits for goods vehicles

	Motorways	Dual carriageways	Other roads
Car derived vans			
Solo	70	70	60
Towing caravan or trailer	60	60	50
Goods vehicles not exceeding 7.5t mlw			
Solo	70	60	50
Articulated	60	60*	50
Drawbar	60	60*	50
Goods vehicles exceeding 7.5t mlw			
Solo	60	50	40
Articulated	60	50	40
Drawbar	60	50	40

mlw: maximum laden weight (ie maximum permissible weight for a vehicle as specified in Construction and Use regulations)

*In Northern Ireland these two limits are 50mph only. Also in NI, learner drivers and those who have only recently passed their driving test (ie when displaying 'L' and 'R' plates respectively) are restricted to a maximum speed of 45mph on all roads where higher limits are otherwise permitted.

Speed limits in Europe
Speed limits applicable to goods vehicles in EU member states (plus Switzerland) are given in Table 8.6.

Bans on goods vehicles
Some EU member states and other neighbouring countries do not allow goods vehicles to use the roads at weekends or on public holidays. Operators should make inquiries about this with the transport association before planning journeys since public holidays vary from country to country and do not always coincide with those of Great Britain.

France, for instance, restricts the movement of goods vehicles over 6 tonnes laden weight on public holidays (eg Bastille Day – 14 July) and at weekends; Germany prohibits the use of goods vehicles over 7.5 tonnes gross weight on Sundays up to 22.00 hours and on public holidays, and goods vehicles may not be driven in Switzerland on Sundays, public holidays and during certain night hours (see Table 8.7).

Road signs
Britain's road sign system follows that of most European countries with the use of internationally recognized signs so those that are familiar on

Table 8.6

Country	Built-up areas	Motorways	Other roads
Austria	50kph	80kph 70kph (road trains)	70kph 60kph (road trains)
Belgium	50kph	90kph (over 7.5t) 70kph min speed	60kph (over 7.5t)
Denmark	50kph	70kph	70kph
Republic of Ireland	48kph	–	64kph
France	50kph	90kph (Over12t) 80kph (DG)	80kph 60kph (DG)
Germany	50kph	80kph	80kph (up to 7.5t) 60kph (over 7.5t)
Great Britain	30mph (48kph)	60mph (96kph)	40mph (64kph)
Greece	50kph 40kph (DG)	70kph (main roads) 50kph (DG)	60kph
Italy	50kph 30kph (DG)	80kph 50kph (DG)	70kph
Luxembourg	60kph 40kph (DG)	90kph 60kph (DG)	75kph (over 5t) 60kph (DG)
Netherlands	50kph	80kph	80kph (A roads) 60kph (B roads)
Portugal	50kph	80kph	
Spain	50kph	90kph	70kph
Switzerland	50kph	80kph	80kph

Source: *IRU Handbook 15th Edition*, 1998
DG = Vehicles carrying dangerous goods
NB: Where member states have no motorways or where common speed limits apply to motorways and other roads (usually classified as being outside built-up areas) these are shown above midway between the two headings.

the roads in Britain will be recognizable abroad. See a current copy of the *Highway Code*. Certain road signs in Belgium and parts of northern Spain (Basque and Catalonian regions) are shown in dual language (eg French and Flemish in Belgium).

Driving on right/priority at junctions
The whole of Europe (except the UK and Republic of Ireland) drives on the right and vehicles must overtake to the left. Priority at road junctions is mainly to traffic approaching from or turning right: *'Priorite a droite'*.

Sources of information
It is essential for operators, when sending vehicles on international journeys, to be aware of the requirements in foreign countries for the following:

Table 8.7   EU member states and neighbouring countries where vehicle bans apply at various times

Country	Goods vehicle ban
Austria	over 3.5 tonnes and when drawing trailer (except for carriage of milk): – after 15.00 hours Saturday – all day Sunday – on public holidays until 22.00 hours
Republic of Ireland	no traffic/vehicle bans in operation but it is not possible to pass through Customs posts (ie from Northern Ireland) except between 09.00 and 17.00 hours daily (weekdays only) except by special request and fee payment
France	vehicles over 6 tonnes laden weight (except those carrying perishables, live animals, newspapers, hydrocarbons and vehicles returning to their home country): – 22.00 hours Saturday (or the day before a public holiday) to 22.00 hours Sundays and public holidays vehicles carrying dangerous goods: – 12.00 hours Saturday (or the day before a public holiday) to 24.00 hours Sunday and public holidays
Germany	vehicles over 7.5 tonnes laden weight (except en route to Berlin and those carrying fresh milk, meat and produce): – Sundays and public holidays
Greece	goods vehicles (except those carrying perishables): – 17.00 hours Saturday to 24.00 hours Sundays and public holidays
Italy	goods vehicles with pmw over 5 tonnes, lorries with trailers (even if unladen) and those carrying dangerous goods: – 08.00 to 22.00 hours Sundays (Jan, Feb, Mar, Oct, Nov, Dec) – 07.00 to 24.00 hours Sundays (May, June, July, Aug, Sept)
Portugal	goods vehicles using certain main national routes: – 14.00 hours to 22.00 hours Saturdays – 06.00 hours to 24.00 hours Sundays and public holidays vehicles carrying dangerous goods: – 12.00 hours to 24.00 hours Saturdays – 06.00 to 24.00 hours Sundays and public holidays
Spain	goods vehicles except those carrying perishables: – Sundays and public holidays 17.00 – 24.00 hours goods vehicles carrying dangerous goods: – Saturday 13.00 hours to Sunday 24.00 hours
Switzerland	vehicles above 3.5 tonnes: – all day Sundays and public holidays – 22.00 to 05.00 hours daily

- Driver licensing.
- Vehicle licensing.
- Traffic regulations.
- Restrictions on vehicle movement.
- Accident procedures.
- Movement of abnormal loads.

Information on these matters may be obtained from a number of sources:

- The motor organizations: AA, RAC, RSAC.
- *Your Lorry Abroad*, International Road Freight Office.
- *International Services Manual*, Freight Transport Association.
- Road Haulage Association.
- Transport authorities for individual countries (eg the DETR in the UK).
- Insurance companies, in the case of accident procedures.

Driving in fog and limited visibility

When driving in fog and limited visibility you should:

- Slow down, keep a safe distance, ensure that you can pull up within your range of vision.
- Do not keep close to the tail lights of the vehicle in front. This gives a false sense of security.
- Check your speed; you may be travelling faster than you think.
- Remember that if you are driving a heavy vehicle you need a greater distance in which to stop.
- Warning signals are there to help and protect. Do observe them.
- See and be seen – use headlights or fog lamps.
- Check and clean your windscreen, lights, reflectors and windows whenever you can.
- If you must drive in fog, allow more time for your journey.

Use of lights in poor visibility
Front and rear position lamps and headlamps must be used during the daytime in poor visibility caused by heavy rain, mist, spray, fog or snow. Rear fog lights, where fitted, should also be used in these conditions. It is an offence to drive in poor visibility without using lights. See also page 263 for section on vehicle lighting.

Segregation
Drivers of cars, light goods vehicles and coaches should move out of the left-hand lane when it is safe to do so, unless they will soon be turning off the motorway. When they want to leave the motorway, they should start their move to the left well before the exit. They should be prepared to miss the exit if they cannot reach it safely.

Drivers of heavy lorries should keep to the left-hand lane but should be ready to let other drivers into the lane at entry points and well before exit points.

Parking, waiting, loading and unloading

Clearways
The road sign indicating a clearway is circular, with a red diagonal cross on a blue background surrounded by a red circle. Vehicles must not stop (other than in an emergency) on the carriageway of a clearway or on the carriageway or verge of an urban clearway during the times shown on the sign which indicates the urban clearway, other than for as long as is necessary to let passengers board or alight from the vehicle.

Parking and overtaking
Vehicles must not park or overtake other vehicles in areas where danger or obstruction may be caused, as follows:

- In a 'no parking' area.
- On a clearway.
- Alongside yellow lines.
- Where there are double white lines.
- Near a road junction.
- Near a bend.
- Near the brow of a hill.
- Near a humpback bridge.
- Near a level crossing.
- Near a bus stop.
- Near a school entrance.
- Near a pedestrian crossing.
- On the right-hand side of the road at night.
- Where the vehicle would obscure a traffic sign.
- On a narrow road.
- On fast main roads and motorways.
- Near entrances and exits used by emergency service vehicles (or by fire hydrants).
- Near roadworks.

- Alongside or opposite another parked vehicle.
- In a parking disc zone unless the vehicle displays a parking disc; in a meter zone unless the meter fee has been paid; at bus stops; on a pavement or cycle track; on flyovers, in tunnels or in underpasses.

The police can request a driver to remove a vehicle causing danger or an obstruction or can forcibly remove it themselves and can prosecute the driver/registered owner.

Parking on pedestrian crossings

A vehicle must not be parked within the area marked by zigzag lines on either side of a zebra crossing or in the zone indicated by metal studs on the approach to a pedestrian crossing. Overtaking is also prohibited in these areas.

Night parking

Vehicles parked on roads overnight must stand on the nearside except when parked in a one-way street or in a recognized parking place.

Goods vehicles *over* 1,525kg unladen must always display lights when parked on roads at night. Goods vehicles *not exceeding* 1,525kg unladen may park without lights on roads where a speed limit is in force (ie on restricted roads) provided they are facing the direction of travel (ie nearside to the kerb) and are not parked within 10 metres (15 yards in Northern Ireland) of a road junction on either side of the road.

Trailers detached from the towing vehicle and vehicles carrying projecting loads must not be parked on roads at night without lights (detached trailers should never be parked on roads or in lay-bys, which are part of the highway).

All parked vehicles must display lights at night when parked on roads where no speed limit is in force.

Loading and unloading

Vehicles may be loaded and unloaded anywhere except where there are signs indicating the contrary. In some areas loading/unloading restrictions are indicated by yellow lines painted on the kerb at right angles (with relevant times given on nearby plates) as follows: single yellow right angle lines indicate loading/unloading restrictions at the times shown on the nearby sign; double yellow right angle lines indicate loading/unloading restrictions at all times.

Loading and unloading in parking meter zones is not allowed during working hours except where a free meter space is available or there is a gap between meter areas. When using a meter bay for loading the meter fee does not have to be paid if the stopping time is 20 minutes or less.

When stopping to load and unload and when leaving the vehicle unattended the engine must be stopped unless it is used for running auxiliary equipment.

Waiting restrictions

Yellow lines painted on the road parallel to the kerb indicate bans on waiting (not to be confused with bans on loading and unloading described above) as follows:

- A complete ban is shown by double yellow parallel lines.
- A partial ban is shown by a single continuous yellow parallel line.

In every case it is essential to consult the nearby sign (usually on a lamp post or wall) indicating the ban to see the precise times when it is in operation.

Traffic control

Traffic is controlled by a variety of road signs and signals designed to restrict speed, direct the flow of vehicles, indicate hazardous situations ahead and generally advise the motor vehicle driver on the use of the road. Traffic signs are divided into categories as shown in Table 8.8.

In addition to these signs there are road markings to indicate no waiting, no parking, prohibited areas, instructions to give way and lane controls (see the *Highway Code* for full details). Bus priority schemes (ie bus lanes) are signposted (relevant information is sometimes also painted on the road surface) as appropriate and these may only be used by passenger vehicles, taxis and cyclists as indicated on the sign.

Lights are used to control traffic at junctions and on motorways to indicate hazards ahead, speed restrictions and lane closures.

H3. SAFE WORKING PRACTICES

The professionally competent transport manager should be able to draw up instructions for drivers to check their compliance with safety requirements on the condition of vehicles, vehicle equipment and loads. These instructions should cover the reporting of vehicle defects by drivers, procedures for safe loading and safe use of vehicles.

Table 8.8

Type	Appearance	Function
Prohibitive	Bordered with red circle (except certain 'no stopping' signs)	Inform the driver what he must or must not do
Compulsory	Blue circles or rectangles	Inform the driver of the direction to be followed
Warning	Mostly bordered with a red triangle	Inform the driver of a variety of traffic situations ahead
Direction	Mostly rectangular with blue, green or white backgrounds Blue = motorways Green = primary routes White = non-primary routes	Indicates routes, road numbers and general directions
Information	All rectangular	Provides the driver with information about road and traffic situations

Driver defect reporting

The law requires that drivers should report defects in their vehicles that affect road safety (it is a condition of operators' licensing). Most transport firms used standardized pre-printed report sheets listing the main components that should be checked daily and reported on, although this is not compulsory so long as a written report is made of defects which come to the driver's attention.

The key safety components that should comprise a driver's pre-journey/daily checklist are:

- brakes/air lines/couplings;
- steering;
- road wheels and tyres;
- suspension;
- lights/direction indicators;
- windscreen wipers/washers;
- mirrors;
- load security.

Safe loading

Legislation makes it clear that where a vehicle or trailer is on the road in an unsafe condition or is loaded in such a way that danger is caused, an offence is committed and prosecution is likely (ie in the C&U regulations). In particular, loads must be securely restrained and where appropriate covered to prevent loose material from falling or being blown from the vehicle. Care must be taken to ensure that the weight of goods loaded is within the maximum permitted limit for the vehicle and its individual axles and that it is distributed correctly to prevent individual axle overload.

Drivers must be instructed as to the maximum weights which may be loaded on their vehicle/trailer and how that weight is to be distributed throughout the load area to comply with legal limits. The driver may have to redistribute his load during a multi-drop journey to avoid transference of excess weight on to the front axle as he unloads from the rear.

Safe use of vehicles

Drivers should be instructed to the effect that vehicles must not be used for a purpose for which they are so unsuited as to cause danger (see the C&U regulations). This phrase can have a number of meanings, particularly where:

- the vehicle's weight-carrying capacity may be exceeded;
- the load area is not large enough to safely contain the load;
- the vehicle is too large/heavy to use on a particular route;
- the vehicle is not designed or equipped to properly handle the load safely.

H4. ACCIDENT PROCEDURES

Duty to stop and give information

In the event of being involved in a road traffic accident, where injury to people (other than the driver himself) or to specified animals (other than those carried in the vehicle) or damage occurs to another vehicle or to roadside property, the driver must stop.

He should remain at the scene at least long enough to provide the requisite information, namely his name and address, the name and address of the vehicle owner, and the registration number of the vehicle, to anybody who has reasonable grounds to request such information.

If he does not give this information to a person requesting it at the scene of the accident, he must report the details to the police *as soon as is reasonably practicable* afterwards but in any case not later than 24 hours after the event.

A police constable can ask the driver to give his name and address and his age, and the name and address of the vehicle owner. The driver may be required to produce his driving licence at the scene of the accident by a police constable, or at the police station when reporting the event or within seven days at a police station of his own choice. The police may ask to see proof of insurance for the vehicle (a certificate of insurance or a temporary cover note) and the vehicle test certificate, if appropriate.

In the case of injury to third persons, an insurance certificate must be shown to a police constable or any other person at the scene of the accident who has reasonable grounds to ask to see it. If the driver is not able to produce the insurance certificate at the time of the accident or within 24 hours at a police station, he will be requested to produce it within seven days at a police station of his own choice. The accident must also be reported to the vehicle owner and the insurers.

For the purposes of these requirements 'roadside property' means items 'constructed on, fixed to, growing on, or otherwise forming part of the land in which the road is situated or land adjacent thereto'. This includes damage to trees, hedges, gardens, gate-posts, street furniture, etc, and other vehicles.

Animals for these purposes are specifically any horse, cattle, ass, mule (in Northern Ireland also a hinnie), sheep, pig, goat or dog.

Injuries to 'people' (which require reporting as stated above) does not include those to the driver. Other people injured in an accident are the 'third party' who may ultimately make a claim direct to the vehicle driver or the insurers for compensation for their injuries.

The *Highway Code* gives additional advice for situations where an accident involves a vehicle carrying dangerous goods. It states that the police and fire brigade should be given as much additional information as possible about the labels and other markings on the vehicle; other people should be kept away from the vehicle and, if it is necessary to act to save life, it should be done with the utmost caution because of the possible presence of dangerous liquids leaking on to the road and dangerous dust or vapours blowing in the wind.

Accident report to the insurers

Drivers are required to report accidents to the vehicle insurers (or via their employer) and the main points to be included in a driver's accident report are:

- the date, time and place of the accident;
- a description of the weather and road conditions at the time;
- the speed of the vehicle;
- the direction of its travel and its position on the road in relationship to other vehicles;
- the position on the road and direction of travel of any other vehicles involved;
- a description of the damage caused to the insured vehicle and any other vehicle;

- a description of the damage or injury caused to any other property (including any other vehicle) or person;
- the names, addresses and the name of the insurers of any other person involved;
- the names and addresses of any witnesses to the accident;
- a note of any comments made by people at the scene of the accident;
- the name or number of any police constable in attendance at the accident;
- details of any instructions given regarding the removal of the vehicle from the scene of the accident.

It is also advisable to provide a sketch of the accident situation showing the relative position of the vehicles involved prior to and immediately after the accident.

Accident claims procedure

In the event of an accident where damage or injury is sustained, the driver should report the event to the vehicle owner (if the driver is not the owner) and to his insurer or the vehicle owner's insurer, usually within seven days. An accident report/claim form should be completed.

At the scene of an accident it is unwise to admit liability, to apologize to the other party for what has occurred or to enter into an argument about responsibility for the accident with the third party or with any other person. Such remarks could prejudice the outcome of any claims arising by compromising the insurer's negotiations. It should be left for the insurers to establish blame and liability when the claim is made.

Where damage or injury is confined to the vehicle and driver and comprehensive insurance cover is operative, a claim can be made for loss or damage, apart from any excess. A vehicle owner can volunteer to pay the first part of an amount of a claim, usually £25 to £250 or even more depending on circumstances, so that for minor damage repairs any 'no claims bonus' on the policy is not jeopardized. Volunteering to pay an excess can result in premium discounts. In special cases the insurers will impose a compulsory excess, often in the case of young or inexperienced drivers. The insurers will assess the claims and will require estimates for repair work to vehicles, property or loss through injury. If claims are met, the 'no claims bonus' will be affected and this will result in a higher premium on renewal of the policy.

Where the damage or injury is confined to the insured vehicle and driver and no comprehensive insurance cover is operative, no claim can be made against the insurers for loss, damage or injury.

If no damage or injury is caused to the driver or the vehicle but is caused to roadside property, other vehicles, animals or people, the insurers will deal with any claims from third parties for loss, damage or injury.

Claims which are received from third parties who have suffered loss or damage should be passed immediately to the insurers for them to deal with. The driver should not enter into correspondence directly with third parties. The insurers will assess the claims and will require estimates for repair work to vehicles, property or loss through injury. If claims are met, the 'no claims bonus' (if applicable) may be affected and this could result in a higher premium on renewal of the policy.

European Accident Statement

Use of the European Accident Statement has already been covered in section E10 of this manual. Its purpose is to provide road accident victims, principally vehicle drivers, with a standardized and widely recognized means of recording accident details, especially relevant driver and vehicle details, nature of the road and weather conditions, position of vehicles prior to and at the moment of impact, witness information, and any other important details. This form of accident recording makes it easier for insurance companies to resolve matters relating to claims for damage repairs and compensation and importantly, where necessary, in apportioning blame which may have a bearing on any claims made.

Legislation

Road Traffic Acts

Road traffic in this country is controlled by many separate pieces of legislation – Acts of Parliament, regulations and statutory orders. Mainly, the legal provisions are to be found in successive Road Traffic Acts, in particular those of 1972, 1974, 1988 and 1991. These, together with the Road Traffic Offenders Act 1988, the Road Traffic Regulation Act of 1984, the Transport Act 1981 and the Highways Act 1980 (plus others), deal with such matters as traffic offences and penalties, vehicle construction and use, plating and testing, licensing of drivers, vehicle insurance requirements, seatbelt fitment and use, speed limits, parking and waiting, motorway driving, powers of police and other enforcement staff and so on.

Accident prevention

Road accidents cause more than 45,000 deaths and a further 1.6 million reported injuries each year in the EU. According to the Health and Safety Executive, in the UK some 70 people are killed in transport-related workplace accidents every year with a further 1,000 major injury accidents and 5,000 injury accidents which cause people to be off work for more than three days. Overall, accidents cost British industry millions of pound annually.

Road traffic accidents involving goods vehicles are mainly caused by:

- driving too fast;
- driving while tired, unwell or under the influence of drink or drugs;
- driving too close to the vehicle in front, especially on motorways – 'tailgating';
- turning across the path of other vehicles;
- not signalling intentions (or signalling too late);
- careless overtaking;
- driving a defective vehicle (inadequate brakes, steering, tyres, lights/signals, etc);
- overloading.

Assessing the risks

It is the statutory duty of road haulage employers under health and safety legislation to assess the risks faced by their employees in loading, unloading and particularly driving goods vehicles (a similar injunction applies to self-employed transport operators). These risks would include:

- people being struck or run over by vehicles manoeuvring in premises;
- people falling from vehicles while loading/unloading/roping and sheeting, etc;
- drivers slipping while entering or alighting from vehicle cabs/load areas;
- maintenance staff being injured while working on/beneath vehicle/ trailers;
- injuries caused by loads falling from vehicles/fork-lift trucks during loading/unloading;
- drivers speeding/taking insufficient care on the road;
- drivers reversing without assistance to guide them.

Risk prevention

Steps must be taken to reduce the identified risks to the absolute minimum by establishing suitable procedures covering the following:

- policies on drinking and drug taking;
- safety controls and monitoring;
- accident/incident reporting;
- accident/risk awareness;
- safety information;
- training and retraining.

Reporting of accidents

Employers, self-employed operators and, where relevant, employees, are required by law to report certain accidents as follows: road traffic accidents causing personal injury, damage to vehicles, animals or property under the Road Traffic Act 1988; and industrial/works accidents causing death or more than three days' incapacity for work under RIDDOR (The Reporting of Injuries, Diseases and Dangerous Occurrences Regulations 1995).

APPENDIX I

Typical examination questions

Readers who wish to prepare themselves for the examination are recommended to test their knowledge with the following typical questions, the answers for which are to be found in Appendix 2. For a more comprehensive test, and for examination practice, a further book called *1001 Typical Questions and Answers* by the author of this manual is available from Kogan Page.

SAMPLE MULTI-CHOICE EXAMINATION QUESTIONS

Select *one* answer only from (a), (b), (c), etc, for each question.
1. Unless a lower speed limit is in force, the maximum permitted speed for any motor vehicle on a UK dual carriageway is
   (a) 40mph
   (b) 50mph
   (c) 60mph
   (d) 70mph

2. A traffic warden may enforce the law for an offence in connection with
   (a) stealing a motor vehicle
   (b) leaving a vehicle parked at night without lights
   (c) failing to stop after an accident
   (d) driving a vehicle with defective tyres

3. Endorsements for speeding offences remain on the driving licence for
   (a) 1 year
   (b) 3 years
   (c) 4 years
   (d) 5 years

4. A transport firm, which is a private limited company, wishes to employ additional labour for a short-term contract. This entails additional outlay of approximately £20,000. How might it reasonably try to raise the extra money?
   (a) by bank overdraft
   (b) a rights share issue
   (c) an additional share issue
   (d) on debenture

5. An increase in the annual rates that a transport company has to pay for its premises will show as
   (a) decreased revenue in the trading account
   (b) decreased revenue in the profit and loss account
   (c) increased expenditure in the profit and loss account
   (d) increased expenditure in the balance sheet

6. Which of the following information must an operator have before 'Return on Capital Employed' can be calculated?
   (a) working capital
   (b) net profit
   (c) debtors
   (d) gross profit

7. A 'cash budget' is a
   (a) plan for future cash expenditure
   (b) plan for future marketing techniques
   (c) record of cash receipts
   (d) record of cash expenditure

8. Effective stock control in a transport company can
   (a) reduce the amount of finance tied up in stocks of spares
   (b) lead to a worsening of the company's cash flow position
   (c) reduce the amount of finance available for other purposes
   (d) lead to the accumulation of excessive stocks of spares

9. A quotation is a notification
   (a) from a supplier to a purchaser detailing the amount owed for work done

(b) from a customer instructing a supplier to supply specified goods or services

(c) from a supplier to a purchaser reminding him how the account stands at a particular date

(d) to a customer specifying a price for carrying out a particular job

10. A transport firm decides that in future, instead of paying its suppliers by cheque, it will pay them any moneys owed direct into their bank accounts. This arrangement is known as
   (a) direct debit
   (b) credit transfer
   (c) deferred payment
   (d) standing order

11. Compulsory Employers' Liability Insurance is designed to meet claims
   (a) by customers injured by defective products
   (b) by employees alleging they have been unfairly dismissed
   (c) by employees injured at work
   (d) for loss of production due to strikes

12. An agent who makes secret profit from activities of the Principal
   (a) can be sued by the Principal for the equivalent sum
   (b) can retain the sum involved regardless of whether or not the Principal has suffered any loss
   (c) must return the sum involved to the person from whom it was obtained
   (d) can keep the sum involved as long as the Principal has not suffered any loss

13. A claim for damages for negligence against a transport operator can *only* be successful if the
   (a) operator has broken some statutory obligation
   (b) operator has committed a criminal offence
   (c) operator has entered into a valid legal contract with the plaintiff
   (d) plaintiff has suffered loss

14. A plc must have an authorized share capital of at least
   (a) £1
   (b) £50,000
   (c) £500,000
   (d) £1,000,000

15. An employee who is dismissed after at least four weeks' service
   (a) is not entitled to a written statement at all

(b) is not entitled to a written statement if he is dismissed for misconduct
(c) must be given a written statement of the reasons if he asks for one
(d) must be given a written statement of the reasons in all cases

16. Under employment legislation, which of the following is entitled to time off work *with pay* to carry out the duties stated?
(a) A person called for jury service
(b) A shop steward for union business
(c) A JP to carry out his public duties
(d) A member of an independent trade union to attend a union meeting

17. Which one of the following benefits is dependent upon an employee having paid a certain number of National Insurance contributions?
(a) Unemployment benefit
(b) Disablement allowance
(c) Income support
(d) Retirement pension

18. An employee with a grievance under UK equal pay legislation may seek redress by application to an Industrial Tribunal during employment or within a maximum period of
(a) 6 months of termination of employment
(b) 9 months of termination of employment
(c) 12 months of termination of employment
(d) at any time

19. For what minimum period must a person who is appointed as a safety representative have normally been employed either by the present employer, or in similar employment elsewhere?
(a) 5 years
(b) 3 years
(c) 2 years
(d) 1 year

20. An application for a trade licence must be submitted to the
(a) Driver and Vehicle Licensing Centre, Swansea
(b) DVLA local office
(c) Goods Vehicle Centre, Swansea
(d) Department of Trade

21. Under EU Regulation 3820/85, a person driving vehicles coming within the scope of the regulation is limited to a maximum period of fortnightly driving of
(a) 88 hours

(b) 90 hours
(c) 92 hours
(d) 96 hours

22. Under EU Regulation 3820/85 the minimum break required after the maximum permitted driving period is
(a) 20 minutes
(b) 30 minutes
(c) 45 minutes
(d) 60 minutes

23. On a two-man tachograph, the chart for the non-driving crew member will record
(a) distance and activity mode only
(b) speed and distance only
(c) speed, activity mode, distance and time
(d) activity mode and time only

24. A new 'plaque' must be fitted to the tachograph after re-calibration every
(a) 6 years
(b) 3 years
(c) 2 years
(d) 1 year

25. The police have the power to enter premises to inspect drivers' hours records
(a) only between 9.00 am and 5.00 pm
(b) at any reasonable time
(c) at any time
(d) they have no such power

26. A driver who is unavoidably delayed on a national road haulage journey which causes him to depart from EU drivers' hours regulations must
(a) contact the Traffic Area Office as soon as possible to advise them of the occurrence
(b) report the circumstances to the police as soon as possible
(c) enter the details on the relevant tachograph chart
(d) report the circumstances within 24 hours to a motor vehicle examiner

27. The holder of a Category C LGV entitlement is also authorized to drive a vehicle of Category
(a) D + E

(b) B
(c) C + E
(d) A

28. A Traffic Commissioner revokes an LGV entitlement. The driver can appeal to the
    (a) Magistrates'/Sheriff's Court
    (b) Minister for Transport
    (c) Transport Tribunal
    (d) High Court

29. A 38-tonne articulated vehicle may travel at a maximum speed on a motorway of
    (a) 40mph
    (b) 50mph
    (c) 60mph
    (d) 70mph

30. At the scene of an accident on the public highway where no injury is involved, a driver is by law bound to provide, if required,
    (a) his driving licence
    (b) his insurance policy
    (c) his certificate of insurance
    (d) his name and address

31. Any legal obligation by a haulage operator to pay for emergency hospital treatment to persons (other than employees) injured in a traffic accident involving one of his haulage vehicles would be covered by
    (a) Fidelity Insurance
    (b) Consequential Loss Insurance
    (c) Third Party Motor Insurance
    (d) Employer's Liability Insurance

32. A road haulage operator can carry his own third-party motor insurance risks provided he deposits a sum of money with the Accountant General of the Supreme Court as a security. This sum is
    (a) £100,000
    (b) £150,000
    (c) £250,000
    (d) £500,000

33. The Code of Practice on the safe loading of vehicles states that to prevent movement of the payload in a forward direction, a load restraint device should be capable of withstanding a force equal to

(a) 50% of the total weight of the load
(b) 75% of the total weight of the load
(c) the total weight of the load
(d) twice the total weight of the load

34. An attendant must accompany a vehicle travelling under the Special
Types Order when the
(a) overall length of the vehicle and load is 18 metres
(b) vehicle and load are 4 metres wide
(c) load projects to the front by 1 metre
(d) load projects to the rear by 2 metres

35. The colours that appear on a sign denoting a vehicle is carrying flammable liquids are
(a) black symbol on a red background
(b) red symbol on a black background
(c) black symbol on a white background
(d) white symbol on a black background

36. Under the Construction & Use Regulations, the maximum permissible weight for a rigid vehicle having four or more axles is
(a) 22,360 kilograms
(b) 26,420 kilograms
(c) 28,450 kilograms
(d) 32,000 kilograms

37. The normal permitted maximum overall length of a road train consisting of a vehicle and one trailer in the UK is
(a) 25 metres
(b) 18.75 metres
(c) 18 metres
(d) 16.5 metres

38. Advance notice must be given to the police when it is proposed to
move on to the public highway a vehicle and load having a rearward
projection exceeding
(a) 1.07 metres
(b) 1.83 metres
(c) 2.9 metres
(d) 3.05 metres

39. A goods vehicle is classed as a motor car if its unladen weight does not
exceed
(a) 3,050kgs

(b) 3,500kgs
(c) 5,075kgs
(d) 7,250kgs

40. Under Plating and Testing Regulations which of the following alterations must be notified to the VI before the vehicle is used on the road
   (a) a change in the structure of the vehicle which varies its carrying capacity
   (b) a change in the colour of the vehicle
   (c) a change in the use of the vehicle
   (d) a change in the owner of the vehicle

41. Under the Construction & Use Regulations every vehicle having a fixed windscreen must have
   (a) at least one automatic wiper
   (b) at least two automatic wipers
   (c) a method of clearing the windscreen which may be manual if this is efficient
   (d) an adequate method of clearing the windscreen with no specific requirement as to method or the number of wipers

42. Rear underrun protectors must be fitted to most new rigid goods vehicles if the GVW exceeds
   (a) 3,500kgs
   (b) 2,040kgs
   (c) 1,525kgs
   (d) 1,020kgs

43. The minimum legal tread depth of an over 3.5 tonne goods vehicle tyre is
   (a) 1mm
   (b) 1.5mm
   (c) 2mm
   (d) 3.5mm

44. In accordance with current lighting regulations, which of the following lamps must be fitted to *all* goods vehicles?
   (a) two front spot lamps
   (b) two rear fog lamps
   (c) rear number plate lamp
   (d) reversing lamps

45. Which of the following persons can issue prohibitions and defect notices?
   (a) an officer of HM Customs and Excise
   (b) a weights and measures officer

(c) a driving/traffic examiner

(d) a Vehicle Inspectorate examiner

46. The weight of a vehicle inclusive of body and parts normally used in operation but exclusive of weight of water, fuel, loose tools and equipment, and batteries, where these are used for propelling the vehicle, is defined as the

(a) kerbside weight

(b) plated weight

(c) tare weight

(d) unladen weight

47. A prohibition notice (PG 9) issued for a vehicle can only be completely removed by the issue of form

(a) PG 9A

(b) PG 9B

(c) PG 9C

(d) PG 10

48. Smith wishes to enter the transport industry for the carriage of goods for hire or reward. He will require a Standard National 'O' licence to operate which of the following vehicles?

(a) a rigid vehicle of 3 tonnes gross plated weight

(b) a rigid vehicle of 5 tonnes unladen weight

(c) a dual purpose vehicle and trailer

(d) an articulated vehicle of 3.5 tonnes combined gross plated weight

49. A road haulage operator applying for an 'O' licence

(a) must lodge one application irrespective of how many operating centres he has throughout Great Britain

(b) must lodge separate applications for each traffic area in which he has an operating centre

(c) must make a single consolidated application to the Department of Transport head office

(d) must make a single consolidated application to the Transport Tribunal

50. A haulier who acquires additional vehicles within the limit authorized by his licence

(a) need not do anything

(b) should have informed the Traffic Commissioner before he acquired them

(c) must inform the Traffic Commissioner within one month of acquiring them

(d) must inform the Traffic Commissioner within three months of acquiring them

51. Which of the following bodies has a statutory right to object to the granting of an operator's licence?
(a) Industrial Training Board
(b) Health and Safety Executive
(c) Freight Transport Association
(d) Department of Environment

52. Records of defects found during preventive maintenance inspections must be retained by the operator for a minimum period of
(a) 6 months
(b) 9 months
(c) 12 months
(d) 15 months

53. An operator parks his vehicles at the premises of a major customer. They are maintained at a commercial garage. The business is run from his home address. The operating centre is
(a) his drivers' homes
(b) his home
(c) the garage
(d) his customer's premises

54. A company applies for a restricted operator's licence. Which one of the following criteria can be *ignored* by the Traffic Commissioner?
(a) the applicant must have sufficient financial resources
(b) the applicant must be a fit and proper person
(c) the applicant must hold a CPC
(d) the arrangements for observing drivers' hours and records must be acceptable

55. Eighteen months after the death of his designated Transport Manager an operator has not employed anybody to take his place and as a result has his Standard Operator's Licence taken away. This constitutes
(a) refusal to grant the licence
(b) suspension of the licence
(c) curtailment of the licence
(d) revocation of his licence

56. Which of the following is a fixed (standing) cost?
(a) lubricating oils used
(b) drivers' guaranteed wages

(c) fuel consumed

(d) tyres supplied on contract

57. A new vehicle costing £49,200 has 6 wheels with tyres worth £200 *each*. If it is to be written down to £6,000 over seven years, what is its annual depreciation using the straight-line method?
    (a) £6,000
    (b) £6,171
    (c) £6,500
    (d) £7,029

58. The term 'Carriage Forward' means payment for transport that
    (a) has already been made by the consignor
    (b) has been made by the consignor's forwarding agent
    (c) will be the responsibility of the consignee
    (d) will be the responsibility of the consignor

59. An organization which is set up specifically to organize the movement of loads by the use of subcontracted hauliers is known as
    (a) an own-account operator
    (b) a warehouse
    (c) a hire and reward operator
    (d) a clearing house

60. A subcontractor is
    (a) a haulage operator who undertakes to perform work on behalf of the original contractor
    (b) an agent who works on a commission basis for a principal
    (c) a haulage operator who subcontracts work to other haulage operators
    (d) an agent who arranges transport for a customer and prepares the necessary customs and transport documentation

61. Joe Bloggs, an LGV driver based in Dover, has during the current week taken the following daily rest periods: Monday, 12 hours in Dover; Tuesday, 12 hours in Paris; Wednesday, 9 hours in Dover; Thursday, 11 hours in London.

    If he takes his daily rest period on Friday in Dover what is the minimum length of rest he must take in accordance with EU drivers' hours regulations?

    (a) 8 hours
    (b) 9 hours
    (c) 11 hours
    (d) 12 hours

62. EC Regulation 3820/85, limiting driving time to a maximum of 9 hours daily, allows the following alternatives
   (a) 9 hours twice in any 7 days
   (b) 10 hours twice in any 7 days
   (c) 10 hours twice in a week
   (d) no alternatives are allowed

63. The minimum weekly rest period required by an LGV driver when operating to an AETR country is
   (a) 24 hours
   (b) 24 hours immediately preceded or followed by a daily rest period
   (c) 45 hours
   (d) 45 hours immediately preceded or followed by a daily rest period

64. If a tachograph breaks down on an international journey the operator must have it repaired, at the latest, as soon as the vehicle returns to his premises. However, the tachograph must be repaired en route if, counting from the day of the breakdown, the vehicle is unable to return to base within
   (a) 2 days
   (b) 3 days
   (c) 5 days
   (d) 7 days

65. A tachograph being used on a heavy goods vehicle on a journey from Tunbridge Wells to Bordeaux must
   (a) be switched off during periods when the driver is taking official breaks from driving
   (b) only be kept running while the vehicle is on the road in England and France (and not during the ferry journey)
   (c) be kept running continuously from the time the driver takes over the vehicle until he finishes the day's work with the vehicle
   (d) only be kept running while the driver is at the wheel of the vehicle

66. An own-account operator will require a journey permit if he is transporting his own goods from the UK to
   (a) Holland
   (b) Belgium
   (c) Turkey
   (d) Germany

67. Which of the following work performed by a British-registered vehicle would be described as cabotage?
   (a) collect Paris and deliver Dublin via London

(b) collect Paris and deliver Hamburg
(c) collect Dover and deliver Calais
(d) collect Paris and deliver Marseilles

68. EU multilateral permits covering hire or reward operations only, are valid for a maximum of
(a) 6 months
(b) 12 months
(c) 18 months
(d) 2 years

69. Transit through Austria is controlled by a points system requiring stamps and a card. This is known as the
(a) Nox system
(b) Pre-entry system
(c) Eco-points system
(d) Road-rail carnet system

70. An international driving permit may be obtained from the RAC or AA provided the applicant has a current valid driving licence and he has satisfied one of the following conditions
(a) he must be domiciled in the UK and be at least 18 years of age
(b) he must be domiciled in the UK and be at least 21 years of age
(c) he must prove a one-year accident-free record
(d) he must have no motoring convictions

71. For a journey to which of the following countries would it be necessary for a UK road haulage driver to have a visa in addition to a passport?
(a) Greece
(b) Slovakia
(c) Italy
(d) Bulgaria

72. Most EU countries limit the amount of fuel that may be allowed to enter in vehicle fuel tanks to
(a) 200 litres
(b) 250 litres
(c) 200 gallons
(d) 250 gallons

73. There is a limit on the amount of fuel that can be imported in the fuel tanks of a heavy goods vehicle when entering some European countries before excise duty is payable.
(a) True
(b) False

74. Under Export Procedures, if pre-entry is chosen, which of the following could be omitted from the Export Entry?
    (a) value
    (b) shipping information
    (c) weight
    (d) tariff number

75. The SAD form in use throughout the EU comprises an eight-part set, certain copies of which remain in the country of dispatch while other copies travel forward with the goods. How many copies travel forward?
    (a) copies 1 to 3
    (b) copies 3 to 6
    (c) copies 2 to 6
    (d) copies 4 to 8

76. A 14-voucher TIR carnet could be used for the international transportation of goods by road from the UK across a maximum of
    (a) 6 frontiers
    (b) 7 frontiers
    (c) 10 frontiers
    (d) 14 frontiers

77. The purpose of a *carnet de passage en douane* is to
    (a) enable a goods vehicle to pass through international frontiers without customs examination
    (b) allow temporary importation of samples and personal effects
    (c) allow temporary importation of exhibition goods without payment of duty, deposit or bond
    (d) allow temporary importation of foreign goods vehicles free of duty or deposit

78. The SITPRO system provides the operator with
    (a) automatic Customs pre-entry
    (b) automatic ECGD cover
    (c) aligned documentation
    (d) Customs clearance at intermediate frontiers

79. A green card which may be carried when travelling abroad is
    (a) evidence of insurance
    (b) an import licence
    (c) a Customs document
    (d) an insurance policy

80. In the case of loss of a consignment of goods despatched under CMR terms the value is calculated by reference to the value at the place and time at which
    (a) they were due for delivery to the consignee
    (b) they were accepted for carriage
    (c) they are believed to have been lost
    (d) the consignee lodges his claim

81. Haulage drivers who are involved in road accidents in Spain are taken into custody irrespective of whether the accident is their fault or not. In order to arrange for the driver's release as quickly as possible the employer should have taken out a
    (a) Bail bond
    (b) Community Transit Guarantee
    (c) Fidelity guarantee
    (d) Fidelity bond

82. If the exchange rate fluctuates, and the French franc is raised in value in relation to the pound sterling, expenses for a UK haulage operator in France will be
    (a) lower
    (b) the same
    (c) higher

83. The AGR Convention establishes
    (a) a system for the carriage of dangerous goods
    (b) a set of conditions of carriage
    (c) a system for the numbering of import quotas
    (d) a system of numbering for road networks

84. The maximum height limit for goods vehicles in most European countries is
    (a) 4.5m
    (b) 4m
    (c) 3.8m
    (d) 3.5m

85. Many French vehicles have yellow headlights. British vehicles must have the same when entering France.
    (a)   True
    (b)   False

86. If a road tanker carrying hydrochloric acid is travelling from Dover to Dusseldorf, which regulations must the vehicle comply with?

(a) ATP Convention
(b) The UK Corrosive Regulations
(c) ADR Convention
(d) ADR and IMDG/Blue Book

87. The ATP Convention applies to journeys made by road or rail, excluding domestic transport, air transport and sea crossings exceeding
(a) 150 kilometres
(b) 100 kilometres
(c) 65 miles
(d) 70 miles

88. It is a requirement that the original vehicle registration document be carried on the vehicle when it is engaged on international road haulage.
(a) True
(b) False

89. Which of the following countries imposes a Sunday driving ban on goods vehicles over 6 tonnes?
(a) Luxembourg
(b) Belgium
(c) France
(d) Finland

90. Which one of the following provides a groupage service?
(a) The Freight Transport Association
(b) International Road Freight Office
(c) The Road Haulage Association
(d) A freight forwarder

91. A transport operator would take out Consequential Loss to protect against
(a) loss of money due to dishonesty of employees
(b) loss of profits in the event of fire
(c) damage to goods in transit
(d) theft of goods in transit

92. The technology which enables transport operators to track the location of vehicles accurately is known as
(a) Real-time computing
(b) Global positioning
(c) Eurostat technology
(d) Ordnance survey

93. A haulier who acquires additional vehicles within the limit authorized by his Operator's Licence, and intending to add them permanently to his fleet
    (a) need not advise the Traffic Area Office
    (b) should have informed the Traffic Commissioner before acquiring the vehicles
    (c) must notify the Traffic Area Office within three months of their acquisition
    (d) must inform the Traffic Commissioner within one month of their acquisition

94. A groupage operator is a firm specializing in
    (a) hiring out goods vehicles to haulage contractors when their own fleets are in full use
    (b) arranging for heavy vehicles to be sent for goods vehicle certification
    (c) consolidating individual consignments into unit loads to fill vehicles and/or containers
    (d) accepting instructions to deliver goods which a principal contractor has been unable to load on to one of his own vehicles

95. When selecting a new vehicle it is important to find out the distance between axles to determine the load-carrying capacity because generally
    (a) the greater the distance the greater the load-carrying capacity
    (b) for double the distance the load-carrying capacity is halved
    (c) for double the distance the load-carrying capacity is doubled
    (d) the greater the distance the lesser the load-carrying capacity

96. Under the Construction & Use Regulations, the maximum permitted weight for a new rigid vehicle having three axles, if at least one of the axles exceeds 9,500kg and the vehicle is not fitted with road-friendly suspension, is
    (a) 25,000kgs
    (b) 28,450kgs
    (c) 30,000kgs
    (d) 32,520kgs

97. Under dangerous goods legislation, a road tanker carrying more than one dangerous substance must display
    (a) a list of the different substances carried
    (b) three orange reflective plates
    (c) a plate containing the word 'multi-load' on the rear of the vehicle
    (d) a substance identification number on each compartment

98. A vehicle owner, who was not driving at the time the vehicle is involved in a road traffic accident, has
(a) a legal obligation to identify the driver to the police only if they intend prosecuting the driver
(b) a legal obligation to identify the driver to the police when requested to do so if the driver is alleged to have committed an offence
(c) no legal obligation to identify the driver to the police
(d) a legal obligation to identify the driver to the police only if someone is injured in the accident

99. Under road traffic law, which of the following details must an LGV driver, involved in a road accident where no personal injury occurs, give the driver of the other vehicle?
(a) his age and LGV driving licence number
(b) the name and address of the vehicle owner's insurance company
(c) his own and the vehicle owner's name and address
(d) his route and destination

100. At what age will a 24-year-old LGV driver next require a medical certificate to renew his LGV driving licence entitlement?
(a) 45 years
(b) 50 years
(c) 55 years
(d) 60 years

The reader will find the correct answers to all these questions within the foregoing text but for ease of reference they are given in Appendix 2.

APPENDIX II

Answers to typical examination questions

Question	Answer	Question	Answer
1	(d)	24	(a)
2	(b)	25	(b)
3	(c)	26	(c)
4	(a)	27	(b)
5	(c)	28	(a)
6	(b)	29	(c)
7	(a)	30	(d)
8	(a)	31	(c)
9	(d)	32	(d)
10	(b)	33	(c)
11	(c)	34	(b)
12	(a)	35	(a)
13	(d)	36	(d)
14	(b)	37	(b)
15	(a)	38	(d)
16	(b)	39	(a)
17	(a)	40	(a)
18	(d)	41	(a)
19	(c)	42	(a)
20	(b)	43	(a)
21	(b)	44	(c)
22	(c)	45	(d)
23	(d)	46	(d)

Question	Answer	Question	Answer
47	(d)	74	(b)
48	(b)	75	(d)
49	(b)	76	(a)
50	(c)	77	(d)
51	(c)	78	(c)
52	(d)	79	(a)
53	(d)	80	(b)
54	(c)	81	(a)
55	(d)	82	(c)
56	(b)	83	(d)
57	(a)	84	(b)
58	(c)	85	(b)
59	(d)	86	(d)
60	(a)	87	(a)
61	(b)	88	(a)
62	(c)	89	(c)
63	(a)	90	(d)
64	(d)	91	(b)
65	(c)	92	(b)
66	(c)	93	(d)
67	(d)	94	(c)
68	(b)	95	(a)
69	(c)	96	(a)
70	(a)	97	(c)
71	(d)	98	(b)
72	(a)	99	(c)
73	(a)	100	(a)

OCR case study scenarios and specimen marks

The following case study scenarios, questions and specimen marks are taken from OCR's specimen papers, for which acknowledgement is hereby given.

AUTHOR'S ADVICE

I advise examination candidates to read both the scenario and the case study examination paper very carefully. It is important to determine precisely what answers the examiner is looking for and not to waste valuable time giving information that is not required. Don't spend time writing long essay-type answers; stick to presenting the facts giving as many as possible and where appropriate qualify those facts with a *brief* explanation. Marks are given for inclusion of key facts, not for waffle, and if the question carries, say, five marks, try to include at least five key facts in your answer.

The specimen marking points shown below are those provided by OCR as being typical of the topics which the examiner would expect you to cover in your answer – these are not the actual answers required. For example, in the National Scenario, question 2 a) and b), the examiner would expect the candidate, at the least, to:

- state the legal requirement for the return of tachograph charts (ie within 21 days);
- outline a system for checking charts for legal compliance;
- list the records which must be made and retained (eg vehicle inspection and service records – for 15 months);

- state what disciplinary procedures may be applied;
- outline the incentives that might be applied to encourage legal compliance;
- refer to the Vehicle Inspectorate Guide to Maintaining Roadworthiness Code of Practice.

In Question 3, note that besides the relevant figures that must be stated, the examiner is expecting a statement about the financial situation of the company (it would be easy to forget to include this after working out the figures and yet this part of the answer alone carries a possible five marks).

In the examinations candidates may use diagrams wherever they will help to answer a question, a non-programmable calculator and a dictionary.

NATIONAL – SCENARIO: RED TRANSPORT LTD

You are the transport manager for Red Transport Ltd. The company was formed 16 years ago and has grown very rapidly during this time. It is involved in the transport of general cargo and some consignments of dangerous goods.

Red Transport Ltd currently operates from six depots nation-wide. All depots have rigid vehicles and also articulated tractor units which operate with trailers exceeding 1,020kg.

In the last few weeks you have carried out work for a new customer ABC Imports Ltd collecting cargo from sea ports. This cargo arrives by sea in unaccompanied trailers. These are collected from the port by Red Transport Ltd.

Vehicles

All vehicles operate six days per week with the exception of bank holiday weeks when they work four days. The company operates the vehicles shown in Table A3.1.

Table A3.1

No. of vehicles	Type	Average quarterly mileage	Average mpg
15	7.5-ton rigid box vehicles	15,600	17
10	17-ton rigid box vehicles	23,400	12
5	17-ton rigid refrigerated box	23,400	11
10	2 x 4 articulated tractor units	31,200	8
Tandem axle trailers		24,000	
Tri-axle trailers		34,000	

Staff

The following staff are employed:

1	Managing Director
1	Sales Manager
1	Accountant
2	Administrators
2	Salespersons
1	Transport Manager
1	Warehouse Manager
1	Traffic Supervisor
35	Drivers
3	Traffic Clerks
6	Warehouse Operatives

Accounts information

The current cost of fuel is £3.25 per gallon. The company does not expect the cost of fuel to increase over the next three months.

Accounting periods for the company are four weeks in the first two months of a quarter and five weeks in the last month of the quarter.

Red Transport Ltd

Balance Sheet Information as at 31 December 1998

FIXED ASSETS	£
Freehold property	250,000
Vehicles	1,765,000
Office furniture and equipment	60,000
Plant and equipment	190,000
CURRENT ASSETS	
Debtors	150,000
Stock	52,000
Cash	2,000
CURRENT LIABILITIES	
Tax	25,000
Bank overdraft	1,000
Creditors	74,000
LONG-TERM LIABILITIES	
Revenue reserves	180,000

Shares issued	2,500,000
Bank loans	400,000
Debentures	185,000

Red Transport Ltd

Trading Account Information, 12 months to 31 December 1998

	£
Sales and haulage work done	1,880,000
Warehouse and rent receipts	610,000
Vehicle running costs	748,000
Vehicle hire	20,000
Subcontractors	2,000
Depreciation of vehicles	317,000
Insurance	80,000
Excise duty	100,000
Operators licences	2,000
Operating wages	525,000

Red Transport Ltd

Profit and Loss Account Information, 12 months to 31 December 1998

	£
Gross profit	to be calculated
Less expenses:	
Directors' remuneration	90,000
Office salaries	190,000
Rates	17,000
Utilities	16,000
Telephone and postage	5,000
Interest charges on loans	48,000
Auditors' fees	14,000
Sundry expenses	26,000

CALENDAR EXTRACT

MONTH 1

M	T	W	T	F	S	S
1*	2	3	4	5	6	7
8	9	10	11	12	13	14
15	16	17	18	19	20	21
22*	23	24	25	26	27	28
29	30	31				

MONTH 2

M	T	W	T	F	S	S
			1	2	3	4
5	6	7	8	9	10	11
12	13	14	15	16	17	18
19	20	21	22	23	24	25
26*	27	28	29	30		

MONTH 3

M	T	W	T	F	S	S
					1	2
3	4	5	6	7	8	9
10	11	12	13	14	15	16
17	18	19	20	21	22	23
24	25	26	27	28	29	30

*Bank Holiday

Read the Case Study Scenario and answer ALL questions.

1. Your customer ABC Imports Ltd has sent you a claim for damage to his goods whilst they were in your possession. Red Transport's Managing Director asked you what rules are likely to apply to the liability of the company. Explain the possible liabilities Red Transport Ltd could have in these circumstances. (10 marks)

OCR specimen marks:

Knowledge that they may be liable to CMR	1 mark
– and reason	3 marks
– SDRs 8.33	2 marks
– From date goods accepted for carriage	1 mark
– Liability does not exceed value of goods	1 mark
– Time limits	1 mark
– Mention of identification of defences	1 mark

2. (a) Explain how you control and monitor legally required transport-related documents in relation to vehicles and drivers to ensure that Red Transport Ltd complies with the regulations and laws relating to them   10 marks

– Issue and return of tachographs	1 mark
– Viability of control	4 marks
– Filing system for vehicle records	1 mark
– Records to be filed	3 marks
– Checking method	1 mark

2. (b) You noticed from returned tachograph charts that one of your drivers, Fred Green, who has been employed for 10 years by the company, consistently breaks transport regulations and has a poor accident record. Explain how you

– would deal with this?	5 marks
– Disciplinary action	1 mark
– Incentives	1 mark
– Code of Practice	3 marks

3. From the Accounts information in the Scenario, calculate the following:
   – capital employed;
   – percentage of direct costs compared to turnover
   – the return on capital employed.

Explain what the financial situation of the company is after assessing the acid test ratio	15 marks
– Capital employed: fixed assets + current assets – current liabilities = £2,369,000	2 marks
– Direct costs to company turnover = 72.04% (ie 72%)	1 mark
– Return on capital employed: £2,490,000 – £1,794,000 = £696,000 gross profit £290,000 – £406,000 = £ 290,000 net profit £290,000 as a % of £2,369,000 = 12.24%	2 marks
– Working capital = current assets – current liabilities: £204,000 – £100,000 = £104,000	1 mark
– Current ratio: £204,000 / £100,000 = 2.04:1	2 marks
– Acid test ratio: £152,000 / £100,000 = 1.52:1	2 marks
– The company is in a healthy position with a: current ratio of 2.04:1 (Ideal 2:1) acid test ratio of 1.52:1 (Ideal 1:1) This means the company has £1.52 for every pound currently owed	5 marks

4. (a) Referring to the calendar extract [above], complete the spreadsheet shown below, setting out your weekly budget for fuel purchases over the next three months   14 marks

	Week 1	Week 2	Week 3	Week 4	Week 5
Month 1					
Month 2					
Month 3					

OCR specimen marks:

	Week 1	Week 2	Week 3	Week 4	Week 5
Month 1	13817	20725	20725	13817	xxxxxxx
Month 2	20725	20725	20725	20725	xxxxxxx
Month 3	13817	20725	20725	20725	20725

   (b) Explain the KEY factors that could affect your budget 6 marks
       – allowance for fuel price increase mentioned   3 marks
       – allowance for increased business mentioned   3 marks

5. Referring to the information on Staff in the Scenario, draw an organizational chart for Red Transport Ltd   5 marks
   – Credible structure   3 marks
   – All staff covered   1 mark
   – Standard of layout   1 mark

6. ABC Imports Ltd deals in machinery and also in dangerous goods. On checking your company records for ABC Imports Ltd, you find the only information recorded is the company name, address and telephone number. What further information would be useful to include on the records?   5 marks

   Any from the following list to a maximum of 5:
   – Fax and/or e-mail   1 mark
   – Type of goods   1 mark
   – Volume/density/quantities/weight   1 mark
   – Dates, service used   1 mark
   – Quotes given   1 mark
   – UN classes for dangerous goods   1 mark

- Special transport requirements   1 mark
- Routes used   1 mark

7. Red Transport Ltd is replacing its 2 x 4 articulated tractor units. Identify and explain the *main* factors to be taken into account. (Consider environmental issues, compatibility with the current fleet, etc.)   10 marks
   - Purchase price
   - Environment/noise pollution
   - Fuel economy/gear ratio/engine size
   - Wheelbase/chassis/fifth-wheel height/number of axles
   - Tax/running costs
   - Driver comfort
   - Purchase costs

   5 marks for list of factors and 5 marks for valid reasons

8. The company carries metal cages loaded with 25-litre drums of sulphuric acid on its tandem axle box trailers. Prepare a schedule of instructions for issue to both warehouse operatives and drivers involved in this traffic   20 marks
   - Accept instructions in various formats:
   - Core
   - Warehouse operatives
   - Drivers   15 marks for actual instructions
   - Credible structure (appropriate style)/logical
     sequence   2 marks
   - Unambiguous/clarity/coherent   3 marks

INTERNATIONAL – SCENARIO: JONES INTERNATIONAL LTD

Jones International Ltd is a young company that has been very successful in international transportation and providing logistics solutions. It has separated the company into *four* main areas of work, each controlled by a general manager. All fleet- and transport-related issues are your responsibility and you report directly to the managing director.

The most successful route you have is to Turkey via Belgium, The Netherlands, Germany, Switzerland and Italy. The company is registered in the UK for VAT purposes and has no agents abroad. The company has insurance to cover its CMR liability.

Section A

Read the Case Study Scenario and answer ALL questions. You should spend approximately 30 minutes on this section of the examination. OCR specimen marks:

1. A two-man crew operates on the Turkish route. What is the maximum amount of time for which they can drive the vehicle in a 30-hour period?   1 mark
   – 20 hours   1 mark

2. One of your vehicles has been involved in an accident in Italy, as a result of which the 'O' licence disc is missing. What other document would your drivers have with them to indicate that the vehicle was operating on an international 'O' Licence?   1 mark
   – Community Authorization   1 mark

3. The route used formerly was via Yugoslavia using the TIR system. What customs transit system do you now use for the majority of the journey?   1 mark
   – Community/Common Transit System   1 mark

4. In which country on the Turkish route would you expect to have to pay vehicle tax for the vehicle to transit?   1 mark
   – Switzerland   1 mark

5. Name the *two* operating companies which operate the 'piggy back' system used in France and Germany   2 marks
   – Novatrans, Kombiverkehr   2 marks

6. What type of cargo would you normally be carrying if the vehicle was operating under the ATP Agreement?   1 mark
   – Perishable goods or refrigerated goods   1 mark

7. Name the *two* international agreements that cover the movement of dangerous goods on the specified route? (Note – the English Channel is crossed by ferry.)   2 marks
   – ADR and IMDG   2 marks

8. The route specified passes through certain countries that require you to obtain a Euro vignette to use their motorway networks. What would be the maximum GVW at which you could operate at in order to avoid this charge?   1 mark
   – 12,000kg   1 mark

9. One of the company's vehicles has been involved in a minor accident whilst travelling under TIR. The vehicle is still roadworthy, but the impact to the vehicle caused the seals on the load compartment to break. What should the driver do with the TIR carnet in these circumstances?　　1 mark
   - Request police or Customs officer to complete the accident report and note the new seal numbers in the report　　1 mark

10. Where would you obtain an ATA Carnet from?　1 mark
    - Chamber of Commerce　　1 mark

11. Where would you obtain Eco-points from?　　1 mark
    - International Road Freight Office (IRFO)　　1 mark

12. For a shipment of cargo requiring full Customs formalities to be carried out which form would you use for this? 1 mark
    - SAD document or C88　　1 mark

Total marks for Section A　　14

Section B

You should spend approximately 30 minutes on this section of the examination.

OCR specimen marks:

13. A customer has made a claim for damage to goods sent through your company to Denmark. The work was subcontracted by yourselves and subcontracted again.
    (a) What action will you take to deal with the claim?　　5 marks
       - Check CMR note　　1 mark
       - Notify claim to subcontractors　　1 mark
       - Notify claim to insurers　　3 marks
    (b) Explain the possible legal obligations of all involved with regards to liability　　9 marks
       - Liability of successive carriers　　3 marks
       - CMR liability of first carrier　　1 mark
       - Possible defences　　1 mark
       - Limit of liability　　1 mark
       - Liability of insolvent carriers　　1 mark
       - Time limits for legal claims　　3 marks

14. The drivers on the Turkish route specified operate as a two-man crew and are out of the country for 18 days at a time. Describe the system that you would use to control their tachograph charts and explain what you would see as being the main obstacles you will need to overcome to ensure good control   10 marks
    – System of control viability   5 marks
    – Problem of chart return   2 marks
    – Problem of cross-reference   2 marks
    – Checking of two individual drivers' charts
    and comparing for that journey   1 mark

15. You have been asked to identify the costs that you would expect the company to incur for movement to Turkey which are in addition to those that would be expected on a national journey. List them   5 marks
    – Any five from the following list at one point each:
    – Tax at Swiss border
    – Driver subsistence
    – Ferry costs
    – Tolls
    – Euro vignette
    – Higher vehicle insurance
    – CMR insurance
    – Telephone calls

Total marks for Section B   29
Total marks for paper   43

Index

Other transport and logistics titles published by Kogan Page:

Published in association with The Institute of Logistics and Transport:

The Certificate of Professional Competence:1001 typical questions and answers, Revised 3rd edn, 2004, David Lowe

The Dangerous Goods Safety Manual:A study guide for DGSAs, 2000, David Lowe

The Handbook of Logistics and Distribution Management, 2nd edn, 2000, Alan Rushton, John Oxley and Phil Croucher

Managing Passenger Logistics, 2000, Paul Fawcett

International Transport, 5th edn, 1999, Rex Faulks

An Introduction to Transport Studies, 3rd edn, 1998, John Hibbs

Also published by Kogan Page:

Applied Transport Economics, 3rd edn, 2005, Stuart Cole

The Directory of UK Food Transport & Logistics 2004, Minto Gordon

Global Logistics and Distribution Planning, 4th edn, 2003, Donald Waters

Managing Transport Operations, 3rd edn, 2002, Edmund J Gubbins

The Professional LGV Driver's Handbook, 2003, David Lowe

The Transport Manager's and Operator's Handbook 2004, 34th edn, David Lowe

Logistics and Retail Management, 2nd edn, 2004, edited by John Fernie and Leigh Sparks

The above titles are available from all good bookshops or direct from the publishers. To obtain more information, please contact the publishers at the address below:

Kogan Page
120 Pentonville Road
London N1 9JN
Tel:020 7278 0433
Fax:020 7837 6348
www.kogan-page.co.uk

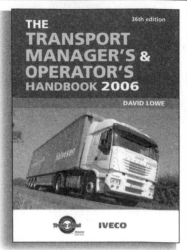